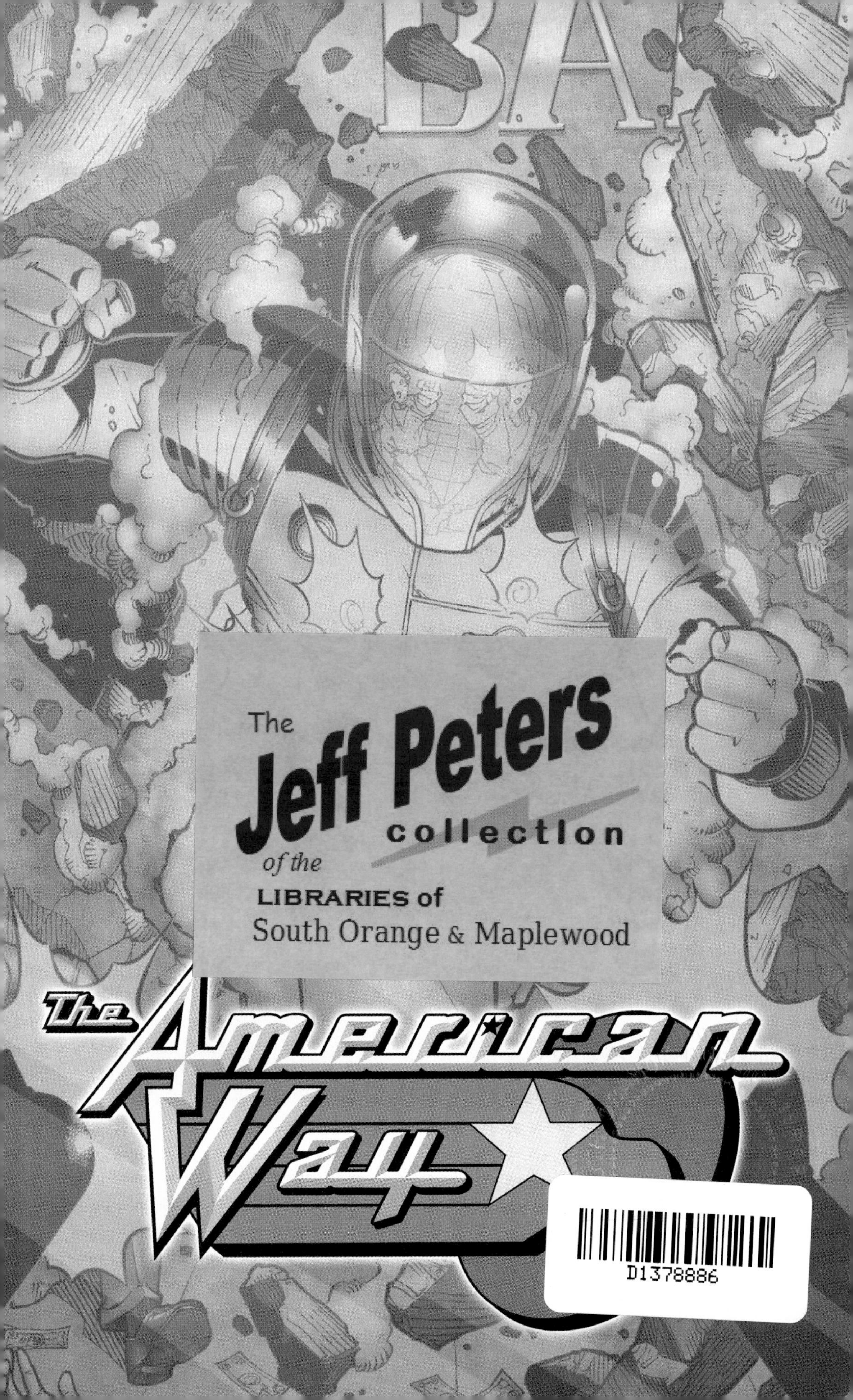
BA
The American Way

Written by
John Ridley

Penciled by
Georges Jeanty

Inked by
Karl Story
with Ray Snyder

Colored by
WildStorm FX

Lettered by
Pat Brosseau, Travis Lanham
& Rob Leigh

Original series covers by
Georges Jeanty, Karl Story
& Randy Mayor

DC Comics, a Warner Bros. Entertainment Company.

ISBN 1-4012-1256-5
ISBN-13: 978-1-4012-1256-8

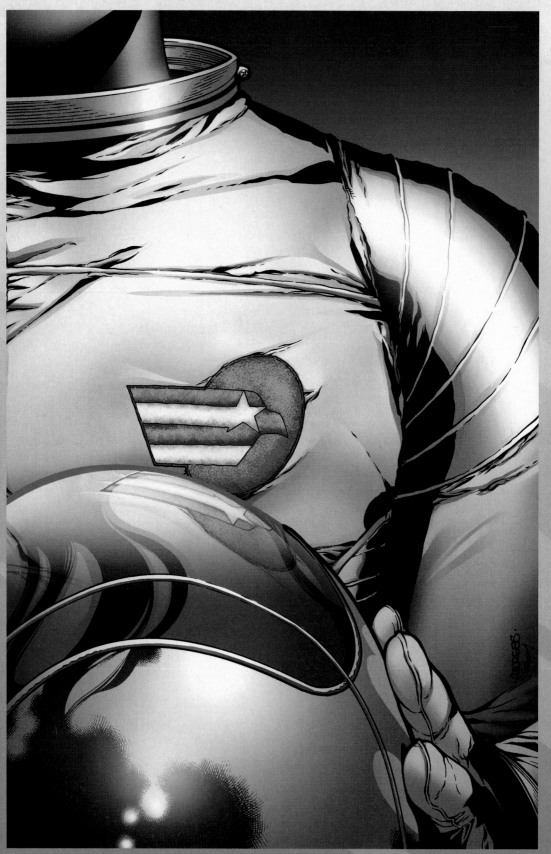

COVER #2

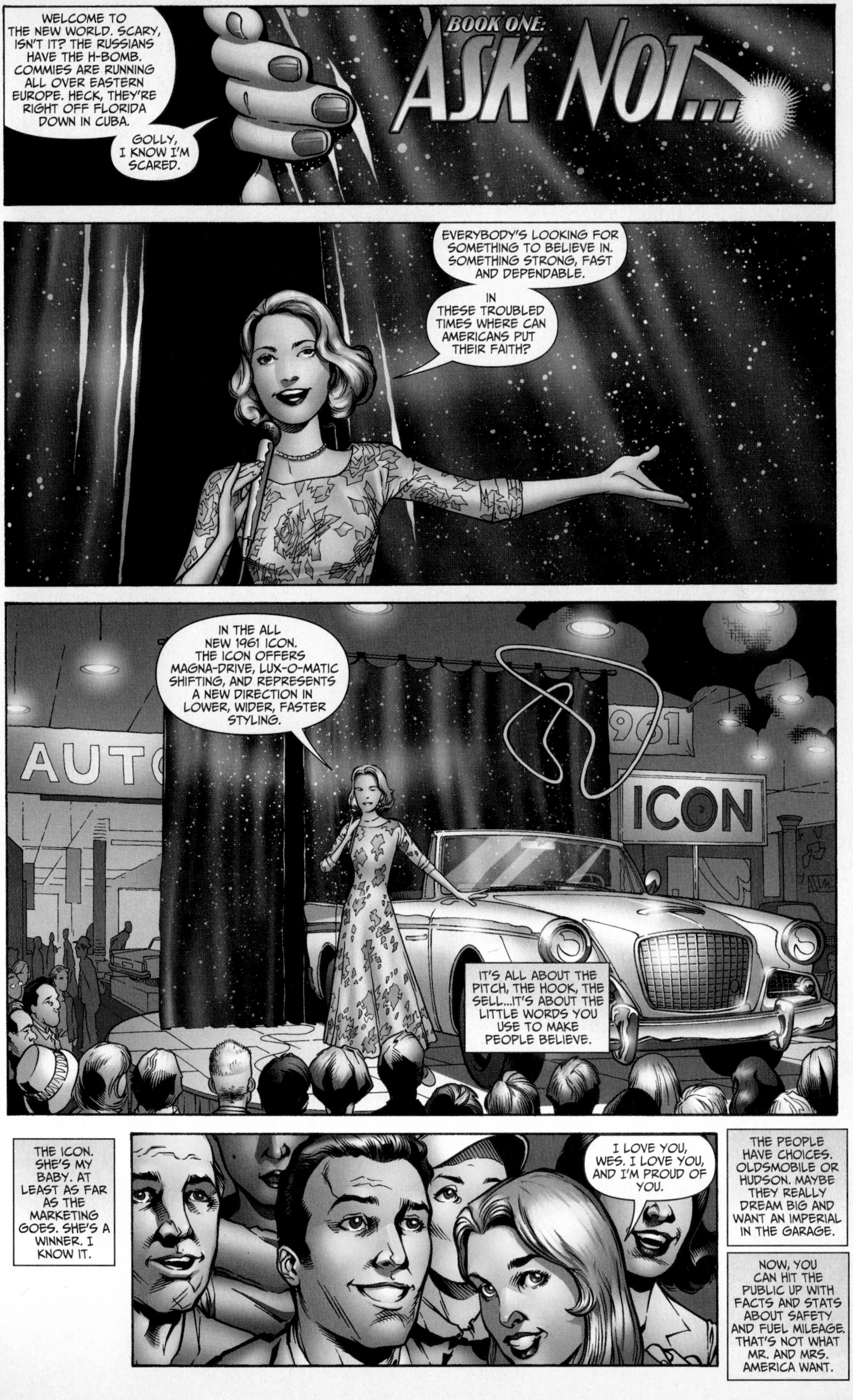
WELCOME TO THE NEW WORLD. SCARY, ISN'T IT? THE RUSSIANS HAVE THE H-BOMB. COMMIES ARE RUNNING ALL OVER EASTERN EUROPE. HECK, THEY'RE RIGHT OFF FLORIDA DOWN IN CUBA.
GOLLY, I KNOW I'M SCARED.
BOOK ONE:
ASK NOT...
EVERYBODY'S LOOKING FOR SOMETHING TO BELIEVE IN. SOMETHING STRONG, FAST AND DEPENDABLE.
IN THESE TROUBLED TIMES WHERE CAN AMERICANS PUT THEIR FAITH?
IN THE ALL NEW 1961 ICON. THE ICON OFFERS MAGNA-DRIVE, LUX-O-MATIC SHIFTING, AND REPRESENTS A NEW DIRECTION IN LOWER, WIDER, FASTER STYLING.
AUTO
1961
ICON
IT'S ALL ABOUT THE PITCH, THE HOOK, THE SELL...IT'S ABOUT THE LITTLE WORDS YOU USE TO MAKE PEOPLE BELIEVE.
THE ICON. SHE'S MY BABY. AT LEAST AS FAR AS THE MARKETING GOES. SHE'S A WINNER. I KNOW IT.
I LOVE YOU, WES. I LOVE YOU, AND I'M PROUD OF YOU.
THE PEOPLE HAVE CHOICES. OLDSMOBILE OR HUDSON. MAYBE THEY REALLY DREAM BIG AND WANT AN IMPERIAL IN THE GARAGE.
NOW, YOU CAN HIT THE PUBLIC UP WITH FACTS AND STATS ABOUT SAFETY AND FUEL MILEAGE. THAT'S NOT WHAT MR. AND MRS. AMERICA WANT.

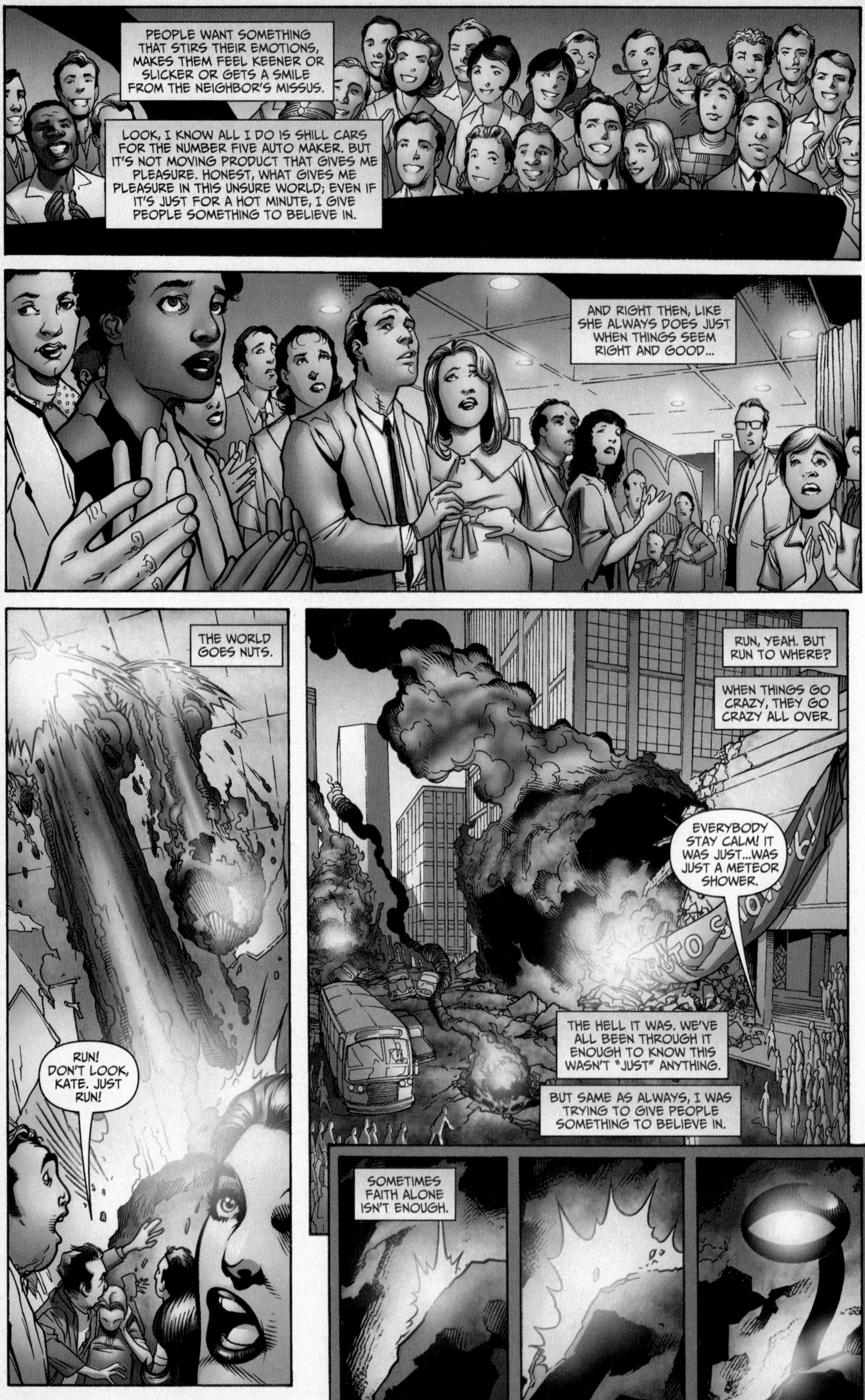
PEOPLE WANT SOMETHING THAT STIRS THEIR EMOTIONS, MAKES THEM FEEL KEENER OR SLICKER OR GETS A SMILE FROM THE NEIGHBOR'S MISSUS.
LOOK, I KNOW ALL I DO IS SHILL CARS FOR THE NUMBER FIVE AUTO MAKER. BUT IT'S NOT MOVING PRODUCT THAT GIVES ME PLEASURE. HONEST, WHAT GIVES ME PLEASURE IN THIS UNSURE WORLD; EVEN IF IT'S JUST FOR A HOT MINUTE, I GIVE PEOPLE SOMETHING TO BELIEVE IN.
AND RIGHT THEN, LIKE SHE ALWAYS DOES JUST WHEN THINGS SEEM RIGHT AND GOOD...
THE WORLD GOES NUTS.
RUN! DON'T LOOK, KATE. JUST RUN!
RUN, YEAH. BUT RUN TO WHERE?
WHEN THINGS GO CRAZY, THEY GO CRAZY ALL OVER.
EVERYBODY STAY CALM! IT WAS JUST...WAS JUST A METEOR SHOWER.
AUTO SHOW
THE HELL IT WAS. WE'VE ALL BEEN THROUGH IT ENOUGH TO KNOW THIS WASN'T "JUST" ANYTHING.
BUT SAME AS ALWAYS, I WAS TRYING TO GIVE PEOPLE SOMETHING TO BELIEVE IN.
SOMETIMES FAITH ALONE ISN'T ENOUGH.

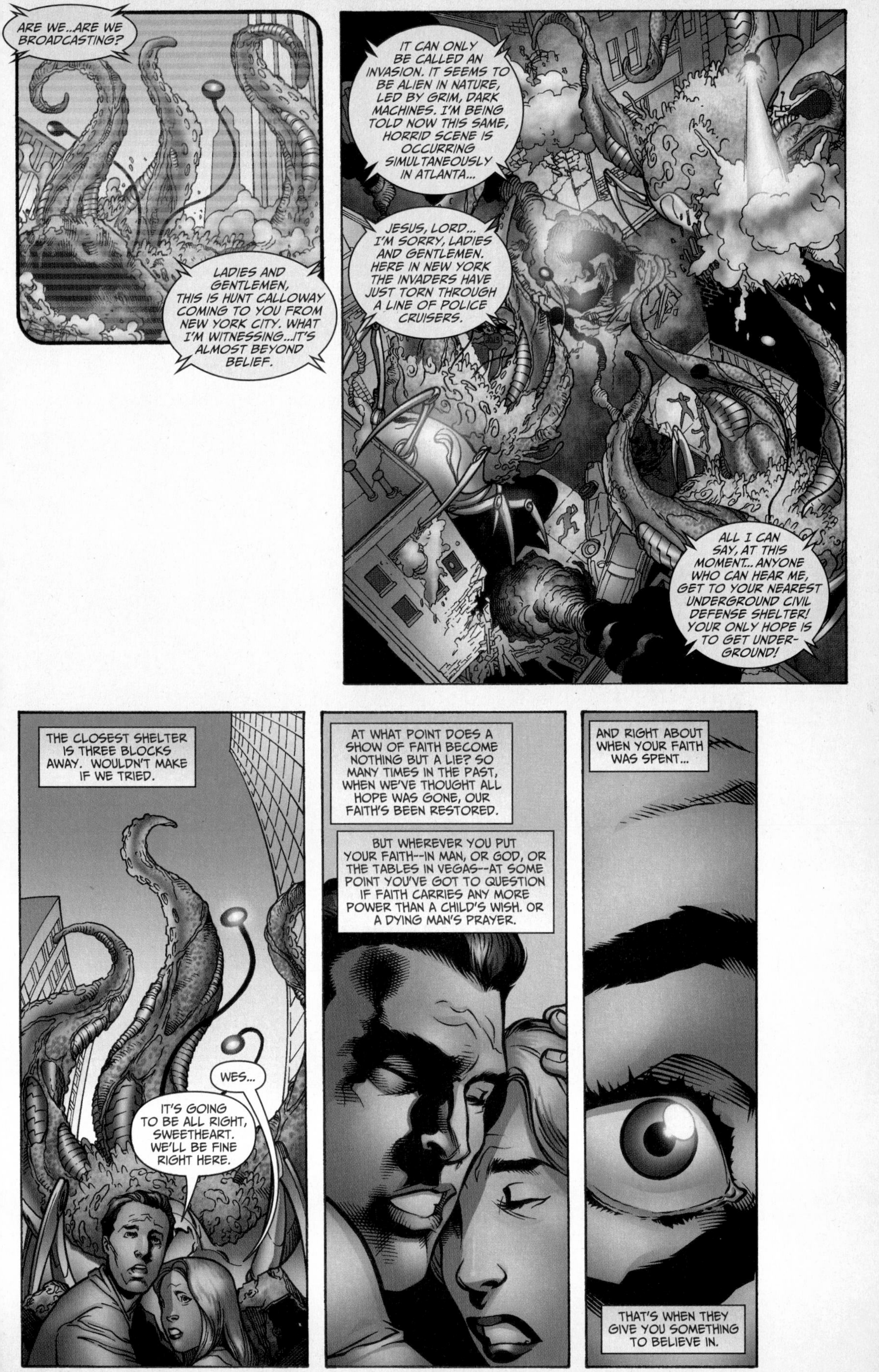
ARE WE...ARE WE BROADCASTING?
LADIES AND GENTLEMEN, THIS IS HUNT CALLOWAY COMING TO YOU FROM NEW YORK CITY. WHAT I'M WITNESSING...IT'S ALMOST BEYOND BELIEF.
IT CAN ONLY BE CALLED AN INVASION. IT SEEMS TO BE ALIEN IN NATURE, LED BY GRIM, DARK MACHINES. I'M BEING TOLD NOW THIS SAME, HORRID SCENE IS OCCURRING SIMULTANEOUSLY IN ATLANTA...
JESUS, LORD... I'M SORRY, LADIES AND GENTLEMEN. HERE IN NEW YORK THE INVADERS HAVE JUST TORN THROUGH A LINE OF POLICE CRUISERS.
ALL I CAN SAY, AT THIS MOMENT... ANYONE WHO CAN HEAR ME, GET TO YOUR NEAREST UNDERGROUND CIVIL DEFENSE SHELTER! YOUR ONLY HOPE IS TO GET UNDER-GROUND!
THE CLOSEST SHELTER IS THREE BLOCKS AWAY. WOULDN'T MAKE IF WE TRIED.
WES...
IT'S GOING TO BE ALL RIGHT, SWEETHEART. WE'LL BE FINE RIGHT HERE.
AT WHAT POINT DOES A SHOW OF FAITH BECOME NOTHING BUT A LIE? SO MANY TIMES IN THE PAST, WHEN WE'VE THOUGHT ALL HOPE WAS GONE, OUR FAITH'S BEEN RESTORED.
BUT WHEREVER YOU PUT YOUR FAITH--IN MAN, OR GOD, OR THE TABLES IN VEGAS--AT SOME POINT YOU'VE GOT TO QUESTION IF FAITH CARRIES ANY MORE POWER THAN A CHILD'S WISH. OR A DYING MAN'S PRAYER.
AND RIGHT ABOUT WHEN YOUR FAITH WAS SPENT...
THAT'S WHEN THEY GIVE YOU SOMETHING TO BELIEVE IN.

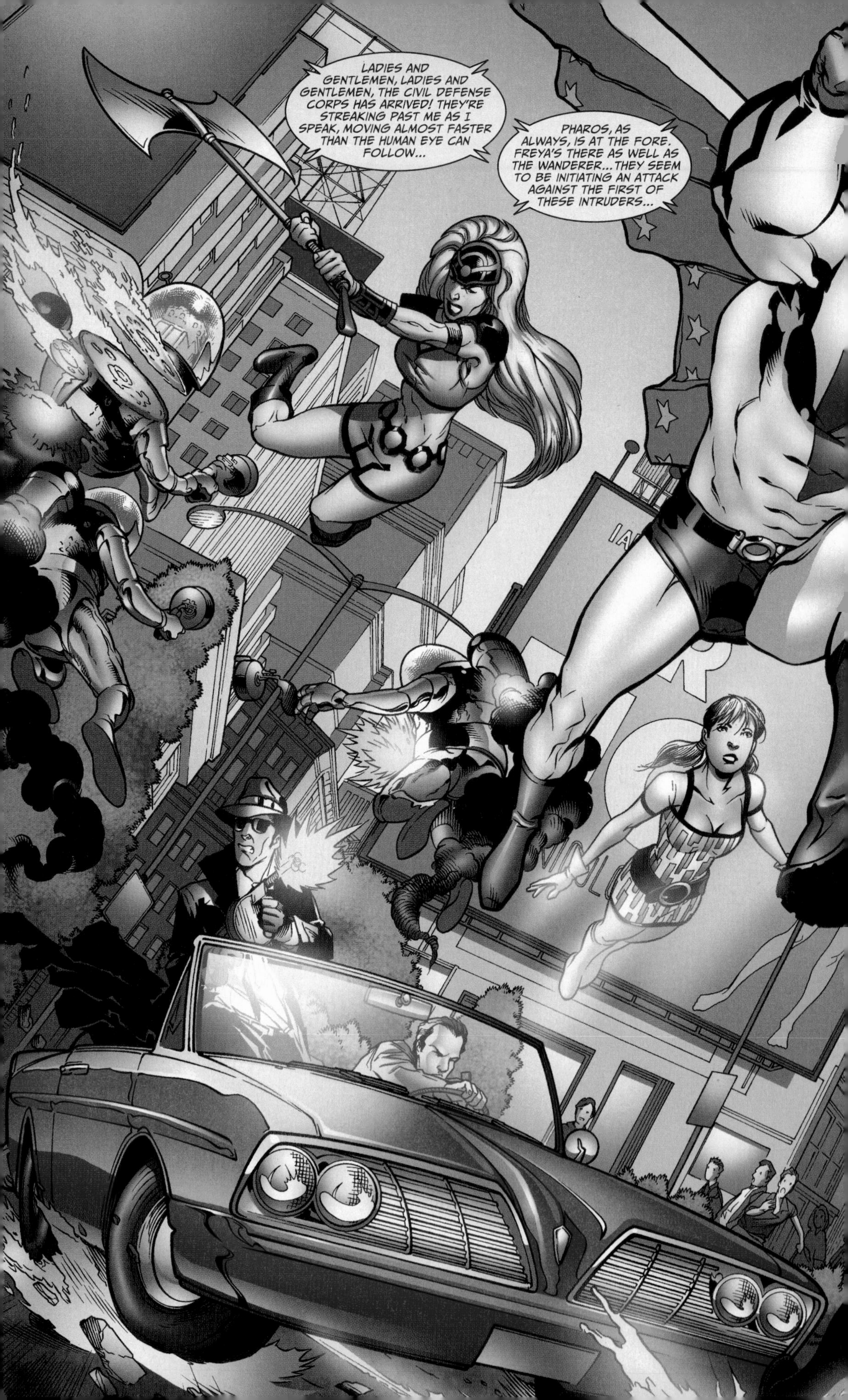
LADIES AND GENTLEMEN, LADIES AND GENTLEMEN, THE CIVIL DEFENSE CORPS HAS ARRIVED! THEY'RE STREAKING PAST ME AS I SPEAK, MOVING ALMOST FASTER THAN THE HUMAN EYE CAN FOLLOW...
PHAROS, AS ALWAYS, IS AT THE FORE. FREYA'S THERE AS WELL AS THE WANDERER...THEY SEEM TO BE INITIATING AN ATTACK AGAINST THE FIRST OF THESE INTRUDERS...

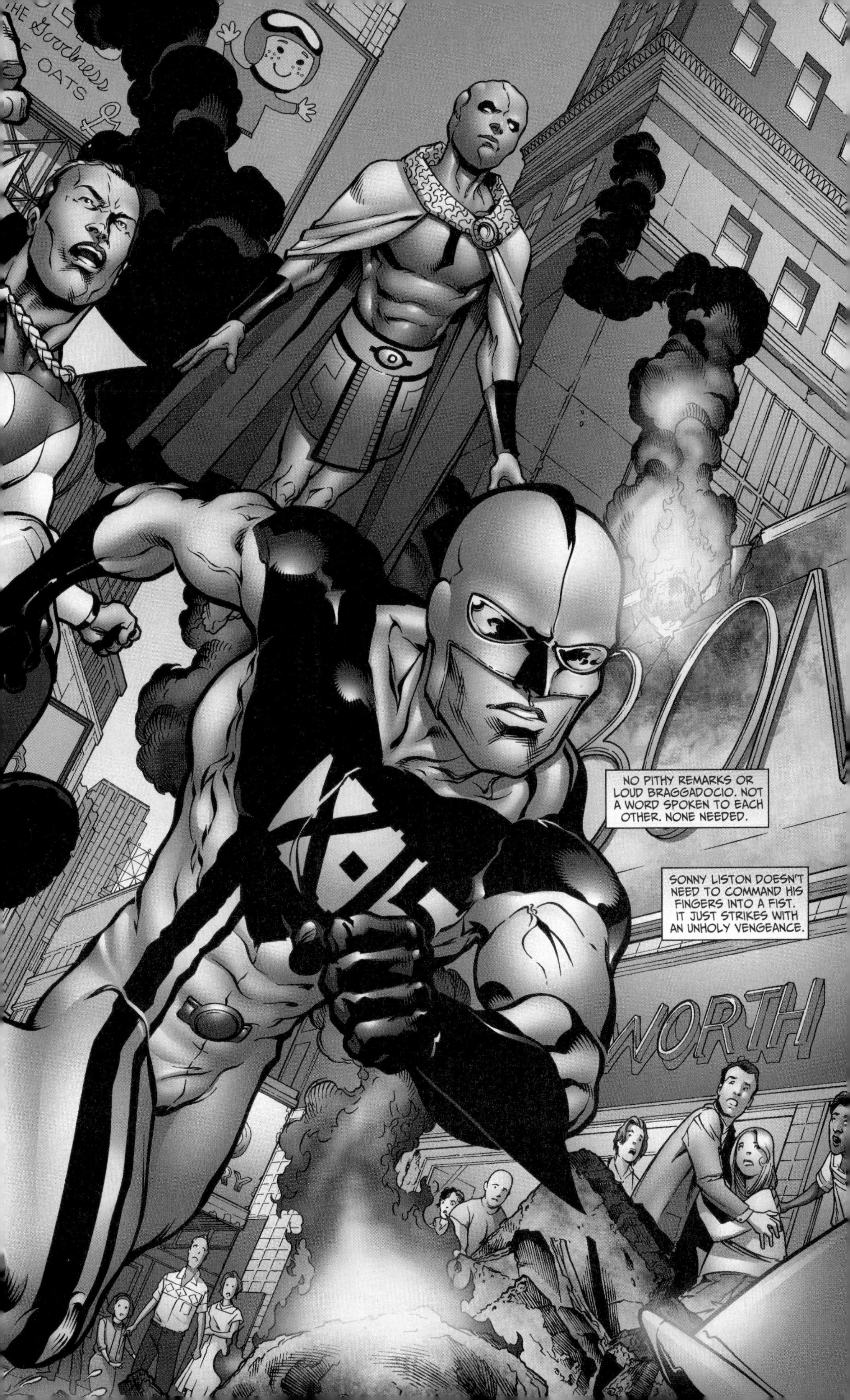
THE Goodness
OF OATS
NO PITHY REMARKS OR LOUD BRAGGADOCIO. NOT A WORD SPOKEN TO EACH OTHER. NONE NEEDED.
SONNY LISTON DOESN'T NEED TO COMMAND HIS FINGERS INTO A FIST. IT JUST STRIKES WITH AN UNHOLY VENGEANCE.
WORTH

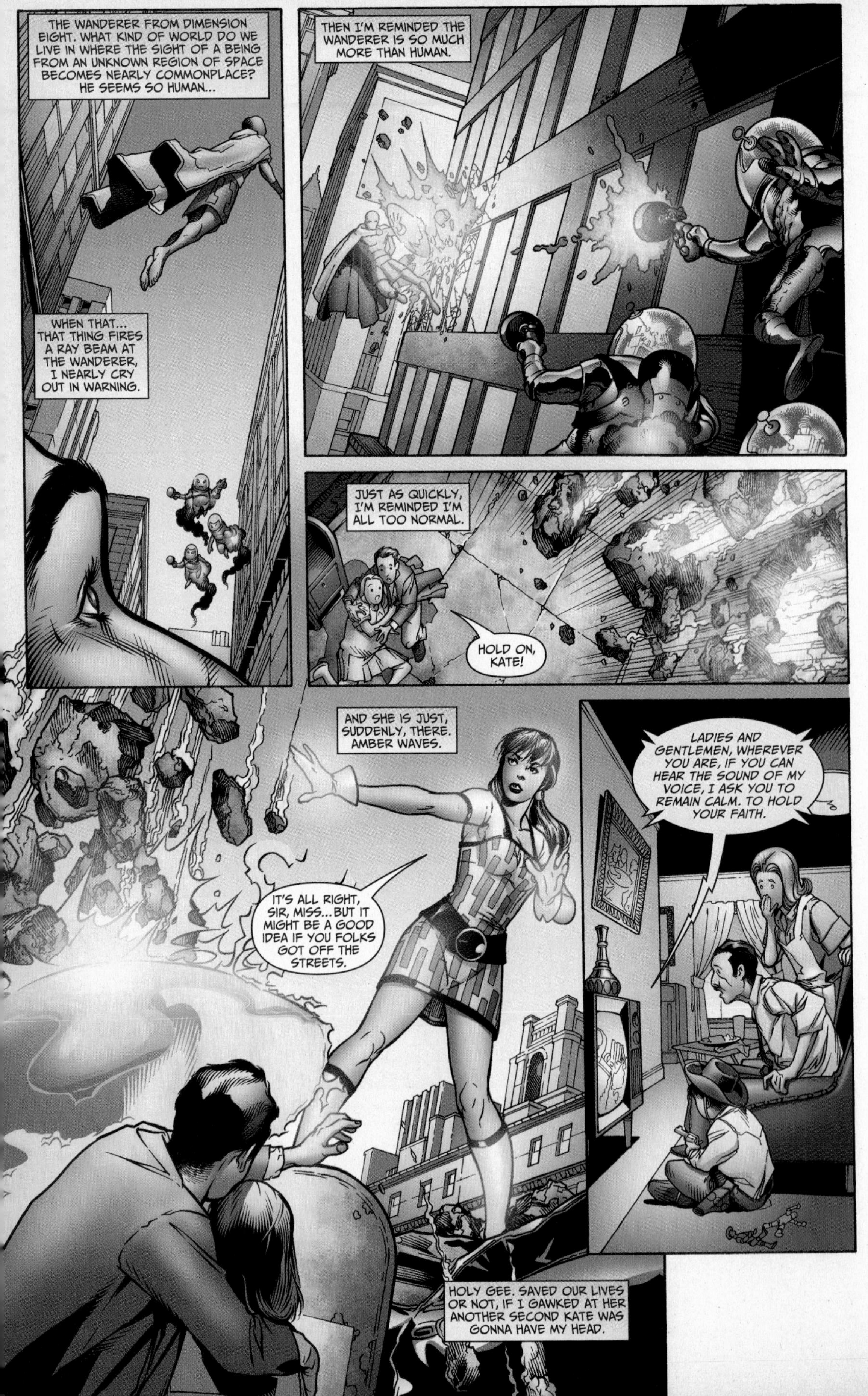
THE WANDERER FROM DIMENSION EIGHT. WHAT KIND OF WORLD DO WE LIVE IN WHERE THE SIGHT OF A BEING FROM AN UNKNOWN REGION OF SPACE BECOMES NEARLY COMMONPLACE? HE SEEMS SO HUMAN...
WHEN THAT... THAT THING FIRES A RAY BEAM AT THE WANDERER, I NEARLY CRY OUT IN WARNING.
THEN I'M REMINDED THE WANDERER IS SO MUCH MORE THAN HUMAN.
JUST AS QUICKLY, I'M REMINDED I'M ALL TOO NORMAL.
HOLD ON, KATE!
AND SHE IS JUST, SUDDENLY, THERE. AMBER WAVES.
IT'S ALL RIGHT, SIR, MISS...BUT IT MIGHT BE A GOOD IDEA IF YOU FOLKS GOT OFF THE STREETS.
LADIES AND GENTLEMEN, WHEREVER YOU ARE, IF YOU CAN HEAR THE SOUND OF MY VOICE, I ASK YOU TO REMAIN CALM. TO HOLD YOUR FAITH.
HOLY GEE. SAVED OUR LIVES OR NOT, IF I GAWKED AT HER ANOTHER SECOND KATE WAS GONNA HAVE MY HEAD.

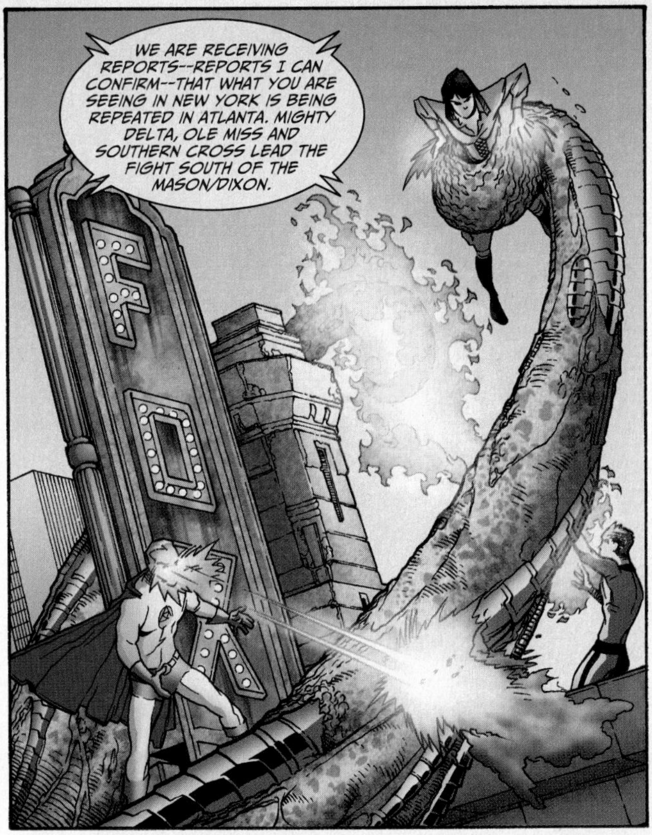
WE ARE RECEIVING REPORTS--REPORTS I CAN CONFIRM--THAT WHAT YOU ARE SEEING IN NEW YORK IS BEING REPEATED IN ATLANTA. MIGHTY DELTA, OLE MISS AND SOUTHERN CROSS LEAD THE FIGHT SOUTH OF THE MASON/DIXON.

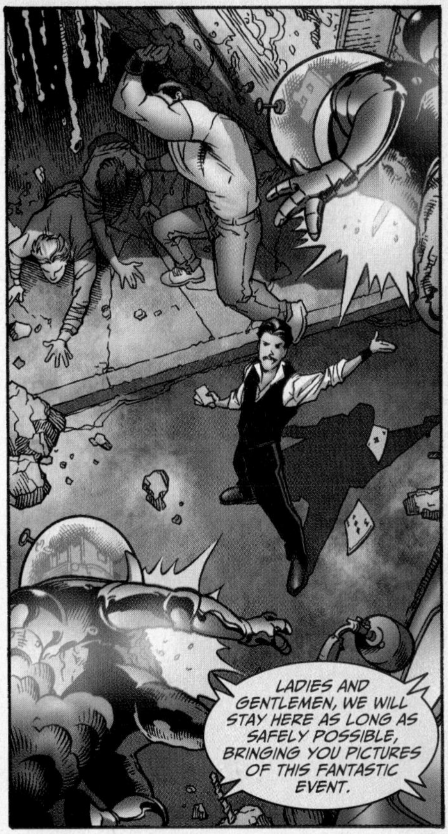
LADIES AND GENTLEMEN, WE WILL STAY HERE AS LONG AS SAFELY POSSIBLE, BRINGING YOU PICTURES OF THIS FANTASTIC EVENT.

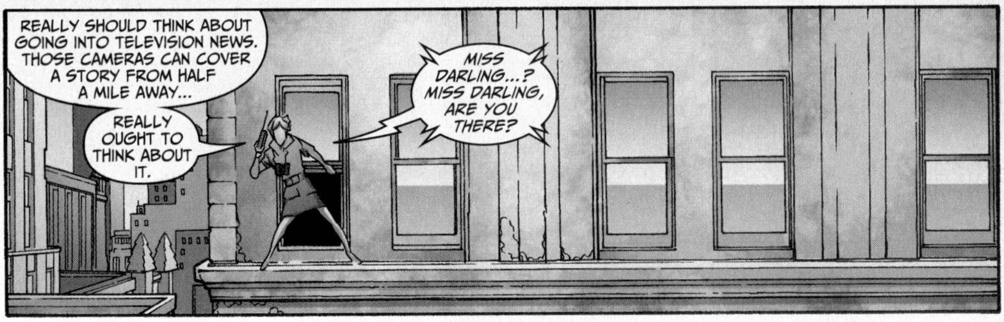
REALLY SHOULD THINK ABOUT GOING INTO TELEVISION NEWS. THOSE CAMERAS CAN COVER A STORY FROM HALF A MILE AWAY...
REALLY OUGHT TO THINK ABOUT IT.
MISS DARLING...? MISS DARLING, ARE YOU THERE?

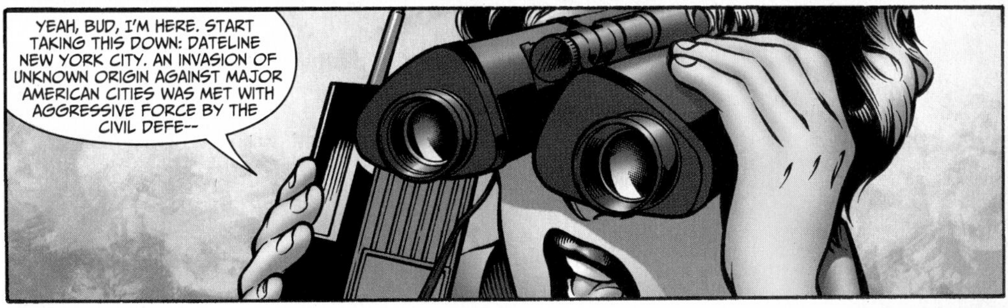
YEAH, BUD, I'M HERE. START TAKING THIS DOWN: DATELINE NEW YORK CITY. AN INVASION OF UNKNOWN ORIGIN AGAINST MAJOR AMERICAN CITIES WAS MET WITH AGGRESSIVE FORCE BY THE CIVIL DEFE--

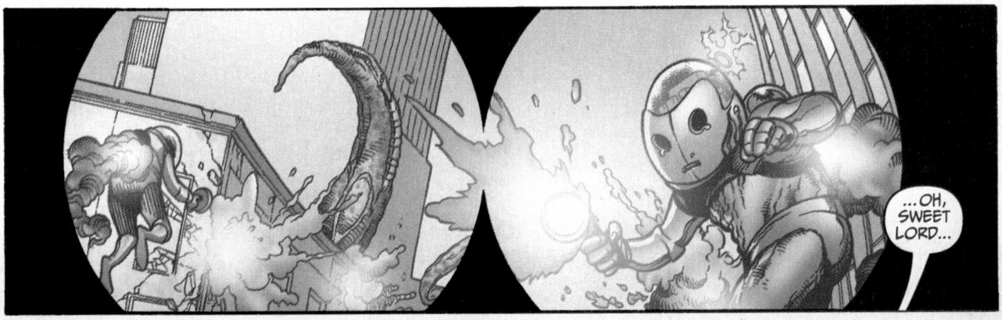
...OH, SWEET LORD...

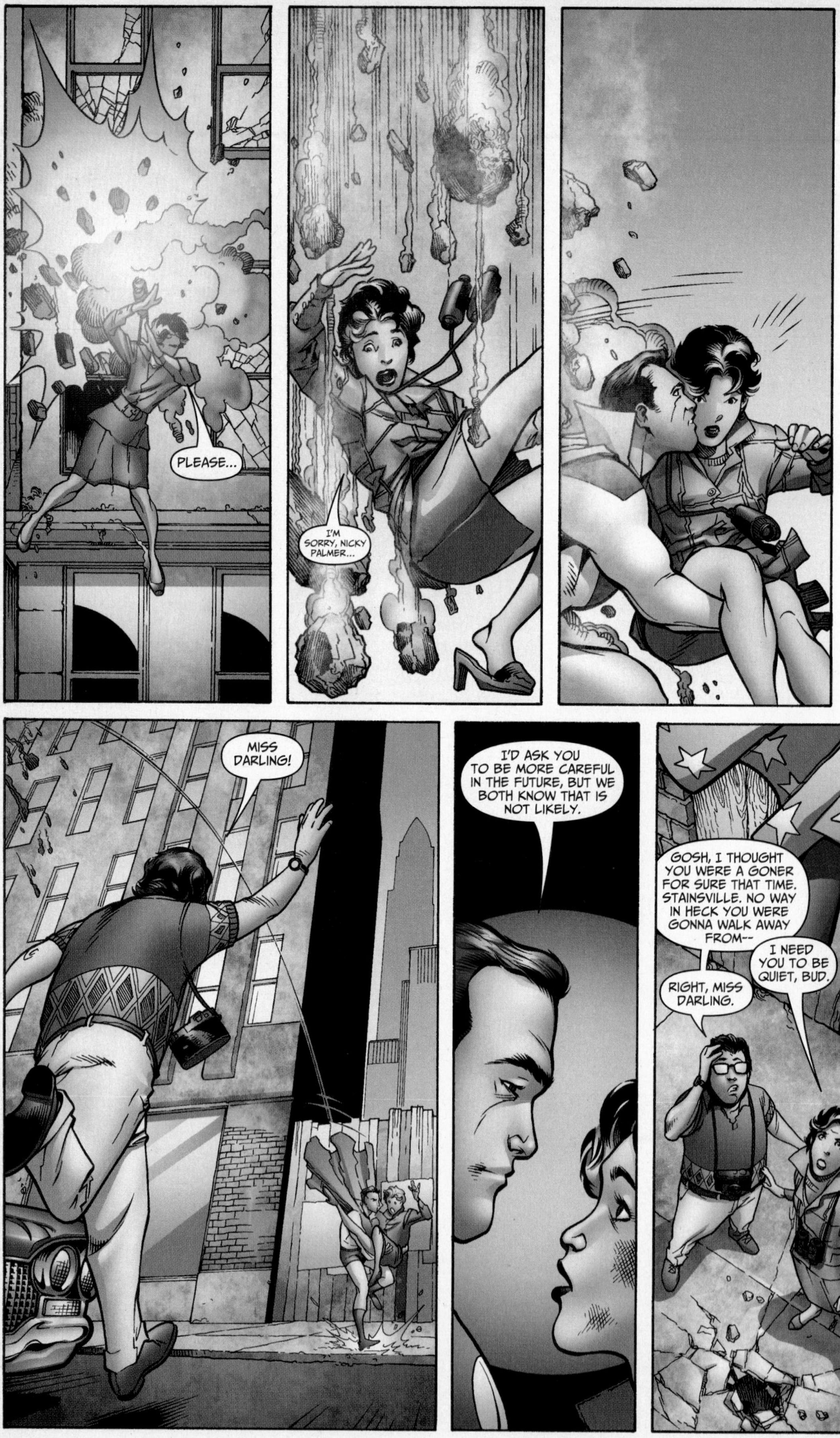
PLEASE...
I'M SORRY, NICKY PALMER...
MISS DARLING!
I'D ASK YOU TO BE MORE CAREFUL IN THE FUTURE, BUT WE BOTH KNOW THAT IS NOT LIKELY.
GOSH, I THOUGHT YOU WERE A GONER FOR SURE THAT TIME. STAINSVILLE. NO WAY IN HECK YOU WERE GONNA WALK AWAY FROM--
I NEED YOU TO BE QUIET, BUD.
RIGHT, MISS DARLING.

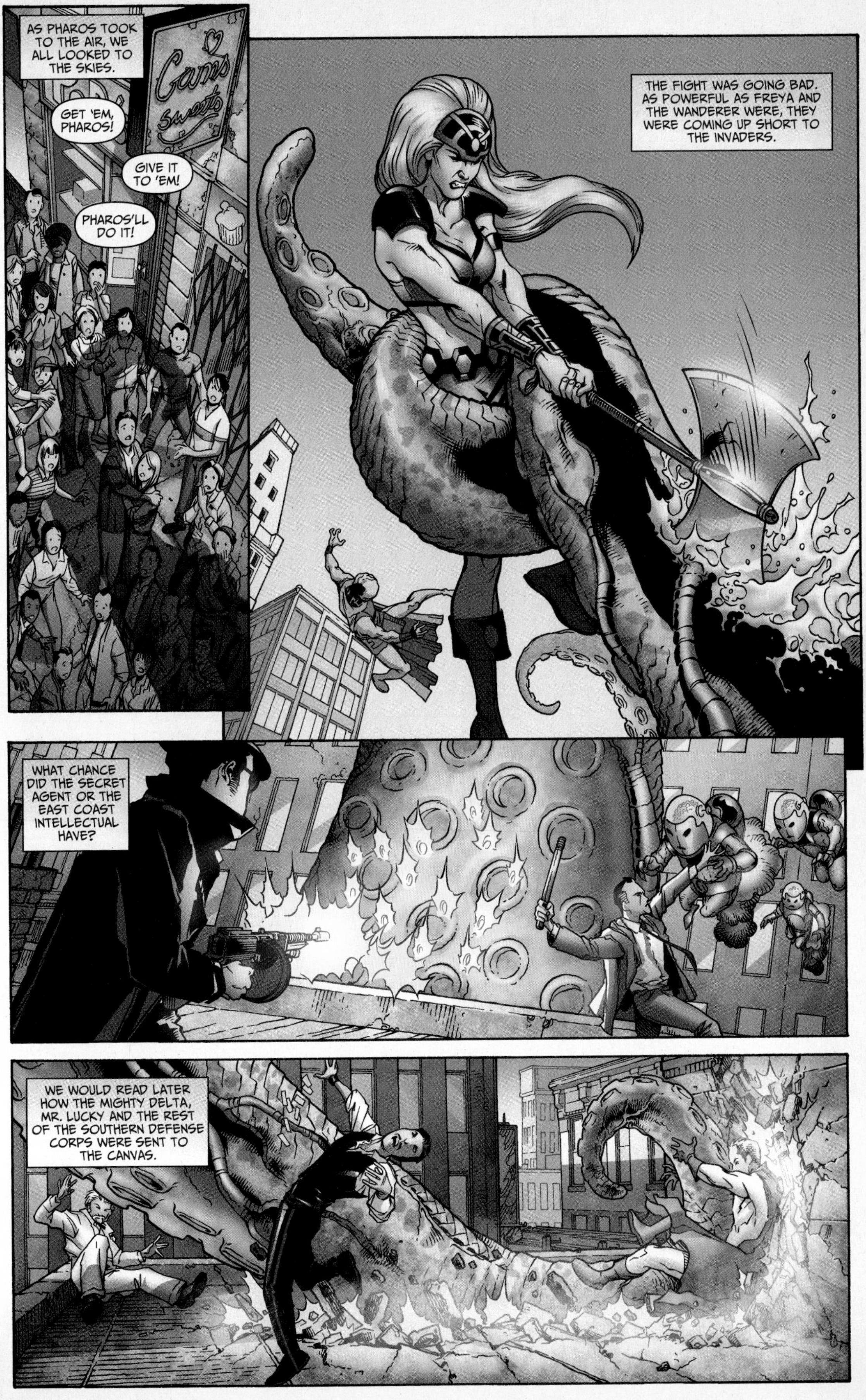

AS PHAROS TOOK TO THE AIR, WE ALL LOOKED TO THE SKIES.
GET 'EM, PHAROS!
GIVE IT TO 'EM!
PHAROS'LL DO IT!
Gam's Sweets
THE FIGHT WAS GOING BAD. AS POWERFUL AS FREYA AND THE WANDERER WERE, THEY WERE COMING UP SHORT TO THE INVADERS.
WHAT CHANCE DID THE SECRET AGENT OR THE EAST COAST INTELLECTUAL HAVE?
WE WOULD READ LATER HOW THE MIGHTY DELTA, MR. LUCKY AND THE REST OF THE SOUTHERN DEFENSE CORPS WERE SENT TO THE CANVAS.

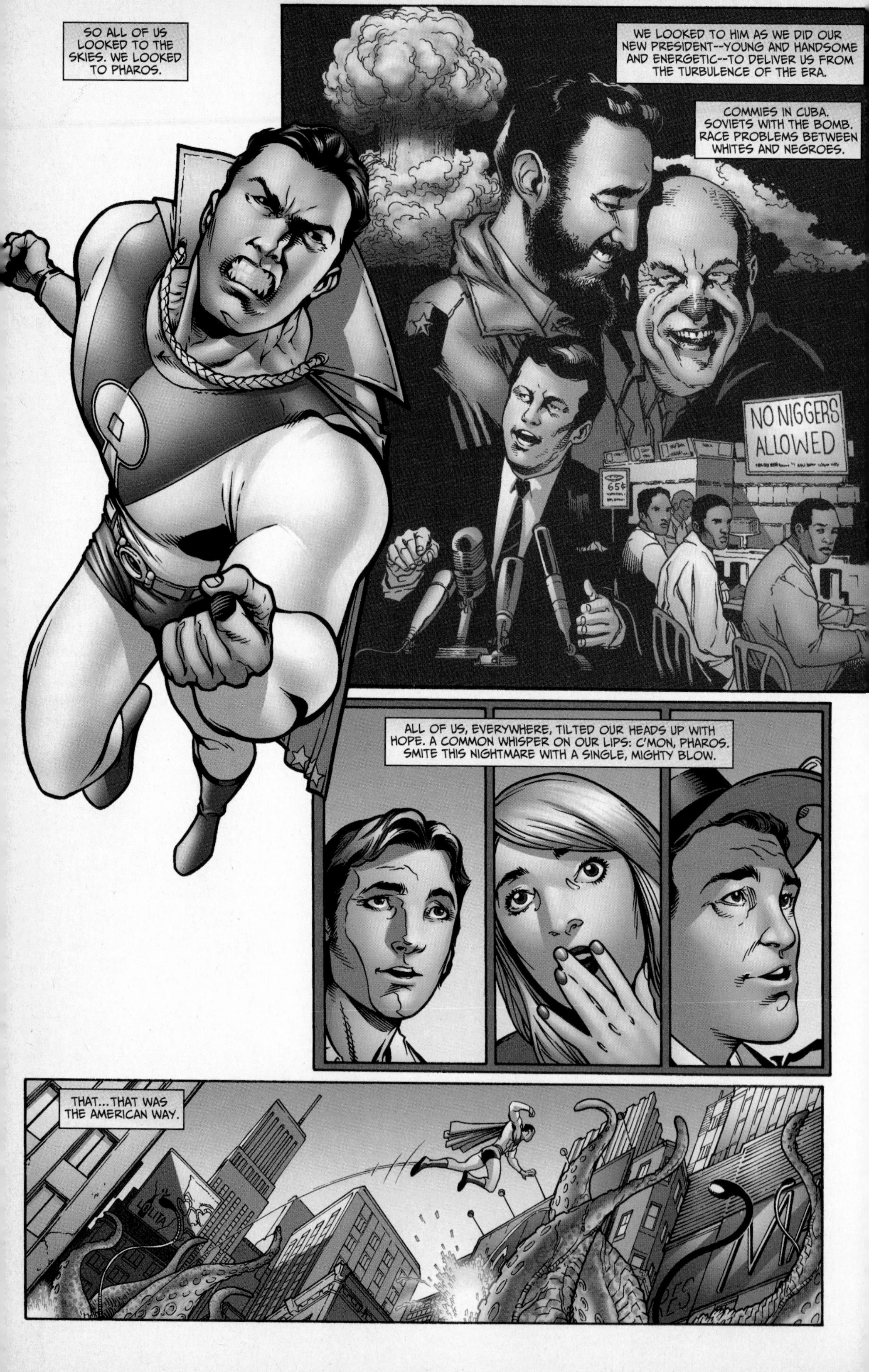
SO ALL OF US LOOKED TO THE SKIES. WE LOOKED TO PHAROS.
WE LOOKED TO HIM AS WE DID OUR NEW PRESIDENT--YOUNG AND HANDSOME AND ENERGETIC--TO DELIVER US FROM THE TURBULENCE OF THE ERA.
COMMIES IN CUBA. SOVIETS WITH THE BOMB. RACE PROBLEMS BETWEEN WHITES AND NEGROES.
NO NIGGERS ALLOWED
65¢
ALL OF US, EVERYWHERE, TILTED OUR HEADS UP WITH HOPE. A COMMON WHISPER ON OUR LIPS: C'MON, PHAROS. SMITE THIS NIGHTMARE WITH A SINGLE, MIGHTY BLOW.
THAT... THAT WAS THE AMERICAN WAY.
LOLITA

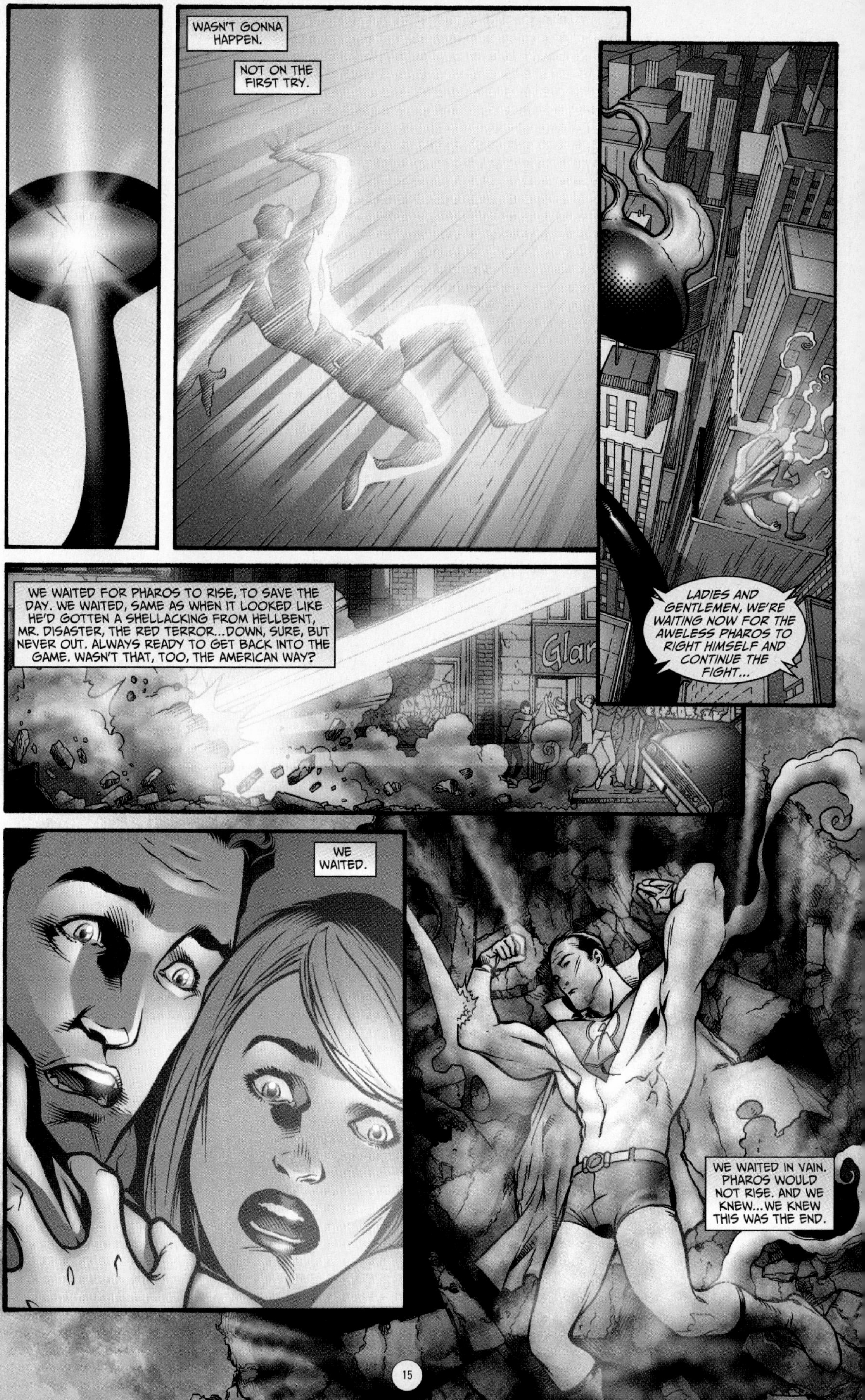

WASN'T GONNA HAPPEN.
NOT ON THE FIRST TRY.
LADIES AND GENTLEMEN, WE'RE WAITING NOW FOR THE AWELESS PHAROS TO RIGHT HIMSELF AND CONTINUE THE FIGHT...
WE WAITED FOR PHAROS TO RISE, TO SAVE THE DAY. WE WAITED, SAME AS WHEN IT LOOKED LIKE HE'D GOTTEN A SHELLACKING FROM HELLBENT, MR. DISASTER, THE RED TERROR...DOWN, SURE, BUT NEVER OUT. ALWAYS READY TO GET BACK INTO THE GAME. WASN'T THAT, TOO, THE AMERICAN WAY?
Glar
WE WAITED.
WE WAITED IN VAIN. PHAROS WOULD NOT RISE. AND WE KNEW...WE KNEW THIS WAS THE END.

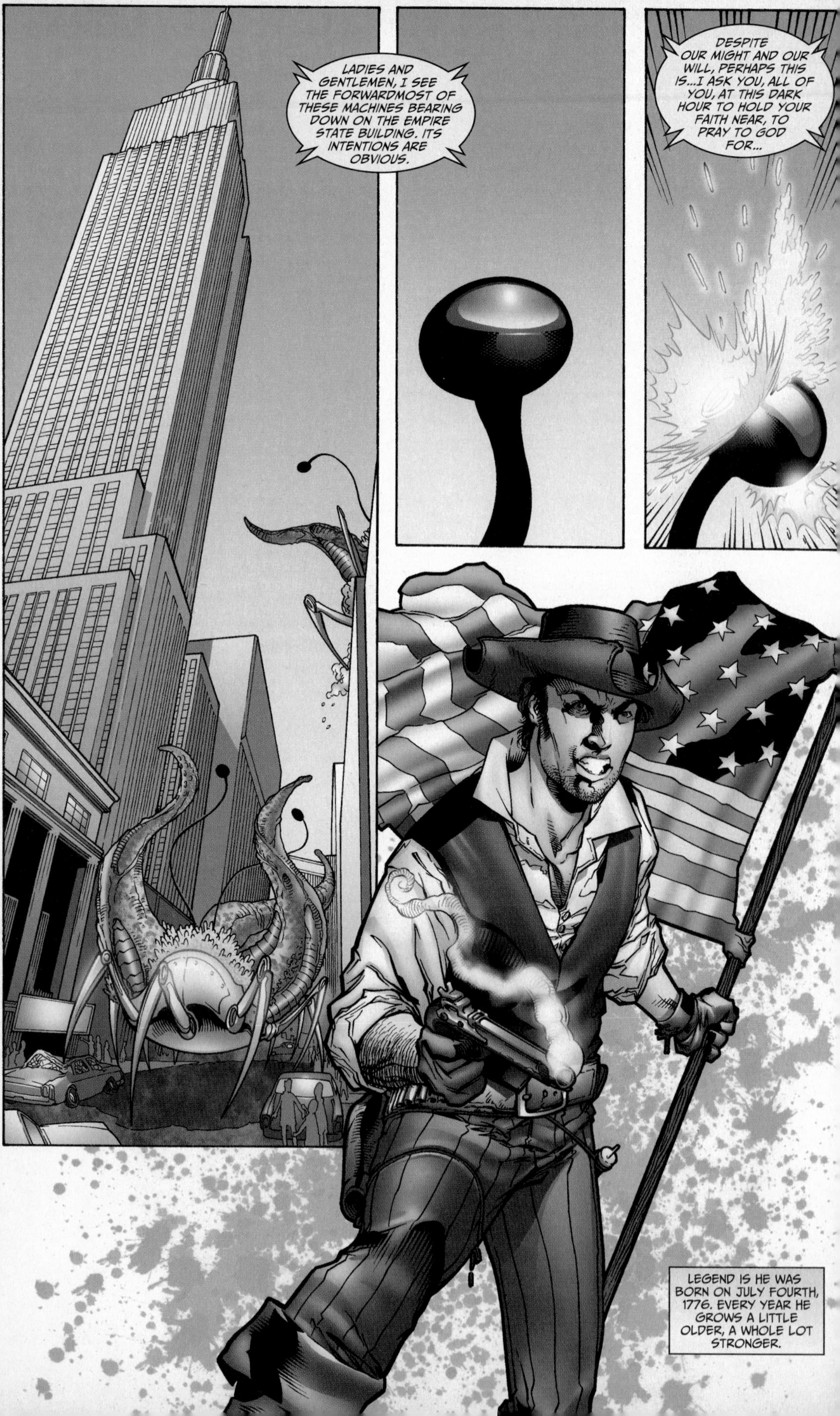
LADIES AND GENTLEMEN, I SEE THE FORWARDMOST OF THESE MACHINES BEARING DOWN ON THE EMPIRE STATE BUILDING. ITS INTENTIONS ARE OBVIOUS.
DESPITE OUR MIGHT AND OUR WILL, PERHAPS THIS IS...I ASK YOU, ALL OF YOU, AT THIS DARK HOUR TO HOLD YOUR FAITH NEAR, TO PRAY TO GOD FOR...
LEGEND IS HE WAS BORN ON JULY FOURTH, 1776. EVERY YEAR HE GROWS A LITTLE OLDER, A WHOLE LOT STRONGER.

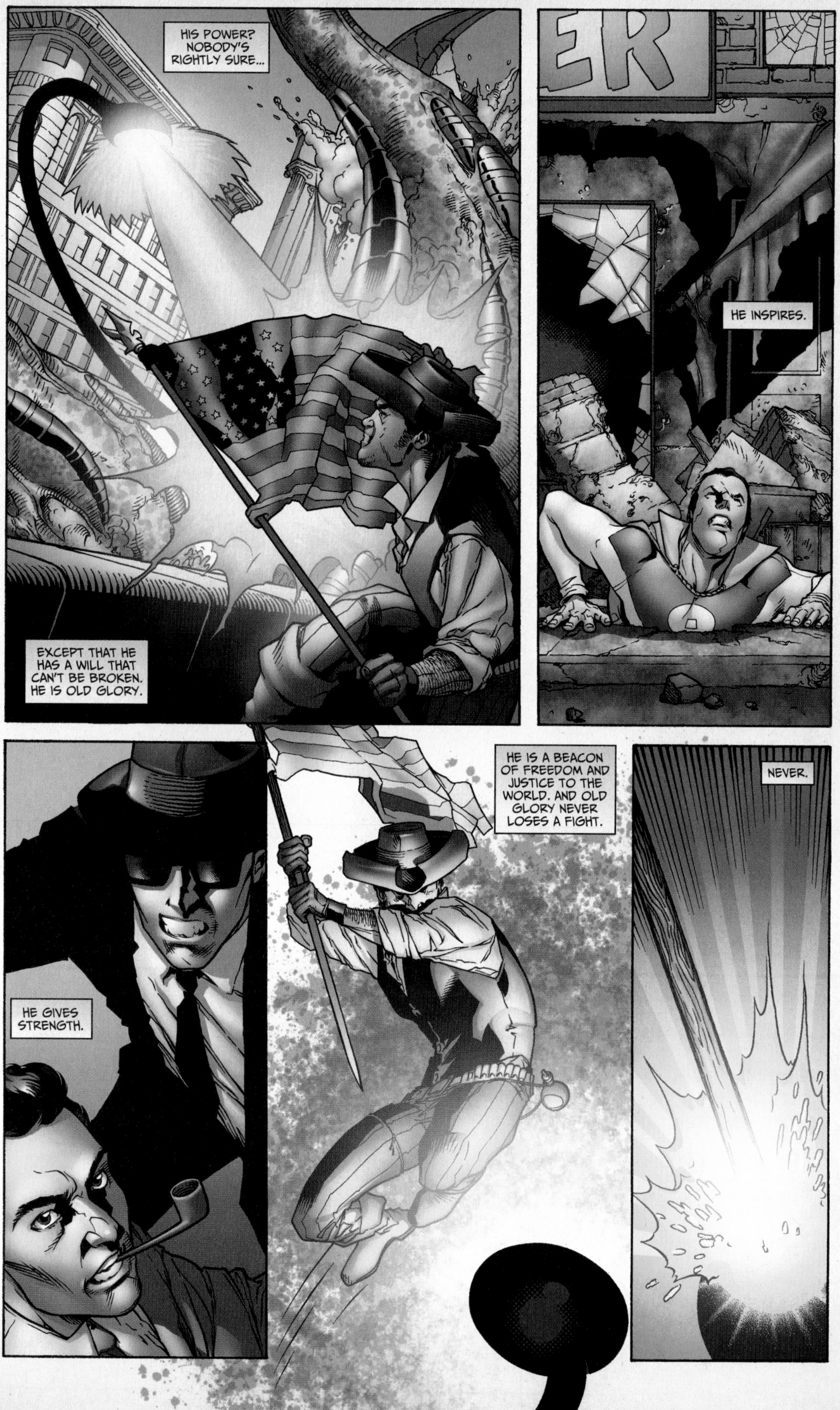
HIS POWER? NOBODY'S RIGHTLY SURE...
EXCEPT THAT HE HAS A WILL THAT CAN'T BE BROKEN. HE IS OLD GLORY.
HE INSPIRES.
HE GIVES STRENGTH.
HE IS A BEACON OF FREEDOM AND JUSTICE TO THE WORLD. AND OLD GLORY NEVER LOSES A FIGHT.
NEVER.

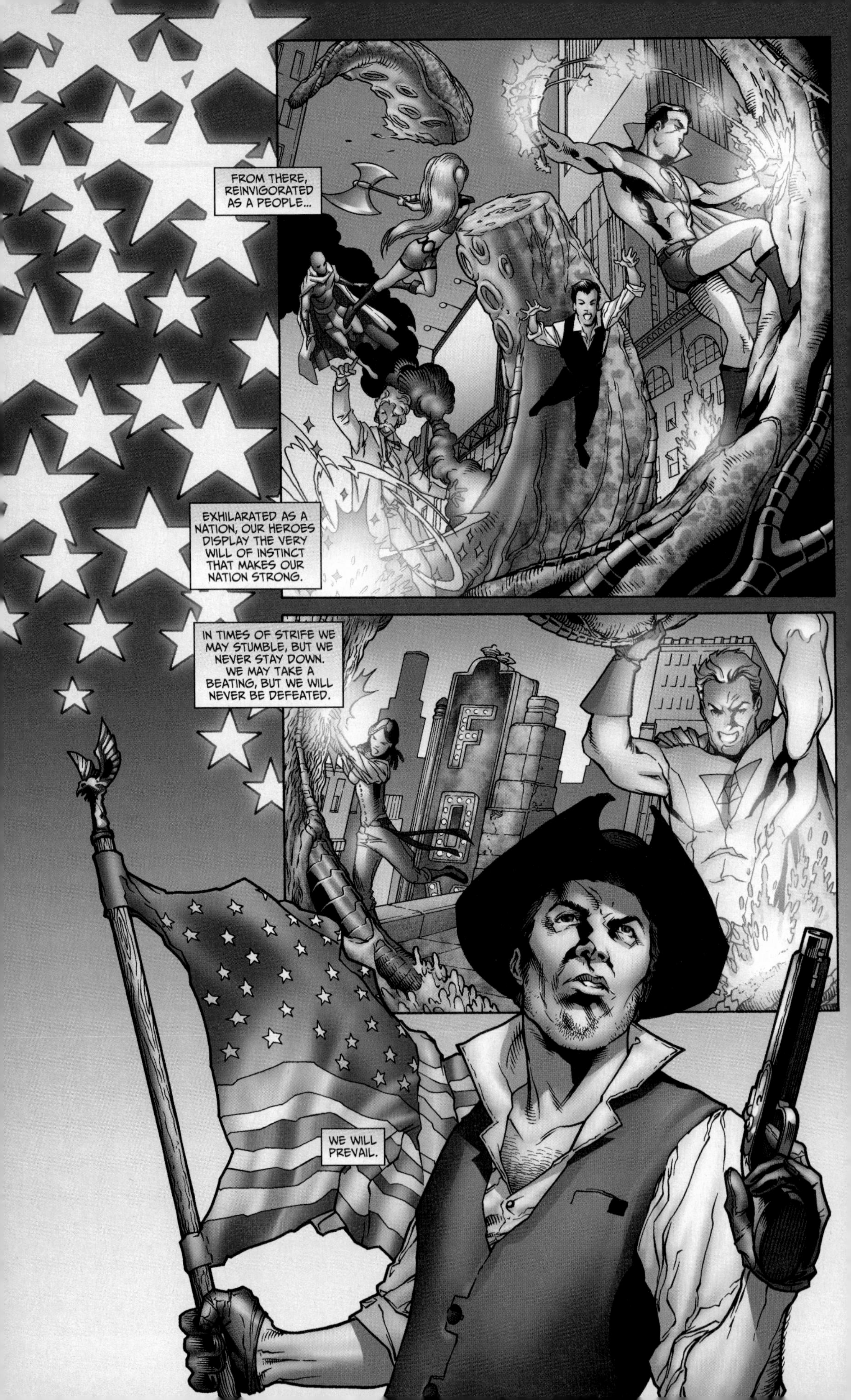
FROM THERE, REINVIGORATED AS A PEOPLE...
EXHILARATED AS A NATION, OUR HEROES DISPLAY THE VERY WILL OF INSTINCT THAT MAKES OUR NATION STRONG.
IN TIMES OF STRIFE WE MAY STUMBLE, BUT WE NEVER STAY DOWN. WE MAY TAKE A BEATING, BUT WE WILL NEVER BE DEFEATED.
WE WILL PREVAIL.

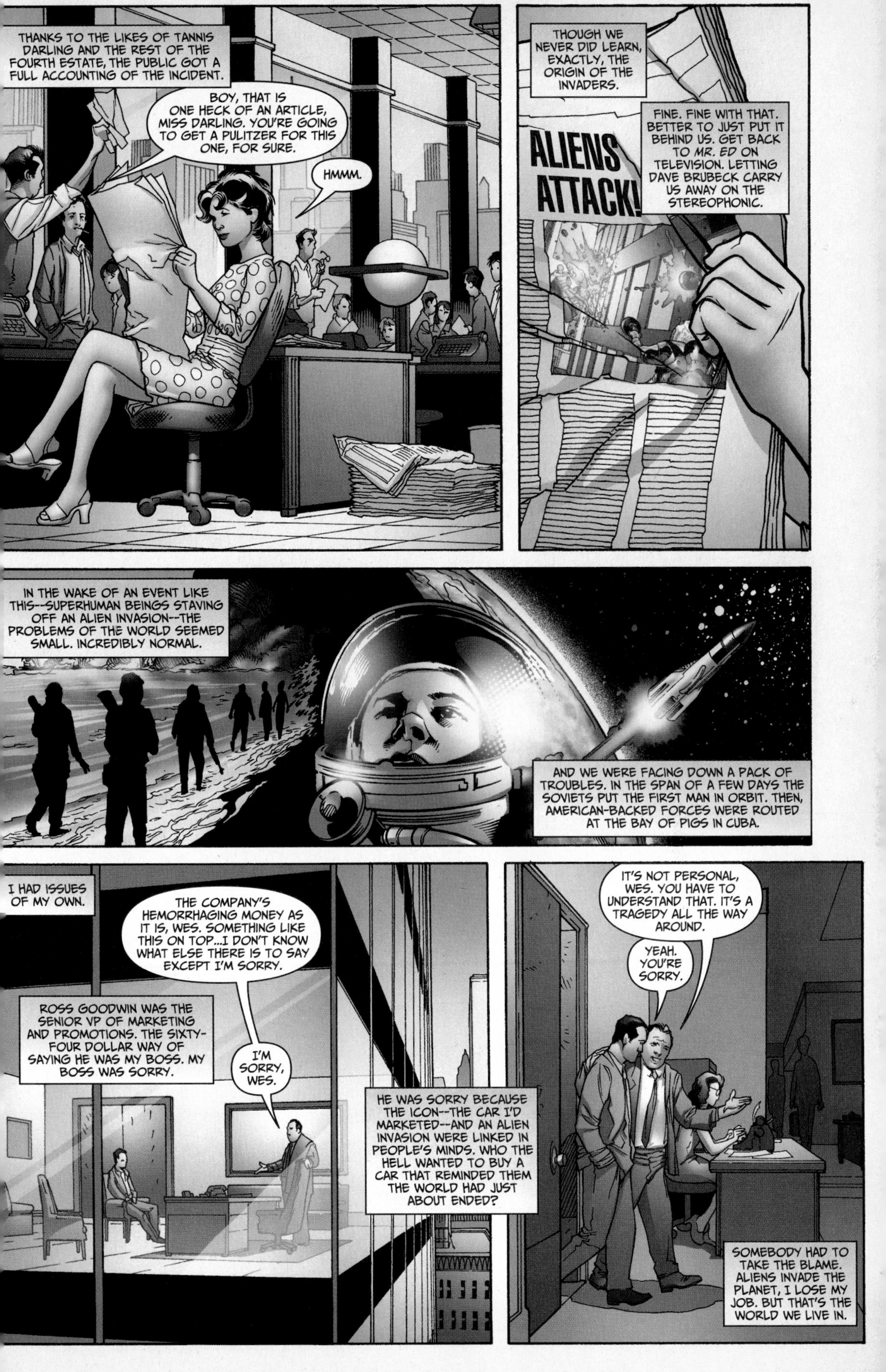
THANKS TO THE LIKES OF TANNIS DARLING AND THE REST OF THE FOURTH ESTATE, THE PUBLIC GOT A FULL ACCOUNTING OF THE INCIDENT.
BOY, THAT IS ONE HECK OF AN ARTICLE, MISS DARLING. YOU'RE GOING TO GET A PULITZER FOR THIS ONE, FOR SURE.
HMMM.
THOUGH WE NEVER DID LEARN, EXACTLY, THE ORIGIN OF THE INVADERS.
FINE. FINE WITH THAT. BETTER TO JUST PUT IT BEHIND US. GET BACK TO MR. ED ON TELEVISION. LETTING DAVE BRUBECK CARRY US AWAY ON THE STEREOPHONIC.
ALIENS ATTACK!
IN THE WAKE OF AN EVENT LIKE THIS--SUPERHUMAN BEINGS STAVING OFF AN ALIEN INVASION--THE PROBLEMS OF THE WORLD SEEMED SMALL. INCREDIBLY NORMAL.
AND WE WERE FACING DOWN A PACK OF TROUBLES. IN THE SPAN OF A FEW DAYS THE SOVIETS PUT THE FIRST MAN IN ORBIT. THEN, AMERICAN-BACKED FORCES WERE ROUTED AT THE BAY OF PIGS IN CUBA.
I HAD ISSUES OF MY OWN.
THE COMPANY'S HEMORRHAGING MONEY AS IT IS, WES. SOMETHING LIKE THIS ON TOP...I DON'T KNOW WHAT ELSE THERE IS TO SAY EXCEPT I'M SORRY.
ROSS GOODWIN WAS THE SENIOR VP OF MARKETING AND PROMOTIONS. THE SIXTY-FOUR DOLLAR WAY OF SAYING HE WAS MY BOSS. MY BOSS WAS SORRY.
I'M SORRY, WES.
HE WAS SORRY BECAUSE THE ICON--THE CAR I'D MARKETED--AND AN ALIEN INVASION WERE LINKED IN PEOPLE'S MINDS. WHO THE HELL WANTED TO BUY A CAR THAT REMINDED THEM THE WORLD HAD JUST ABOUT ENDED?
IT'S NOT PERSONAL, WES. YOU HAVE TO UNDERSTAND THAT. IT'S A TRAGEDY ALL THE WAY AROUND.
YEAH. YOU'RE SORRY.
SOMEBODY HAD TO TAKE THE BLAME. ALIENS INVADE THE PLANET, I LOSE MY JOB. BUT THAT'S THE WORLD WE LIVE IN.

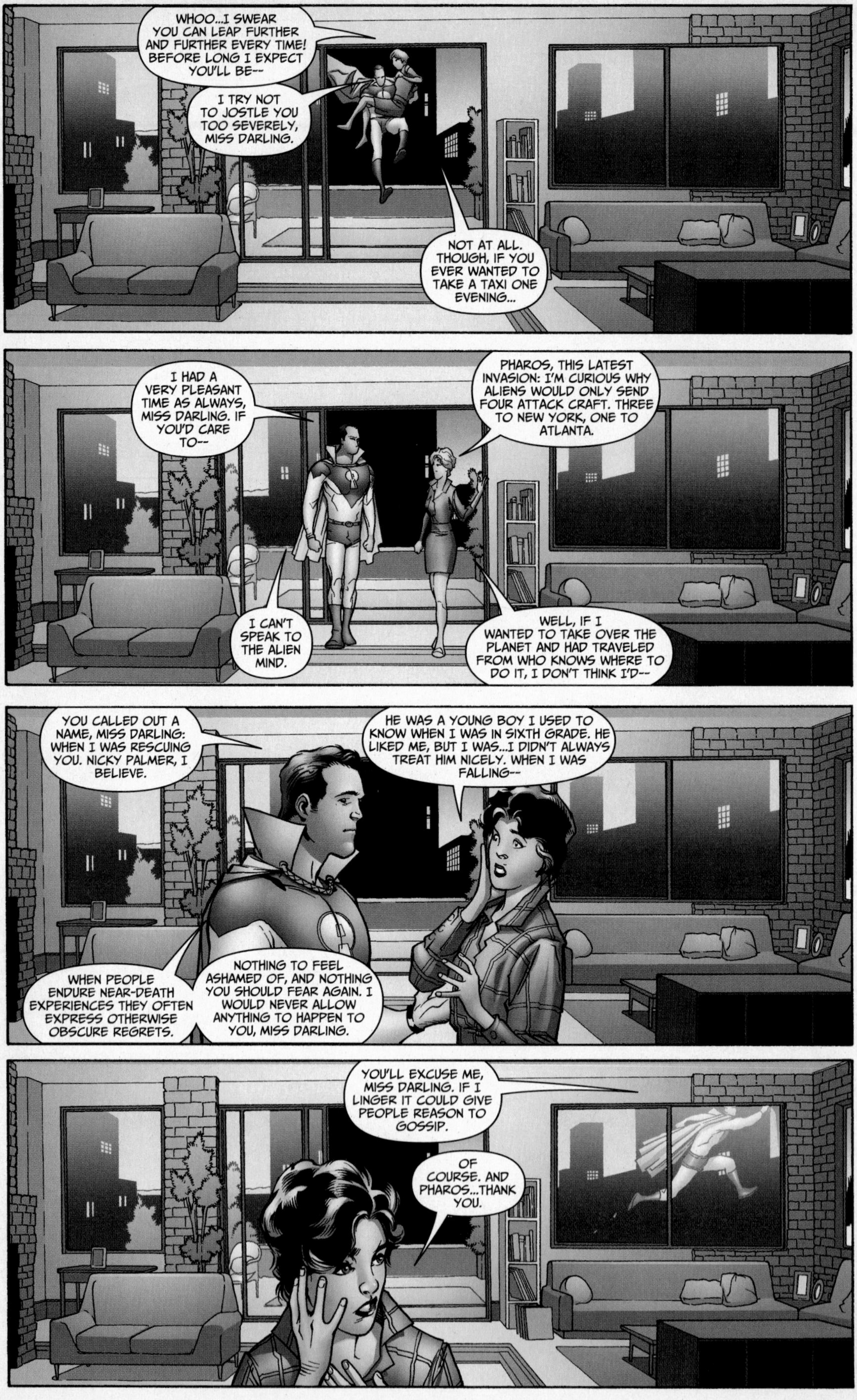
WHOO...I SWEAR YOU CAN LEAP FURTHER AND FURTHER EVERY TIME! BEFORE LONG I EXPECT YOU'LL BE--
I TRY NOT TO JOSTLE YOU TOO SEVERELY, MISS DARLING.
NOT AT ALL. THOUGH, IF YOU EVER WANTED TO TAKE A TAXI ONE EVENING...
I HAD A VERY PLEASANT TIME AS ALWAYS, MISS DARLING. IF YOU'D CARE TO--
PHAROS, THIS LATEST INVASION: I'M CURIOUS WHY ALIENS WOULD ONLY SEND FOUR ATTACK CRAFT. THREE TO NEW YORK, ONE TO ATLANTA.
I CAN'T SPEAK TO THE ALIEN MIND.
WELL, IF I WANTED TO TAKE OVER THE PLANET AND HAD TRAVELED FROM WHO KNOWS WHERE TO DO IT, I DON'T THINK I'D--
YOU CALLED OUT A NAME, MISS DARLING: WHEN I WAS RESCUING YOU. NICKY PALMER, I BELIEVE.
HE WAS A YOUNG BOY I USED TO KNOW WHEN I WAS IN SIXTH GRADE. HE LIKED ME, BUT I WAS...I DIDN'T ALWAYS TREAT HIM NICELY. WHEN I WAS FALLING--
WHEN PEOPLE ENDURE NEAR-DEATH EXPERIENCES THEY OFTEN EXPRESS OTHERWISE OBSCURE REGRETS.
NOTHING TO FEEL ASHAMED OF, AND NOTHING YOU SHOULD FEAR AGAIN. I WOULD NEVER ALLOW ANYTHING TO HAPPEN TO YOU, MISS DARLING.
YOU'LL EXCUSE ME, MISS DARLING. IF I LINGER IT COULD GIVE PEOPLE REASON TO GOSSIP.
OF COURSE. AND PHAROS...THANK YOU.

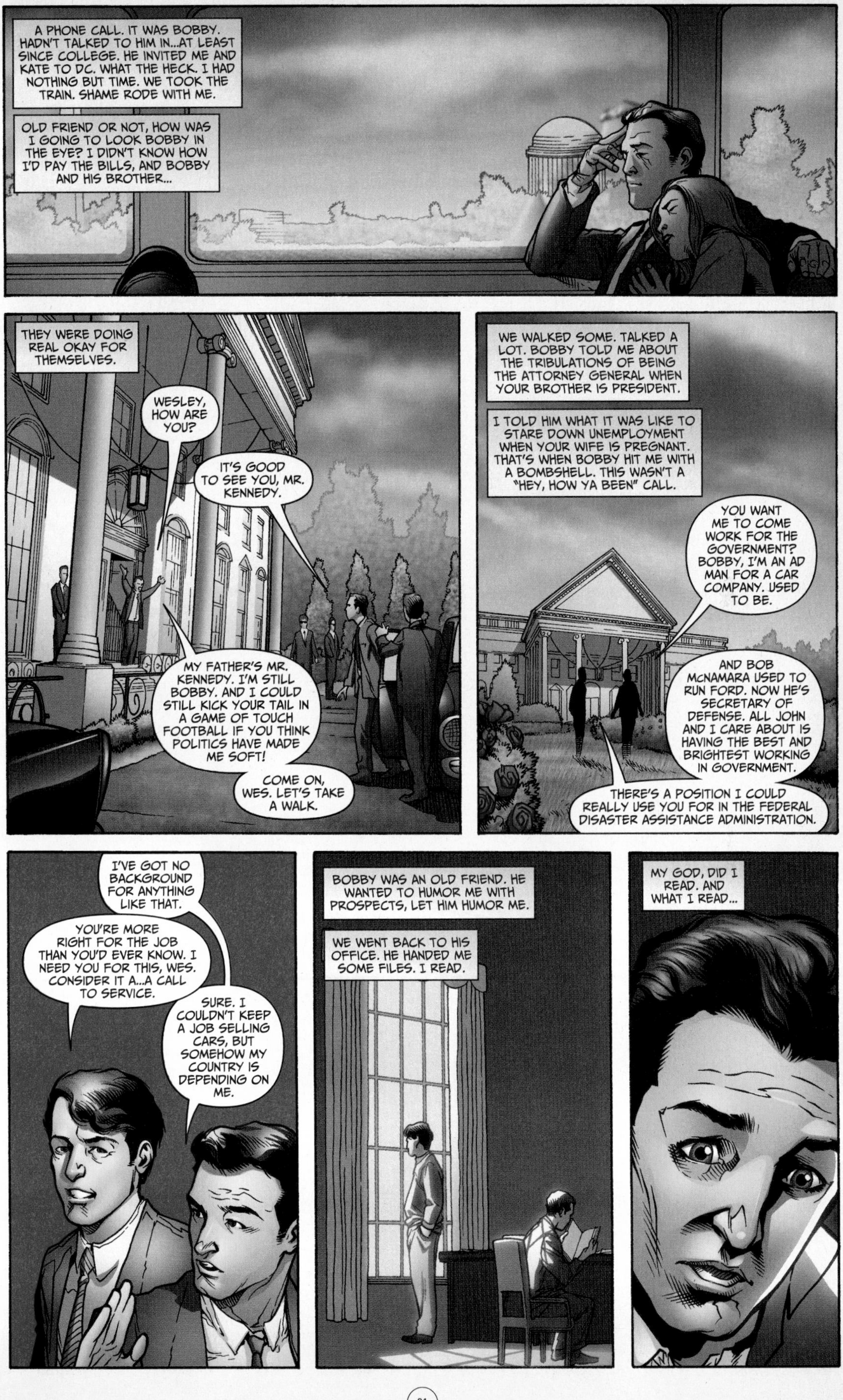
A PHONE CALL. IT WAS BOBBY. HADN'T TALKED TO HIM IN...AT LEAST SINCE COLLEGE. HE INVITED ME AND KATE TO DC. WHAT THE HECK. I HAD NOTHING BUT TIME. WE TOOK THE TRAIN. SHAME RODE WITH ME.
OLD FRIEND OR NOT, HOW WAS I GOING TO LOOK BOBBY IN THE EYE? I DIDN'T KNOW HOW I'D PAY THE BILLS, AND BOBBY AND HIS BROTHER...
THEY WERE DOING REAL OKAY FOR THEMSELVES.
WESLEY, HOW ARE YOU?
IT'S GOOD TO SEE YOU, MR. KENNEDY.
MY FATHER'S MR. KENNEDY. I'M STILL BOBBY. AND I COULD STILL KICK YOUR TAIL IN A GAME OF TOUCH FOOTBALL IF YOU THINK POLITICS HAVE MADE ME SOFT!
COME ON, WES. LET'S TAKE A WALK.
WE WALKED SOME. TALKED A LOT. BOBBY TOLD ME ABOUT THE TRIBULATIONS OF BEING THE ATTORNEY GENERAL WHEN YOUR BROTHER IS PRESIDENT.
I TOLD HIM WHAT IT WAS LIKE TO STARE DOWN UNEMPLOYMENT WHEN YOUR WIFE IS PREGNANT. THAT'S WHEN BOBBY HIT ME WITH A BOMBSHELL. THIS WASN'T A "HEY, HOW YA BEEN" CALL.
YOU WANT ME TO COME WORK FOR THE GOVERNMENT? BOBBY, I'M AN AD MAN FOR A CAR COMPANY. USED TO BE.
AND BOB McNAMARA USED TO RUN FORD. NOW HE'S SECRETARY OF DEFENSE. ALL JOHN AND I CARE ABOUT IS HAVING THE BEST AND BRIGHTEST WORKING IN GOVERNMENT.
THERE'S A POSITION I COULD REALLY USE YOU FOR IN THE FEDERAL DISASTER ASSISTANCE ADMINISTRATION.
I'VE GOT NO BACKGROUND FOR ANYTHING LIKE THAT.
YOU'RE MORE RIGHT FOR THE JOB THAN YOU'D EVER KNOW. I NEED YOU FOR THIS, WES. CONSIDER IT A...A CALL TO SERVICE.
SURE. I COULDN'T KEEP A JOB SELLING CARS, BUT SOMEHOW MY COUNTRY IS DEPENDING ON ME.
BOBBY WAS AN OLD FRIEND. HE WANTED TO HUMOR ME WITH PROSPECTS, LET HIM HUMOR ME.
WE WENT BACK TO HIS OFFICE. HE HANDED ME SOME FILES. I READ.
MY GOD, DID I READ. AND WHAT I READ...

I READ ABOUT THE FIRST SUPERHUMAN. BARELY MORE THAN A STRONG MAN AT A CIRCUS, BUT WITH HIDE THAT COULDN'T BE PIERCED. THE GOVERNMENT KNEW IT WOULDN'T BE LONG BEFORE MORE OF HIS KIND FOLLOWED.

MORE, BUT WOULD THEY BE AMERICAN, OR ENEMIES OF AMERICA? THE GOVERNMENT WASN'T TAKING THE CHANCE.

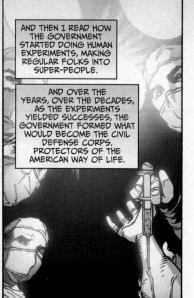

AND THEN I READ HOW THE GOVERNMENT STARTED DOING HUMAN EXPERIMENTS, MAKING REGULAR FOLKS INTO SUPER-PEOPLE.

AND OVER THE YEARS, OVER THE DECADES, AS THE EXPERIMENTS YIELDED SUCCESSES, THE GOVERNMENT FORMED WHAT WOULD BECOME THE CIVIL DEFENSE CORPS. PROTECTORS OF THE AMERICAN WAY OF LIFE.

AND TO MAKE SURE ALL OF HER ENEMIES GOT THE PICTURE, THE GOVERNMENT PUT ON A SHOW. THE SHOW WAS BIG AND PUBLIC AND TOOK PLACE WITH REGULARITY. A SHOW STARING THE CDC.

THE CDC AND THE SS ASSASSINS. THE CDC AND THE JAPOTEURS OR MAYBE THE BIG COMBO. THE CDC AND WHATEVER PERSONIFICATION OF EVIL THE GOVERNMENT CARED TO HAVE THEIR HEROES GIVE A CERTIFIED LICKING TO IN TIME FOR THE FOOTAGE TO MAKE THE EVENING NEWS.

THERE WAS A REASON THE CDC'S BATTLES, AS DESTRUCTIVE AS THEY WERE, NEVER ENDED WITH CIVILIAN DEATHS. A REASON VILLAINS AND INVADERS ATTACKED IN A MANNER THAT NEARLY GUARANTEED THEIR DEFEAT...

IT'D BEEN PLANNED THAT WAY. THE HEROES, THE VILLAINS WOULD FIGHT TO THE DEATH ONLY TO RETURN HOME, SLAP BACKS AND DRINK BEERS.

THE CIVIL DEFENSE CORPS. AMERICA'S HEROES. NOTHING BUT LIES.

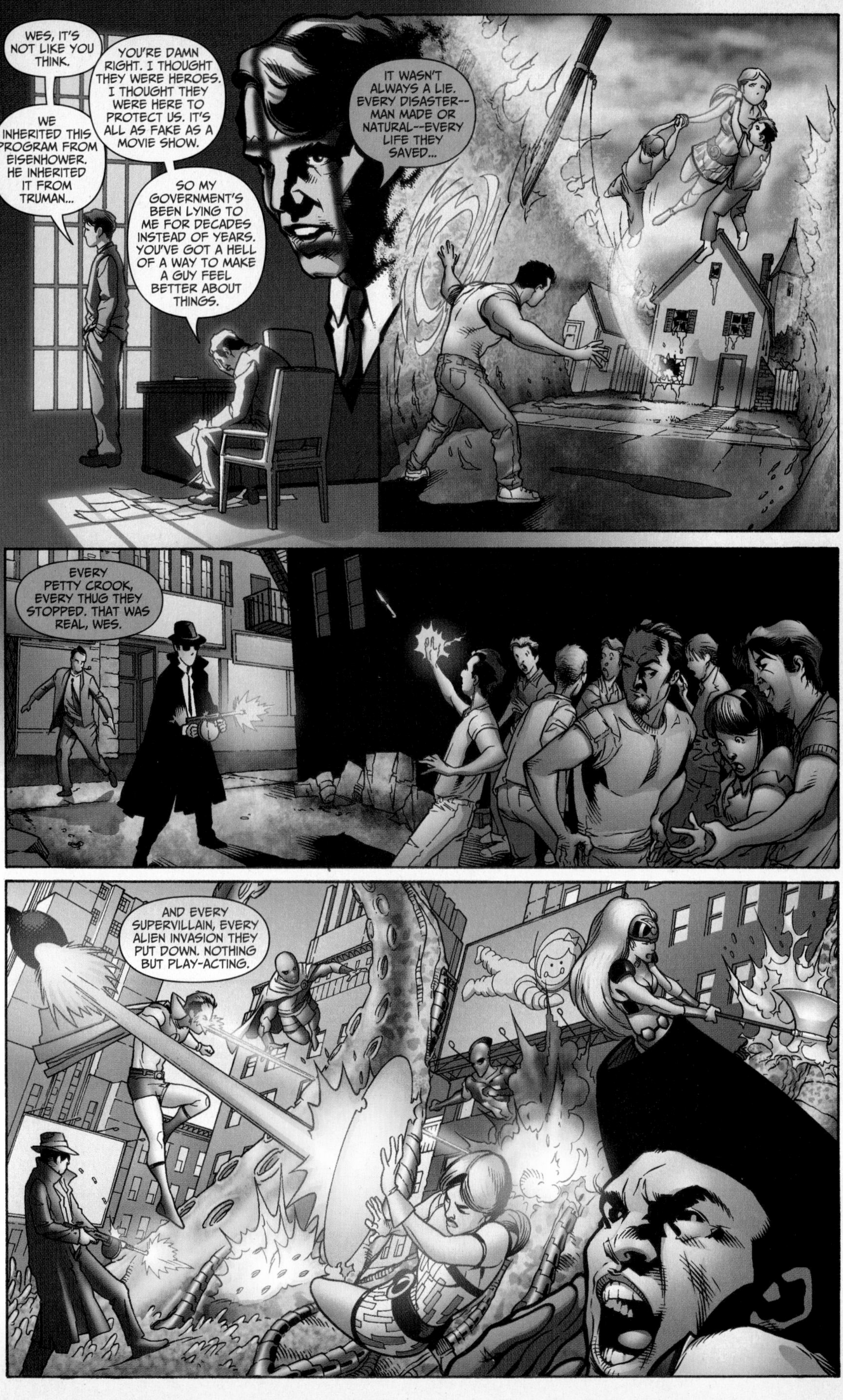
WES, IT'S NOT LIKE YOU THINK.
WE INHERITED THIS PROGRAM FROM EISENHOWER. HE INHERITED IT FROM TRUMAN...
YOU'RE DAMN RIGHT. I THOUGHT THEY WERE HEROES. I THOUGHT THEY WERE HERE TO PROTECT US. IT'S ALL AS FAKE AS A MOVIE SHOW.
SO MY GOVERNMENT'S BEEN LYING TO ME FOR DECADES INSTEAD OF YEARS. YOU'VE GOT A HELL OF A WAY TO MAKE A GUY FEEL BETTER ABOUT THINGS.
IT WASN'T ALWAYS A LIE. EVERY DISASTER--MAN MADE OR NATURAL--EVERY LIFE THEY SAVED...
EVERY PETTY CROOK, EVERY THUG THEY STOPPED. THAT WAS REAL, WES.
AND EVERY SUPERVILLAIN, EVERY ALIEN INVASION THEY PUT DOWN. NOTHING BUT PLAY-ACTING.

GOD, BOBBY. THE WANDERER ISN'T EVEN AN ALIEN. JUST SOME GUY IN A MASK AND SUIT.

PEOPLE FEAR OUTER SPACE. AN ALIEN OF OUR OWN HELPS EASE TENSIONS. THAT'S WHAT THIS IS ABOUT: PUTTING DOWN FEARS.

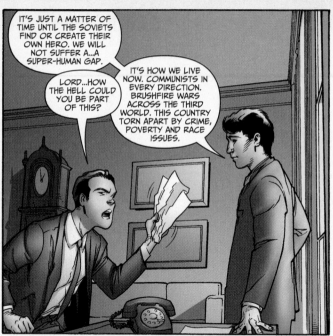

IT'S JUST A MATTER OF TIME UNTIL THE SOVIETS FIND OR CREATE THEIR OWN HERO. WE WILL NOT SUFFER A...A SUPER-HUMAN GAP.

LORD...HOW THE HELL COULD YOU BE PART OF THIS?

IT'S HOW WE LIVE NOW. COMMUNISTS IN EVERY DIRECTION. BRUSHFIRE WARS ACROSS THE THIRD WORLD. THIS COUNTRY TORN APART BY CRIME, POVERTY AND RACE ISSUES.

THE CIVIL DEFENSE CORPS ISN'T SOME ORWELLIAN FRAUD TO PLACATE THE MASSES.

IT'S ABOUT GIVING PEOPLE HOPE. GIVING THEM SOMETHING TO BELIEVE IN.

BELIEF IN WHAT? IT'S A CARNIVAL ACT. THE ONLY THINGS YOU'RE MISSING ARE A MIDGET AND A GEEK. ARE ANY OF THESE...THESE HEROES REAL?

SOME WERE BORN WITH SUPERIOR ABILITIES.

OTHERS ARE GENETICALLY ENHANCED THROUGH OUR...MEDICAL RESEARCH.

THE CAPTAIN, MR. LUCKY; THEIR ABILITIES SEEM TO BE, WELL, WE'RE NOT SURE. FREYA...SHE MIGHT ACTUALLY BE SOME KIND OF SUPERIOR BEING.

YOU MEAN A GOD? SHE MIGHT BE A GOD AND YOU'VE KEPT THIS A SECRET?

THE COUNTRY'S BARELY READY TO ACCEPT A CATHOLIC PRESIDENT. HOW DO YOU THINK THEY'D TAKE THE POSSIBILITY THERE MIGHT BE GODS OTHER THAN A CHRISTIAN ONE?

AND PHAROS?

WE DON'T REALLY KNOW THAT MUCH ABOUT HIM EXCEPT THAT HE SEEMS INCORRUPTIBLE.

AND HE'S GROWING MORE POWERFUL EVERY DAY.

WES, I'VE TOLD YOU ALL THIS BECAUSE I NEED YOUR HELP.

HELP HOW? HELP LIE?

I NEED YOU TO SELL. WE'RE IN A PROPAGANDA WAR AS MUCH AS IT IS A COLD WAR. THE SOVIETS HAVE SPUTNIK AND GAGARIN. WE'VE GOT THE MIGHTY DELTA AND PHAROS. WE NEED TO SELL AMERICA AND THE WHOLE WORLD ON FREEDOM AND DEMOCRACY AND THE BELIEF THEIR LIFE WON'T END TOMORROW IN ATOMIC ASH.

I WENT BACK TO THE HOTEL. I TOLD KATE NOTHING. WHAT WAS I SUPPOSED TO TELL HER? THAT EVERYTHING SHE EVER BELIEVED WAS A LIE?

I TRIED TO PLAY THINGS STRAIGHT; I'D JUST HAD A VISIT WITH AN OLD FRIEND. SHE COULD SEE IT'D BEEN MORE THAN THAT. KATE OFFERED NO QUICK FIXES OR EASY PLATITUDES FOR MY MOOD.

KATE OFFERED ONLY HER PRESENCE. HER QUIET STRENGTH AND HER UNQUESTIONING DEVOTION. I WAS A FAILURE. AN OUT-OF-WORK SHILL. BUT STILL SHE BELIEVED IN ME.

SO WHAT WAS THE TRUTH? WERE THE CIVIL DEFENSE CORPS KEEPERS OF THE AMERICAN DREAM, OR BREAD AND CIRCUSES FOR THE MASSES?

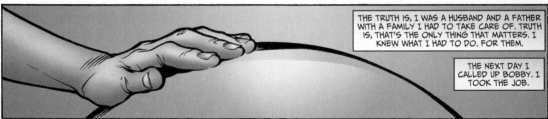

THE TRUTH IS, I WAS A HUSBAND AND A FATHER WITH A FAMILY I HAD TO TAKE CARE OF. TRUTH IS, THAT'S THE ONLY THING THAT MATTERS. I KNEW WHAT I HAD TO DO. FOR THEM.

THE NEXT DAY I CALLED UP BOBBY. I TOOK THE JOB.

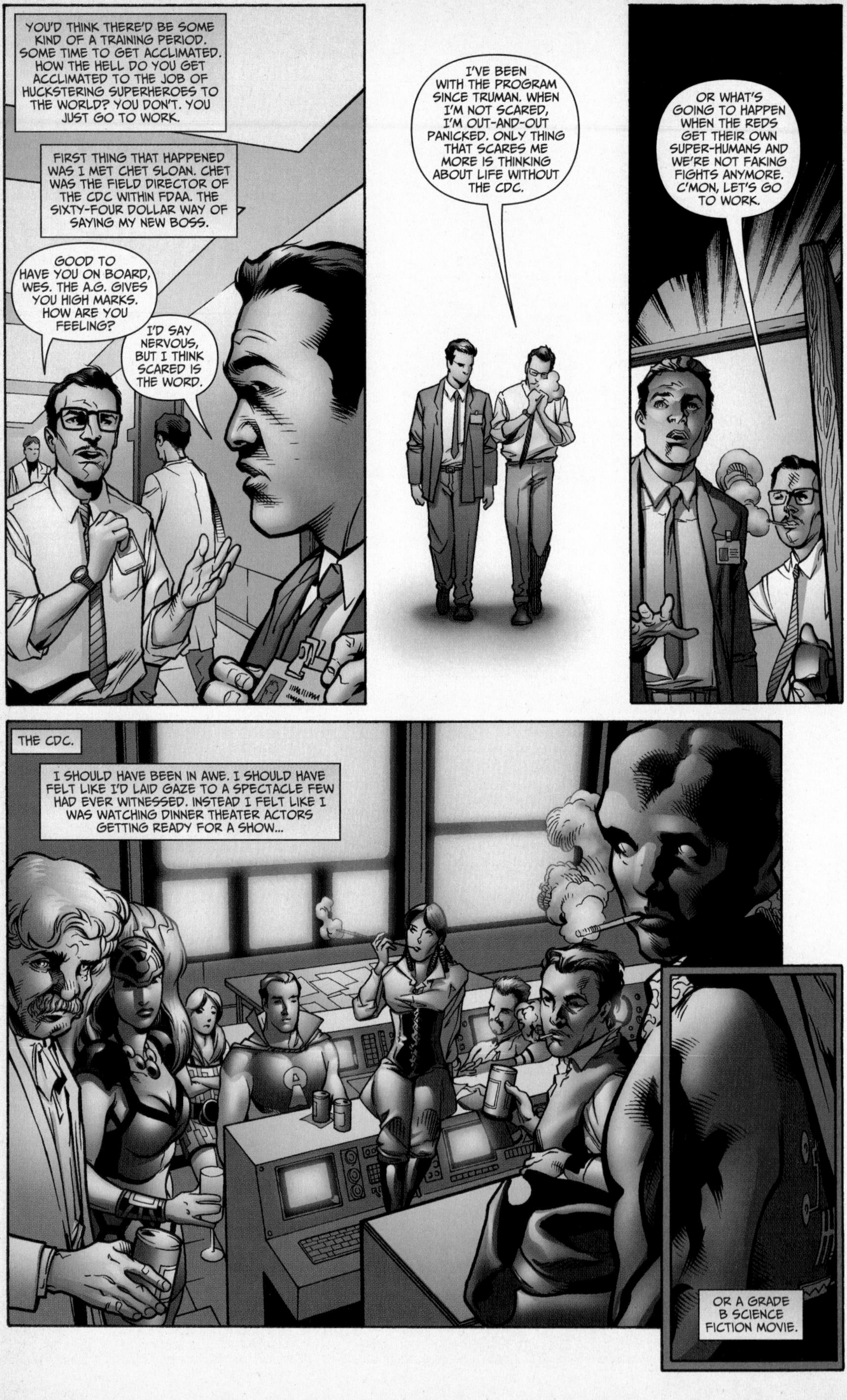
YOU'D THINK THERE'D BE SOME KIND OF A TRAINING PERIOD. SOME TIME TO GET ACCLIMATED. HOW THE HELL DO YOU GET ACCLIMATED TO THE JOB OF HUCKSTERING SUPERHEROES TO THE WORLD? YOU DON'T. YOU JUST GO TO WORK.
FIRST THING THAT HAPPENED WAS I MET CHET SLOAN. CHET WAS THE FIELD DIRECTOR OF THE CDC WITHIN FDAA. THE SIXTY-FOUR DOLLAR WAY OF SAYING MY NEW BOSS.
GOOD TO HAVE YOU ON BOARD, WES. THE A.G. GIVES YOU HIGH MARKS. HOW ARE YOU FEELING?
I'D SAY NERVOUS, BUT I THINK SCARED IS THE WORD.
I'VE BEEN WITH THE PROGRAM SINCE TRUMAN. WHEN I'M NOT SCARED, I'M OUT-AND-OUT PANICKED. ONLY THING THAT SCARES ME MORE IS THINKING ABOUT LIFE WITHOUT THE CDC.
OR WHAT'S GOING TO HAPPEN WHEN THE REDS GET THEIR OWN SUPER-HUMANS AND WE'RE NOT FAKING FIGHTS ANYMORE. C'MON, LET'S GO TO WORK.
THE CDC.
I SHOULD HAVE BEEN IN AWE. I SHOULD HAVE FELT LIKE I'D LAID GAZE TO A SPECTACLE FEW HAD EVER WITNESSED. INSTEAD I FELT LIKE I WAS WATCHING DINNER THEATER ACTORS GETTING READY FOR A SHOW...
OR A GRADE B SCIENCE FICTION MOVIE.

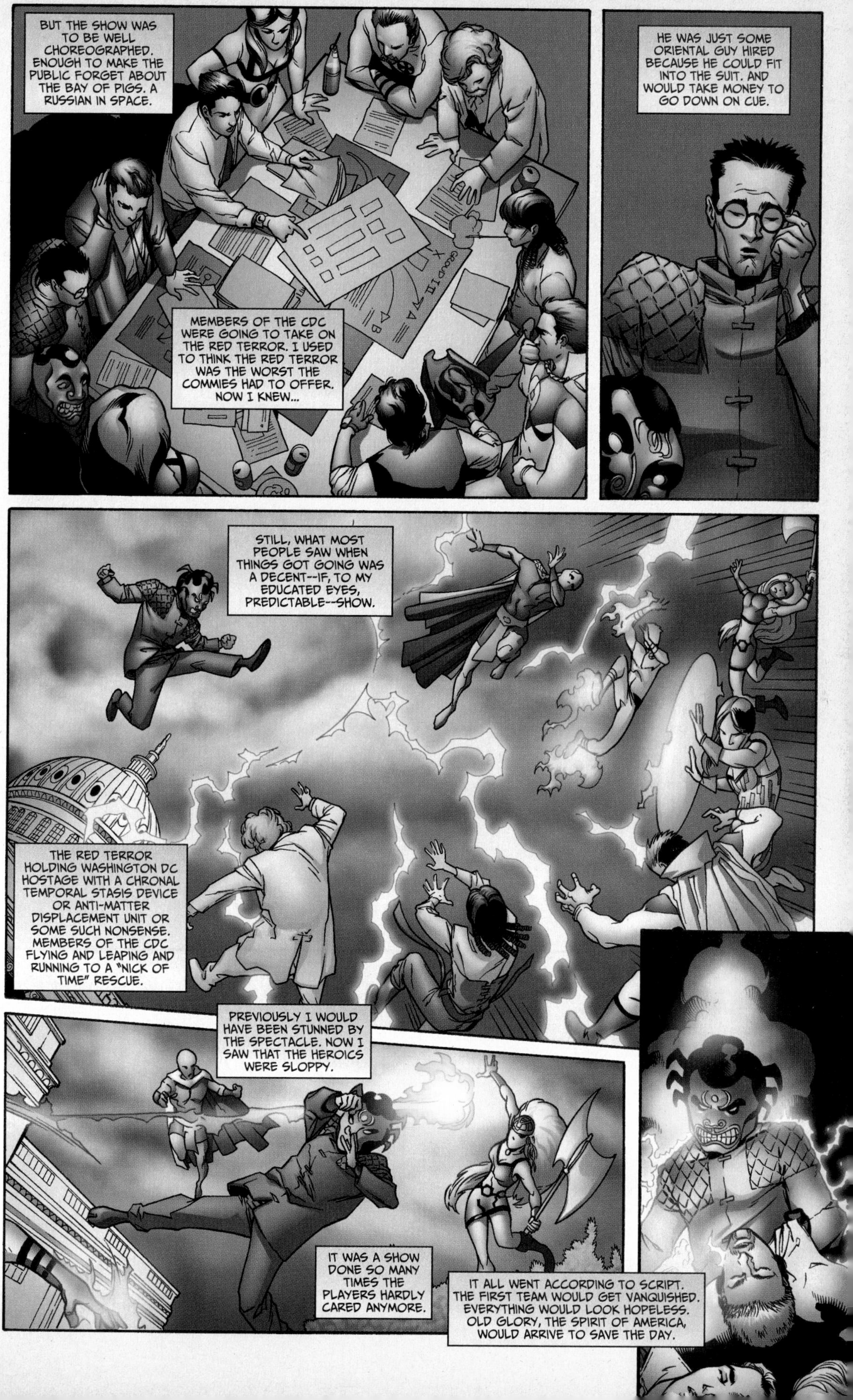

BUT THE SHOW WAS TO BE WELL CHOREOGRAPHED. ENOUGH TO MAKE THE PUBLIC FORGET ABOUT THE BAY OF PIGS. A RUSSIAN IN SPACE.
MEMBERS OF THE CDC WERE GOING TO TAKE ON THE RED TERROR. I USED TO THINK THE RED TERROR WAS THE WORST THE COMMIES HAD TO OFFER. NOW I KNEW...
HE WAS JUST SOME ORIENTAL GUY HIRED BECAUSE HE COULD FIT INTO THE SUIT. AND WOULD TAKE MONEY TO GO DOWN ON CUE.
STILL, WHAT MOST PEOPLE SAW WHEN THINGS GOT GOING WAS A DECENT--IF, TO MY EDUCATED EYES, PREDICTABLE--SHOW.
THE RED TERROR HOLDING WASHINGTON DC HOSTAGE WITH A CHRONAL TEMPORAL STASIS DEVICE OR ANTI-MATTER DISPLACEMENT UNIT OR SOME SUCH NONSENSE. MEMBERS OF THE CDC FLYING AND LEAPING AND RUNNING TO A "NICK OF TIME" RESCUE.
PREVIOUSLY I WOULD HAVE BEEN STUNNED BY THE SPECTACLE. NOW I SAW THAT THE HEROICS WERE SLOPPY.
IT WAS A SHOW DONE SO MANY TIMES THE PLAYERS HARDLY CARED ANYMORE.
IT ALL WENT ACCORDING TO SCRIPT. THE FIRST TEAM WOULD GET VANQUISHED. EVERYTHING WOULD LOOK HOPELESS. OLD GLORY, THE SPIRIT OF AMERICA, WOULD ARRIVE TO SAVE THE DAY.

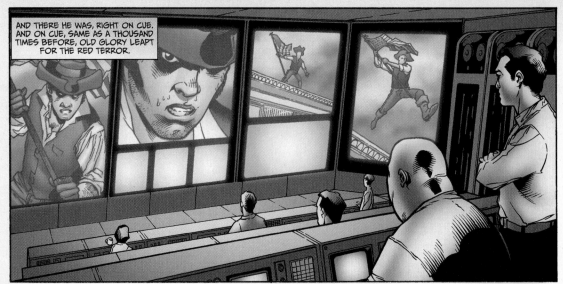

AND THERE HE WAS, RIGHT ON CUE. AND ON CUE, SAME AS A THOUSAND TIMES BEFORE, OLD GLORY LEAPT FOR THE RED TERROR.

AND THEN...I CAN'T SAY IF IT WAS BECAUSE OF MY VANTAGE POINT OF TRUTH, FROM KNOWING WHAT I WAS WATCHING WAS SUPPOSED TO BE FAKE. BUT I JUST...WE ALL COULD TELL SOMETHING WAS WRONG.

SOMETHING WAS HAPPENING WAY OFF SCRIPT.

THE IMPOSSIBLE WAS HAPPENING.

ON THE JOB LESS THAN A DAY. MY FIRST ASSIGNMENT: TELL THE WORLD OLD GLORY IS DEAD.

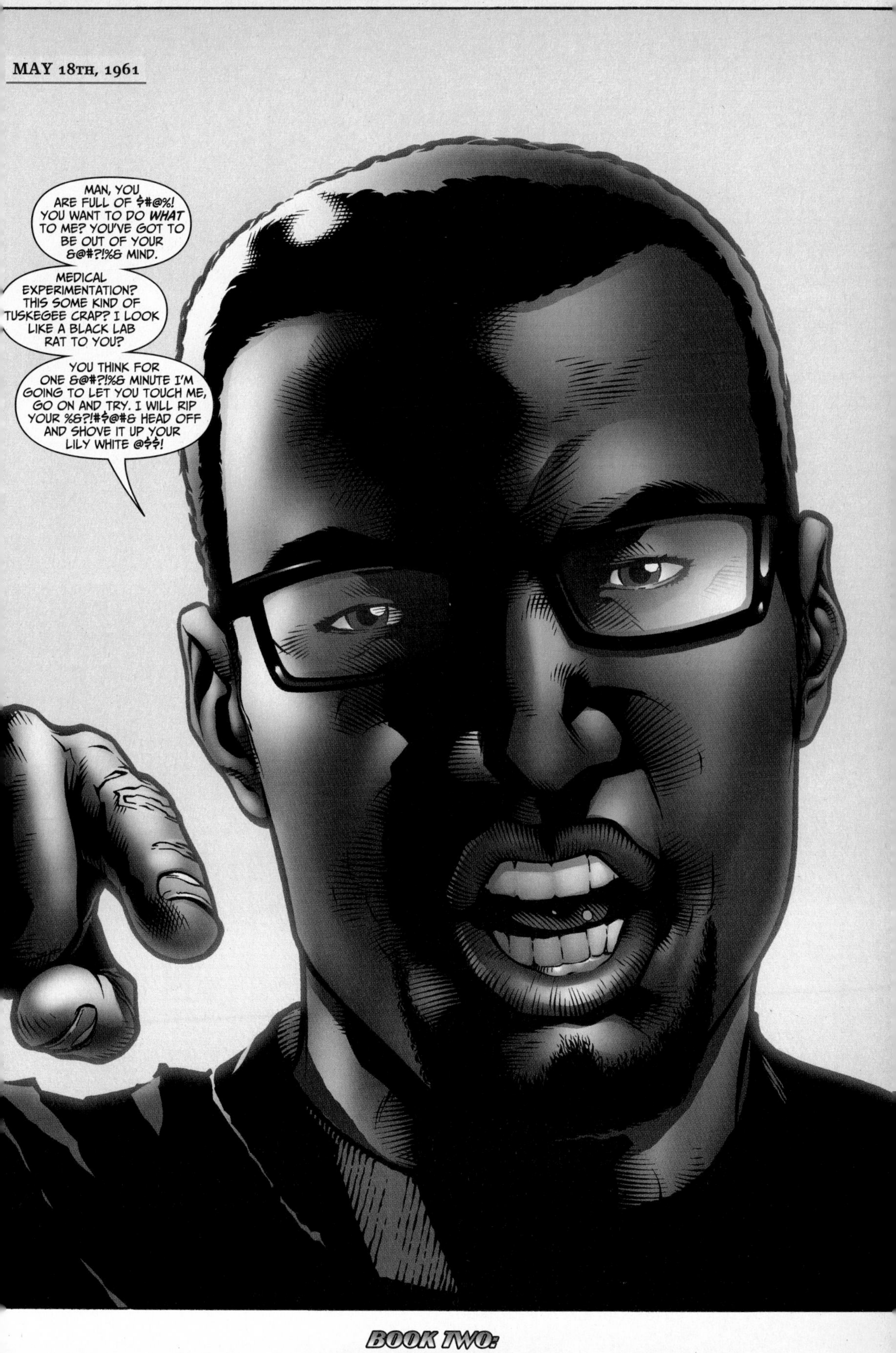
MAY 18TH, 1961
MAN, YOU ARE FULL OF $#@%! YOU WANT TO DO *WHAT* TO ME? YOU'VE GOT TO BE OUT OF YOUR &@#?!%& MIND.
MEDICAL EXPERIMENTATION? THIS SOME KIND OF TUSKEGEE CRAP? I LOOK LIKE A BLACK LAB RAT TO YOU?
YOU THINK FOR ONE &@#?!%& MINUTE I'M GOING TO LET YOU TOUCH ME, GO ON AND TRY. I WILL RIP YOUR %&?!#$@#& HEAD OFF AND SHOVE IT UP YOUR LILY WHITE @$$!

BOOK TWO:

A NEW GENERATION

RIGHT. EXCUSE US, WOULD YOU, MR. FISHER?

WE'RE JUST GONNA...IN THE HALL...FOR A SECOND.

YOU'RE RIBBING ME, YEAH?

DO I LOOK LIKE I'M KIDDING?

YOU'RE TELLING ME THAT FOUL-MOUTHED HOT HEAD IS GOING TO SAVE AMERICA?

THIS WAS *YOUR* IDEA. AND YOU GOT ME TO BACK YOUR PLAY. NOW IT'S MY HIDE ON THE LINE. I'M RUNNING THE CIVIL DEFENSE CORPS. YOU'RE JUST AN EX-CAR SALESMAN.

ALL OUR TESTING-- PSYCHOLOGICAL AND PHYSIOLOGICAL--TELLS US JASON FISHER IS THE BEST CANDIDATE FOR GENE MANIPULATION. HE HAS WHAT IT TAKES TO BE A HERO.

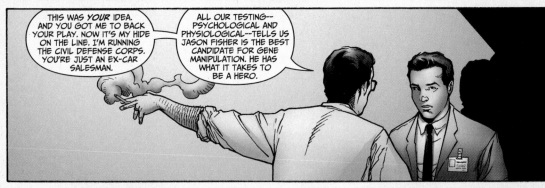

AND YOU'D BETTER GET HIM TO COME AROUND TO THINGS OR WE'RE ALL HEADING TO HELL WITHOUT THE HANDCART.

YEAH, WELL, THIS WAS MY IDEA. AND AT THE TIME IT SEEMED LIKE A HELL OF A GOOD ONE.

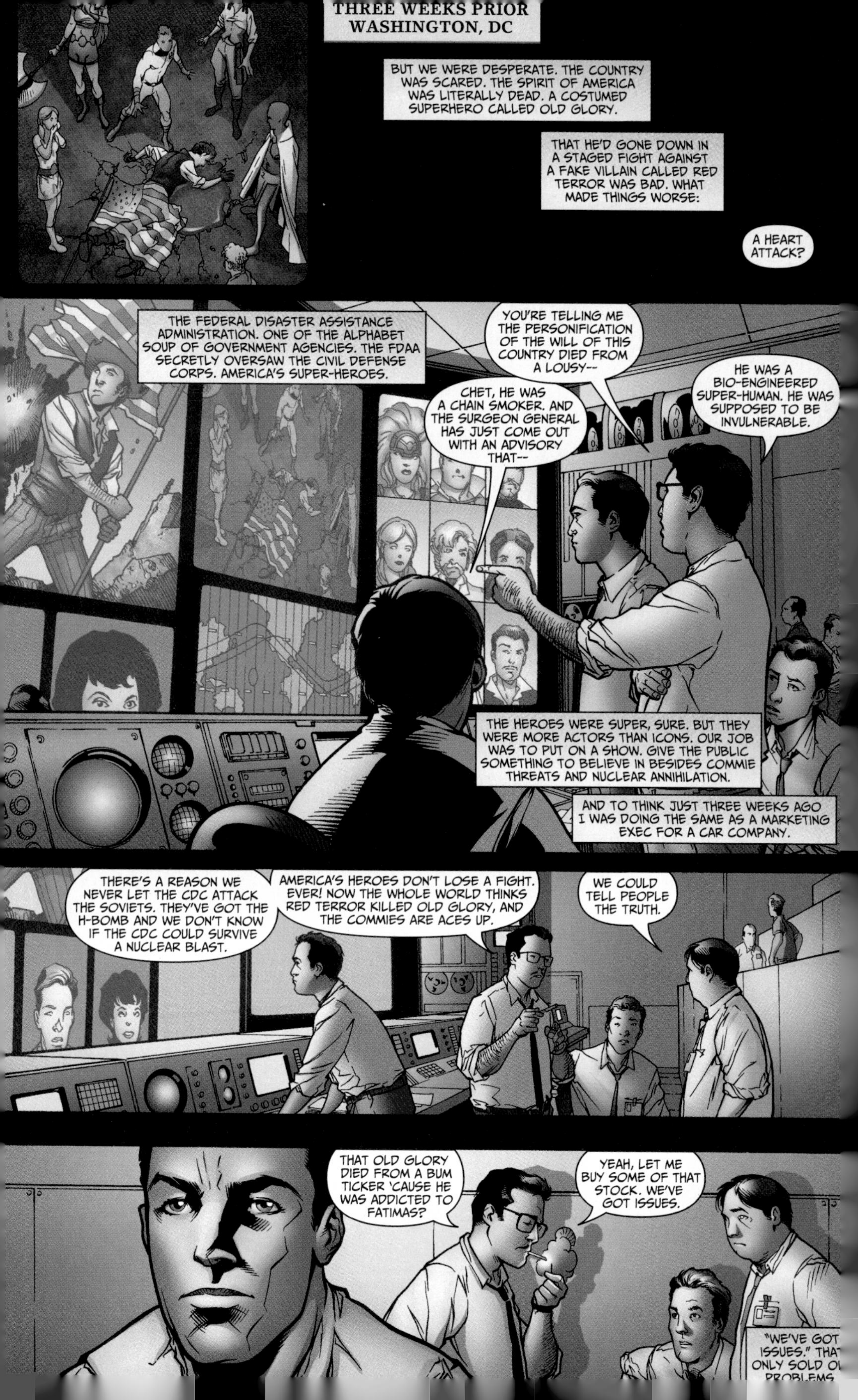
THREE WEEKS PRIOR
WASHINGTON, DC
BUT WE WERE DESPERATE. THE COUNTRY WAS SCARED. THE SPIRIT OF AMERICA WAS LITERALLY DEAD. A COSTUMED SUPERHERO CALLED OLD GLORY.
THAT HE'D GONE DOWN IN A STAGED FIGHT AGAINST A FAKE VILLAIN CALLED RED TERROR WAS BAD. WHAT MADE THINGS WORSE:
A HEART ATTACK?
THE FEDERAL DISASTER ASSISTANCE ADMINISTRATION. ONE OF THE ALPHABET SOUP OF GOVERNMENT AGENCIES. THE FDAA SECRETLY OVERSAW THE CIVIL DEFENSE CORPS. AMERICA'S SUPER-HEROES.
YOU'RE TELLING ME THE PERSONIFICATION OF THE WILL OF THIS COUNTRY DIED FROM A LOUSY--
CHET, HE WAS A CHAIN SMOKER. AND THE SURGEON GENERAL HAS JUST COME OUT WITH AN ADVISORY THAT--
HE WAS A BIO-ENGINEERED SUPER-HUMAN. HE WAS SUPPOSED TO BE INVULNERABLE.
THE HEROES WERE SUPER, SURE. BUT THEY WERE MORE ACTORS THAN ICONS. OUR JOB WAS TO PUT ON A SHOW. GIVE THE PUBLIC SOMETHING TO BELIEVE IN BESIDES COMMIE THREATS AND NUCLEAR ANNIHILATION.
AND TO THINK JUST THREE WEEKS AGO I WAS DOING THE SAME AS A MARKETING EXEC FOR A CAR COMPANY.
THERE'S A REASON WE NEVER LET THE CDC ATTACK THE SOVIETS. THEY'VE GOT THE H-BOMB AND WE DON'T KNOW IF THE CDC COULD SURVIVE A NUCLEAR BLAST.
AMERICA'S HEROES DON'T LOSE A FIGHT. EVER! NOW THE WHOLE WORLD THINKS RED TERROR KILLED OLD GLORY, AND THE COMMIES ARE ACES UP.
WE COULD TELL PEOPLE THE TRUTH.
THAT OLD GLORY DIED FROM A BUM TICKER 'CAUSE HE WAS ADDICTED TO FATIMAS?
YEAH, LET ME BUY SOME OF THAT STOCK. WE'VE GOT ISSUES.
"WE'VE GOT ISSUES." THA
ONLY SOLD O
PROBLEMS

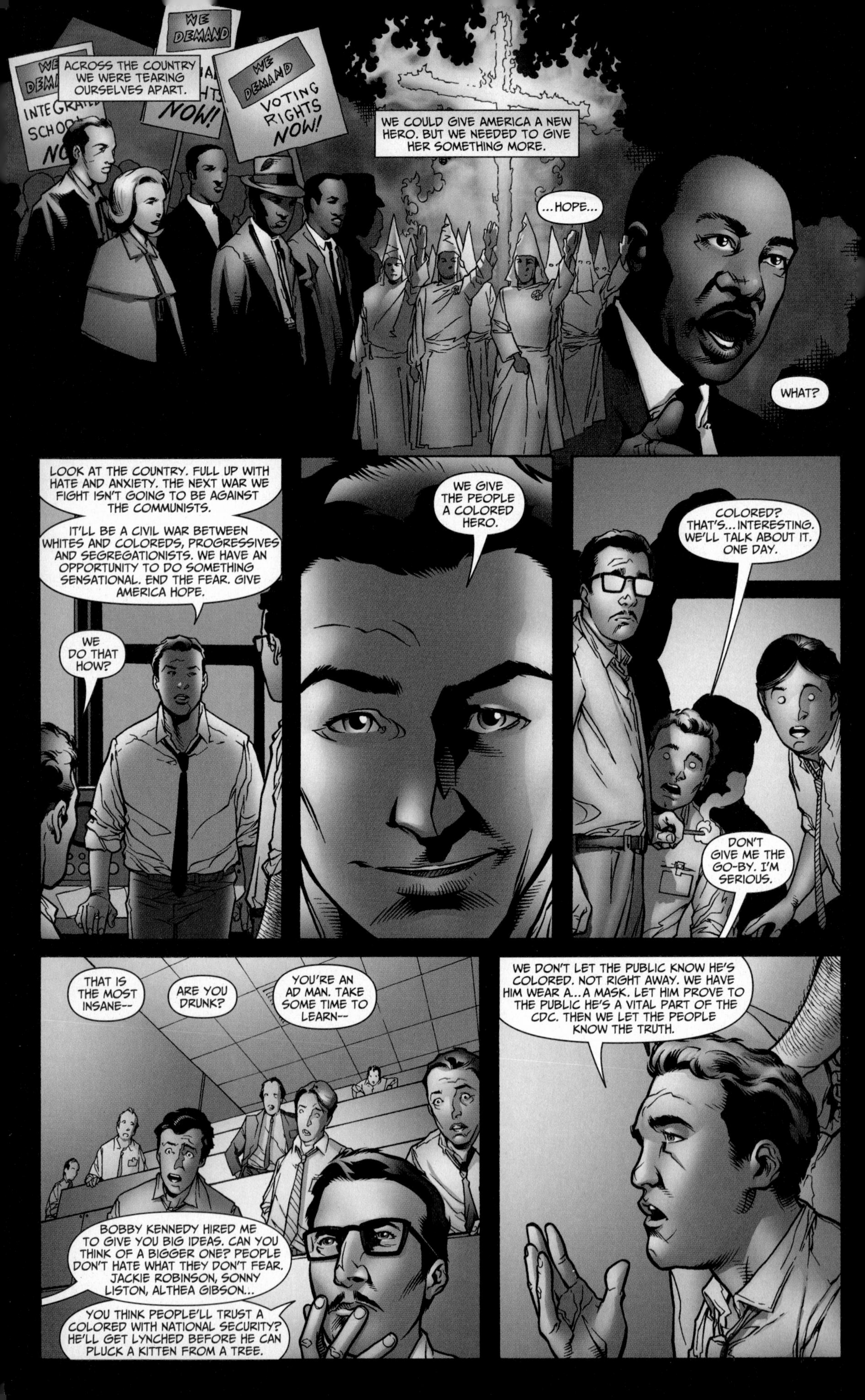
WE DEMAND
WE DEMAND INTEGRATED SCHOOLS NOW
ACROSS THE COUNTRY WE WERE TEARING OURSELVES APART.
WE DEMAND VOTING RIGHTS NOW!
WE COULD GIVE AMERICA A NEW HERO. BUT WE NEEDED TO GIVE HER SOMETHING MORE.
...HOPE...
WHAT?
LOOK AT THE COUNTRY. FULL UP WITH HATE AND ANXIETY. THE NEXT WAR WE FIGHT ISN'T GOING TO BE AGAINST THE COMMUNISTS.
IT'LL BE A CIVIL WAR BETWEEN WHITES AND COLOREDS, PROGRESSIVES AND SEGREGATIONISTS. WE HAVE AN OPPORTUNITY TO DO SOMETHING SENSATIONAL. END THE FEAR. GIVE AMERICA HOPE.
WE DO THAT HOW?
WE GIVE THE PEOPLE A COLORED HERO.
COLORED? THAT'S...INTERESTING. WE'LL TALK ABOUT IT. ONE DAY.
DON'T GIVE ME THE GO-BY. I'M SERIOUS.
THAT IS THE MOST INSANE--
ARE YOU DRUNK?
YOU'RE AN AD MAN. TAKE SOME TIME TO LEARN--
BOBBY KENNEDY HIRED ME TO GIVE YOU BIG IDEAS. CAN YOU THINK OF A BIGGER ONE? PEOPLE DON'T HATE WHAT THEY DON'T FEAR. JACKIE ROBINSON, SONNY LISTON, ALTHEA GIBSON...
YOU THINK PEOPLE'LL TRUST A COLORED WITH NATIONAL SECURITY? HE'LL GET LYNCHED BEFORE HE CAN PLUCK A KITTEN FROM A TREE.
WE DON'T LET THE PUBLIC KNOW HE'S COLORED. NOT RIGHT AWAY. WE HAVE HIM WEAR A...A MASK. LET HIM PROVE TO THE PUBLIC HE'S A VITAL PART OF THE CDC. THEN WE LET THE PEOPLE KNOW THE TRUTH.

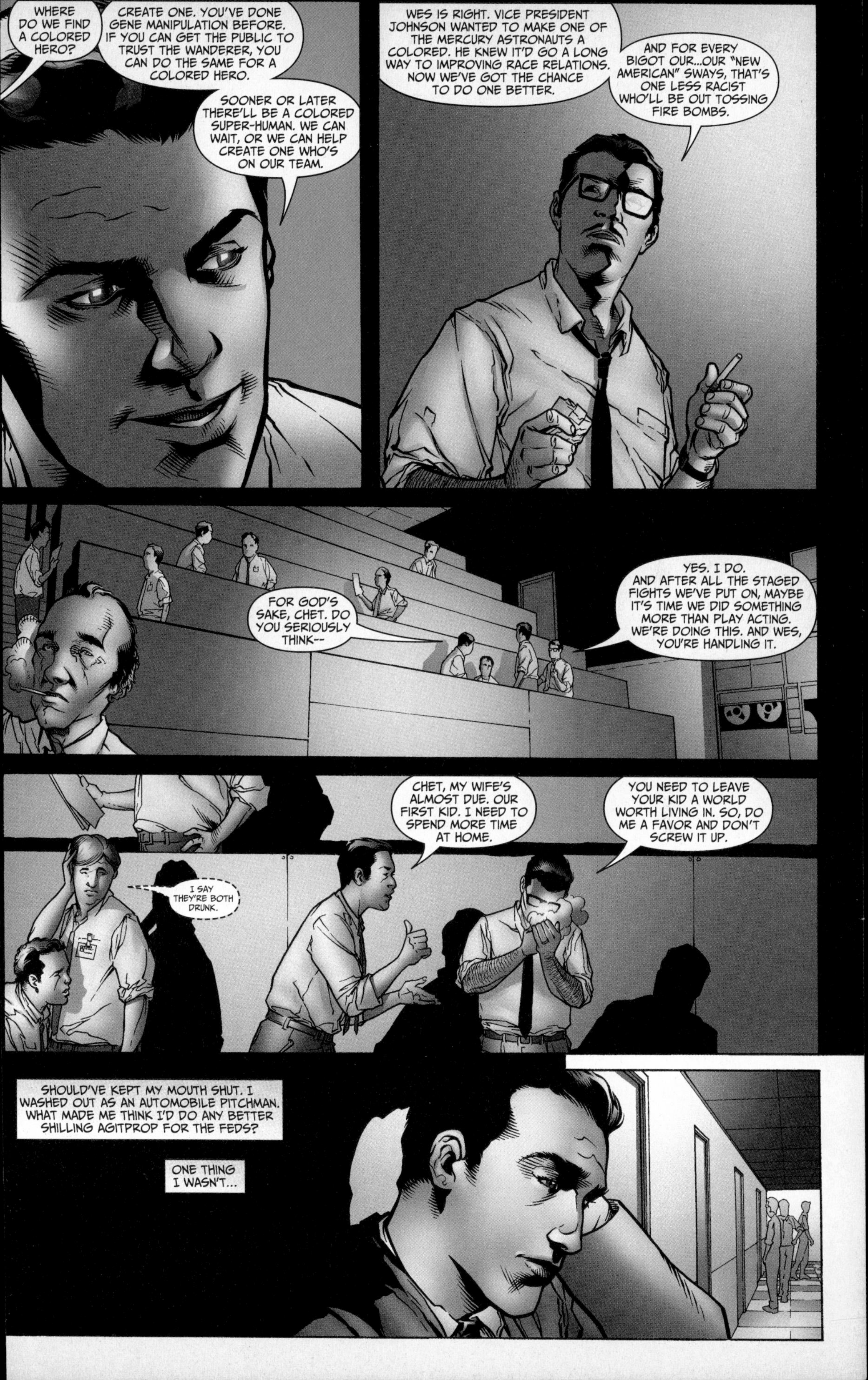
WHERE DO WE FIND A COLORED HERO?
CREATE ONE. YOU'VE DONE GENE MANIPULATION BEFORE. IF YOU CAN GET THE PUBLIC TO TRUST THE WANDERER, YOU CAN DO THE SAME FOR A COLORED HERO.
SOONER OR LATER THERE'LL BE A COLORED SUPER-HUMAN. WE CAN WAIT, OR WE CAN HELP CREATE ONE WHO'S ON OUR TEAM.
WES IS RIGHT. VICE PRESIDENT JOHNSON WANTED TO MAKE ONE OF THE MERCURY ASTRONAUTS A COLORED. HE KNEW IT'D GO A LONG WAY TO IMPROVING RACE RELATIONS. NOW WE'VE GOT THE CHANCE TO DO ONE BETTER.
AND FOR EVERY BIGOT OUR...OUR "NEW AMERICAN" SWAYS, THAT'S ONE LESS RACIST WHO'LL BE OUT TOSSING FIRE BOMBS.
FOR GOD'S SAKE, CHET. DO YOU SERIOUSLY THINK--
YES. I DO. AND AFTER ALL THE STAGED FIGHTS WE'VE PUT ON, MAYBE IT'S TIME WE DID SOMETHING MORE THAN PLAY ACTING. WE'RE DOING THIS. AND WES, YOU'RE HANDLING IT.
I SAY THEY'RE BOTH DRUNK.
CHET, MY WIFE'S ALMOST DUE. OUR FIRST KID. I NEED TO SPEND MORE TIME AT HOME.
YOU NEED TO LEAVE YOUR KID A WORLD WORTH LIVING IN. SO, DO ME A FAVOR AND DON'T SCREW IT UP.
SHOULD'VE KEPT MY MOUTH SHUT. I WASHED OUT AS AN AUTOMOBILE PITCHMAN. WHAT MADE ME THINK I'D DO ANY BETTER SHILLING AGITPROP FOR THE FEDS?
ONE THING I WASN'T...

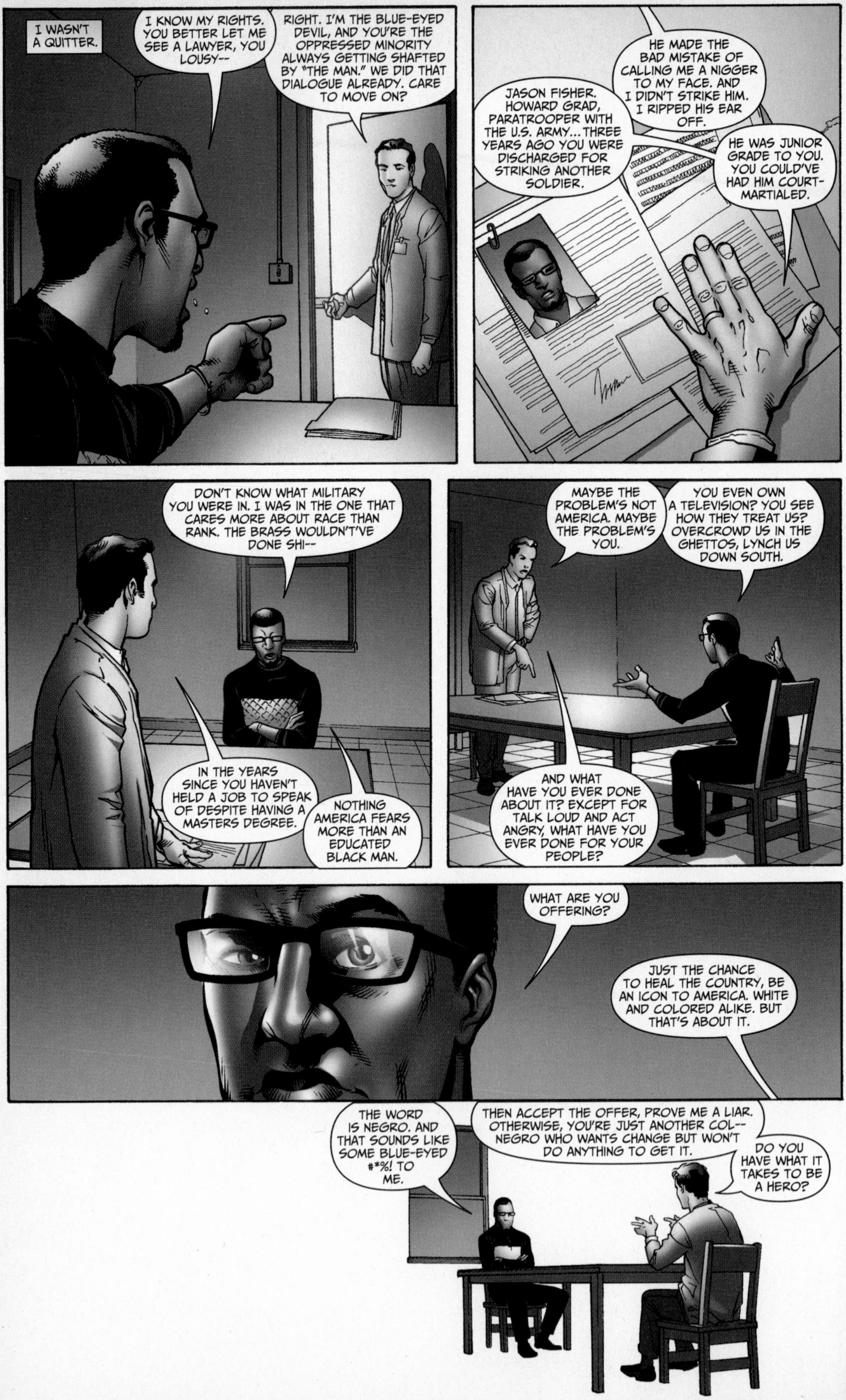
I WASN'T A QUITTER.
I KNOW MY RIGHTS. YOU BETTER LET ME SEE A LAWYER, YOU LOUSY--
RIGHT. I'M THE BLUE-EYED DEVIL, AND YOU'RE THE OPPRESSED MINORITY ALWAYS GETTING SHAFTED BY "THE MAN." WE DID THAT DIALOGUE ALREADY. CARE TO MOVE ON?
JASON FISHER. HOWARD GRAD, PARATROOPER WITH THE U.S. ARMY... THREE YEARS AGO YOU WERE DISCHARGED FOR STRIKING ANOTHER SOLDIER.
HE MADE THE BAD MISTAKE OF CALLING ME A NIGGER TO MY FACE. AND I DIDN'T STRIKE HIM. I RIPPED HIS EAR OFF.
HE WAS JUNIOR GRADE TO YOU. YOU COULD'VE HAD HIM COURT-MARTIALED.
DON'T KNOW WHAT MILITARY YOU WERE IN. I WAS IN THE ONE THAT CARES MORE ABOUT RACE THAN RANK. THE BRASS WOULDN'T'VE DONE SHI--
IN THE YEARS SINCE YOU HAVEN'T HELD A JOB TO SPEAK OF DESPITE HAVING A MASTERS DEGREE.
NOTHING AMERICA FEARS MORE THAN AN EDUCATED BLACK MAN.
MAYBE THE PROBLEM'S NOT AMERICA. MAYBE THE PROBLEM'S YOU.
YOU EVEN OWN A TELEVISION? YOU SEE HOW THEY TREAT US? OVERCROWD US IN THE GHETTOS, LYNCH US DOWN SOUTH.
AND WHAT HAVE YOU EVER DONE ABOUT IT? EXCEPT FOR TALK LOUD AND ACT ANGRY, WHAT HAVE YOU EVER DONE FOR YOUR PEOPLE?
WHAT ARE YOU OFFERING?
JUST THE CHANCE TO HEAL THE COUNTRY, BE AN ICON TO AMERICA. WHITE AND COLORED ALIKE. BUT THAT'S ABOUT IT.
THE WORD IS NEGRO. AND THAT SOUNDS LIKE SOME BLUE-EYED #*%! TO ME.
THEN ACCEPT THE OFFER, PROVE ME A LIAR. OTHERWISE, YOU'RE JUST ANOTHER COL-- NEGRO WHO WANTS CHANGE BUT WON'T DO ANYTHING TO GET IT.
DO YOU HAVE WHAT IT TAKES TO BE A HERO?

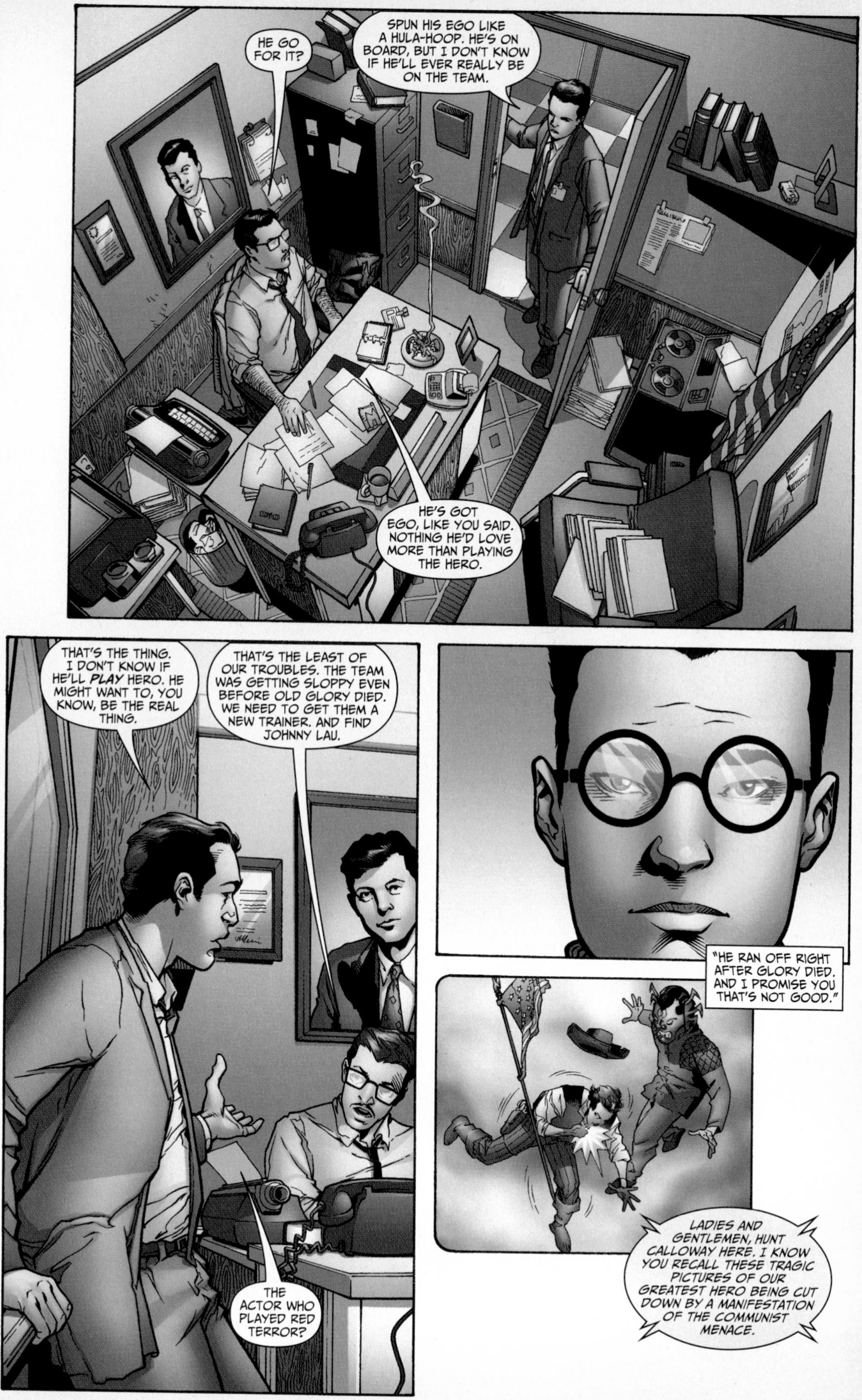
HE GO FOR IT?
SPUN HIS EGO LIKE A HULA-HOOP. HE'S ON BOARD, BUT I DON'T KNOW IF HE'LL EVER REALLY BE ON THE TEAM.
HE'S GOT EGO, LIKE YOU SAID. NOTHING HE'D LOVE MORE THAN PLAYING THE HERO.
THAT'S THE THING. I DON'T KNOW IF HE'LL *PLAY* HERO. HE MIGHT WANT TO, YOU KNOW, BE THE REAL THING.
THAT'S THE LEAST OF OUR TROUBLES. THE TEAM WAS GETTING SLOPPY EVEN BEFORE OLD GLORY DIED. WE NEED TO GET THEM A NEW TRAINER. AND FIND JOHNNY LAU.
THE ACTOR WHO PLAYED RED TERROR?
"HE RAN OFF RIGHT AFTER GLORY DIED. AND I PROMISE YOU THAT'S NOT GOOD."
LADIES AND GENTLEMEN, HUNT CALLOWAY HERE. I KNOW YOU RECALL THESE TRAGIC PICTURES OF OUR GREATEST HERO BEING CUT DOWN BY A MANIFESTATION OF THE COMMUNIST MENACE.

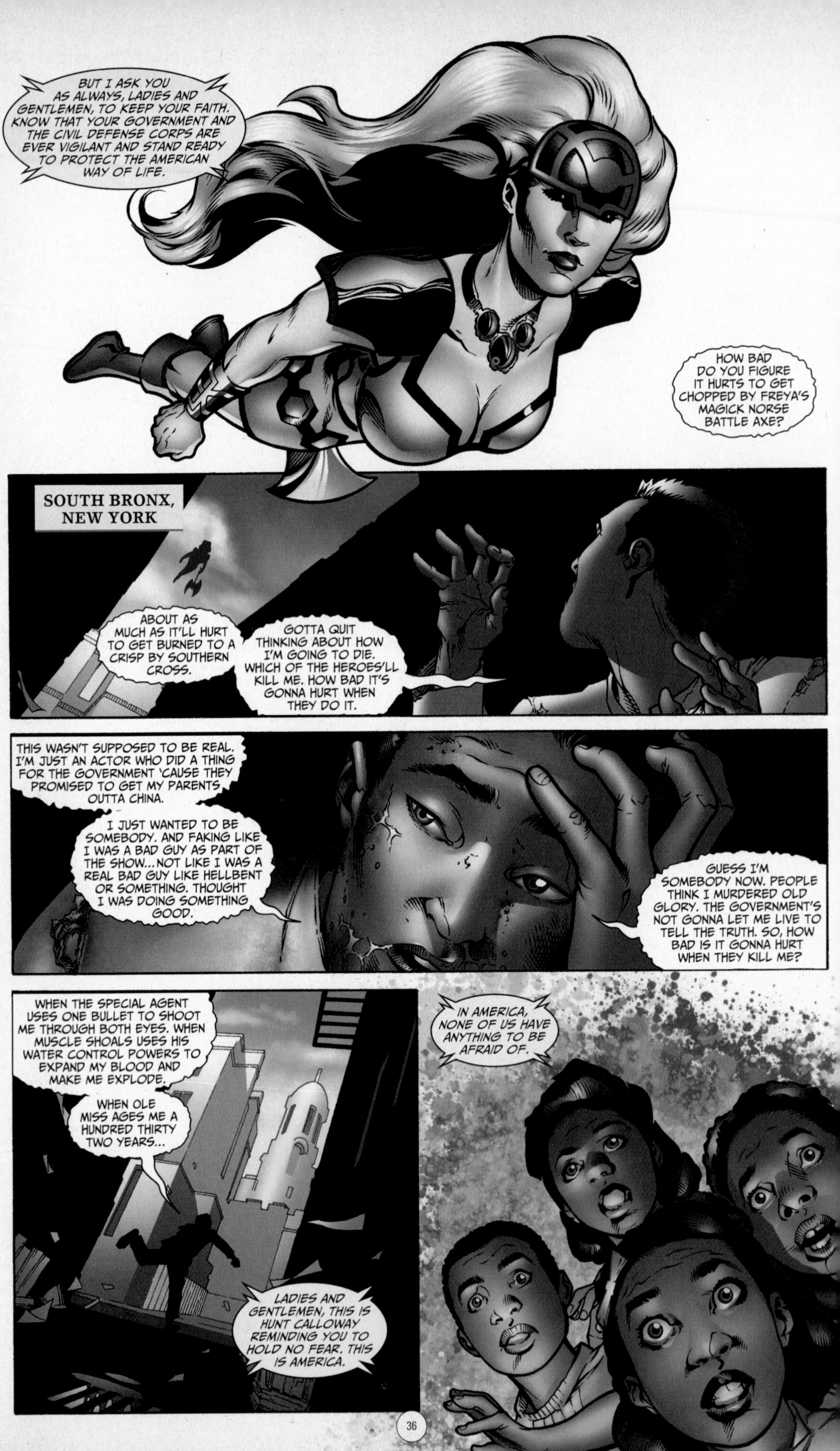
BUT I ASK YOU AS ALWAYS, LADIES AND GENTLEMEN, TO KEEP YOUR FAITH. KNOW THAT YOUR GOVERNMENT AND THE CIVIL DEFENSE CORPS ARE EVER VIGILANT AND STAND READY TO PROTECT THE AMERICAN WAY OF LIFE.
HOW BAD DO YOU FIGURE IT HURTS TO GET CHOPPED BY FREYA'S MAGICK NORSE BATTLE AXE?
SOUTH BRONX, NEW YORK
ABOUT AS MUCH AS IT'LL HURT TO GET BURNED TO A CRISP BY SOUTHERN CROSS.
GOTTA QUIT THINKING ABOUT HOW I'M GOING TO DIE. WHICH OF THE HEROES'LL KILL ME. HOW BAD IT'S GONNA HURT WHEN THEY DO IT.
THIS WASN'T SUPPOSED TO BE REAL. I'M JUST AN ACTOR WHO DID A THING FOR THE GOVERNMENT 'CAUSE THEY PROMISED TO GET MY PARENTS OUTTA CHINA.
I JUST WANTED TO BE SOMEBODY. AND FAKING LIKE I WAS A BAD GUY AS PART OF THE SHOW...NOT LIKE I WAS A REAL BAD GUY LIKE HELLBENT OR SOMETHING. THOUGHT I WAS DOING SOMETHING GOOD.
GUESS I'M SOMEBODY NOW. PEOPLE THINK I MURDERED OLD GLORY. THE GOVERNMENT'S NOT GONNA LET ME LIVE TO TELL THE TRUTH. SO, HOW BAD IS IT GONNA HURT WHEN THEY KILL ME?
WHEN THE SPECIAL AGENT USES ONE BULLET TO SHOOT ME THROUGH BOTH EYES. WHEN MUSCLE SHOALS USES HIS WATER CONTROL POWERS TO EXPAND MY BLOOD AND MAKE ME EXPLODE.
WHEN OLE MISS AGES ME A HUNDRED THIRTY TWO YEARS...
LADIES AND GENTLEMEN, THIS IS HUNT CALLOWAY REMINDING YOU TO HOLD NO FEAR. THIS IS AMERICA.
IN AMERICA, NONE OF US HAVE ANYTHING TO BE AFRAID OF.

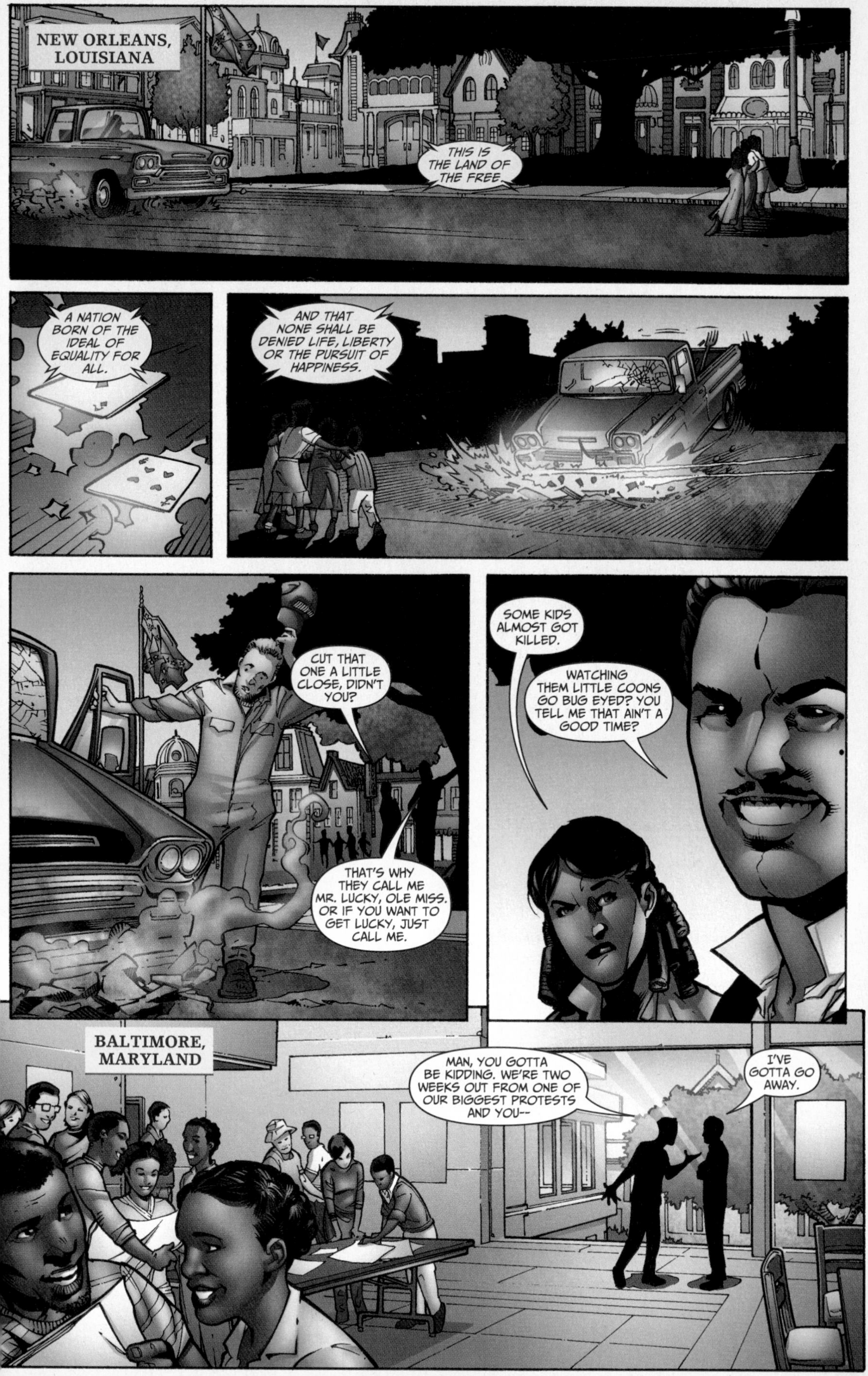
NEW ORLEANS, LOUISIANA
THIS IS THE LAND OF THE FREE.
A NATION BORN OF THE IDEAL OF EQUALITY FOR ALL.
AND THAT NONE SHALL BE DENIED LIFE, LIBERTY OR THE PURSUIT OF HAPPINESS.
CUT THAT ONE A LITTLE CLOSE, DIDN'T YOU?
THAT'S WHY THEY CALL ME MR. LUCKY, OLE MISS. OR IF YOU WANT TO GET LUCKY, JUST CALL ME.
SOME KIDS ALMOST GOT KILLED.
WATCHING THEM LITTLE COONS GO BUG EYED? YOU TELL ME THAT AIN'T A GOOD TIME?
BALTIMORE, MARYLAND
MAN, YOU GOTTA BE KIDDING. WE'RE TWO WEEKS OUT FROM ONE OF OUR BIGGEST PROTESTS AND YOU--
I'VE GOTTA GO AWAY.

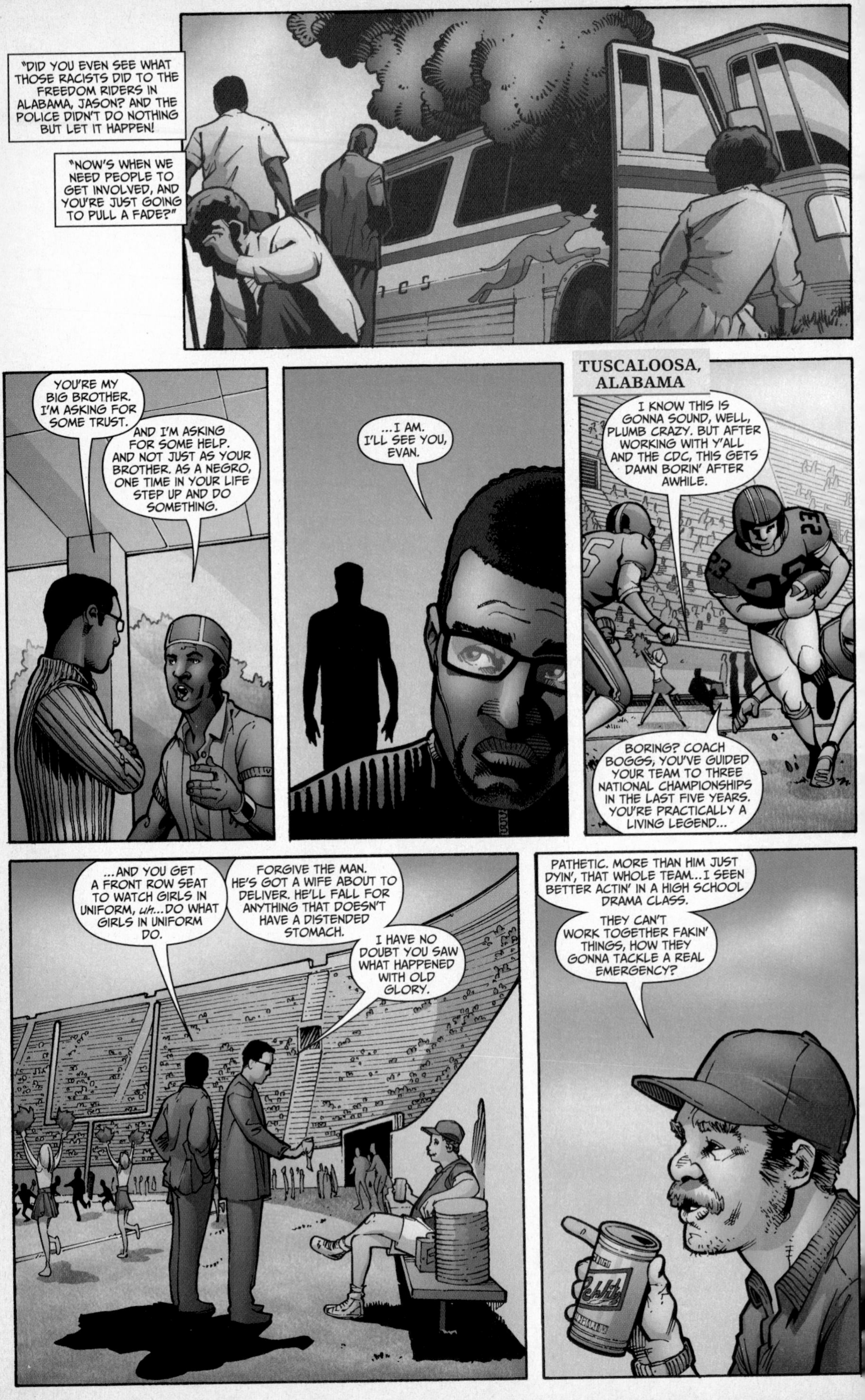
"DID YOU EVEN SEE WHAT THOSE RACISTS DID TO THE FREEDOM RIDERS IN ALABAMA, JASON? AND THE POLICE DIDN'T DO NOTHING BUT LET IT HAPPEN!
"NOW'S WHEN WE NEED PEOPLE TO GET INVOLVED, AND YOU'RE JUST GOING TO PULL A FADE?"
YOU'RE MY BIG BROTHER. I'M ASKING FOR SOME TRUST.
AND I'M ASKING FOR SOME HELP. AND NOT JUST AS YOUR BROTHER. AS A NEGRO, ONE TIME IN YOUR LIFE STEP UP AND DO SOMETHING.
...I AM. I'LL SEE YOU, EVAN.
TUSCALOOSA, ALABAMA
I KNOW THIS IS GONNA SOUND, WELL, PLUMB CRAZY. BUT AFTER WORKING WITH Y'ALL AND THE CDC, THIS GETS DAMN BORIN' AFTER AWHILE.
BORING? COACH BOGGS, YOU'VE GUIDED YOUR TEAM TO THREE NATIONAL CHAMPIONSHIPS IN THE LAST FIVE YEARS. YOU'RE PRACTICALLY A LIVING LEGEND...
...AND YOU GET A FRONT ROW SEAT TO WATCH GIRLS IN UNIFORM, *uh*...DO WHAT GIRLS IN UNIFORM DO.
FORGIVE THE MAN. HE'S GOT A WIFE ABOUT TO DELIVER. HE'LL FALL FOR ANYTHING THAT DOESN'T HAVE A DISTENDED STOMACH.
I HAVE NO DOUBT YOU SAW WHAT HAPPENED WITH OLD GLORY.
PATHETIC. MORE THAN HIM JUST DYIN', THAT WHOLE TEAM...I SEEN BETTER ACTIN' IN A HIGH SCHOOL DRAMA CLASS.
THEY CAN'T WORK TOGETHER FAKIN' THINGS, HOW THEY GONNA TACKLE A REAL EMERGENCY?

AND YOU KNOW, SOONER OR LATER, IT'S GONNA GET REAL.

THAT'S WHY WE WANT YOU TO COME BACK, COACH. WORK WITH THE TEAM. HALF OF THEM ARE SOUTHERNERS. I THINK THEY GET TIRED OF DEALING WITH US EAST COASTERS ALL THE TIME.

AND THERE ARE SOME... CHANGES WE'RE MAKING. HAVING YOU AROUND COULD SMOOTH THEM OVER.

WOULD LOVE TO GET BACK INTO THINGS, BUT THE MISSUS...SHE'S THE ONE WHO NAGGED ME BACK INTO COACHIN' COLLEGE BALL. COULDN'T STAND LIVIN' IN DC.

YEP, I WOULD SURELY LOVE TO COME BACK. EXCEPT FOR THE MISSUS.

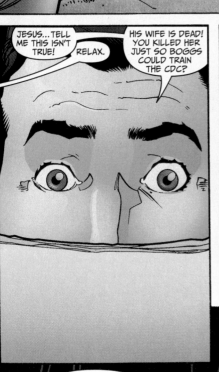

JESUS...TELL ME THIS ISN'T TRUE!

RELAX.

HIS WIFE IS DEAD! YOU KILLED HER JUST SO BOGGS COULD TRAIN THE CDC?

SURE. WE WERE GOING TO USE ALL THE RESOURCES OF THE U.S. GOVERNMENT TO ASSASSINATE THE WIFE OF A COLLEGE FOOTBALL COACH...

THEN WE DECIDED TO JUST GIVE HER A MILLION BUCKS IF SHE'D GO TO MILWAUKEE AND DISAPPEAR.

MILWAUKEE?

IT'S LIKE BEING DEAD...ONLY NOT AS PLEASANT. LOOK, WES, I KNOW WHAT WE DO HERE WOULD MAKE THE POPE LOSE HIS FAITH, BUT WE DON'T KILL BECAUSE IT'S EXPEDIENT.

HOW ARE THINGS WITH FISHER?

HE'S STARTED HIS GENE THERAPY. HE SHOULD BE READY FOR REAL WORLD TESTING IN A FEW WEEKS.

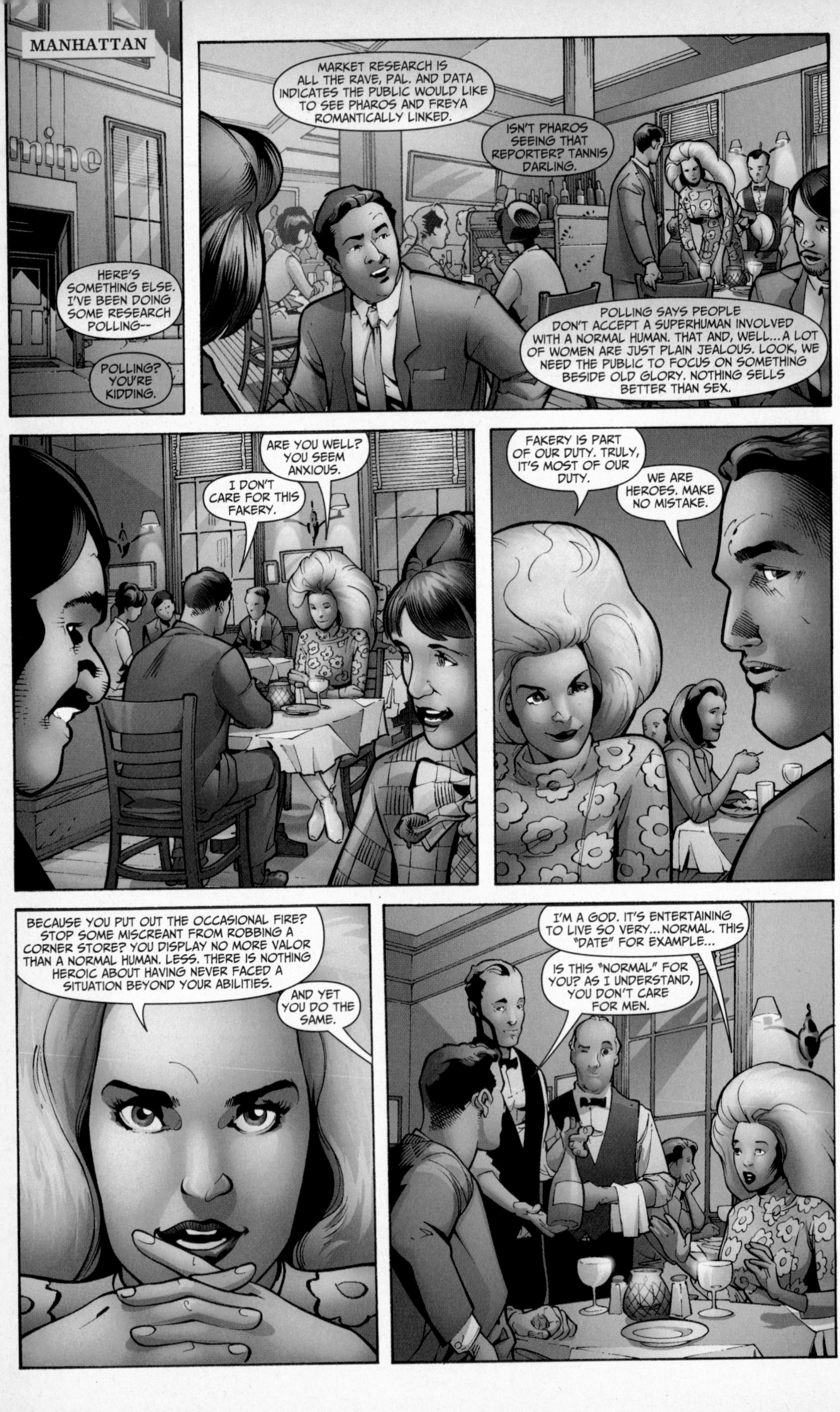
MANHATTAN
mine
HERE'S SOMETHING ELSE. I'VE BEEN DOING SOME RESEARCH POLLING--
POLLING? YOU'RE KIDDING.
MARKET RESEARCH IS ALL THE RAVE, PAL. AND DATA INDICATES THE PUBLIC WOULD LIKE TO SEE PHAROS AND FREYA ROMANTICALLY LINKED.
ISN'T PHAROS SEEING THAT REPORTER? TANNIS DARLING.
POLLING SAYS PEOPLE DON'T ACCEPT A SUPERHUMAN INVOLVED WITH A NORMAL HUMAN. THAT AND, WELL... A LOT OF WOMEN ARE JUST PLAIN JEALOUS. LOOK, WE NEED THE PUBLIC TO FOCUS ON SOMETHING BESIDE OLD GLORY. NOTHING SELLS BETTER THAN SEX.
ARE YOU WELL? YOU SEEM ANXIOUS.
I DON'T CARE FOR THIS FAKERY.
FAKERY IS PART OF OUR DUTY. TRULY, IT'S MOST OF OUR DUTY.
WE ARE HEROES. MAKE NO MISTAKE.
BECAUSE YOU PUT OUT THE OCCASIONAL FIRE? STOP SOME MISCREANT FROM ROBBING A CORNER STORE? YOU DISPLAY NO MORE VALOR THAN A NORMAL HUMAN. LESS. THERE IS NOTHING HEROIC ABOUT HAVING NEVER FACED A SITUATION BEYOND YOUR ABILITIES.
AND YET YOU DO THE SAME.
I'M A GOD. IT'S ENTERTAINING TO LIVE SO VERY... NORMAL. THIS "DATE" FOR EXAMPLE...
IS THIS "NORMAL" FOR YOU? AS I UNDERSTAND, YOU DON'T CARE FOR MEN.

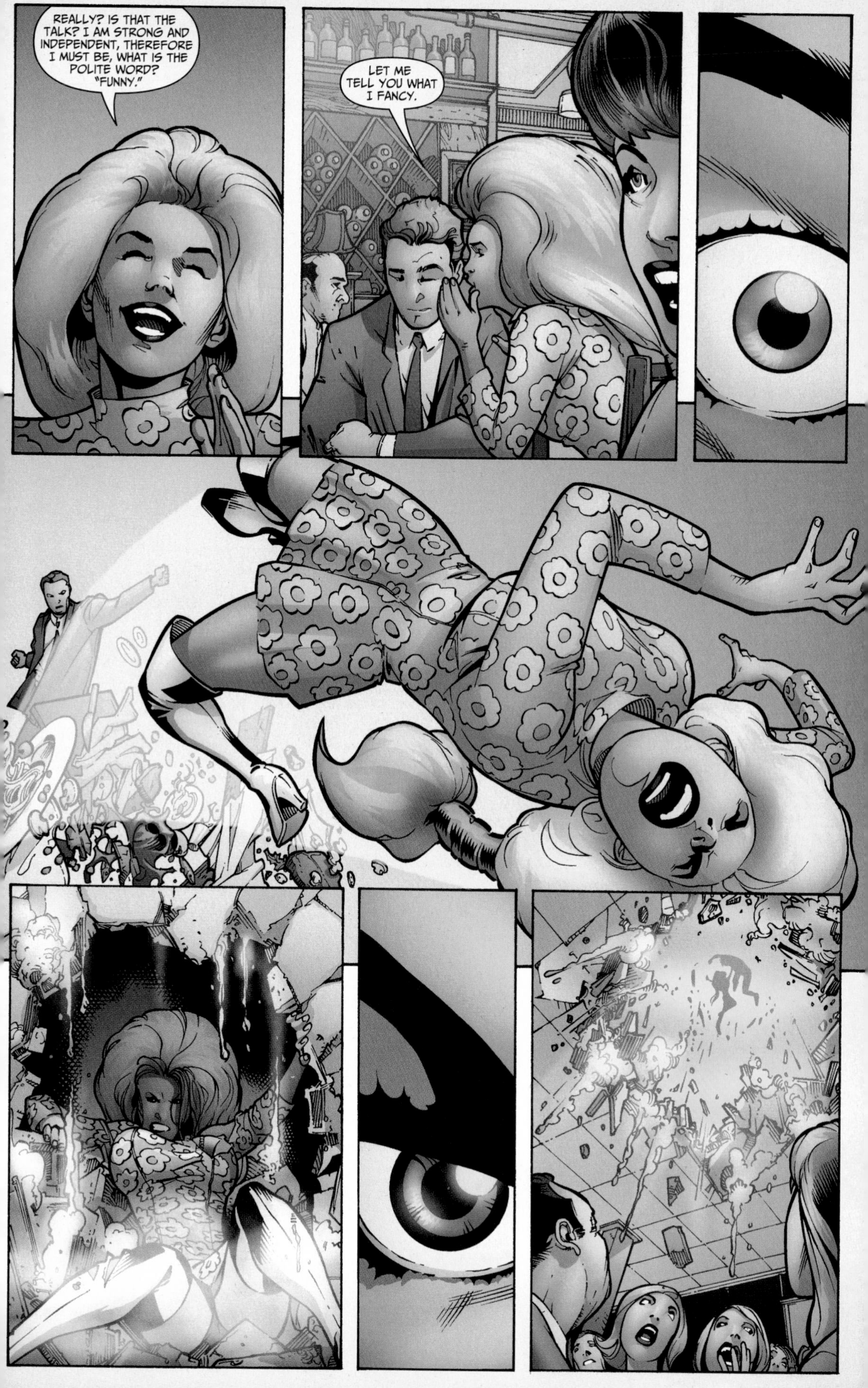
REALLY? IS THAT THE TALK? I AM STRONG AND INDEPENDENT, THEREFORE I MUST BE, WHAT IS THE POLITE WORD? "FUNNY."
LET ME TELL YOU WHAT I FANCY.

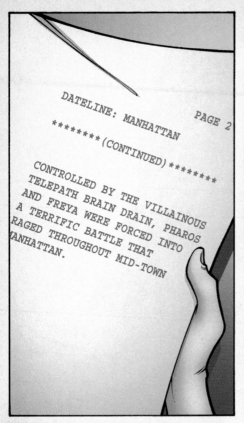

DATELINE: MANHATTAN

********* (CONTINUED) *********

CONTROLLED BY THE VILLAINOUS TELEPATH BRAIN DRAIN, PHAROS AND FREYA WERE FORCED INTO A TERRIFIC BATTLE THAT RAGED THROUGHOUT MID-TOWN MANHATTAN.

HOLY MACKEREL! BRAIN DRAIN! THAT EXPLAINS WHY PHAROS WAS OUT WITH FREYA IN THE FIRST PLACE. NO WAY HE'D EVER BE DISRESPECTFUL TO YOU, MISS DARLING.

BUD, HUSH UP.

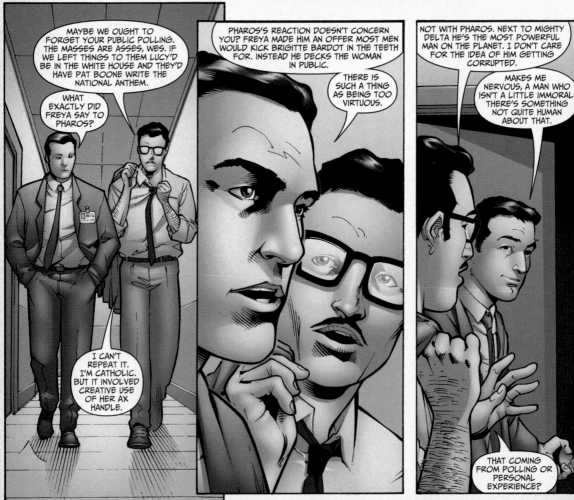

MAYBE WE OUGHT TO FORGET YOUR PUBLIC POLLING. THE MASSES ARE ASSES, WES. IF WE LEFT THINGS TO THEM LUCY'D BE IN THE WHITE HOUSE AND THEY'D HAVE PAT BOONE WRITE THE NATIONAL ANTHEM.

WHAT EXACTLY DID FREYA SAY TO PHAROS?

I CAN'T REPEAT IT. I'M CATHOLIC. BUT IT INVOLVED CREATIVE USE OF HER AX HANDLE.

PHAROS'S REACTION DOESN'T CONCERN YOU? FREYA MADE HIM AN OFFER MOST MEN WOULD KICK BRIGITTE BARDOT IN THE TEETH FOR. INSTEAD HE DECKS THE WOMAN IN PUBLIC.

THERE IS SUCH A THING AS BEING TOO VIRTUOUS.

NOT WITH PHAROS. NEXT TO MIGHTY DELTA HE'S THE MOST POWERFUL MAN ON THE PLANET. I DON'T CARE FOR THE IDEA OF HIM GETTING CORRUPTED.

MAKES ME NERVOUS, A MAN WHO ISN'T A LITTLE IMMORAL. THERE'S SOMETHING NOT QUITE HUMAN ABOUT THAT.

THAT COMING FROM POLLING OR PERSONAL EXPERIENCE?

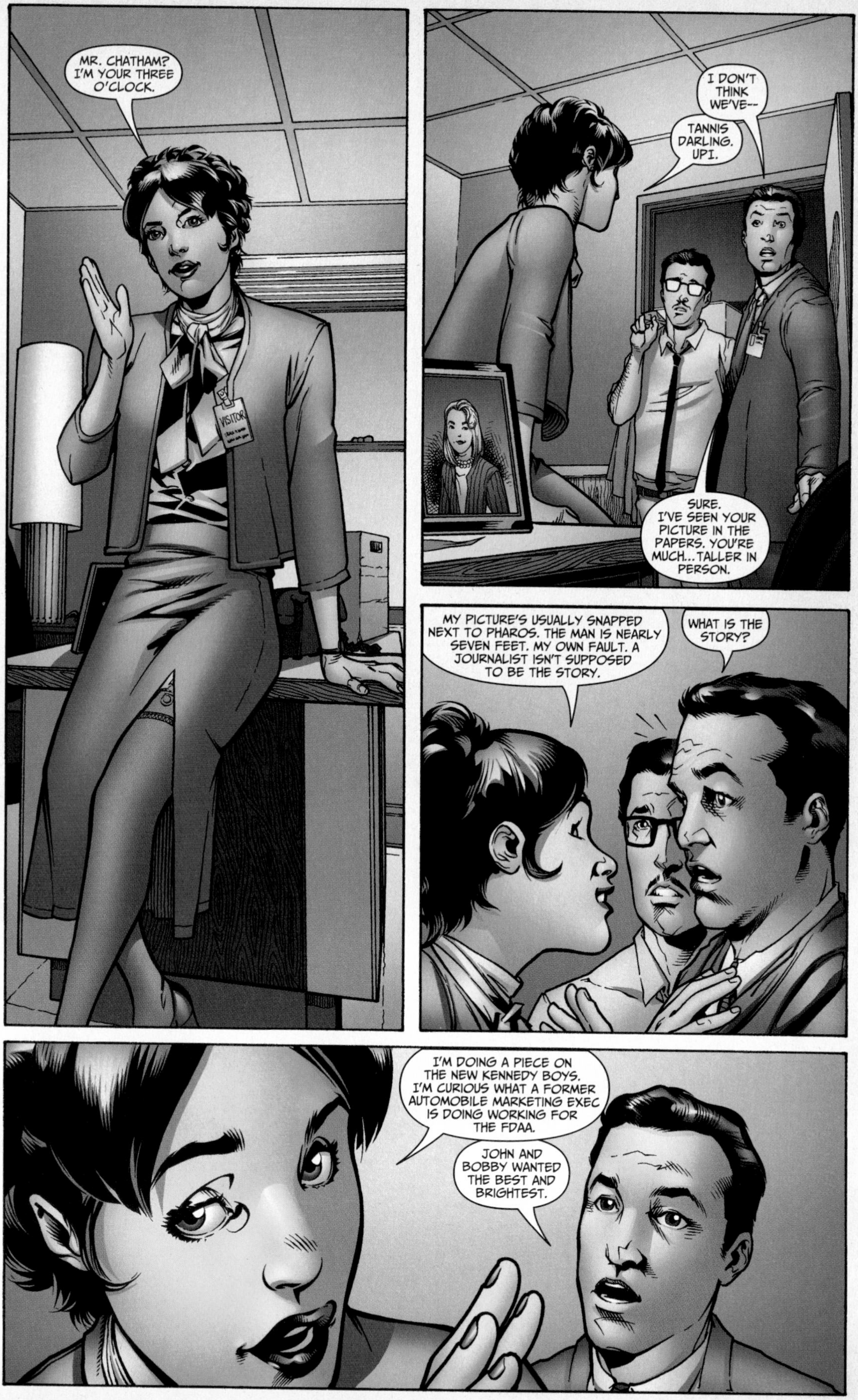
MR. CHATHAM? I'M YOUR THREE O'CLOCK.
VISITOR
I DON'T THINK WE'VE--
TANNIS DARLING. UPI.
SURE. I'VE SEEN YOUR PICTURE IN THE PAPERS. YOU'RE MUCH...TALLER IN PERSON.
MY PICTURE'S USUALLY SNAPPED NEXT TO PHAROS. THE MAN IS NEARLY SEVEN FEET. MY OWN FAULT. A JOURNALIST ISN'T SUPPOSED TO BE THE STORY.
WHAT IS THE STORY?
I'M DOING A PIECE ON THE NEW KENNEDY BOYS. I'M CURIOUS WHAT A FORMER AUTOMOBILE MARKETING EXEC IS DOING WORKING FOR THE FDAA.
JOHN AND BOBBY WANTED THE BEST AND BRIGHTEST.

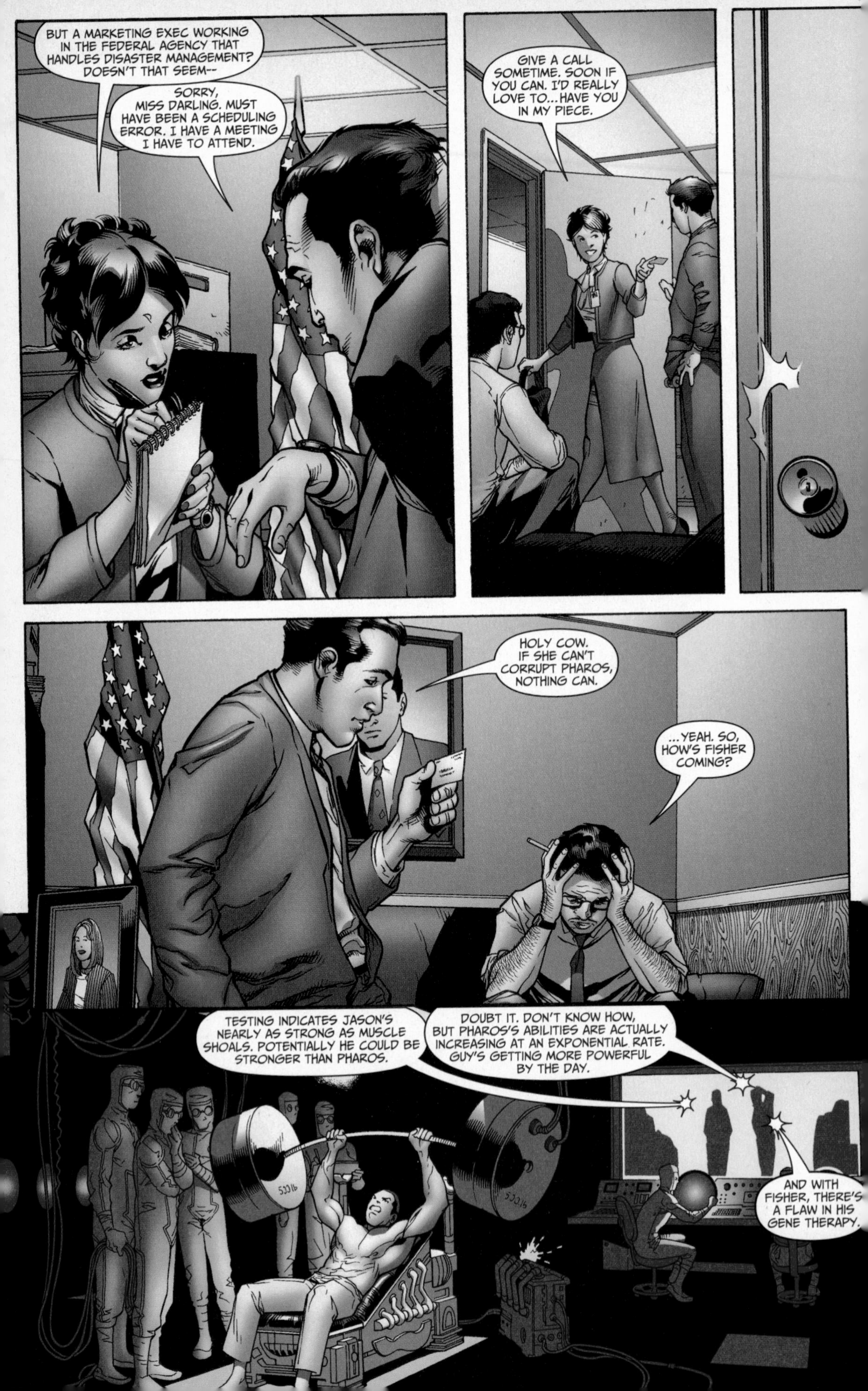
BUT A MARKETING EXEC WORKING IN THE FEDERAL AGENCY THAT HANDLES DISASTER MANAGEMENT? DOESN'T THAT SEEM--
SORRY, MISS DARLING. MUST HAVE BEEN A SCHEDULING ERROR. I HAVE A MEETING I HAVE TO ATTEND.
GIVE A CALL SOMETIME. SOON IF YOU CAN. I'D REALLY LOVE TO...HAVE YOU IN MY PIECE.
HOLY COW. IF SHE CAN'T CORRUPT PHAROS, NOTHING CAN.
...YEAH. SO, HOW'S FISHER COMING?
TESTING INDICATES JASON'S NEARLY AS STRONG AS MUSCLE SHOALS. POTENTIALLY HE COULD BE STRONGER THAN PHAROS.
DOUBT IT. DON'T KNOW HOW, BUT PHAROS'S ABILITIES ARE ACTUALLY INCREASING AT AN EXPONENTIAL RATE. GUY'S GETTING MORE POWERFUL BY THE DAY.
AND WITH FISHER, THERE'S A FLAW IN HIS GENE THERAPY.

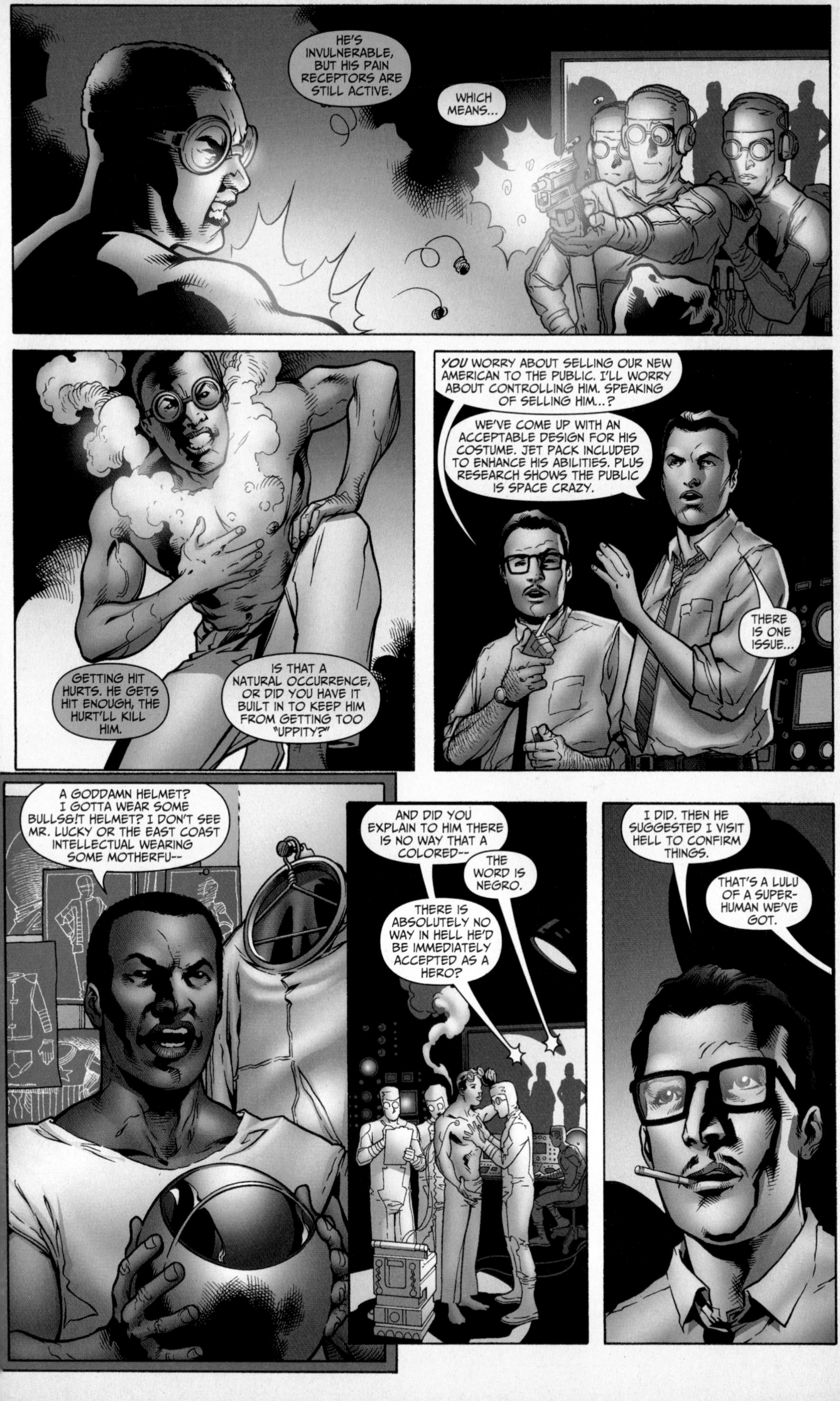
HE'S INVULNERABLE, BUT HIS PAIN RECEPTORS ARE STILL ACTIVE.
WHICH MEANS...
GETTING HIT HURTS. HE GETS HIT ENOUGH, THE HURT'LL KILL HIM.
IS THAT A NATURAL OCCURRENCE, OR DID YOU HAVE IT BUILT IN TO KEEP HIM FROM GETTING TOO "UPPITY?"
YOU WORRY ABOUT SELLING OUR NEW AMERICAN TO THE PUBLIC. I'LL WORRY ABOUT CONTROLLING HIM. SPEAKING OF SELLING HIM...?
WE'VE COME UP WITH AN ACCEPTABLE DESIGN FOR HIS COSTUME. JET PACK INCLUDED TO ENHANCE HIS ABILITIES. PLUS RESEARCH SHOWS THE PUBLIC IS SPACE CRAZY.
THERE IS ONE ISSUE...
A GODDAMN HELMET? I GOTTA WEAR SOME BULLS&!T HELMET? I DON'T SEE MR. LUCKY OR THE EAST COAST INTELLECTUAL WEARING SOME MOTHERFU--
AND DID YOU EXPLAIN TO HIM THERE IS NO WAY THAT A COLORED--
THE WORD IS NEGRO.
THERE IS ABSOLUTELY NO WAY IN HELL HE'D BE IMMEDIATELY ACCEPTED AS A HERO?
I DID. THEN HE SUGGESTED I VISIT HELL TO CONFIRM THINGS.
THAT'S A LULU OF A SUPER-HUMAN WE'VE GOT.

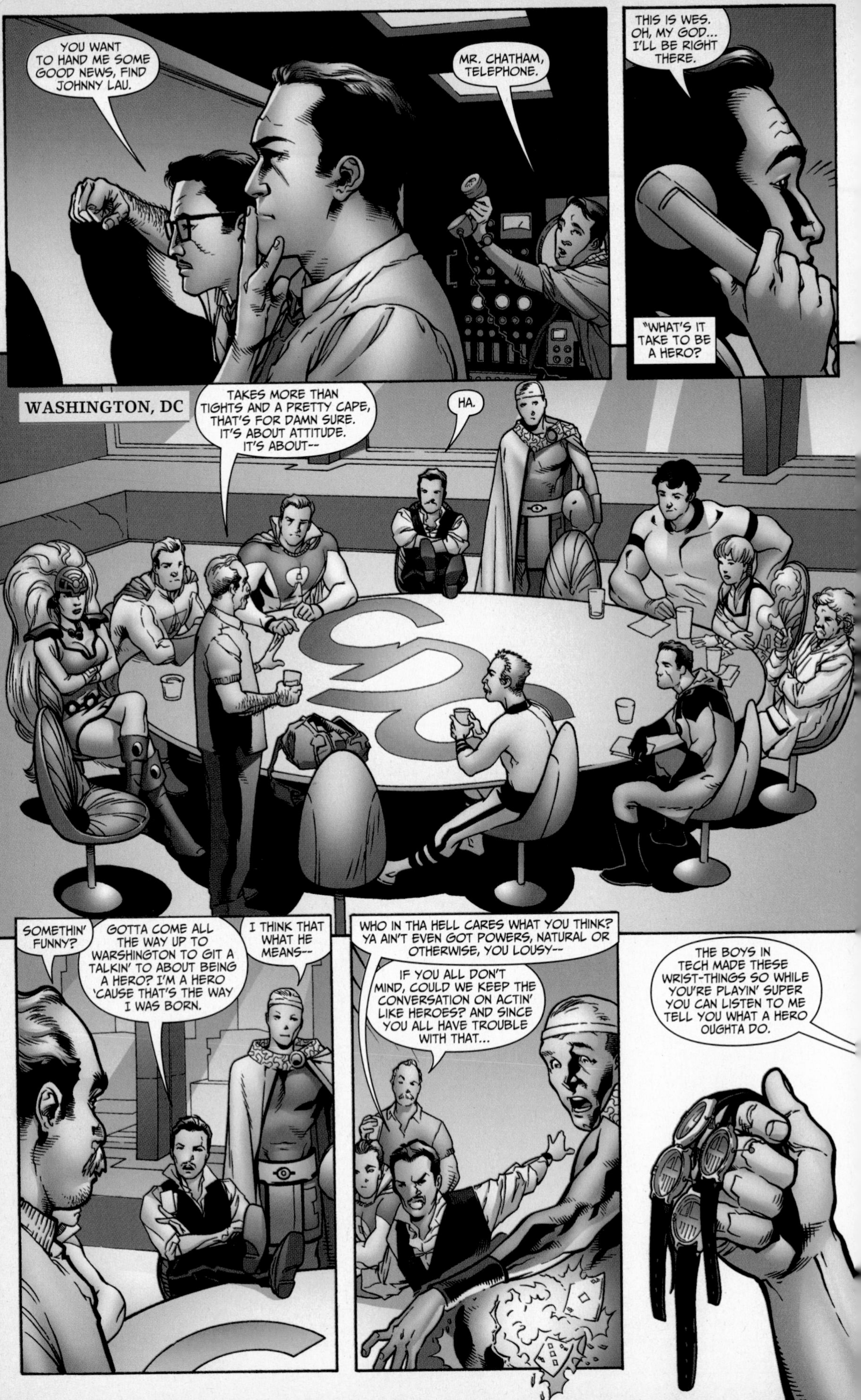
YOU WANT TO HAND ME SOME GOOD NEWS, FIND JOHNNY LAU.
MR. CHATHAM, TELEPHONE.
THIS IS WES. OH, MY GOD... I'LL BE RIGHT THERE.
"WHAT'S IT TAKE TO BE A HERO?
WASHINGTON, DC
TAKES MORE THAN TIGHTS AND A PRETTY CAPE, THAT'S FOR DAMN SURE. IT'S ABOUT ATTITUDE. IT'S ABOUT--
HA.
SOMETHIN' FUNNY?
GOTTA COME ALL THE WAY UP TO WARSHINGTON TO GIT A TALKIN' TO ABOUT BEING A HERO? I'M A HERO 'CAUSE THAT'S THE WAY I WAS BORN.
I THINK THAT WHAT HE MEANS--
WHO IN THA HELL CARES WHAT YOU THINK? YA AIN'T EVEN GOT POWERS, NATURAL OR OTHERWISE, YOU LOUSY--
IF YOU ALL DON'T MIND, COULD WE KEEP THE CONVERSATION ON ACTIN' LIKE HEROES? AND SINCE YOU ALL HAVE TROUBLE WITH THAT...
THE BOYS IN TECH MADE THESE WRIST-THINGS SO WHILE YOU'RE PLAYIN' SUPER YOU CAN LISTEN TO ME TELL YOU WHAT A HERO OUGHTA DO.

SURE, LET'S TALK ABOUT HEROES.

WHAT'S THAT, CAPTAIN?

YOU KNOW I'M JUST AN OL' STORYTELLER, BUT MY STORIES HAVE A WAY OF COMIN' TRUE. I'M THINKING IT'S ABOUT TIME TO TELL A NEW TALE.

A REUBEN SANDWICH. A REUBEN WITH A BUNCH OF SAUERKRAUT AND ONE OF THEM BIG DILL PICKLES. SOON AS I GET SOMEWHERE I'M GETTING ME A REUBEN...

THAT'S A CRAZY THOUGHT. I HATE DILL PICKLES. MUST BE GETTING SLEEP DEPRIVED. CAN'T START GOING NUTS.

JUST GOTTA STAY AWAKE, STAY CLEAR OF HALF A DOZEN SUPER-PEOPLE WHO ARE TRYING TO KILL ME... THEN I'M GETTING ME A REU--

THE SECRET AGENT! THEY FOUND ME!

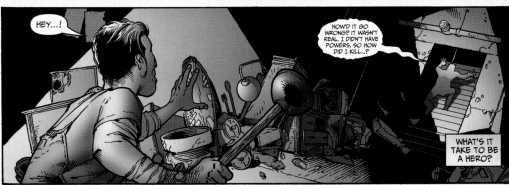

HEY...!

HOW'D IT GO WRONG? IT WASN'T REAL. I DIDN'T HAVE POWERS, SO HOW DID I KILL...?

WHAT'S IT TAKE TO BE A HERO?

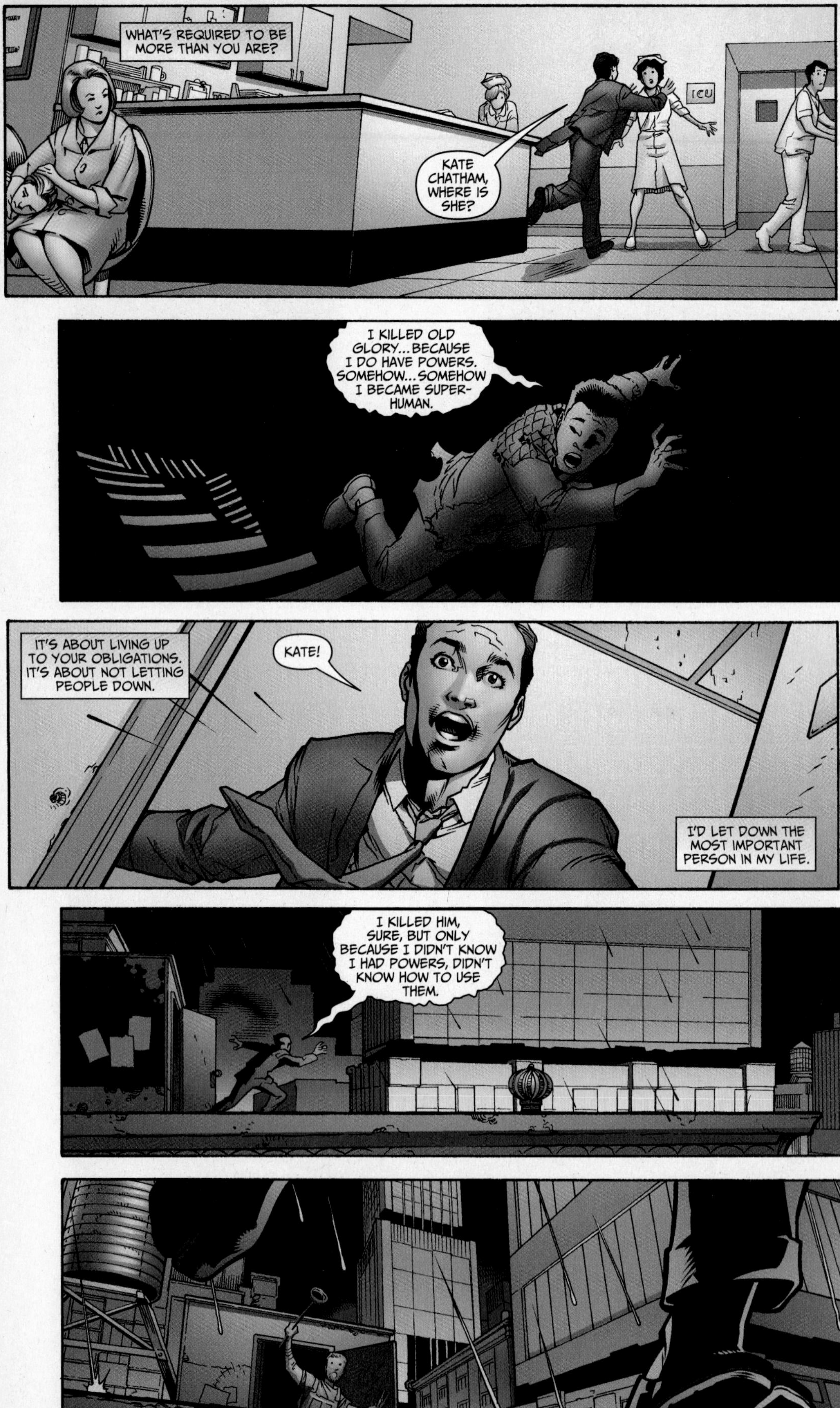
WHAT'S REQUIRED TO BE MORE THAN YOU ARE?
ICU
KATE CHATHAM, WHERE IS SHE?
I KILLED OLD GLORY...BECAUSE I DO HAVE POWERS. SOMEHOW...SOMEHOW I BECAME SUPER-HUMAN.
IT'S ABOUT LIVING UP TO YOUR OBLIGATIONS. IT'S ABOUT NOT LETTING PEOPLE DOWN.
KATE!
I'D LET DOWN THE MOST IMPORTANT PERSON IN MY LIFE.
I KILLED HIM, SURE, BUT ONLY BECAUSE I DIDN'T KNOW I HAD POWERS, DIDN'T KNOW HOW TO USE THEM.

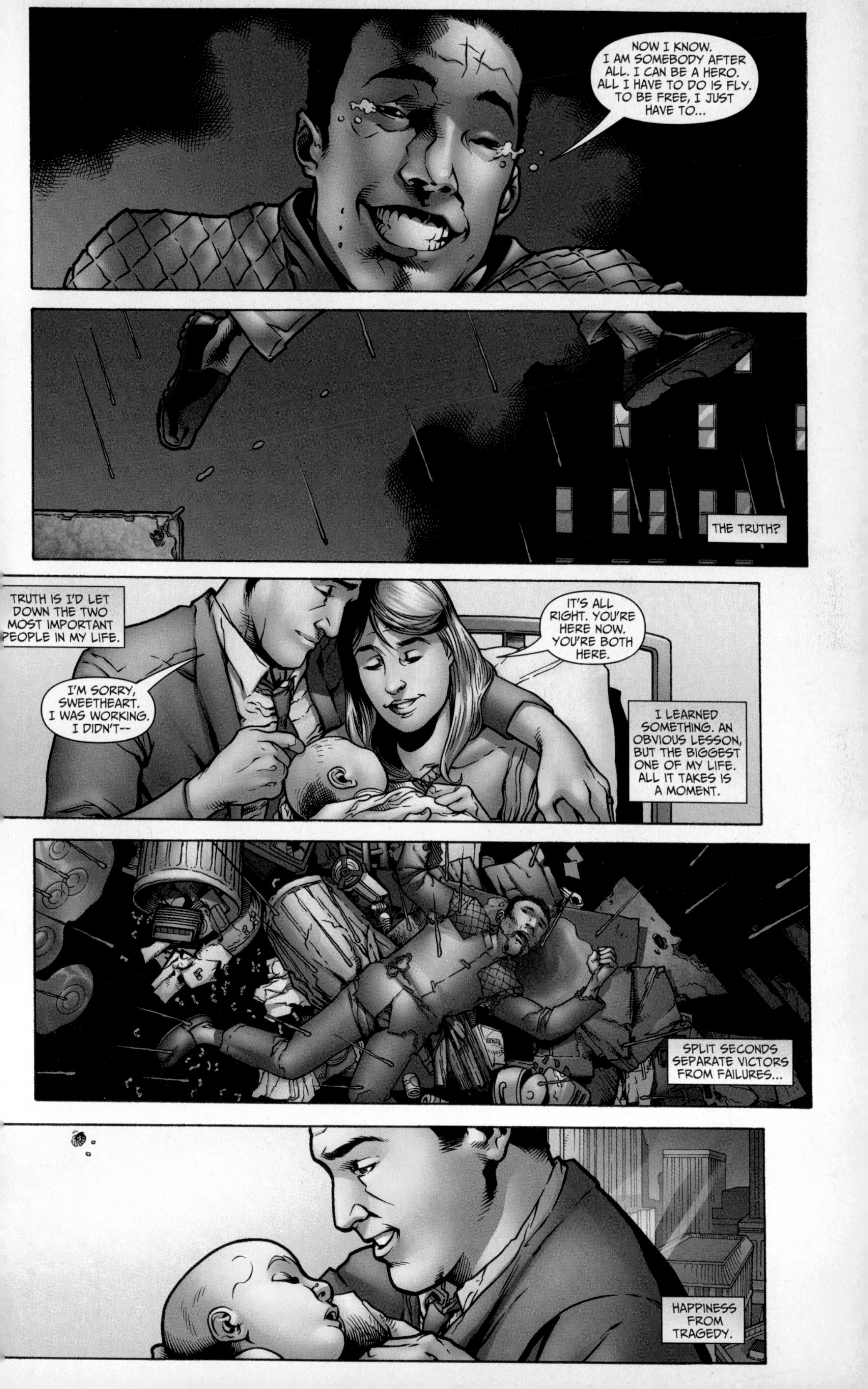
NOW I KNOW. I AM SOMEBODY AFTER ALL. I CAN BE A HERO. ALL I HAVE TO DO IS FLY. TO BE FREE, I JUST HAVE TO...
THE TRUTH?
TRUTH IS I'D LET DOWN THE TWO MOST IMPORTANT PEOPLE IN MY LIFE.
I'M SORRY, SWEETHEART. I WAS WORKING. I DIDN'T--
IT'S ALL RIGHT. YOU'RE HERE NOW. YOU'RE BOTH HERE.
I LEARNED SOMETHING. AN OBVIOUS LESSON, BUT THE BIGGEST ONE OF MY LIFE. ALL IT TAKES IS A MOMENT.
SPLIT SECONDS SEPARATE VICTORS FROM FAILURES...
HAPPINESS FROM TRAGEDY.

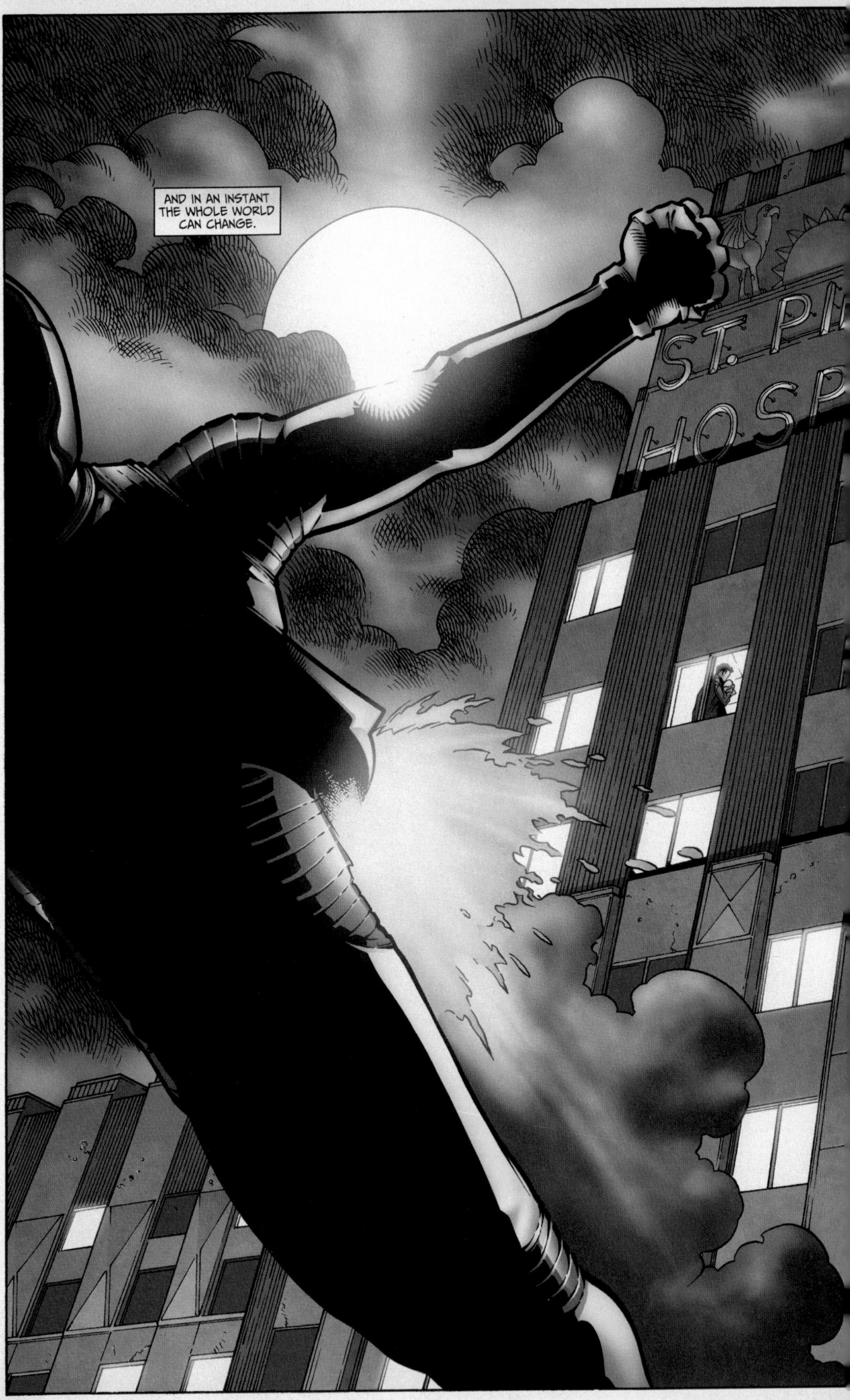
AND IN AN INSTANT THE WHOLE WORLD CAN CHANGE.
ST. PI
HOSP

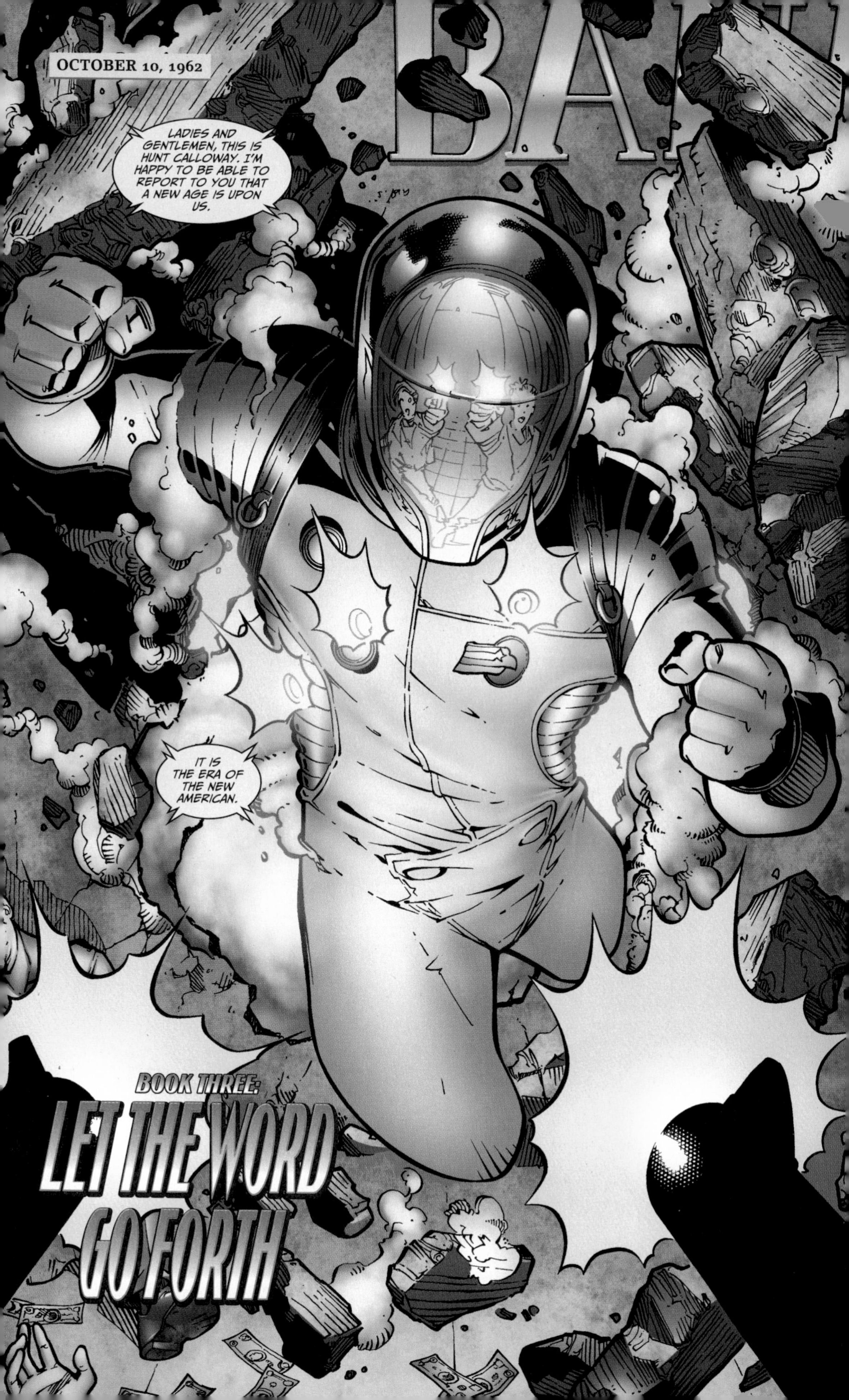
OCTOBER 10, 1962
LADIES AND GENTLEMEN, THIS IS HUNT CALLOWAY. I'M HAPPY TO BE ABLE TO REPORT TO YOU THAT A NEW AGE IS UPON US.
IT IS THE ERA OF THE NEW AMERICAN.
BOOK THREE:
LET THE WORD GO FORTH

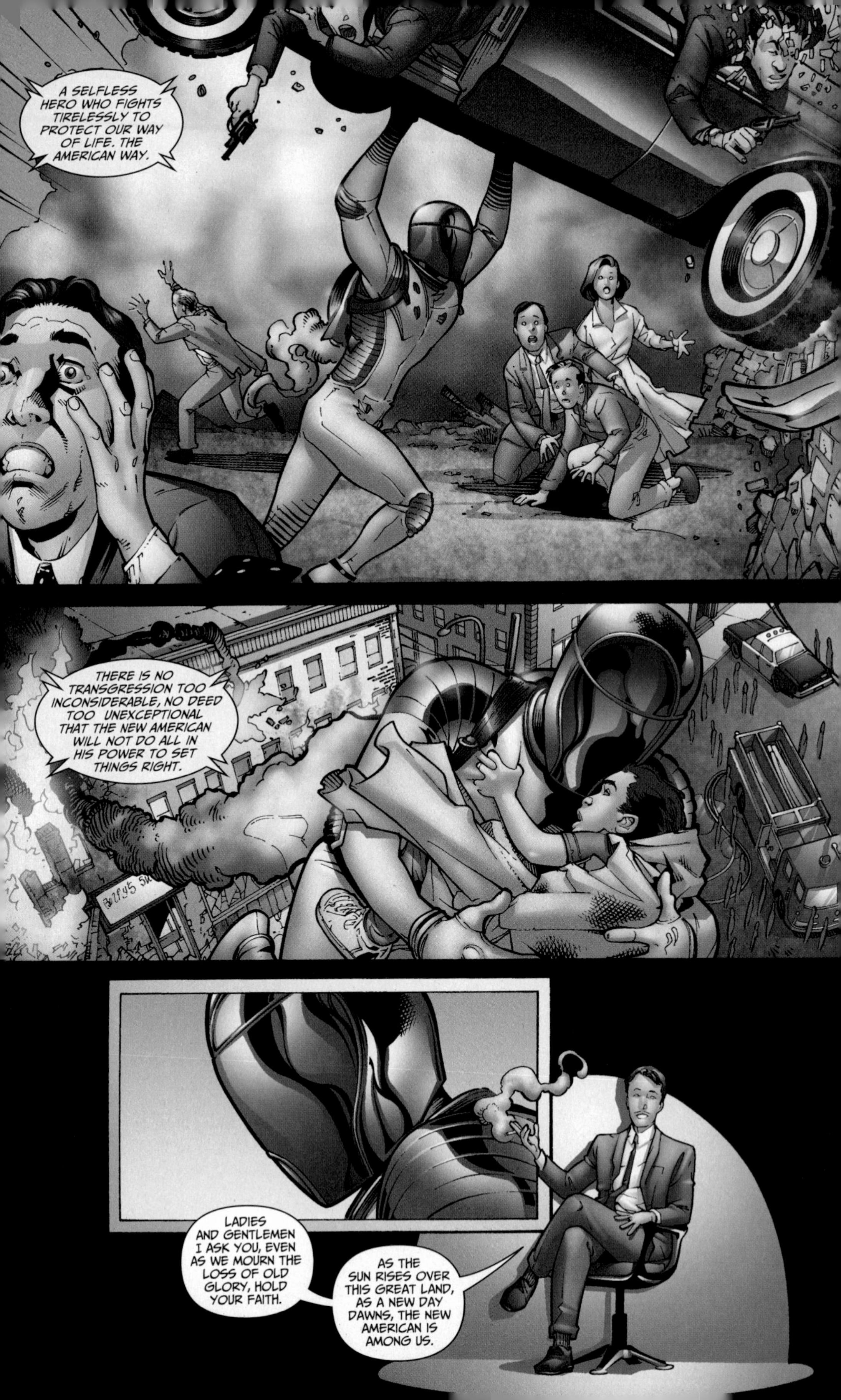
A SELFLESS HERO WHO FIGHTS TIRELESSLY TO PROTECT OUR WAY OF LIFE. THE AMERICAN WAY.
THERE IS NO TRANSGRESSION TOO INCONSIDERABLE, NO DEED TOO UNEXCEPTIONAL THAT THE NEW AMERICAN WILL NOT DO ALL IN HIS POWER TO SET THINGS RIGHT.
LADIES AND GENTLEMEN I ASK YOU, EVEN AS WE MOURN THE LOSS OF OLD GLORY, HOLD YOUR FAITH.
AS THE SUN RISES OVER THIS GREAT LAND, AS A NEW DAY DAWNS, THE NEW AMERICAN IS AMONG US.

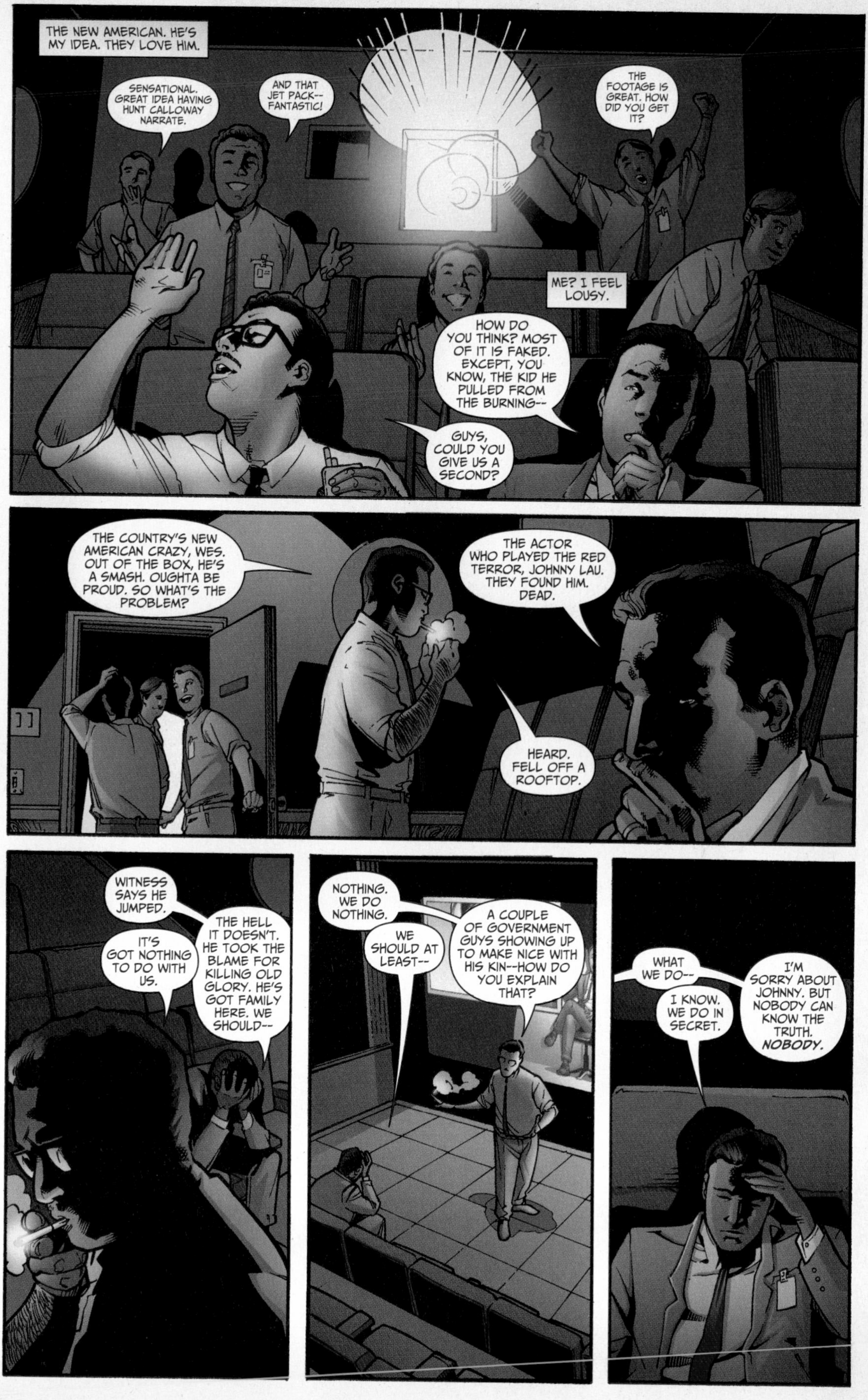
THE NEW AMERICAN. HE'S MY IDEA. THEY LOVE HIM.
SENSATIONAL. GREAT IDEA HAVING HUNT CALLOWAY NARRATE.
AND THAT JET PACK-- FANTASTIC!
THE FOOTAGE IS GREAT. HOW DID YOU GET IT?
ME? I FEEL LOUSY.
HOW DO YOU THINK? MOST OF IT IS FAKED. EXCEPT, YOU KNOW, THE KID HE PULLED FROM THE BURNING--
GUYS, COULD YOU GIVE US A SECOND?
THE COUNTRY'S NEW AMERICAN CRAZY, WES. OUT OF THE BOX, HE'S A SMASH. OUGHTA BE PROUD. SO WHAT'S THE PROBLEM?
THE ACTOR WHO PLAYED THE RED TERROR, JOHNNY LAU. THEY FOUND HIM. DEAD.
HEARD. FELL OFF A ROOFTOP.
WITNESS SAYS HE JUMPED.
IT'S GOT NOTHING TO DO WITH US.
THE HELL IT DOESN'T. HE TOOK THE BLAME FOR KILLING OLD GLORY. HE'S GOT FAMILY HERE. WE SHOULD--
NOTHING. WE DO NOTHING.
WE SHOULD AT LEAST--
A COUPLE OF GOVERNMENT GUYS SHOWING UP TO MAKE NICE WITH HIS KIN--HOW DO YOU EXPLAIN THAT?
WHAT WE DO--
I KNOW. WE DO IN SECRET.
I'M SORRY ABOUT JOHNNY. BUT NOBODY CAN KNOW THE TRUTH. *NOBODY.*

WELL?

EVERYBODY LOVES YOU. YOU'RE A SENSATION. A REGULAR AMERICAN HERO.

SO, HOW LONG DO I HAVE TO WEAR THE HELMET?

AS LONG AS IT TAKES TO GET TO A PLACE THE PUBLIC COULD ACCEPT THE NEW AMERICAN IS A NEGRO. ANOTHER COUPLE OF YEARS. OR FOUR. MINIMUM.

WHEN I AGREED TO THIS GIG, YOU TOLD ME I COULD BE A HERO TO NEGROES AND WHITES. NOW I COME TO FIND OUT EVERYTHING'S FAKED. NOTHING BUT A SHOW AND A SCAM.

NOBODY EVEN KNOWS WHAT COLOR I AM.

SO, I'M A LYING SACK OF CRAP. YOU'VE GOT SUPER-POWERS. YOU COULD KILL ME 45 DIFFERENT WAYS WITH JUST YOUR EMPTY HANDS AND A BAD THOUGHT. WHY DON'T YOU JUST DO ME THE FAVOR?

IF NOT, I'VE GOT THINGS TO DEAL WITH.

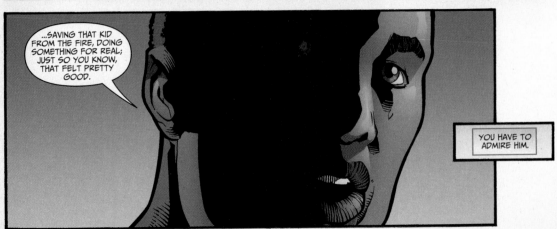

...SAVING THAT KID FROM THE FIRE, DOING SOMETHING FOR REAL; JUST SO YOU KNOW, THAT FELT PRETTY GOOD.

YOU HAVE TO ADMIRE HIM.

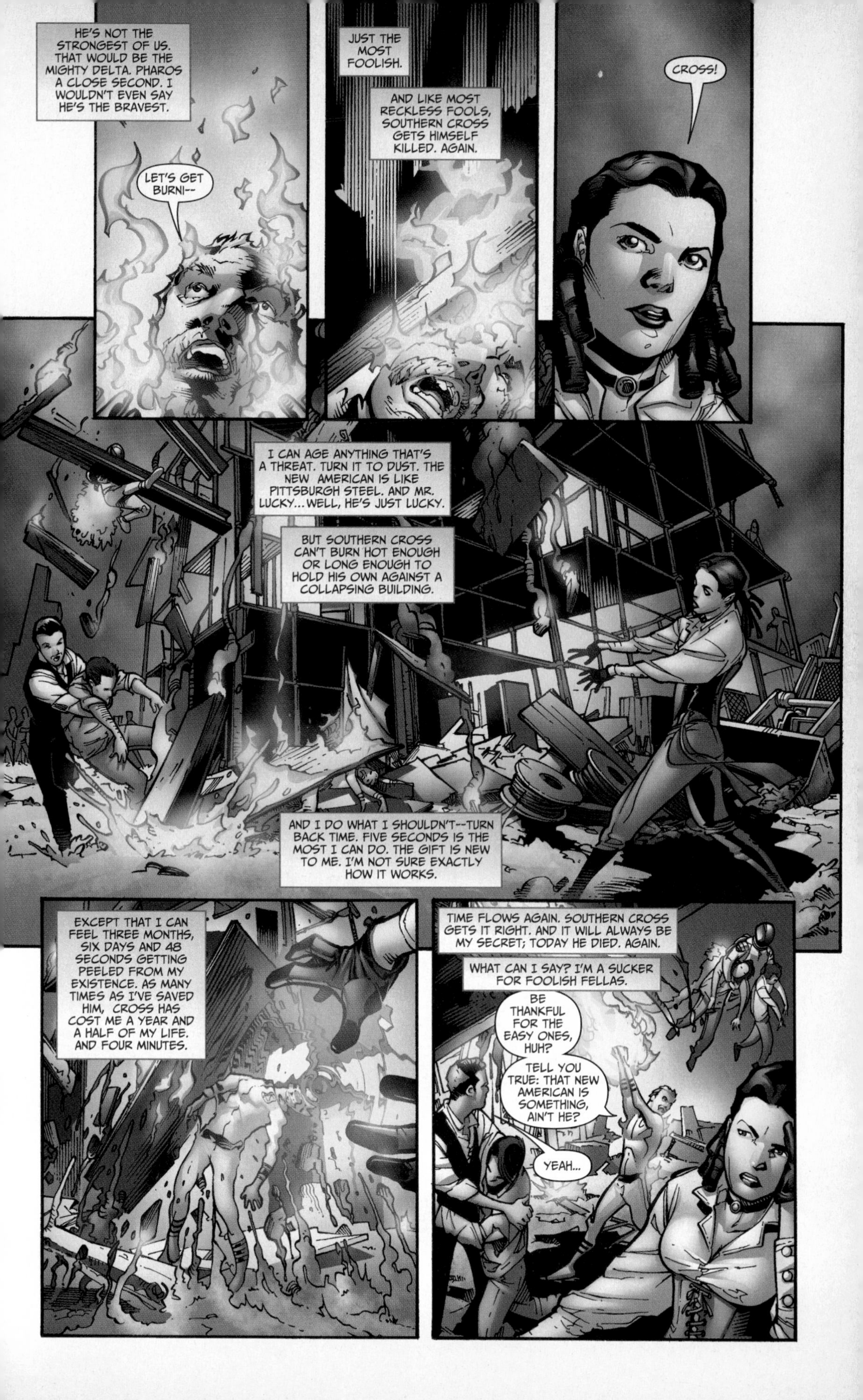
HE'S NOT THE STRONGEST OF US. THAT WOULD BE THE MIGHTY DELTA. PHAROS A CLOSE SECOND. I WOULDN'T EVEN SAY HE'S THE BRAVEST.
LET'S GET BURNI--
JUST THE MOST FOOLISH.
AND LIKE MOST RECKLESS FOOLS, SOUTHERN CROSS GETS HIMSELF KILLED. AGAIN.
CROSS!
I CAN AGE ANYTHING THAT'S A THREAT. TURN IT TO DUST. THE NEW AMERICAN IS LIKE PITTSBURGH STEEL. AND MR. LUCKY...WELL, HE'S JUST LUCKY.
BUT SOUTHERN CROSS CAN'T BURN HOT ENOUGH OR LONG ENOUGH TO HOLD HIS OWN AGAINST A COLLAPSING BUILDING.
AND I DO WHAT I SHOULDN'T--TURN BACK TIME. FIVE SECONDS IS THE MOST I CAN DO. THE GIFT IS NEW TO ME. I'M NOT SURE EXACTLY HOW IT WORKS.
EXCEPT THAT I CAN FEEL THREE MONTHS, SIX DAYS AND 48 SECONDS GETTING PEELED FROM MY EXISTENCE. AS MANY TIMES AS I'VE SAVED HIM, CROSS HAS COST ME A YEAR AND A HALF OF MY LIFE. AND FOUR MINUTES.
TIME FLOWS AGAIN. SOUTHERN CROSS GETS IT RIGHT. AND IT WILL ALWAYS BE MY SECRET; TODAY HE DIED. AGAIN.
WHAT CAN I SAY? I'M A SUCKER FOR FOOLISH FELLAS.
BE THANKFUL FOR THE EASY ONES, HUH?
TELL YOU TRUE: THAT NEW AMERICAN IS SOMETHING, AIN'T HE?
YEAH...

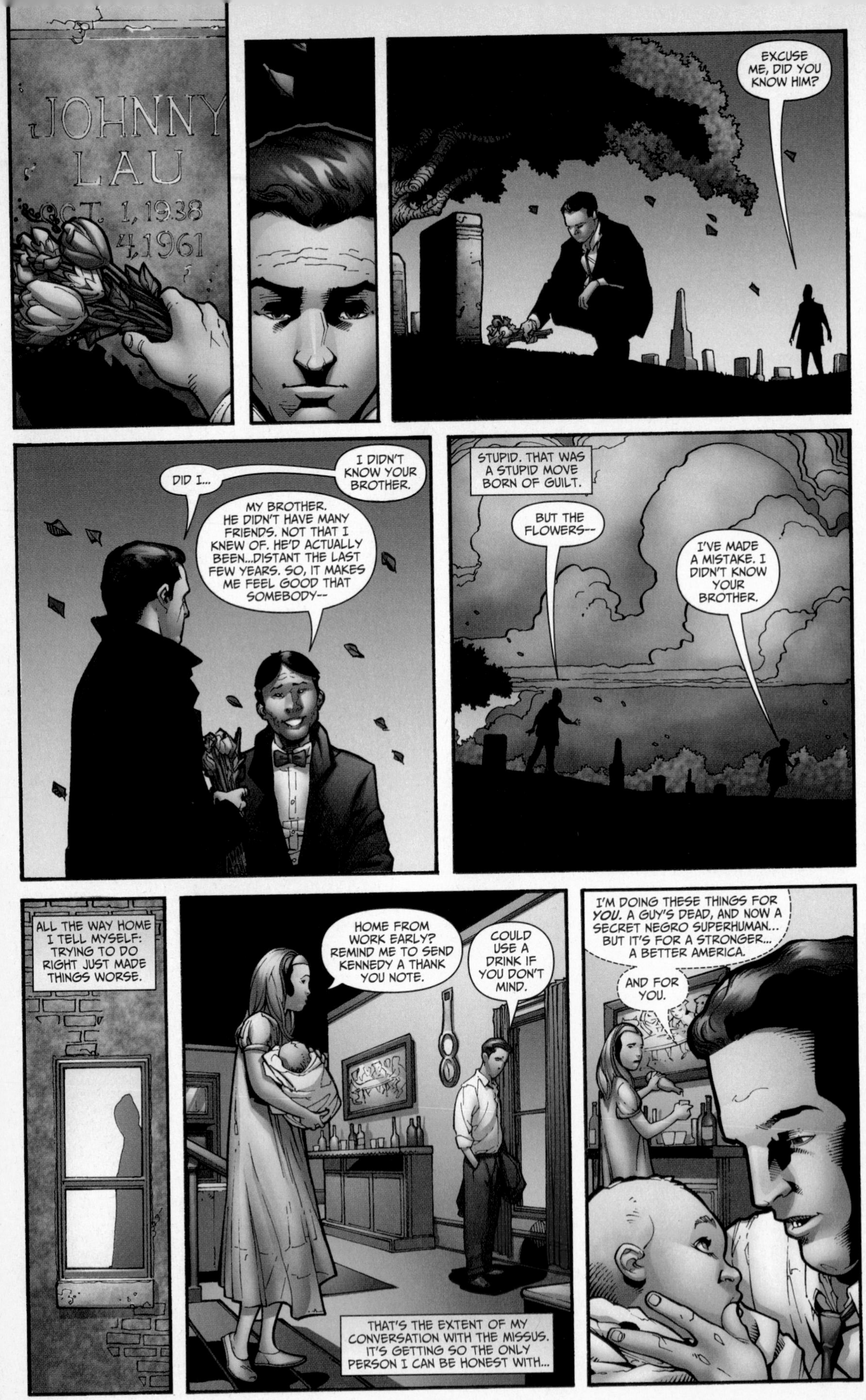
JOHNNY
LAU
OCT. 1, 1938
4, 1961
EXCUSE ME, DID YOU KNOW HIM?
DID I...
I DIDN'T KNOW YOUR BROTHER.
MY BROTHER. HE DIDN'T HAVE MANY FRIENDS. NOT THAT I KNEW OF. HE'D ACTUALLY BEEN...DISTANT THE LAST FEW YEARS. SO, IT MAKES ME FEEL GOOD THAT SOMEBODY--
STUPID. THAT WAS A STUPID MOVE BORN OF GUILT.
BUT THE FLOWERS--
I'VE MADE A MISTAKE. I DIDN'T KNOW YOUR BROTHER.
ALL THE WAY HOME I TELL MYSELF: TRYING TO DO RIGHT JUST MADE THINGS WORSE.
HOME FROM WORK EARLY? REMIND ME TO SEND KENNEDY A THANK YOU NOTE.
COULD USE A DRINK IF YOU DON'T MIND.
THAT'S THE EXTENT OF MY CONVERSATION WITH THE MISSUS. IT'S GETTING SO THE ONLY PERSON I CAN BE HONEST WITH...
I'M DOING THESE THINGS FOR *YOU*. A GUY'S DEAD, AND NOW A SECRET NEGRO SUPERHUMAN... BUT IT'S FOR A STRONGER... A BETTER AMERICA.
AND FOR YOU.

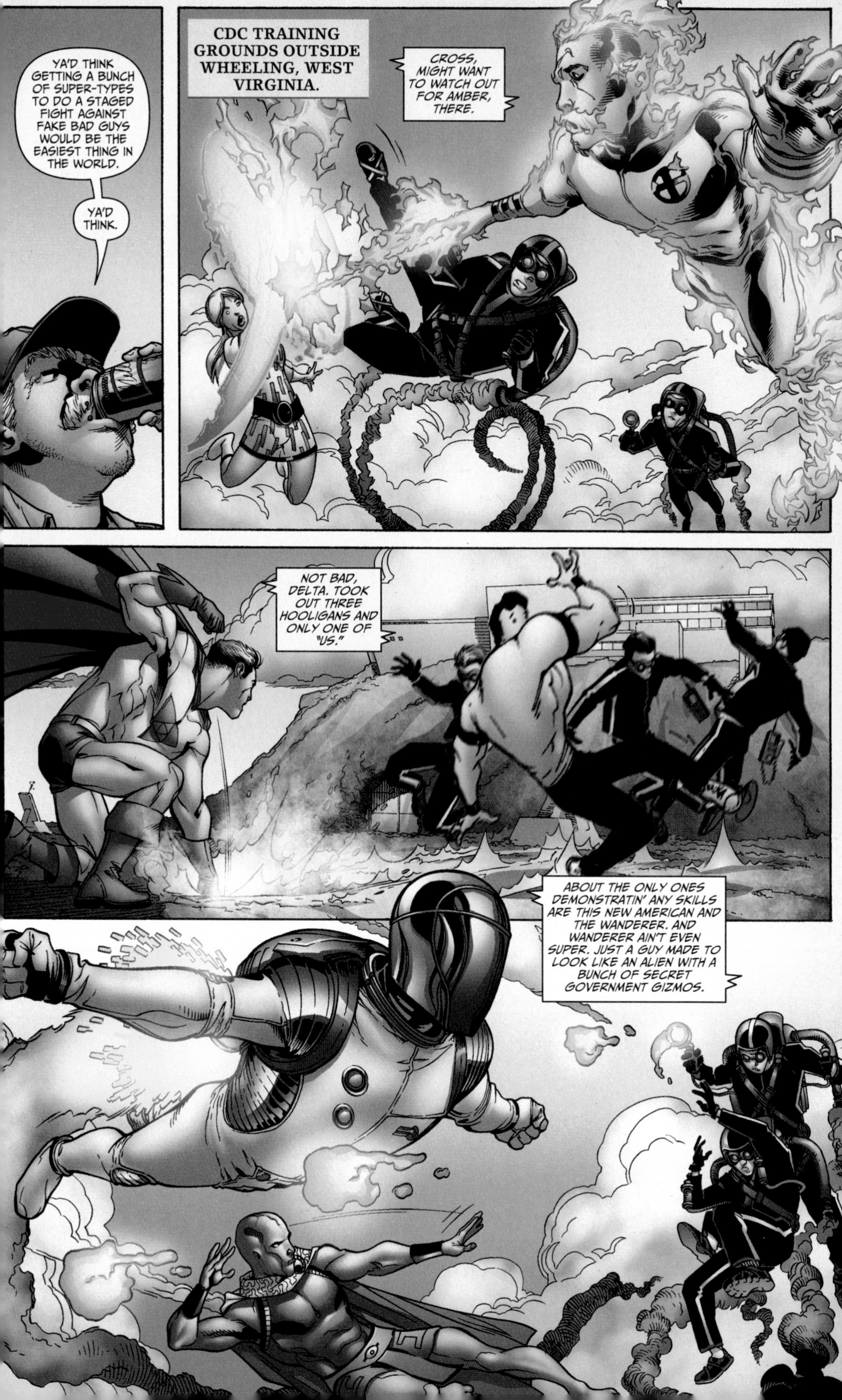

YA'D THINK GETTING A BUNCH OF SUPER-TYPES TO DO A STAGED FIGHT AGAINST FAKE BAD GUYS WOULD BE THE EASIEST THING IN THE WORLD.
YA'D THINK.
CDC TRAINING GROUNDS OUTSIDE WHEELING, WEST VIRGINIA.
CROSS, MIGHT WANT TO WATCH OUT FOR AMBER, THERE.
NOT BAD, DELTA. TOOK OUT THREE HOOLIGANS AND ONLY ONE OF "US."
ABOUT THE ONLY ONES DEMONSTRATIN' ANY SKILLS ARE THIS NEW AMERICAN AND THE WANDERER. AND WANDERER AIN'T EVEN SUPER. JUST A GUY MADE TO LOOK LIKE AN ALIEN WITH A BUNCH OF SECRET GOVERNMENT GIZMOS.

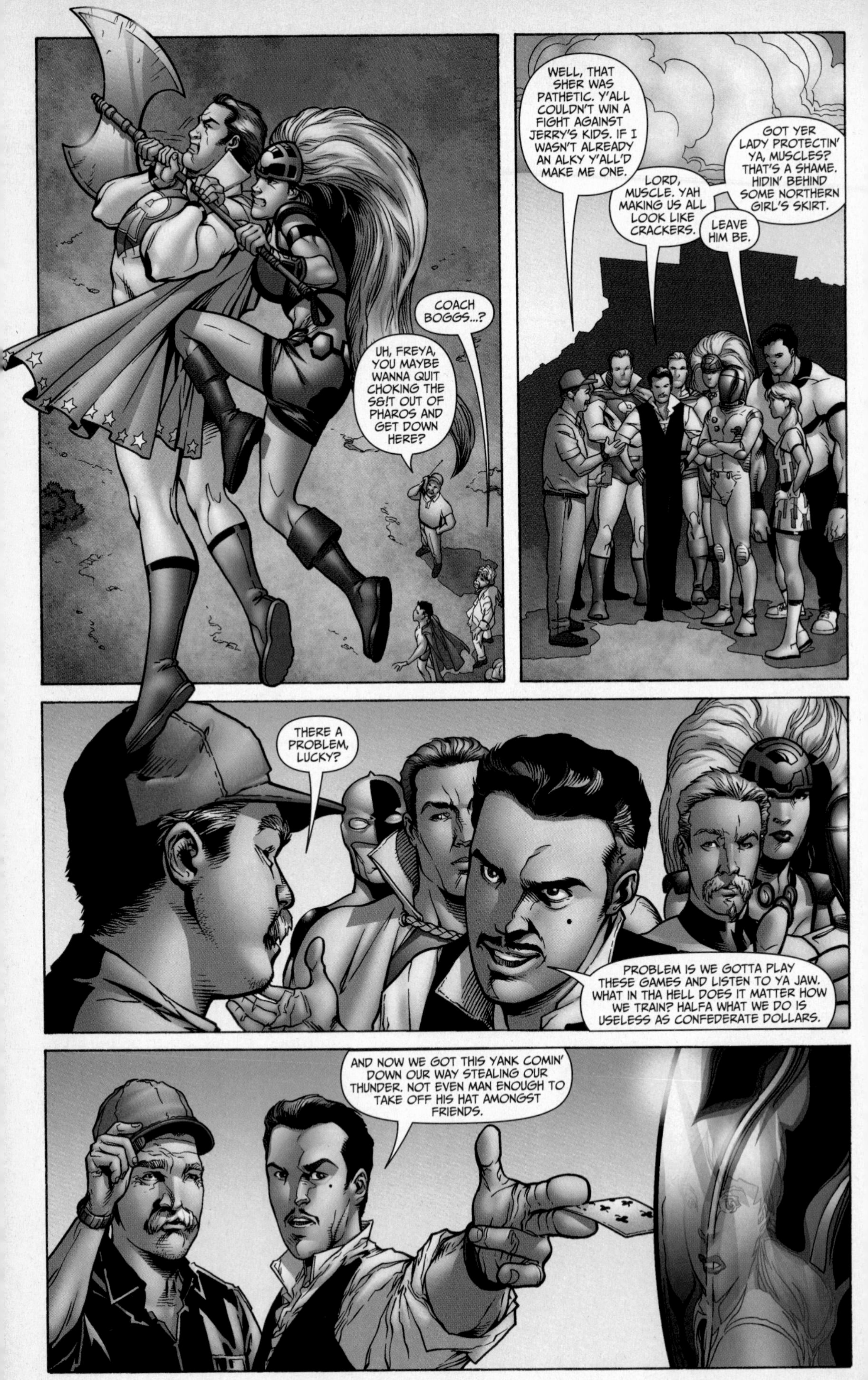
COACH BOGGS...?
UH, FREYA, YOU MAYBE WANNA QUIT CHOKING THE S&!T OUT OF PHAROS AND GET DOWN HERE?
WELL, THAT SHER WAS PATHETIC. Y'ALL COULDN'T WIN A FIGHT AGAINST JERRY'S KIDS. IF I WASN'T ALREADY AN ALKY Y'ALL'D MAKE ME ONE.
LORD, MUSCLE. YAH MAKING US ALL LOOK LIKE CRACKERS.
GOT YER LADY PROTECTIN' YA, MUSCLES? THAT'S A SHAME. HIDIN' BEHIND SOME NORTHERN GIRL'S SKIRT.
LEAVE HIM BE.
THERE A PROBLEM, LUCKY?
PROBLEM IS WE GOTTA PLAY THESE GAMES AND LISTEN TO YA JAW. WHAT IN THA HELL DOES IT MATTER HOW WE TRAIN? HALFA WHAT WE DO IS USELESS AS CONFEDERATE DOLLARS.
AND NOW WE GOT THIS YANK COMIN' DOWN OUR WAY STEALING OUR THUNDER. NOT EVEN MAN ENOUGH TO TAKE OFF HIS HAT AMONGST FRIENDS.

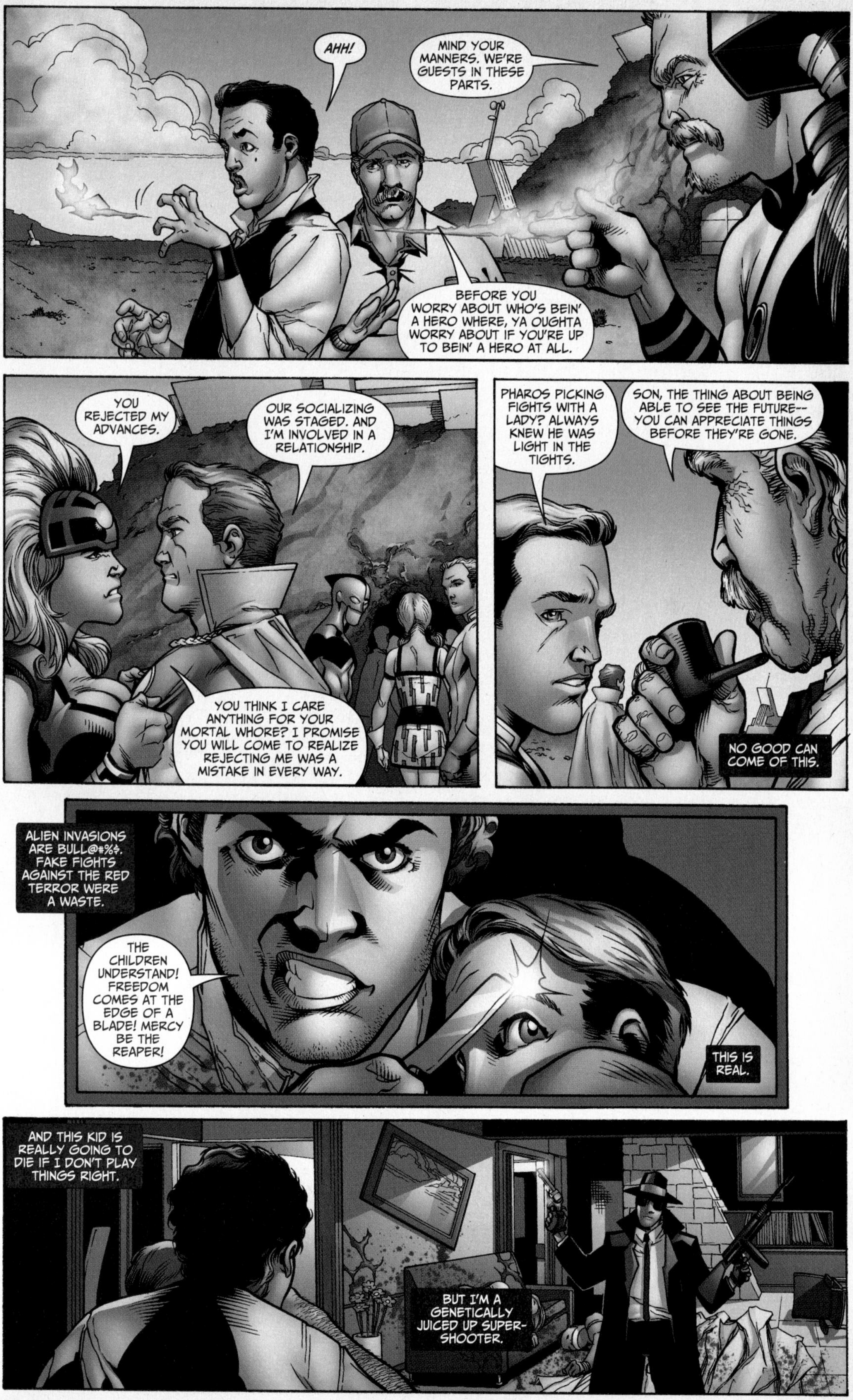
AHH!
MIND YOUR MANNERS. WE'RE GUESTS IN THESE PARTS.
BEFORE YOU WORRY ABOUT WHO'S BEIN' A HERO WHERE, YA OUGHTA WORRY ABOUT IF YOU'RE UP TO BEIN' A HERO AT ALL.
YOU REJECTED MY ADVANCES.
OUR SOCIALIZING WAS STAGED. AND I'M INVOLVED IN A RELATIONSHIP.
YOU THINK I CARE ANYTHING FOR YOUR MORTAL WHORE? I PROMISE YOU WILL COME TO REALIZE REJECTING ME WAS A MISTAKE IN EVERY WAY.
PHAROS PICKING FIGHTS WITH A LADY? ALWAYS KNEW HE WAS LIGHT IN THE TIGHTS.
SON, THE THING ABOUT BEING ABLE TO SEE THE FUTURE-- YOU CAN APPRECIATE THINGS BEFORE THEY'RE GONE.
NO GOOD CAN COME OF THIS.
ALIEN INVASIONS ARE BULL@#%$. FAKE FIGHTS AGAINST THE RED TERROR WERE A WASTE.
THE CHILDREN UNDERSTAND! FREEDOM COMES AT THE EDGE OF A BLADE! MERCY BE THE REAPER!
THIS IS REAL.
AND THIS KID IS REALLY GOING TO DIE IF I DON'T PLAY THINGS RIGHT.
BUT I'M A GENETICALLY JUICED UP SUPER-SHOOTER.

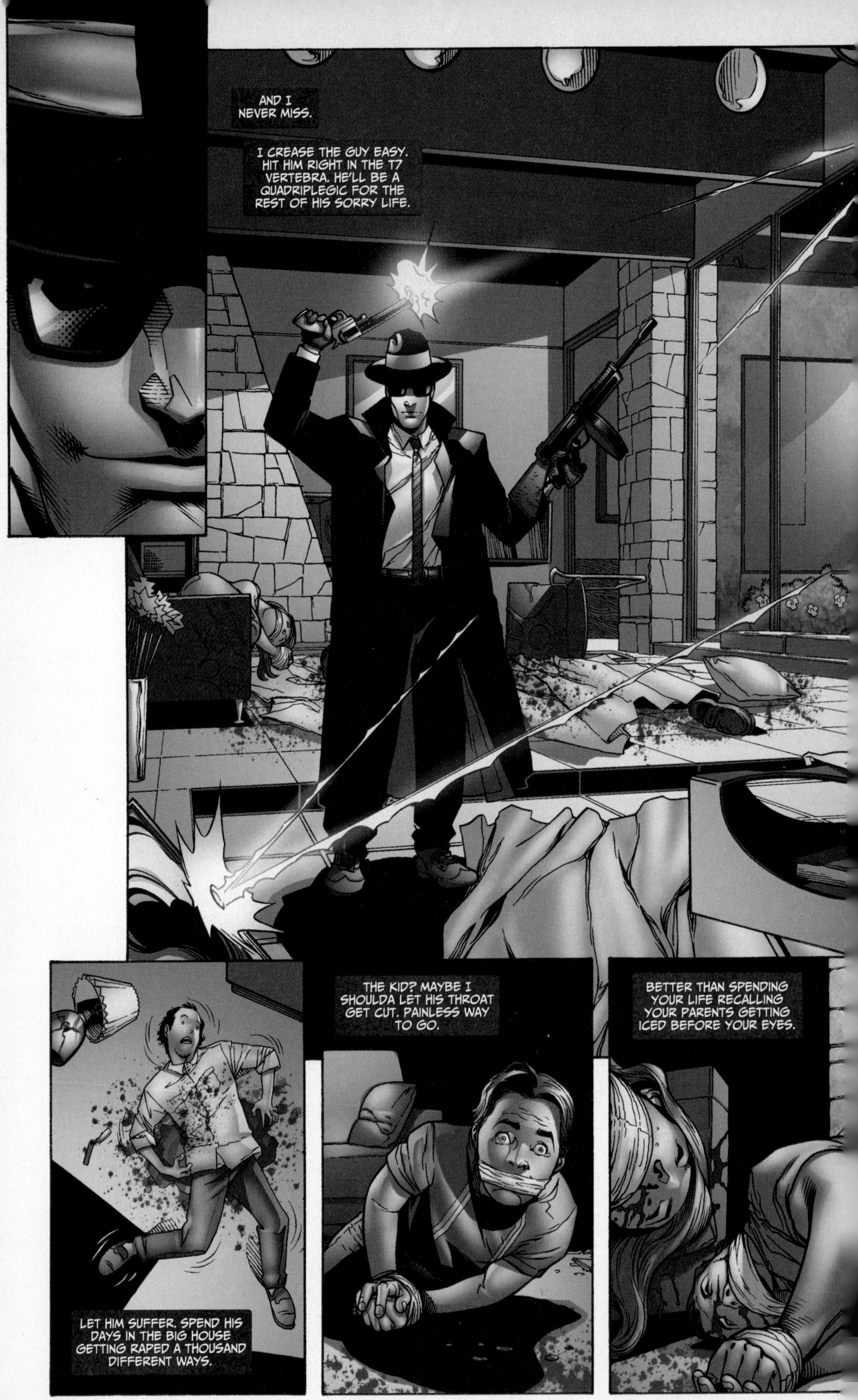
AND I NEVER MISS.
I CREASE THE GUY EASY. HIT HIM RIGHT IN THE T7 VERTEBRA. HE'LL BE A QUADRIPLEGIC FOR THE REST OF HIS SORRY LIFE.
LET HIM SUFFER. SPEND HIS DAYS IN THE BIG HOUSE GETTING RAPED A THOUSAND DIFFERENT WAYS.
THE KID? MAYBE I SHOULDA LET HIS THROAT GET CUT. PAINLESS WAY TO GO.
BETTER THAN SPENDING YOUR LIFE RECALLING YOUR PARENTS GETTING ICED BEFORE YOUR EYES.

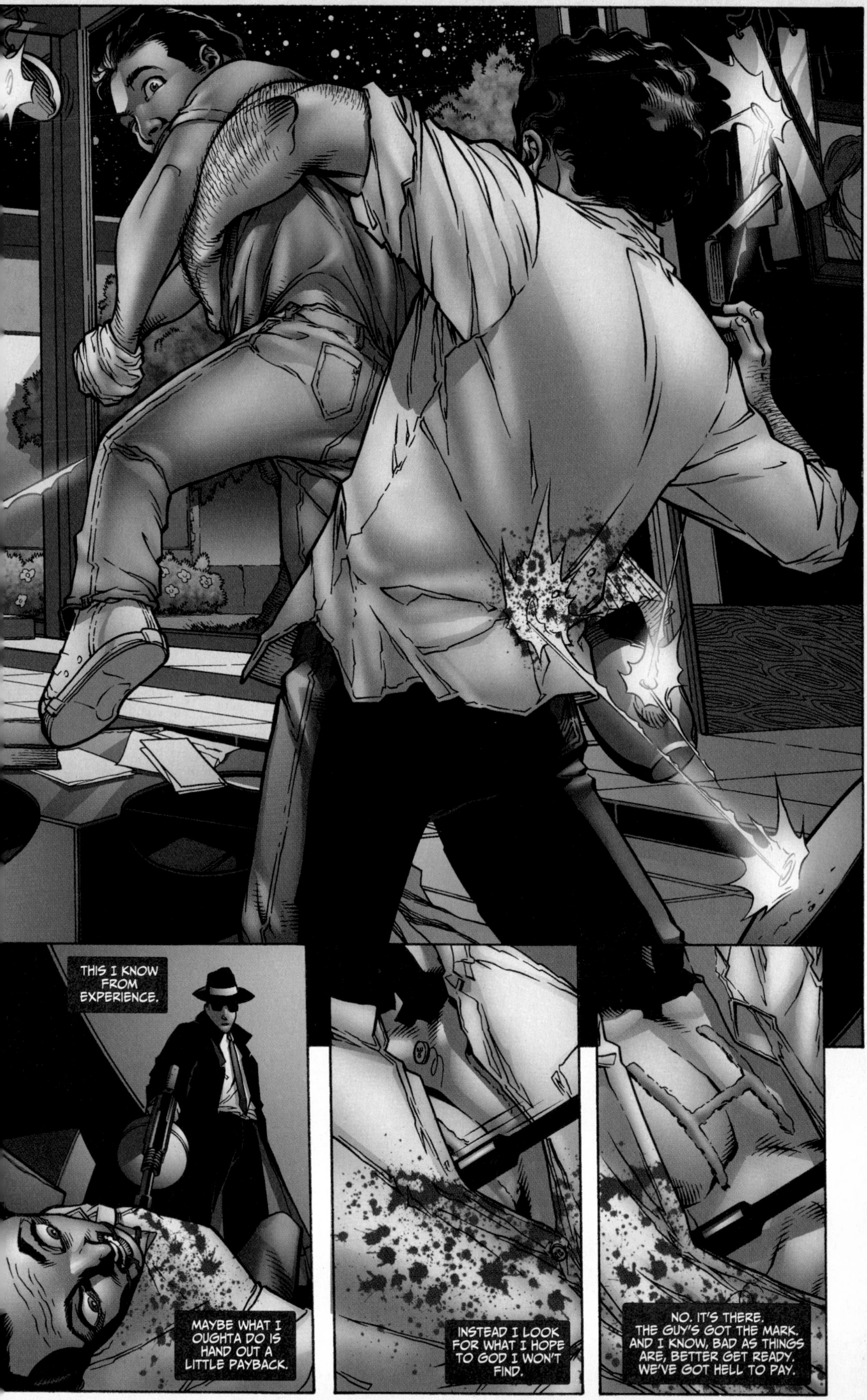
THIS I KNOW FROM EXPERIENCE.
MAYBE WHAT I OUGHTA DO IS HAND OUT A LITTLE PAYBACK.
INSTEAD I LOOK FOR WHAT I HOPE TO GOD I WON'T FIND.
NO. IT'S THERE. THE GUY'S GOT THE MARK. AND I KNOW, BAD AS THINGS ARE, BETTER GET READY. WE'VE GOT HELL TO PAY.

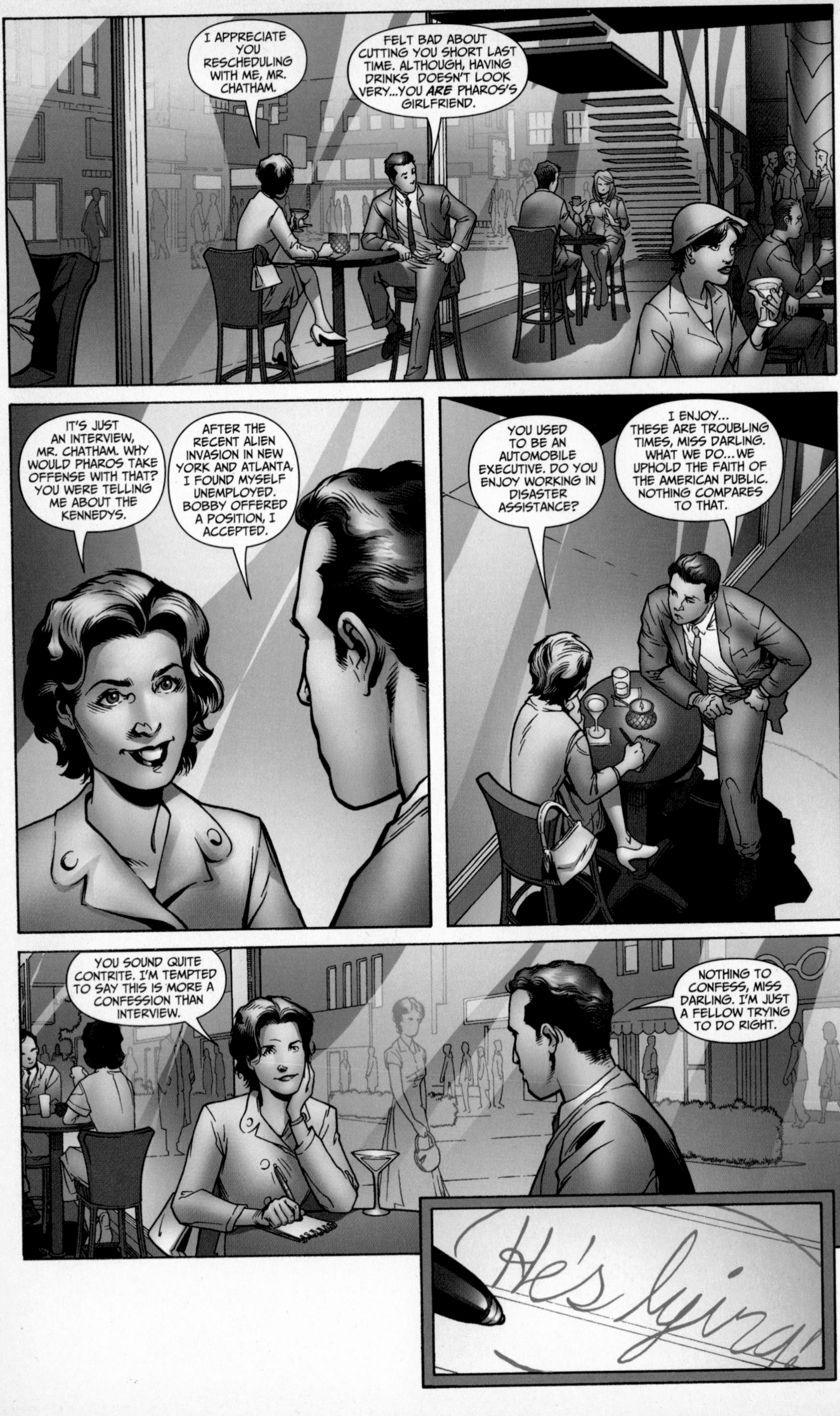
I APPRECIATE YOU RESCHEDULING WITH ME, MR. CHATHAM.
FELT BAD ABOUT CUTTING YOU SHORT LAST TIME. ALTHOUGH, HAVING DRINKS DOESN'T LOOK VERY...YOU *ARE* PHAROS'S GIRLFRIEND.
IT'S JUST AN INTERVIEW, MR. CHATHAM. WHY WOULD PHAROS TAKE OFFENSE WITH THAT? YOU WERE TELLING ME ABOUT THE KENNEDYS.
AFTER THE RECENT ALIEN INVASION IN NEW YORK AND ATLANTA, I FOUND MYSELF UNEMPLOYED. BOBBY OFFERED A POSITION, I ACCEPTED.
YOU USED TO BE AN AUTOMOBILE EXECUTIVE. DO YOU ENJOY WORKING IN DISASTER ASSISTANCE?
I ENJOY... THESE ARE TROUBLING TIMES, MISS DARLING. WHAT WE DO...WE UPHOLD THE FAITH OF THE AMERICAN PUBLIC. NOTHING COMPARES TO THAT.
YOU SOUND QUITE CONTRITE. I'M TEMPTED TO SAY THIS IS MORE A CONFESSION THAN INTERVIEW.
NOTHING TO CONFESS, MISS DARLING. I'M JUST A FELLOW TRYING TO DO RIGHT.
He's lying!

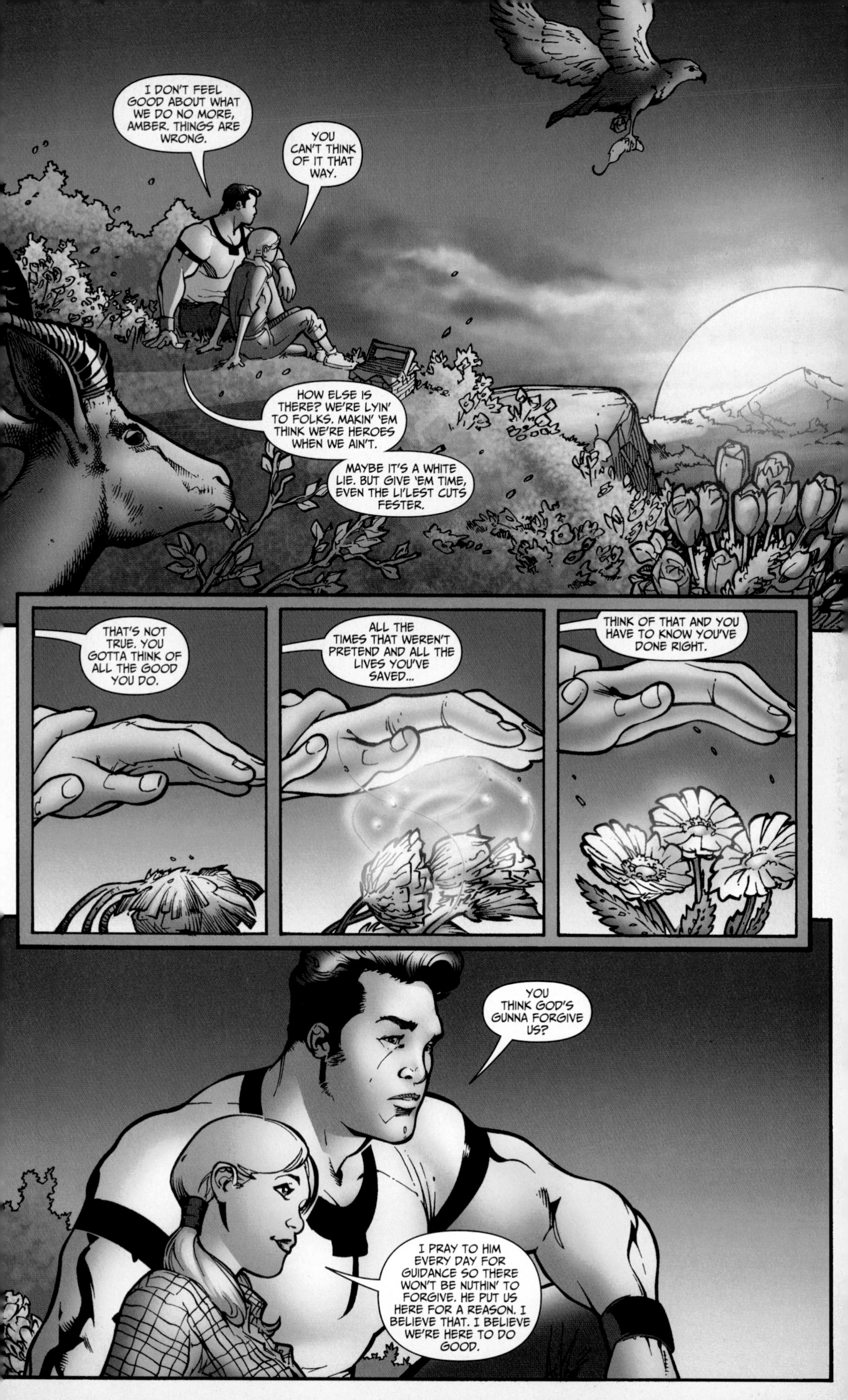
I DON'T FEEL GOOD ABOUT WHAT WE DO NO MORE, AMBER. THINGS ARE WRONG.
YOU CAN'T THINK OF IT THAT WAY.
HOW ELSE IS THERE? WE'RE LYIN' TO FOLKS. MAKIN' 'EM THINK WE'RE HEROES WHEN WE AIN'T.
MAYBE IT'S A WHITE LIE. BUT GIVE 'EM TIME, EVEN THE LI'LEST CUTS FESTER.
THAT'S NOT TRUE. YOU GOTTA THINK OF ALL THE GOOD YOU DO.
ALL THE TIMES THAT WEREN'T PRETEND AND ALL THE LIVES YOU'VE SAVED...
THINK OF THAT AND YOU HAVE TO KNOW YOU'VE DONE RIGHT.
YOU THINK GOD'S GUNNA FORGIVE US?
I PRAY TO HIM EVERY DAY FOR GUIDANCE SO THERE WON'T BE NUTHIN' TO FORGIVE. HE PUT US HERE FOR A REASON. I BELIEVE THAT. I BELIEVE WE'RE HERE TO DO GOOD.

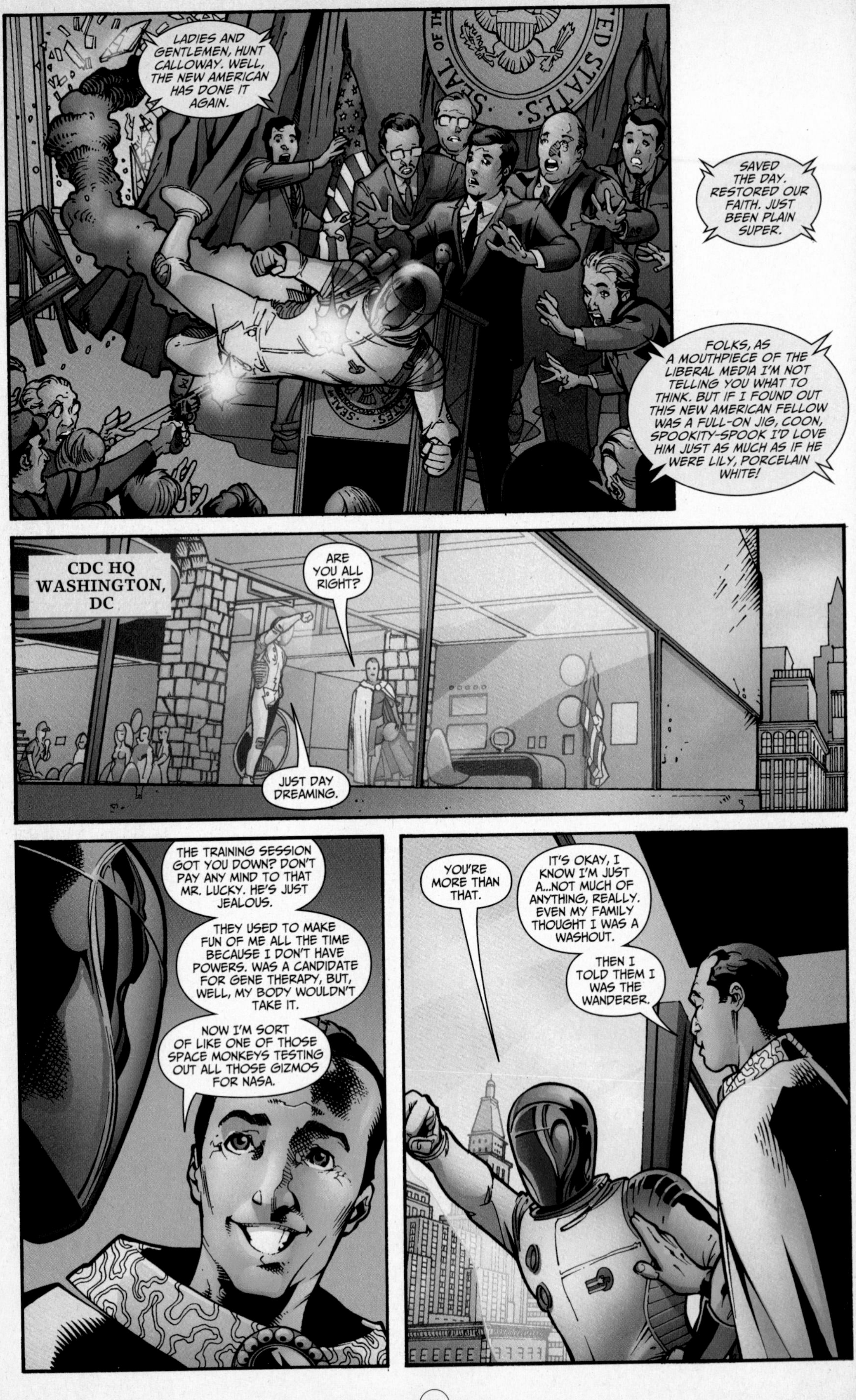

LADIES AND GENTLEMEN, HUNT CALLOWAY. WELL, THE NEW AMERICAN HAS DONE IT AGAIN.
SAVED THE DAY. RESTORED OUR FAITH. JUST BEEN PLAIN SUPER.
FOLKS, AS A MOUTHPIECE OF THE LIBERAL MEDIA I'M NOT TELLING YOU WHAT TO THINK. BUT IF I FOUND OUT THIS NEW AMERICAN FELLOW WAS A FULL-ON JIG, COON, SPOOKITY-SPOOK I'D LOVE HIM JUST AS MUCH AS IF HE WERE LILY, PORCELAIN WHITE!
CDC HQ WASHINGTON, DC
ARE YOU ALL RIGHT?
JUST DAY DREAMING.
THE TRAINING SESSION GOT YOU DOWN? DON'T PAY ANY MIND TO THAT MR. LUCKY. HE'S JUST JEALOUS.
THEY USED TO MAKE FUN OF ME ALL THE TIME BECAUSE I DON'T HAVE POWERS. WAS A CANDIDATE FOR GENE THERAPY, BUT, WELL, MY BODY WOULDN'T TAKE IT.
NOW I'M SORT OF LIKE ONE OF THOSE SPACE MONKEYS TESTING OUT ALL THOSE GIZMOS FOR NASA.
IT'S OKAY, I KNOW I'M JUST A...NOT MUCH OF ANYTHING, REALLY. EVEN MY FAMILY THOUGHT I WAS A WASHOUT.
YOU'RE MORE THAN THAT.
THEN I TOLD THEM I WAS THE WANDERER.

YOU TOLD YOUR FAMILY?

I KNOW. WHAT WE DO WE'RE SUPPOSED TO DO IN SECRET. BUT I CAN'T HAVE MY FAMILY THINKING I'M A FAILURE.

THEY'RE PROUD OF ME. THEY'RE NOT GOING TO TELL ANYONE THE TRUTH.

HE TOLD THEM WHAT?

GOOD LORD. WE'VE GOT PEOPLE OUTSIDE THE GOVERNMENT WHO KNOW THE WANDERER'S JUST A GUY IN A SUIT.

IT'S JUST HIS FAMILY.

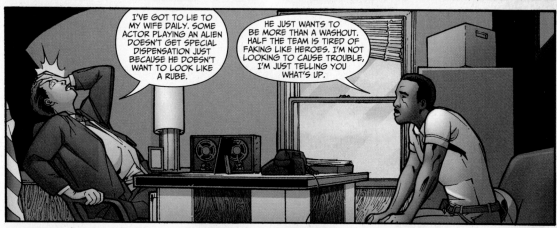

I'VE GOT TO LIE TO MY WIFE DAILY. SOME ACTOR PLAYING AN ALIEN DOESN'T GET SPECIAL DISPENSATION JUST BECAUSE HE DOESN'T WANT TO LOOK LIKE A RUBE.

HE JUST WANTS TO BE MORE THAN A WASHOUT. HALF THE TEAM IS TIRED OF FAKING LIKE HEROES. I'M NOT LOOKING TO CAUSE TROUBLE, I'M JUST TELLING YOU WHAT'S UP.

WHY? YOU AND ME HAVE BEEN AT ODDS SINCE I RECRUITED YOU.

I KNOW IT SOUNDS... I DON'T KNOW. SOFT AS HELL. BUT YOU SAVE A LIFE, YOU GET USED TO THE FEELING.

AND YOU GET TO THINKING MAYBE ALL OF US CAN DO BETTER. SO, YOU WANT TO DO GOOD BY ME--LET'S DO BETTER.

I GOTTA WONDER-- DOES HE REALLY BELIEVE IT'S THAT EASY TO DO RIGHT?

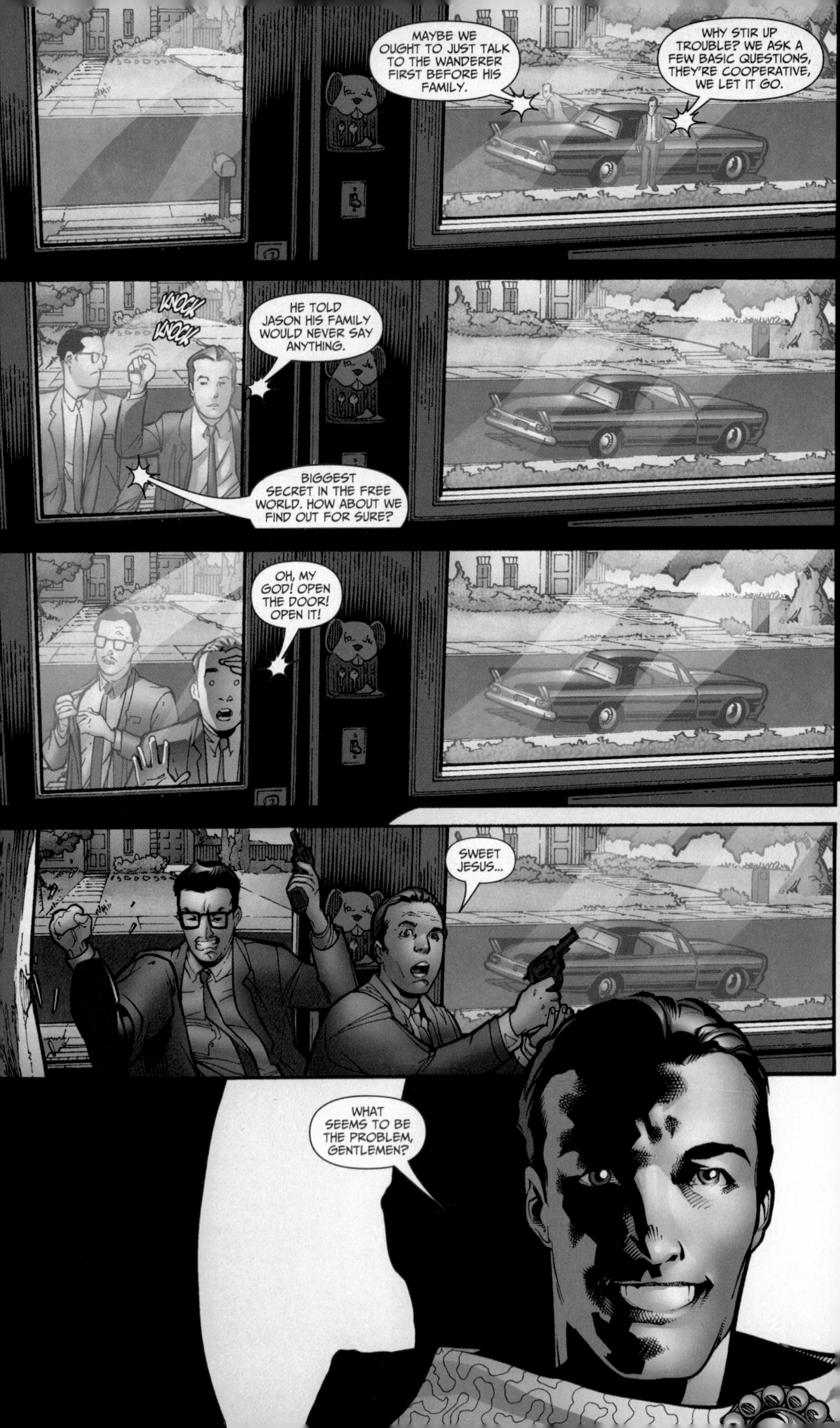
MAYBE WE OUGHT TO JUST TALK TO THE WANDERER FIRST BEFORE HIS FAMILY.
WHY STIR UP TROUBLE? WE ASK A FEW BASIC QUESTIONS, THEY'RE COOPERATIVE, WE LET IT GO.
KNOCK KNOCK
HE TOLD JASON HIS FAMILY WOULD NEVER SAY ANYTHING.
BIGGEST SECRET IN THE FREE WORLD. HOW ABOUT WE FIND OUT FOR SURE?
OH, MY GOD! OPEN THE DOOR! OPEN IT!
SWEET JESUS...
WHAT SEEMS TO BE THE PROBLEM, GENTLEMEN?

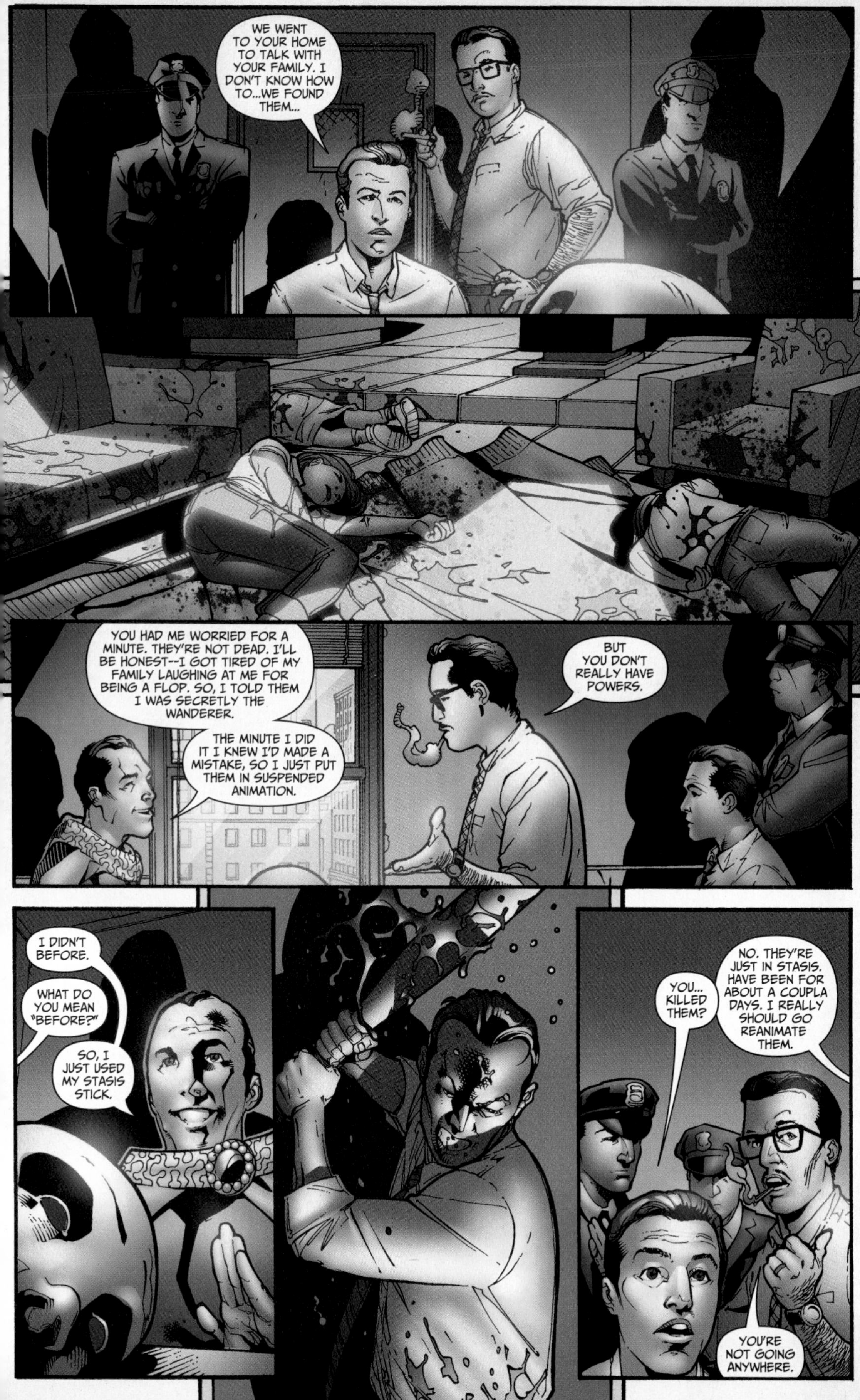
WE WENT TO YOUR HOME TO TALK WITH YOUR FAMILY. I DON'T KNOW HOW TO...WE FOUND THEM...
YOU HAD ME WORRIED FOR A MINUTE. THEY'RE NOT DEAD. I'LL BE HONEST--I GOT TIRED OF MY FAMILY LAUGHING AT ME FOR BEING A FLOP. SO, I TOLD THEM I WAS SECRETLY THE WANDERER.
THE MINUTE I DID IT I KNEW I'D MADE A MISTAKE, SO I JUST PUT THEM IN SUSPENDED ANIMATION.
BUT YOU DON'T REALLY HAVE POWERS.
I DIDN'T BEFORE.
WHAT DO YOU MEAN "BEFORE?"
SO, I JUST USED MY STASIS STICK.
YOU... KILLED THEM?
NO. THEY'RE JUST IN STASIS. HAVE BEEN FOR ABOUT A COUPLA DAYS. I REALLY SHOULD GO REANIMATE THEM.
YOU'RE NOT GOING ANYWHERE.

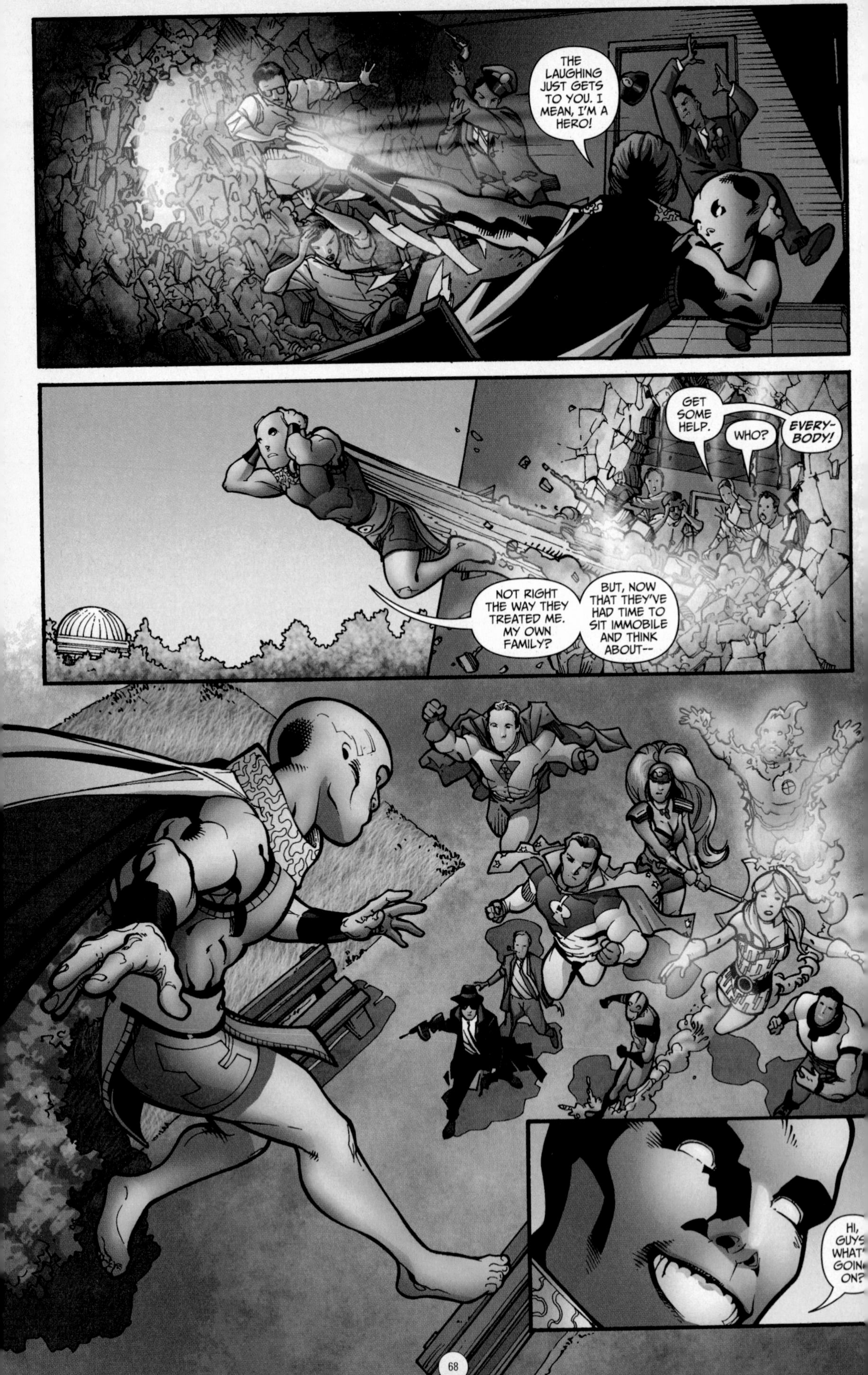

THE LAUGHING JUST GETS TO YOU. I MEAN, I'M A HERO!
GET SOME HELP.
WHO?
EVERY-BODY!
NOT RIGHT THE WAY THEY TREATED ME. MY OWN FAMILY?
BUT, NOW THAT THEY'VE HAD TIME TO SIT IMMOBILE AND THINK ABOUT--
HI, GUYS WHAT' GOIN ON?

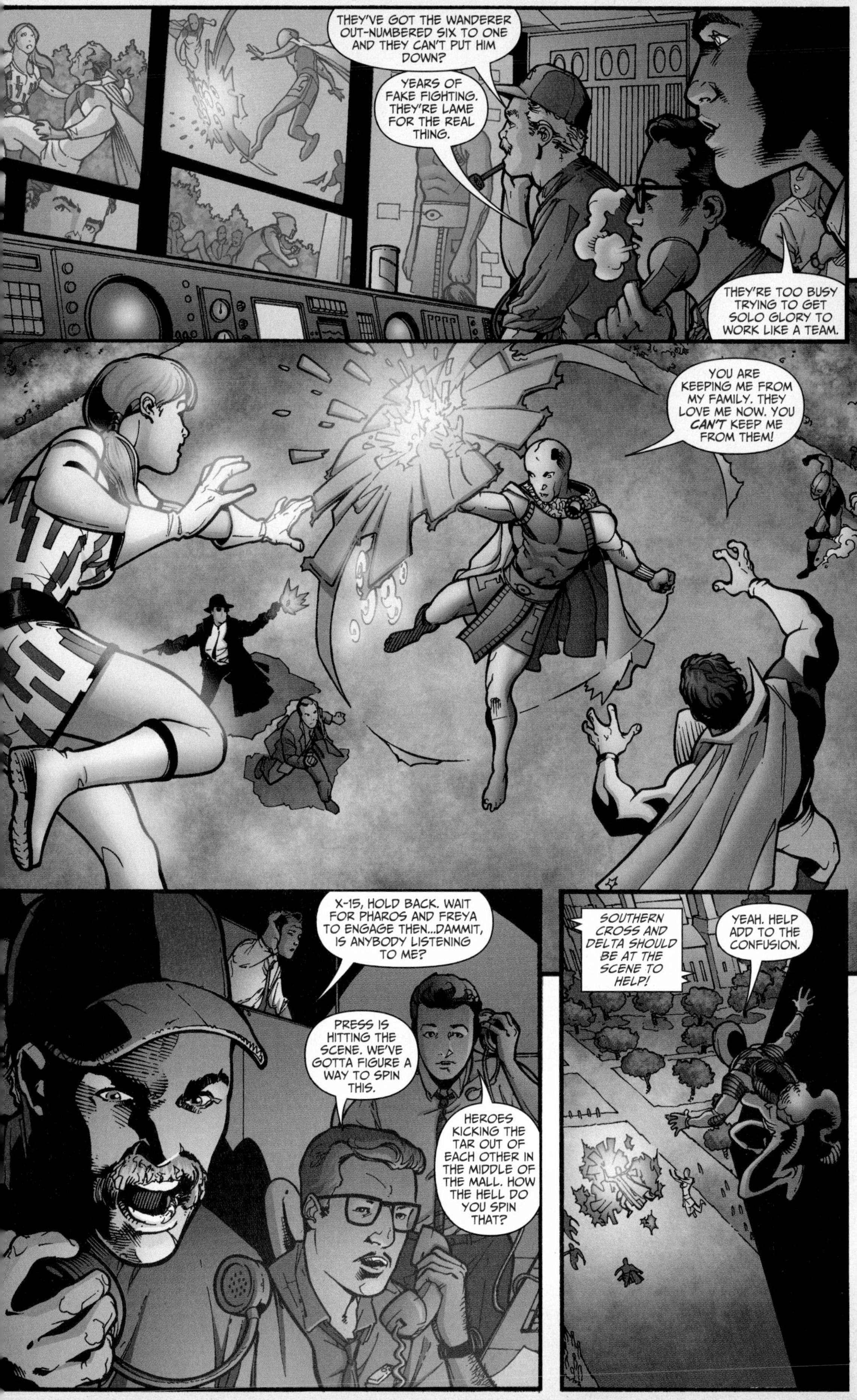
THEY'VE GOT THE WANDERER OUT-NUMBERED SIX TO ONE AND THEY CAN'T PUT HIM DOWN?
YEARS OF FAKE FIGHTING. THEY'RE LAME FOR THE REAL THING.
THEY'RE TOO BUSY TRYING TO GET SOLO GLORY TO WORK LIKE A TEAM.
YOU ARE KEEPING ME FROM MY FAMILY. THEY LOVE ME NOW. YOU *CAN'T* KEEP ME FROM THEM!
X-15, HOLD BACK. WAIT FOR PHAROS AND FREYA TO ENGAGE THEN...DAMMIT, IS ANYBODY LISTENING TO ME?
PRESS IS HITTING THE SCENE. WE'VE GOTTA FIGURE A WAY TO SPIN THIS.
HEROES KICKING THE TAR OUT OF EACH OTHER IN THE MIDDLE OF THE MALL. HOW THE HELL DO YOU SPIN THAT?
SOUTHERN CROSS AND DELTA SHOULD BE AT THE SCENE TO HELP!
YEAH. HELP ADD TO THE CONFUSION.

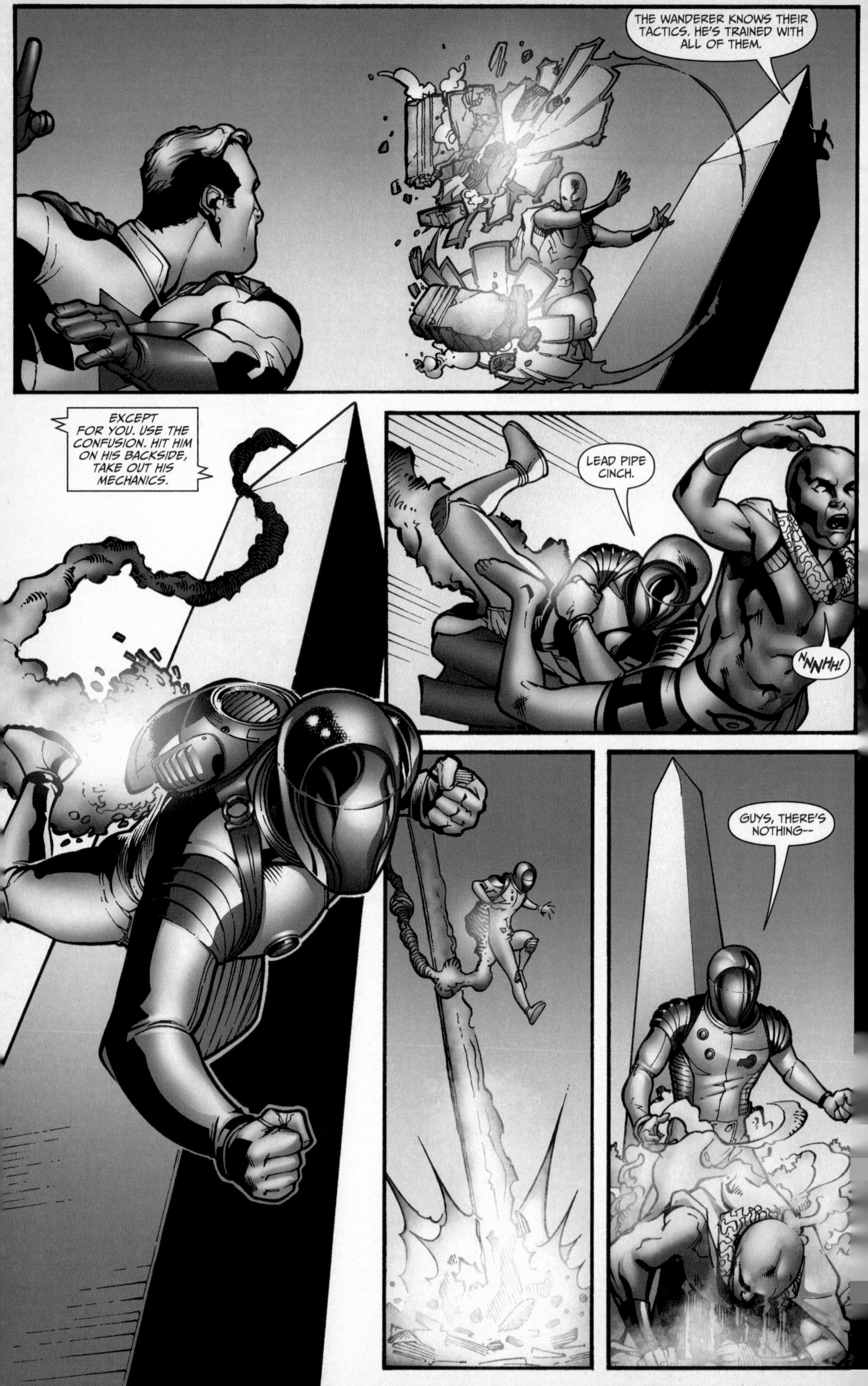

THE WANDERER KNOWS THEIR TACTICS. HE'S TRAINED WITH ALL OF THEM.
EXCEPT FOR YOU. USE THE CONFUSION. HIT HIM ON HIS BACKSIDE, TAKE OUT HIS MECHANICS.
LEAD PIPE CINCH.
NNNHH!
GUYS, THERE'S NOTHING--

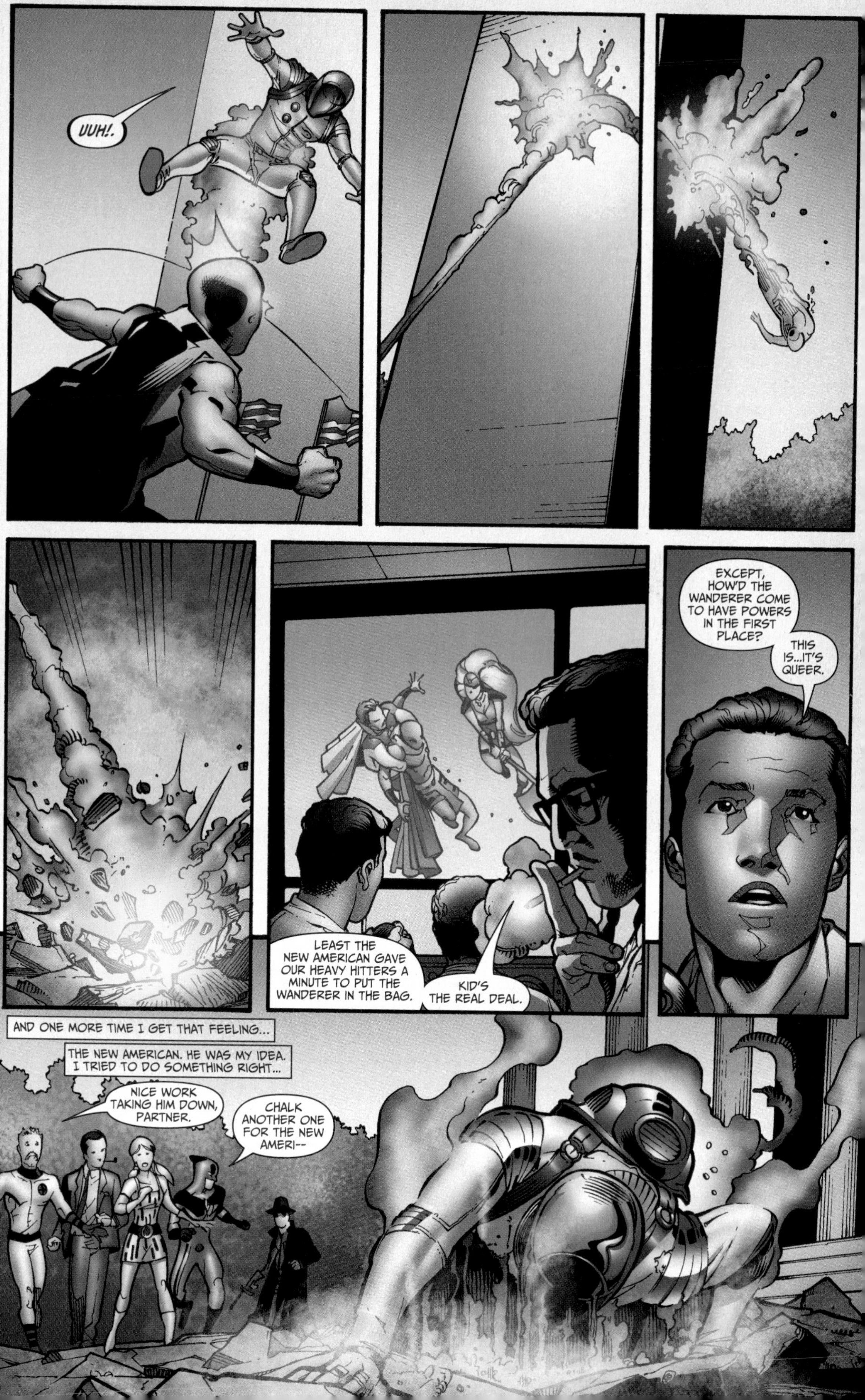
UUH!.
EXCEPT, HOW'D THE WANDERER COME TO HAVE POWERS IN THE FIRST PLACE?
THIS IS...IT'S QUEER.
LEAST THE NEW AMERICAN GAVE OUR HEAVY HITTERS A MINUTE TO PUT THE WANDERER IN THE BAG.
KID'S THE REAL DEAL.
AND ONE MORE TIME I GET THAT FEELING...
THE NEW AMERICAN. HE WAS MY IDEA. I TRIED TO DO SOMETHING RIGHT...
NICE WORK TAKING HIM DOWN, PARTNER.
CHALK ANOTHER ONE FOR THE NEW AMERI--

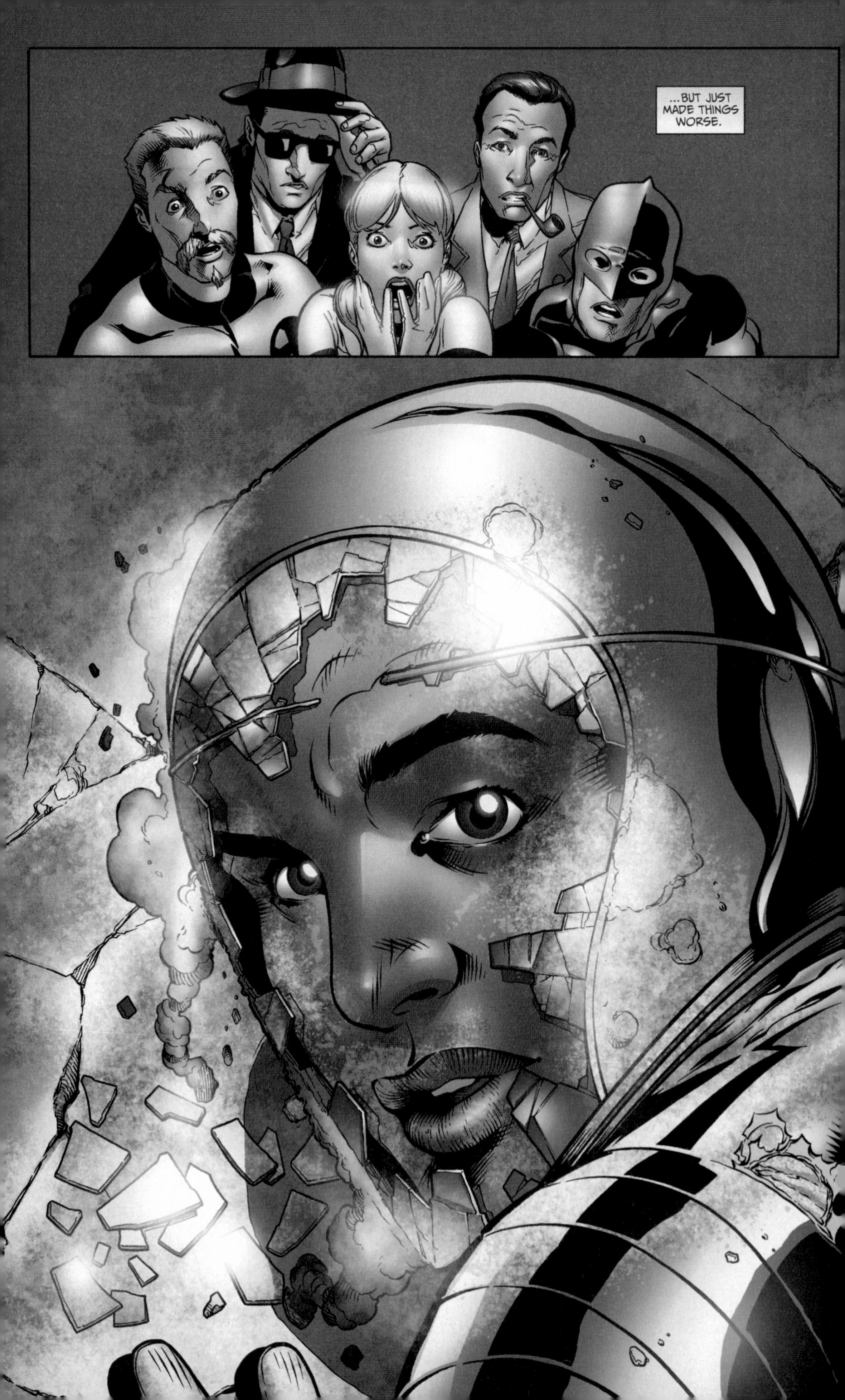
...BUT JUST MADE THINGS WORSE.

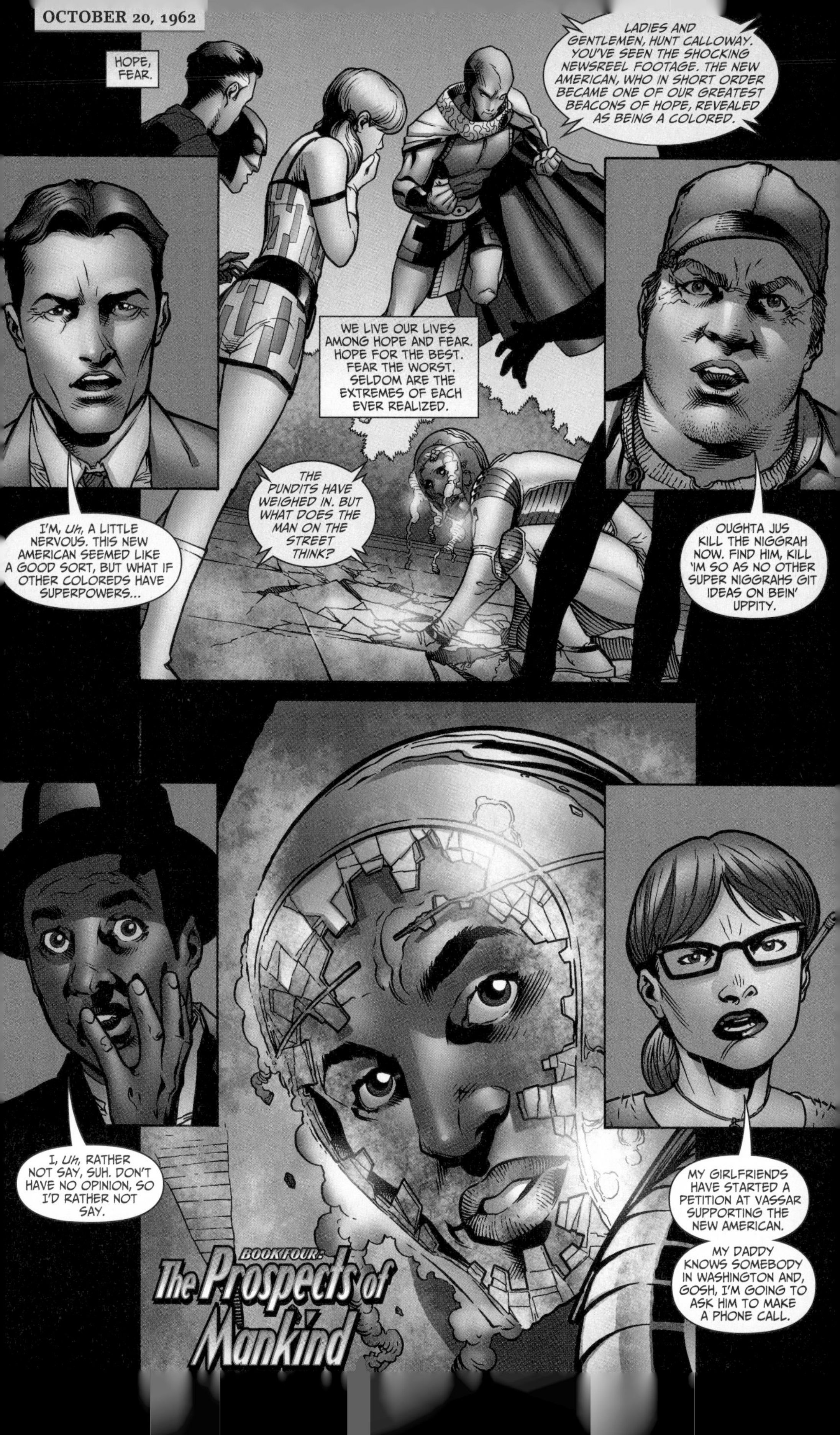
OCTOBER 20, 1962
HOPE, FEAR.
LADIES AND GENTLEMEN, HUNT CALLOWAY. YOU'VE SEEN THE SHOCKING NEWSREEL FOOTAGE. THE NEW AMERICAN, WHO IN SHORT ORDER BECAME ONE OF OUR GREATEST BEACONS OF HOPE, REVEALED AS BEING A COLORED.
WE LIVE OUR LIVES AMONG HOPE AND FEAR. HOPE FOR THE BEST. FEAR THE WORST. SELDOM ARE THE EXTREMES OF EACH EVER REALIZED.
THE PUNDITS HAVE WEIGHED IN. BUT WHAT DOES THE MAN ON THE STREET THINK?
I'M, *UH*, A LITTLE NERVOUS. THIS NEW AMERICAN SEEMED LIKE A GOOD SORT, BUT WHAT IF OTHER COLOREDS HAVE SUPERPOWERS...
OUGHTA JUS KILL THE NIGGRAH NOW. FIND HIM, KILL 'IM SO AS NO OTHER SUPER NIGGRAHS GIT IDEAS ON BEIN' UPPITY.
I, *UH*, RATHER NOT SAY, SUH. DON'T HAVE NO OPINION, SO I'D RATHER NOT SAY.
MY GIRLFRIENDS HAVE STARTED A PETITION AT VASSAR SUPPORTING THE NEW AMERICAN.
MY DADDY KNOWS SOMEBODY IN WASHINGTON AND, GOSH, I'M GOING TO ASK HIM TO MAKE A PHONE CALL.
BOOK FOUR:
The Prospects of Mankind

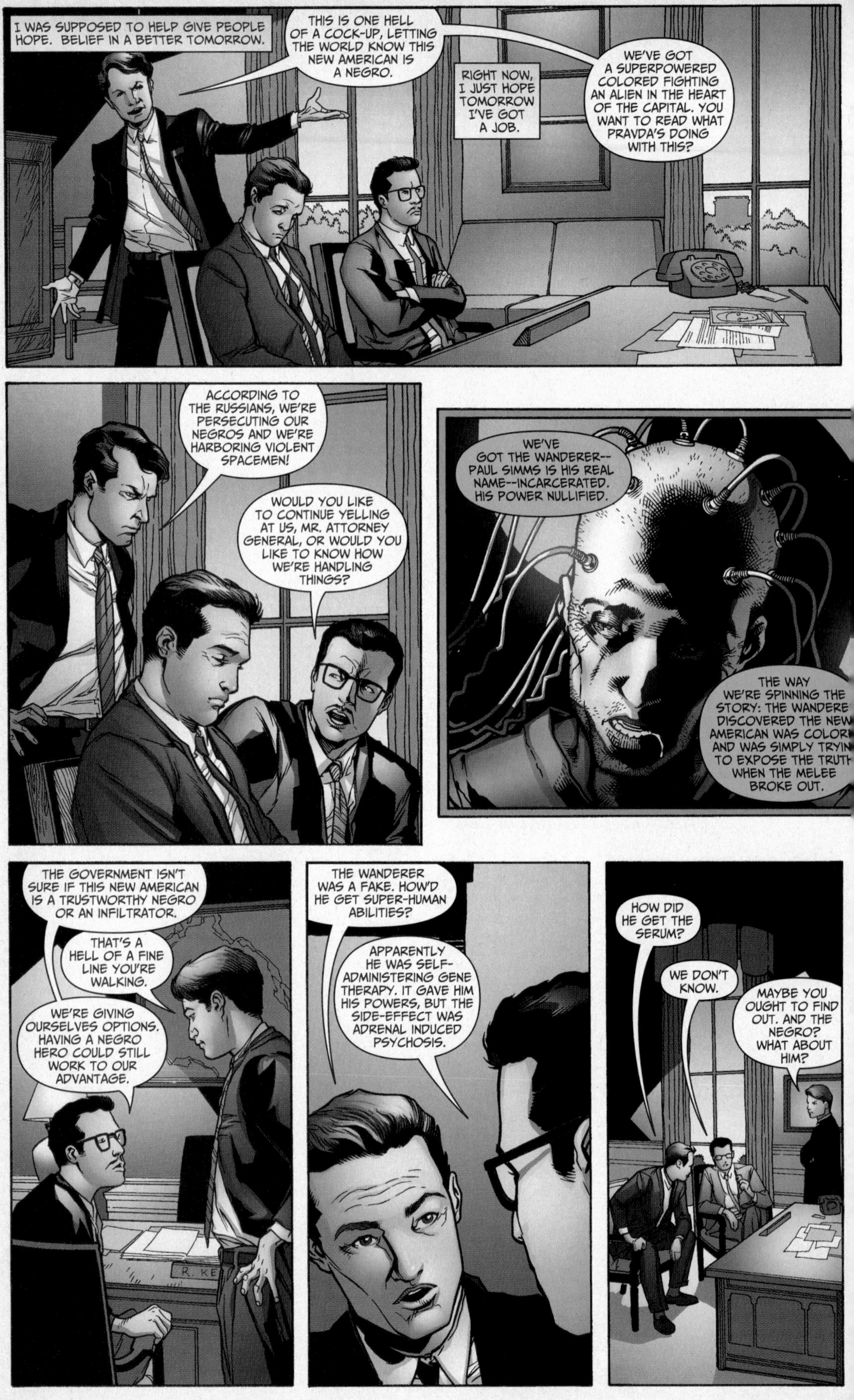
I WAS SUPPOSED TO HELP GIVE PEOPLE HOPE. BELIEF IN A BETTER TOMORROW.
THIS IS ONE HELL OF A COCK-UP, LETTING THE WORLD KNOW THIS NEW AMERICAN IS A NEGRO.
RIGHT NOW, I JUST HOPE TOMORROW I'VE GOT A JOB.
WE'VE GOT A SUPERPOWERED COLORED FIGHTING AN ALIEN IN THE HEART OF THE CAPITAL. YOU WANT TO READ WHAT PRAVDA'S DOING WITH THIS?
ACCORDING TO THE RUSSIANS, WE'RE PERSECUTING OUR NEGROS AND WE'RE HARBORING VIOLENT SPACEMEN!
WOULD YOU LIKE TO CONTINUE YELLING AT US, MR. ATTORNEY GENERAL, OR WOULD YOU LIKE TO KNOW HOW WE'RE HANDLING THINGS?
WE'VE GOT THE WANDERER--PAUL SIMMS IS HIS REAL NAME--INCARCERATED. HIS POWER NULLIFIED.
THE WAY WE'RE SPINNING THE STORY: THE WANDERE DISCOVERED THE NEW AMERICAN WAS COLOR AND WAS SIMPLY TRYIN TO EXPOSE THE TRUTH WHEN THE MELEE BROKE OUT.
THE GOVERNMENT ISN'T SURE IF THIS NEW AMERICAN IS A TRUSTWORTHY NEGRO OR AN INFILTRATOR.
THAT'S A HELL OF A FINE LINE YOU'RE WALKING.
WE'RE GIVING OURSELVES OPTIONS. HAVING A NEGRO HERO COULD STILL WORK TO OUR ADVANTAGE.
R. KE
THE WANDERER WAS A FAKE. HOW'D HE GET SUPER-HUMAN ABILITIES?
APPARENTLY HE WAS SELF-ADMINISTERING GENE THERAPY. IT GAVE HIM HIS POWERS, BUT THE SIDE-EFFECT WAS ADRENAL INDUCED PSYCHOSIS.
HOW DID HE GET THE SERUM?
WE DON'T KNOW.
MAYBE YOU OUGHT TO FIND OUT. AND THE NEGRO? WHAT ABOUT HIM?

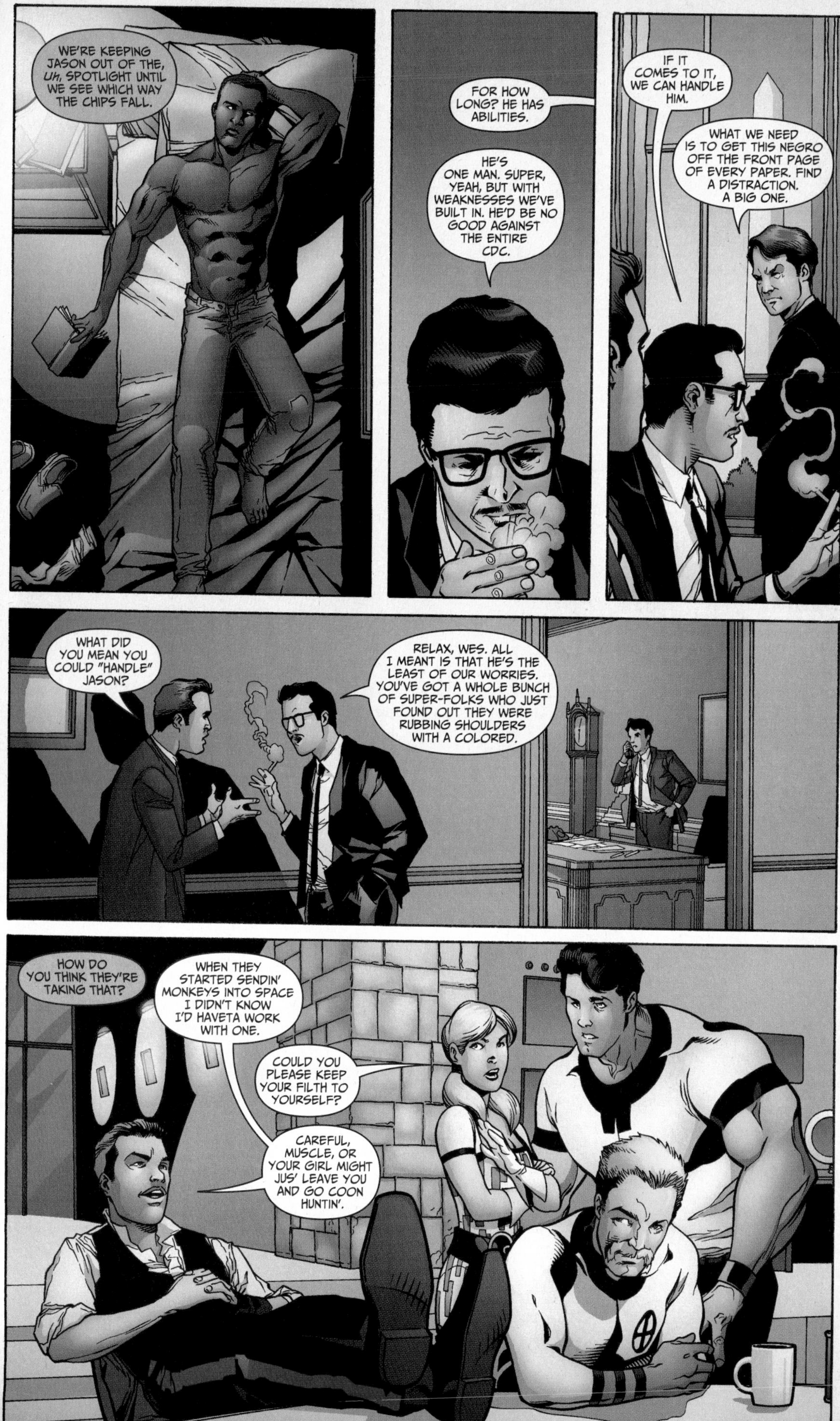
WE'RE KEEPING JASON OUT OF THE, *Uh*, SPOTLIGHT UNTIL WE SEE WHICH WAY THE CHIPS FALL.
FOR HOW LONG? HE HAS ABILITIES.
HE'S ONE MAN. SUPER, YEAH, BUT WITH WEAKNESSES WE'VE BUILT IN. HE'D BE NO GOOD AGAINST THE ENTIRE CDC.
IF IT COMES TO IT, WE CAN HANDLE HIM.
WHAT WE NEED IS TO GET THIS NEGRO OFF THE FRONT PAGE OF EVERY PAPER. FIND A DISTRACTION. A BIG ONE.
WHAT DID YOU MEAN YOU COULD "HANDLE" JASON?
RELAX, WES. ALL I MEANT IS THAT HE'S THE LEAST OF OUR WORRIES. YOU'VE GOT A WHOLE BUNCH OF SUPER-FOLKS WHO JUST FOUND OUT THEY WERE RUBBING SHOULDERS WITH A COLORED.
HOW DO YOU THINK THEY'RE TAKING THAT?
WHEN THEY STARTED SENDIN' MONKEYS INTO SPACE I DIDN'T KNOW I'D HAVETA WORK WITH ONE.
COULD YOU PLEASE KEEP YOUR FILTH TO YOURSELF?
CAREFUL, MUSCLE, OR YOUR GIRL MIGHT JUS' LEAVE YOU AND GO COON HUNTIN'.

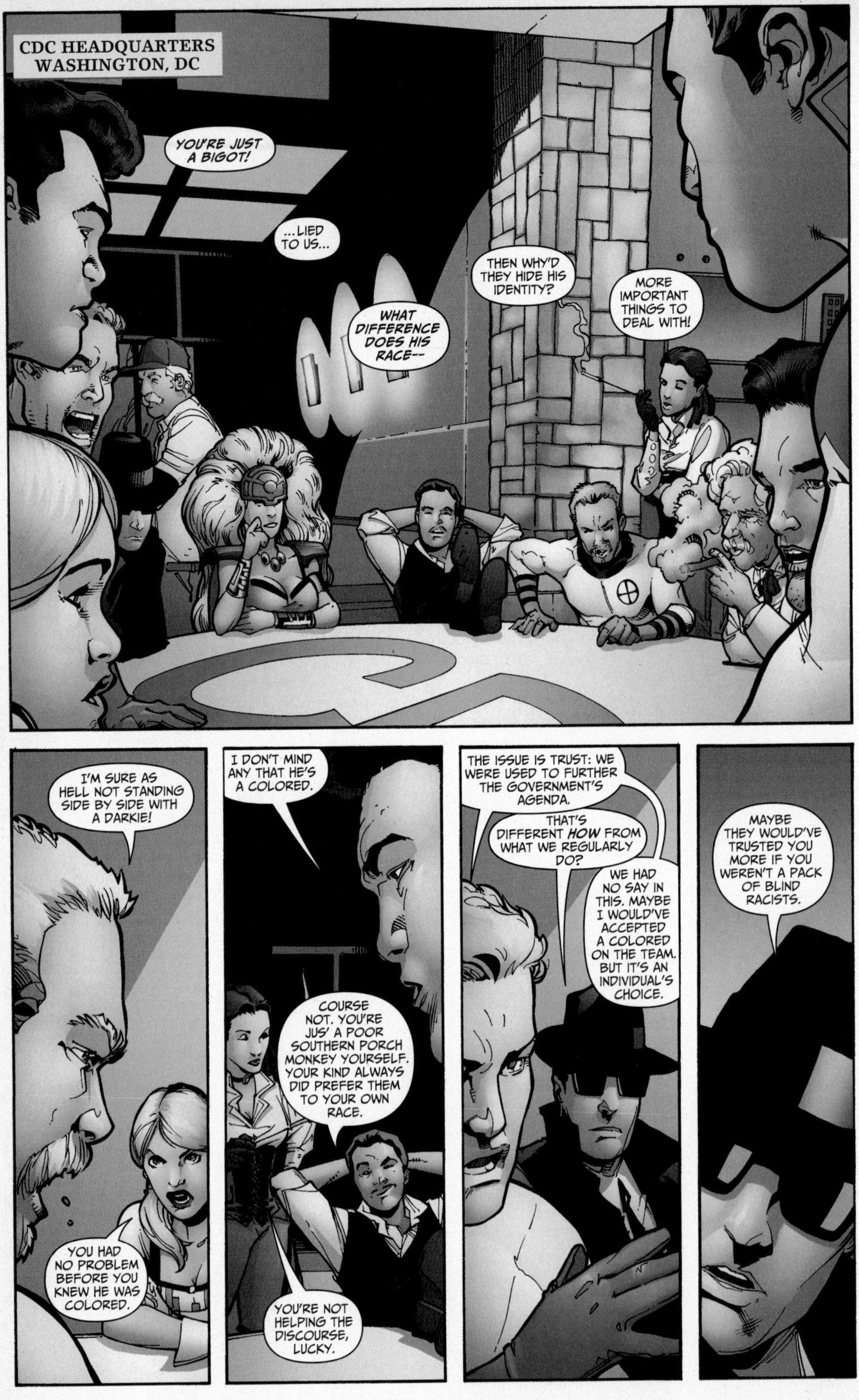

CDC HEADQUARTERS WASHINGTON, DC
YOU'RE JUST A BIGOT!
...LIED TO US...
WHAT DIFFERENCE DOES HIS RACE--
THEN WHY'D THEY HIDE HIS IDENTITY?
MORE IMPORTANT THINGS TO DEAL WITH!
I'M SURE AS HELL NOT STANDING SIDE BY SIDE WITH A DARKIE!
YOU HAD NO PROBLEM BEFORE YOU KNEW HE WAS COLORED.
I DON'T MIND ANY THAT HE'S A COLORED.
COURSE NOT. YOU'RE JUS' A POOR SOUTHERN PORCH MONKEY YOURSELF. YOUR KIND ALWAYS DID PREFER THEM TO YOUR OWN RACE.
YOU'RE NOT HELPING THE DISCOURSE, LUCKY.
THE ISSUE IS TRUST: WE WERE USED TO FURTHER THE GOVERNMENT'S AGENDA.
THAT'S DIFFERENT HOW FROM WHAT WE REGULARLY DO?
WE HAD NO SAY IN THIS. MAYBE I WOULD'VE ACCEPTED A COLORED ON THE TEAM. BUT IT'S AN INDIVIDUAL'S CHOICE.
MAYBE THEY WOULD'VE TRUSTED YOU MORE IF YOU WEREN'T A PACK OF BLIND RACISTS.

YOUR ARGUING IS AS POINTLESS AS IT IS AMUSING. YOU ACT SUPERIOR, BUT FROM MY VANTAGE ARE ALL MERE MORTALS.

QUIT THE "GODDESS" BITS. YOU'RE JUST A DELUDED WENCH WITH A SHARP TOY.

MY NORSE MAGICK BATTLE AX HAS BEEN BLESSED BY ODIN HIMSELF. ANY TIME YOU WISH TO TEST MY DELUSIONS OR THE SHARPNESS OF MY "TOY" YOU ARE INVITED.

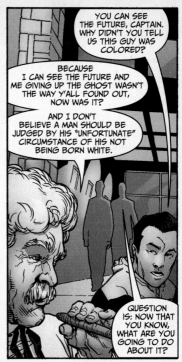

YOU CAN SEE THE FUTURE, CAPTAIN. WHY DIDN'T YOU TELL US THIS GUY WAS COLORED?

BECAUSE I CAN SEE THE FUTURE AND ME GIVING UP THE GHOST WASN'T THE WAY Y'ALL FOUND OUT, NOW WAS IT?

AND I DON'T BELIEVE A MAN SHOULD BE JUDGED BY HIS "UNFORTUNATE" CIRCUMSTANCE OF HIS NOT BEING BORN WHITE.

QUESTION IS: NOW THAT YOU KNOW, WHAT ARE YOU GOING TO DO ABOUT IT?

IF IT ISN'T OUR EAST-COAST MINDERS.

DO YOU UNDERSTAND THE OPPORTUNITY YOU HAVE? IF YOU EMBRACE A NEGRO DO YOU KNOW WHAT KIND OF MESSAGE THAT WILL SEND TO THE PUBLIC?

THIS IS YOUR CHOICE: SHOW AMERICA A NEGRO CAN BE A HERO SAME AS WHITES, OR LET PREJUDICE FESTER AND THE COUNTRY BURN WITH RACE HATE.

WHAT THE HELL YOU SELLIN', PITCHMAN? BAD ENOUGH YOU SHINE US INTO THINKING THIS COON'S A HERO—

CROSS—

HELL NO! I AIN'T GONNA BE PART OF TELLING WHITES NIGGERS ARE GOOD AS US.

AND IF Y'ALL KENNEDY BOYS THINK YOU CAN WHISTLE AND WE'LL JUS' DANCE—

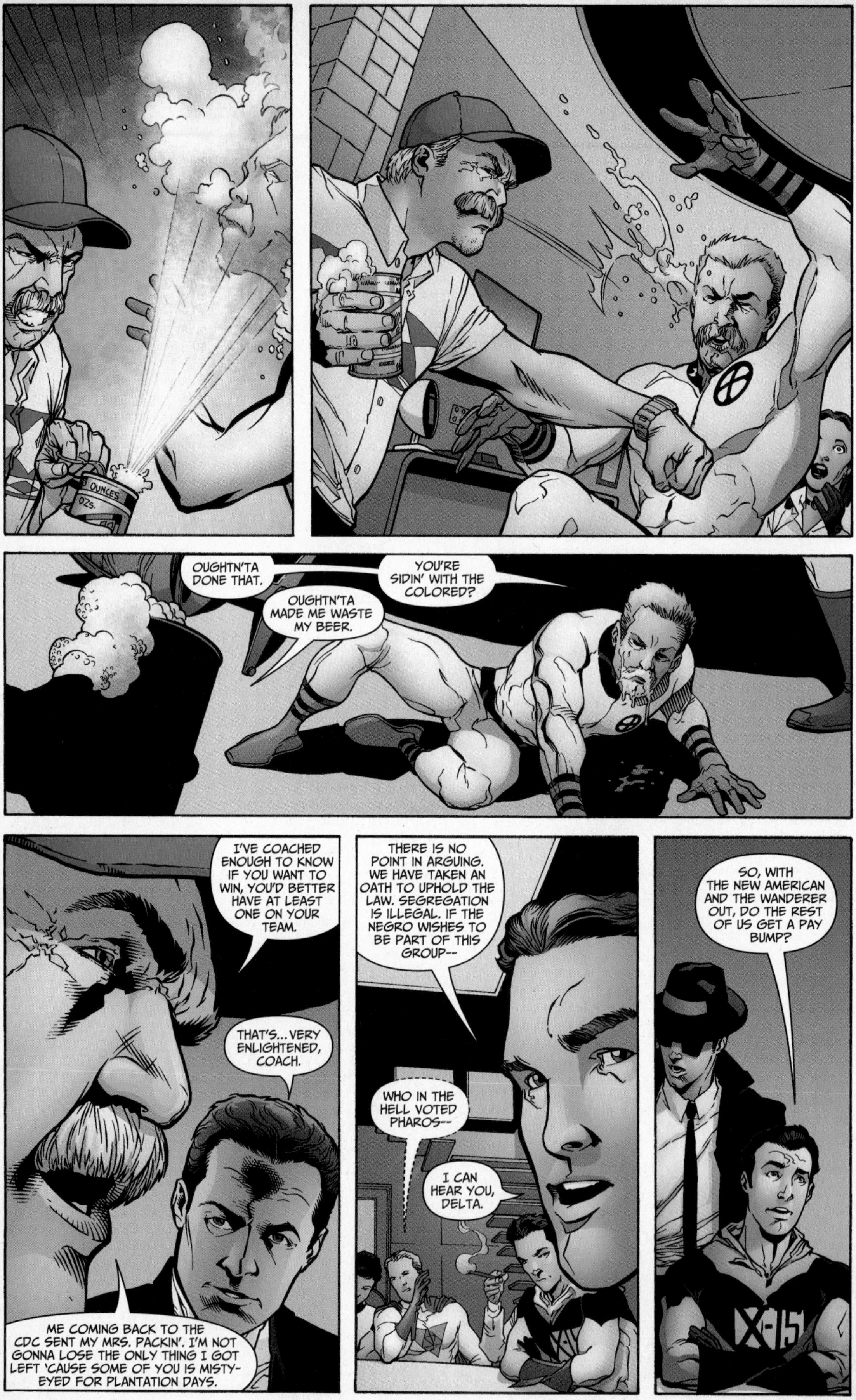
OUNCES
OZS.
OUGHTN'TA DONE THAT.
OUGHTN'TA MADE ME WASTE MY BEER.
YOU'RE SIDIN' WITH THE COLORED?
I'VE COACHED ENOUGH TO KNOW IF YOU WANT TO WIN, YOU'D BETTER HAVE AT LEAST ONE ON YOUR TEAM.
THAT'S...VERY ENLIGHTENED, COACH.
ME COMING BACK TO THE CDC SENT MY MRS. PACKIN'. I'M NOT GONNA LOSE THE ONLY THING I GOT LEFT 'CAUSE SOME OF YOU IS MISTY-EYED FOR PLANTATION DAYS.
THERE IS NO POINT IN ARGUING. WE HAVE TAKEN AN OATH TO UPHOLD THE LAW. SEGREGATION IS ILLEGAL. IF THE NEGRO WISHES TO BE PART OF THIS GROUP--
WHO IN THE HELL VOTED PHAROS--
I CAN HEAR YOU, DELTA.
SO, WITH THE NEW AMERICAN AND THE WANDERER OUT, DO THE REST OF US GET A PAY BUMP?
X-15

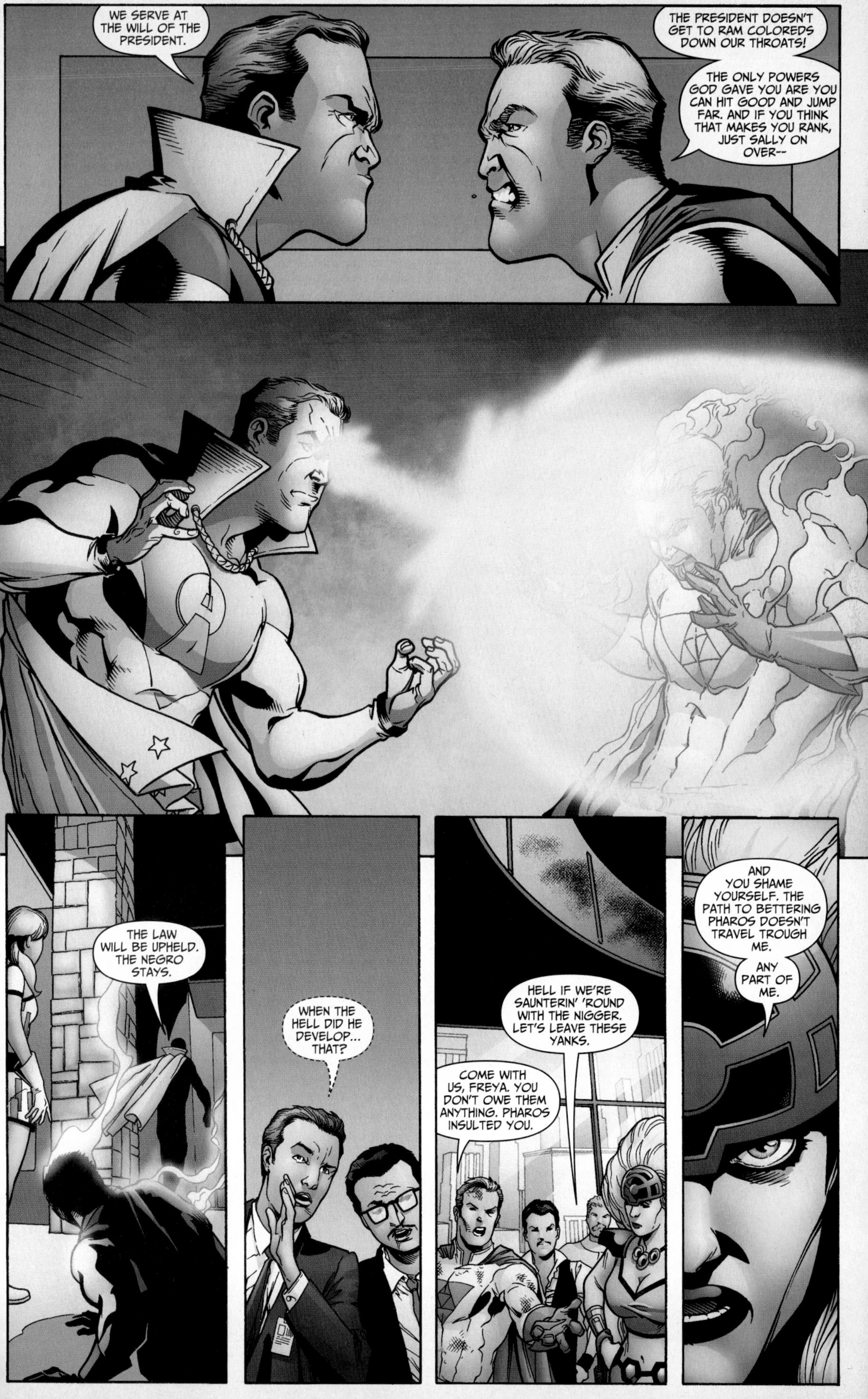
WE SERVE AT THE WILL OF THE PRESIDENT.
THE PRESIDENT DOESN'T GET TO RAM COLOREDS DOWN OUR THROATS!
THE ONLY POWERS GOD GAVE YOU ARE YOU CAN HIT GOOD AND JUMP FAR. AND IF YOU THINK THAT MAKES YOU RANK, JUST SALLY ON OVER--
THE LAW WILL BE UPHELD. THE NEGRO STAYS.
WHEN THE HELL DID HE DEVELOP... THAT?
HELL IF WE'RE SAUNTERIN' 'ROUND WITH THE NIGGER. LET'S LEAVE THESE YANKS.
COME WITH US, FREYA. YOU DON'T OWE THEM ANYTHING. PHAROS INSULTED YOU.
AND YOU SHAME YOURSELF. THE PATH TO BETTERING PHAROS DOESN'T TRAVEL TROUGH ME.
ANY PART OF ME.

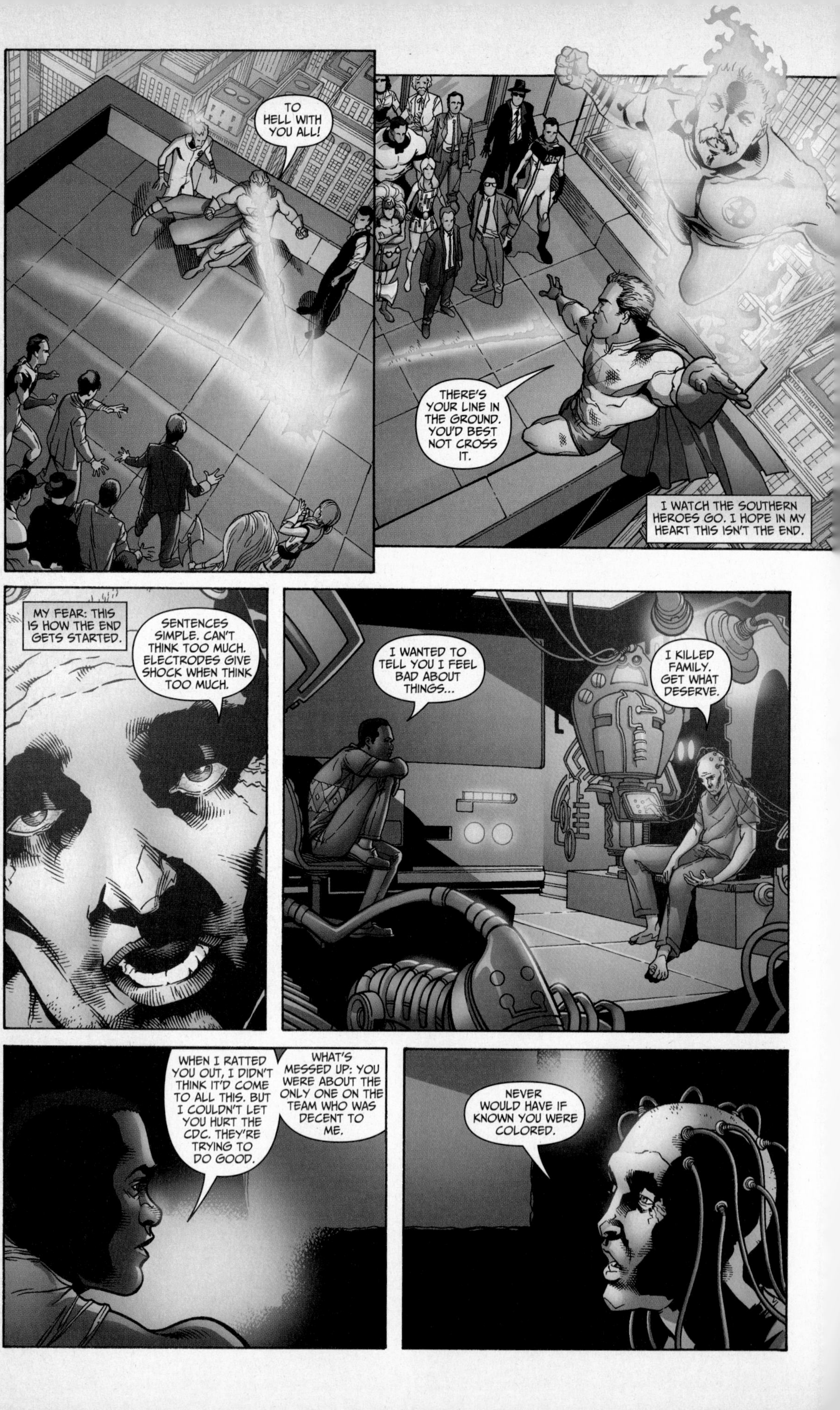
TO HELL WITH YOU ALL!
THERE'S YOUR LINE IN THE GROUND. YOU'D BEST NOT CROSS IT.
I WATCH THE SOUTHERN HEROES GO. I HOPE IN MY HEART THIS ISN'T THE END.
MY FEAR: THIS IS HOW THE END GETS STARTED.
SENTENCES SIMPLE. CAN'T THINK TOO MUCH. ELECTRODES GIVE SHOCK WHEN THINK TOO MUCH.
I WANTED TO TELL YOU I FEEL BAD ABOUT THINGS...
I KILLED FAMILY. GET WHAT DESERVE.
WHEN I RATTED YOU OUT, I DIDN'T THINK IT'D COME TO ALL THIS. BUT I COULDN'T LET YOU HURT THE CDC. THEY'RE TRYING TO DO GOOD.
WHAT'S MESSED UP: YOU WERE ABOUT THE ONLY ONE ON THE TEAM WHO WAS DECENT TO ME.
NEVER WOULD HAVE IF KNOWN YOU WERE COLORED.

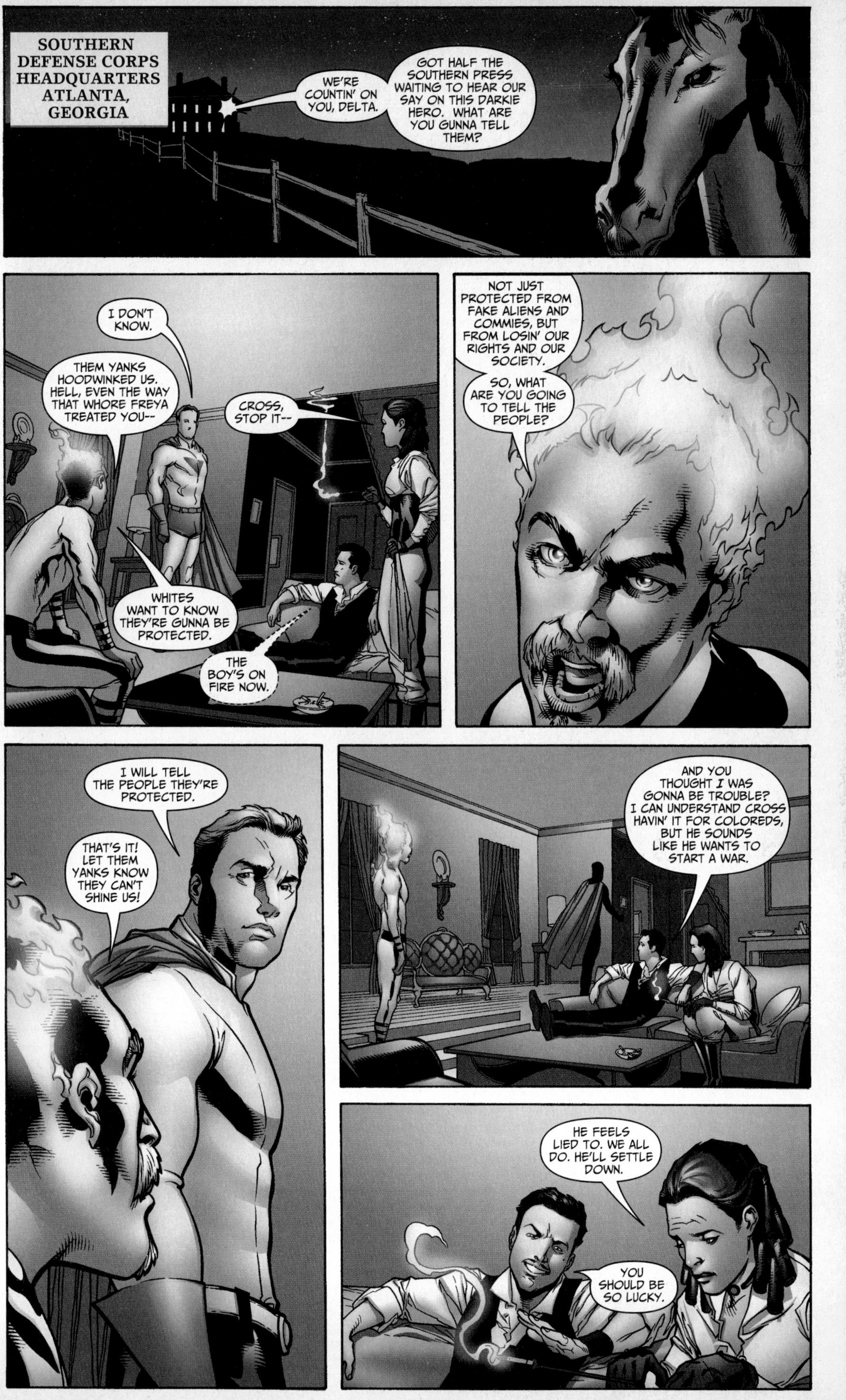
SOUTHERN DEFENSE CORPS HEADQUARTERS ATLANTA, GEORGIA
WE'RE COUNTIN' ON YOU, DELTA.
GOT HALF THE SOUTHERN PRESS WAITING TO HEAR OUR SAY ON THIS DARKIE HERO. WHAT ARE YOU GUNNA TELL THEM?
I DON'T KNOW.
THEM YANKS HOODWINKED US. HELL, EVEN THE WAY THAT WHORE FREYA TREATED YOU--
CROSS, STOP IT--
WHITES WANT TO KNOW THEY'RE GUNNA BE PROTECTED.
THE BOY'S ON FIRE NOW.
NOT JUST PROTECTED FROM FAKE ALIENS AND COMMIES, BUT FROM LOSIN' OUR RIGHTS AND OUR SOCIETY.
SO, WHAT ARE YOU GOING TO TELL THE PEOPLE?
I WILL TELL THE PEOPLE THEY'RE PROTECTED.
THAT'S IT! LET THEM YANKS KNOW THEY CAN'T SHINE US!
AND YOU THOUGHT I WAS GONNA BE TROUBLE? I CAN UNDERSTAND CROSS HAVIN' IT FOR COLOREDS, BUT HE SOUNDS LIKE HE WANTS TO START A WAR.
HE FEELS LIED TO. WE ALL DO. HE'LL SETTLE DOWN.
YOU SHOULD BE SO LUCKY.

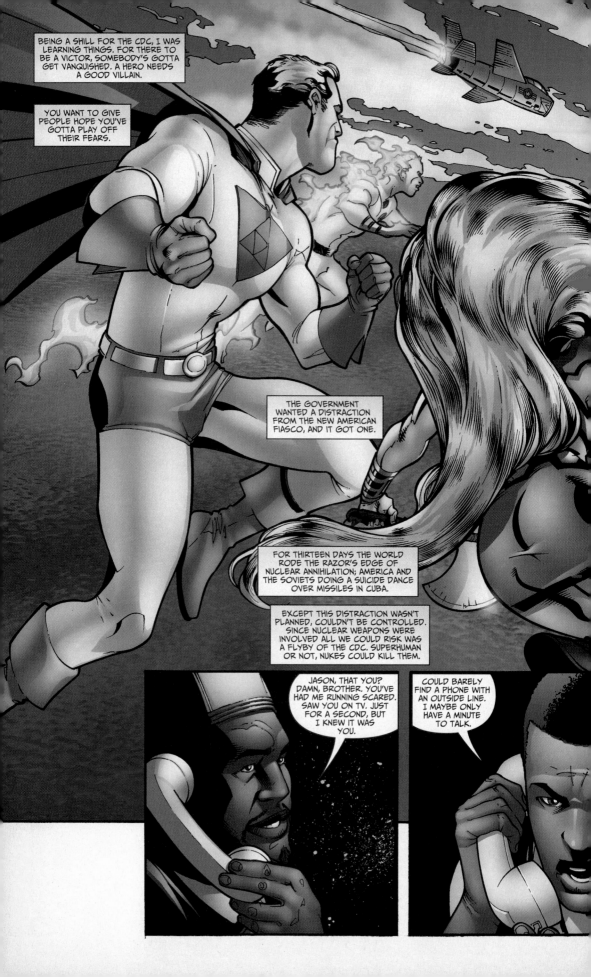

BEING A SHILL FOR THE CDC, I WAS LEARNING THINGS. FOR THERE TO BE A VICTOR, SOMEBODY'S GOTTA GET VANQUISHED. A HERO NEEDS A GOOD VILLAIN.

YOU WANT TO GIVE PEOPLE HOPE YOU'VE GOTTA PLAY OFF THEIR FEARS.

THE GOVERNMENT WANTED A DISTRACTION FROM THE NEW AMERICAN FIASCO, AND IT GOT ONE.

FOR THIRTEEN DAYS THE WORLD RODE THE RAZOR'S EDGE OF NUCLEAR ANNIHILATION; AMERICA AND THE SOVIETS DOING A SUICIDE DANCE OVER MISSILES IN CUBA.

EXCEPT THIS DISTRACTION WASN'T PLANNED, COULDN'T BE CONTROLLED. SINCE NUCLEAR WEAPONS WERE INVOLVED ALL WE COULD RISK WAS A FLYBY OF THE CDC. SUPERHUMAN OR NOT, NUKES COULD KILL THEM.

JASON, THAT YOU? DAMN, BROTHER. YOU'VE HAD ME RUNNING SCARED. SAW YOU ON TV. JUST FOR A SECOND, BUT I KNEW IT WAS YOU.

COULD BARELY FIND A PHONE WITH AN OUTSIDE LINE. I MAYBE ONLY HAVE A MINUTE TO TALK.

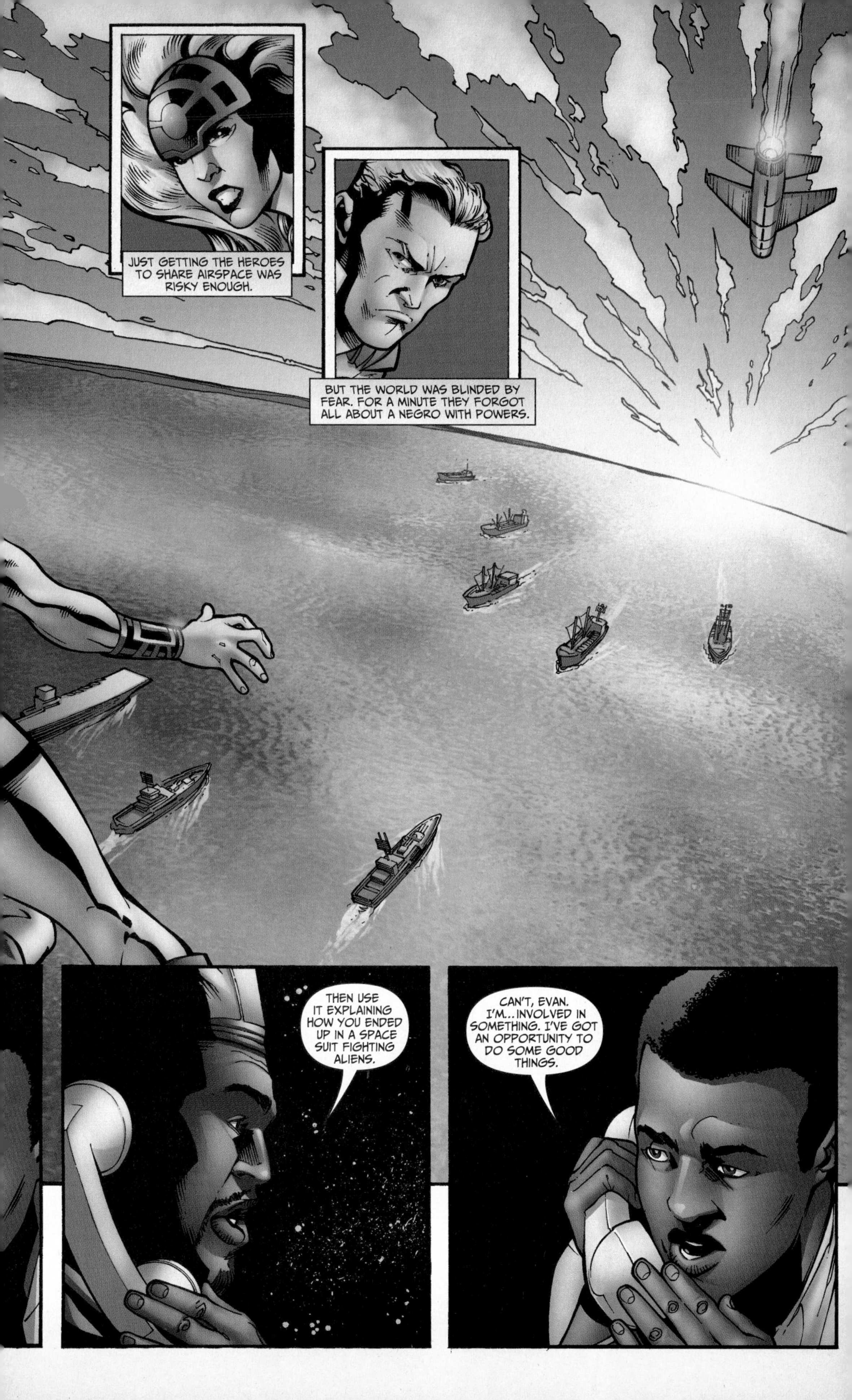
JUST GETTING THE HEROES TO SHARE AIRSPACE WAS RISKY ENOUGH.
BUT THE WORLD WAS BLINDED BY FEAR. FOR A MINUTE THEY FORGOT ALL ABOUT A NEGRO WITH POWERS.
THEN USE IT EXPLAINING HOW YOU ENDED UP IN A SPACE SUIT FIGHTING ALIENS.
CAN'T, EVAN. I'M...INVOLVED IN SOMETHING. I'VE GOT AN OPPORTUNITY TO DO SOME GOOD THINGS.

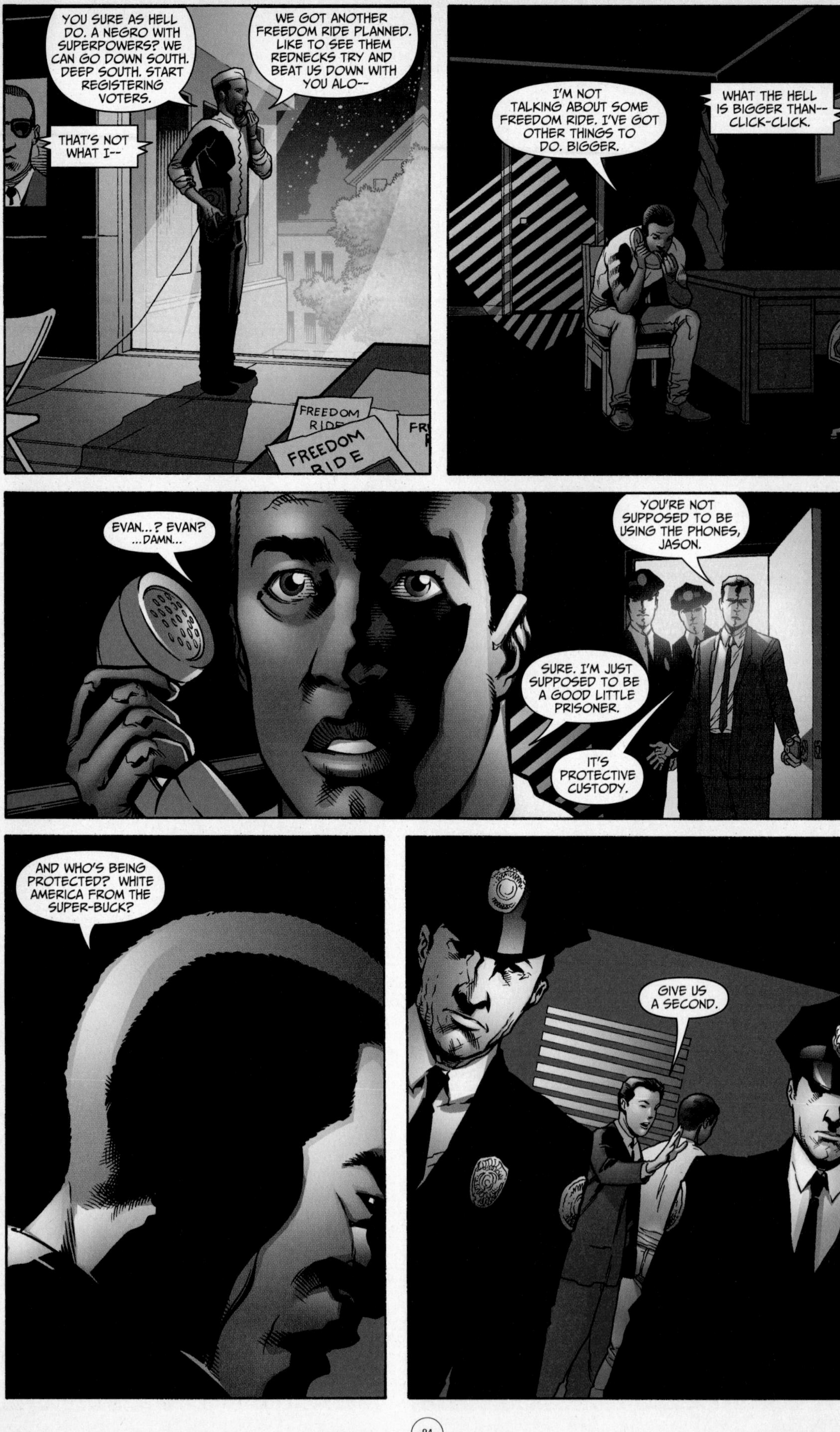
YOU SURE AS HELL DO. A NEGRO WITH SUPERPOWERS? WE CAN GO DOWN SOUTH. DEEP SOUTH. START REGISTERING VOTERS.
THAT'S NOT WHAT I--
WE GOT ANOTHER FREEDOM RIDE PLANNED. LIKE TO SEE THEM REDNECKS TRY AND BEAT US DOWN WITH YOU ALO--
FREEDOM RIDE
FREEDOM RIDE
I'M NOT TALKING ABOUT SOME FREEDOM RIDE. I'VE GOT OTHER THINGS TO DO. BIGGER.
WHAT THE HELL IS BIGGER THAN--CLICK-CLICK.
EVAN...? EVAN? ...DAMN...
YOU'RE NOT SUPPOSED TO BE USING THE PHONES, JASON.
SURE. I'M JUST SUPPOSED TO BE A GOOD LITTLE PRISONER.
IT'S PROTECTIVE CUSTODY.
AND WHO'S BEING PROTECTED? WHITE AMERICA FROM THE SUPER-BUCK?
GIVE US A SECOND.

THIS ISN'T HOW I WANTED THINGS. AFTER YOU'D PROVEN YOURSELF, THEN WE COULD'VE REVEALED YOU'RE A NEGRO. A FEW YEARS, AND--

A FEW YEARS OF HIDING BEHIND A MASK? C'MON, MAN. IT'S BEEN TWO HUNDRED YEARS, AND TO MOST WHITES WE'RE STILL NOTHING BUT "NIGGERS."

HOPE? YOU CAN BARELY SAY THE WORD. TOLD YOU WHEN I MET YOU I THOUGHT YOU WERE FULL OF S&!T.

I FIND OUT YOU REALLY ARE, I DON'T CARE ABOUT CONSEQUENCES. THERE'S GONNA BE TROUBLE. AND I'M BRINGING IT

MY BROTHER SAYS I OUGHTA TAKE MY NEW POWERS DOWN SOUTH, FIND A FEW BIGOTS AND--

KILL 'EM? KILL 'EM FOR KILLING NEGROS, AND GIVE THEM REASON TO KILL MORE NEGROS?

MAN, I LOVE YOU LIBERAL WHITES. JUST GIVE EVERYBODY A HUG, THE WORLD'LL BE FINE.

A WORLD FULL OF RETRIBUTION KILLINGS ISN'T ONE I WANT MY SON GROWING UP IN.

THERE'S STILL A CHANCE FOR US TO DO BETTER. TO GIVE PEOPLE... HOPE.

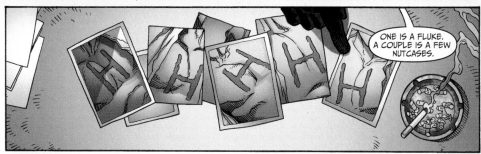

ONE IS A FLUKE. A COUPLE IS A FEW NUTCASES.

I'VE NAILED FIVE PSYCHOS IN THE LAST YEAR WEARING AN H. HELLBENT.

SELF-INFLICTED. YOU'D THINK THESE DAYS THEY'D JUST GET A TATTOO LIKE MOST YOUNG MISCREANTS.

YEAH. HELLBENT HAVING FOLLOWERS. MAYBE HE DOES. THANKS TO THE LIBERAL MEDIA KILLERS GET MADE INTO CELEBRITIES.

ALL THE MORE REASON WE SHOULD KEEP LETTING HIM TAKE PUBLIC LICKINGS FROM THE CDC.

I BELIEVE WHAT HAS THE SECRET AGENT CONCERNED--

HELLBENT'S DIFFERENT THAN THE NORMAL CHARADE WE PERPETRATE. IT'S REAL CRIME, AND YOU KNOW I'VE GOT NO TASTE FOR THAT.

HE'S A MENTAL CASE WHO DOES OUR BIDDING.

HELLBENT IS A HOMICIDAL GENIUS WITH AN INSATIABLE BLOOD LUST. REGARDLESS OF THE "ARRANGEMENT" YOU HAVE WITH HIM, I BELIEVE THERE'S MORE TO HIS FOLLOWING THAN EVIDENT.

AND YOU'RE SUPPOSED TO BE THE SMARTEST GUY IN AMERICA. WELL, WHEN YOUR SUPER-DUPER BRAIN BOX FIGURES THINGS OUT, LET ME KNOW.

SUCH AS?

I'M NOT CERTAIN.

YOU'RE DANCING WITH THE DEVIL. I GOT NO TASTE FOR IT.

IT'S BEEN IN THE DRINK FOR MONTHS. WHAT THE WATER DIDN'T DECOMPOSE, THE FISH ATE.

THE CORONER'S GOTTA MAKE IT OFFICIAL, BUT I'VE BEEN DOING THIS ENOUGH YEARS TO KNOW IT'S MURDER.

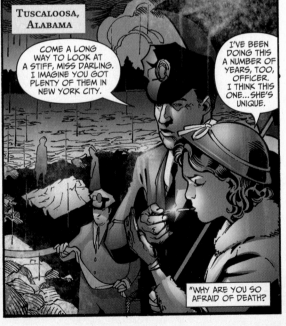

TUSCALOOSA, ALABAMA

COME A LONG WAY TO LOOK AT A STIFF, MISS DARLING. I IMAGINE YOU GOT PLENTY OF THEM IN NEW YORK CITY.

I'VE BEEN DOING THIS A NUMBER OF YEARS, TOO, OFFICER. I THINK THIS ONE...SHE'S UNIQUE.

"WHY ARE YOU SO AFRAID OF DEATH?

THE INFLUENZA PANDEMIC OF 1918 KILLED HALF A MILLION PEOPLE IN AMERICA. THIRTY MILLION WORLD WIDE.

ADULTS WERE SO TERRORIZED THEY STAYED LOCKED IN THEIR HOUSES FOR DAYS ON END FOR FEAR OF CATCHING THEIR DEATH OF COLD.

BUT THE CHILDREN, YOU KNOW THEY MADE A RHYME. "I HAD A LITTLE BIRD/HIS NAME WAS ENZA/ I OPENED THE WINDOW/AND INFLUENZA."

THE CHILDREN UNDERSTAND. MERCY BE THE REAPER. DON'T FEAR DEATH. THEN MAYBE YOU WOULDN'T FEAR ME.

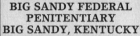

BIG SANDY FEDERAL PENITENTIARY
BIG SANDY, KENTUCKY

YOU'RE A REGULAR NUTCASE, HELLBENT. AND NOBODY'S SCARED OF YOU.

REALLY...?

YOU GO TO A LOT OF EFFORT FOR PEOPLE WHO AREN'T SCARED.

OVERKILL, I WOULD SAY. THE SHOOTING STARTS YOU'LL TAKE A BULLET, TOO.

LIKE I SAID. I'M NOT SCARED.

THIS ONE IS. STINKS LIKE AN OLD MAN TWO MINUTES FROM DYING.

LOVELY. HE'S NEW, AND HE BELIEVES YOUR PRESS. BUT YOU'RE NOT SOME GENIUS MANIAC. JUST A GUY WHO GETS HARD AS TEAK FOR KILLING.

WHICH, ON OCCASION, WE LET YOU DO.

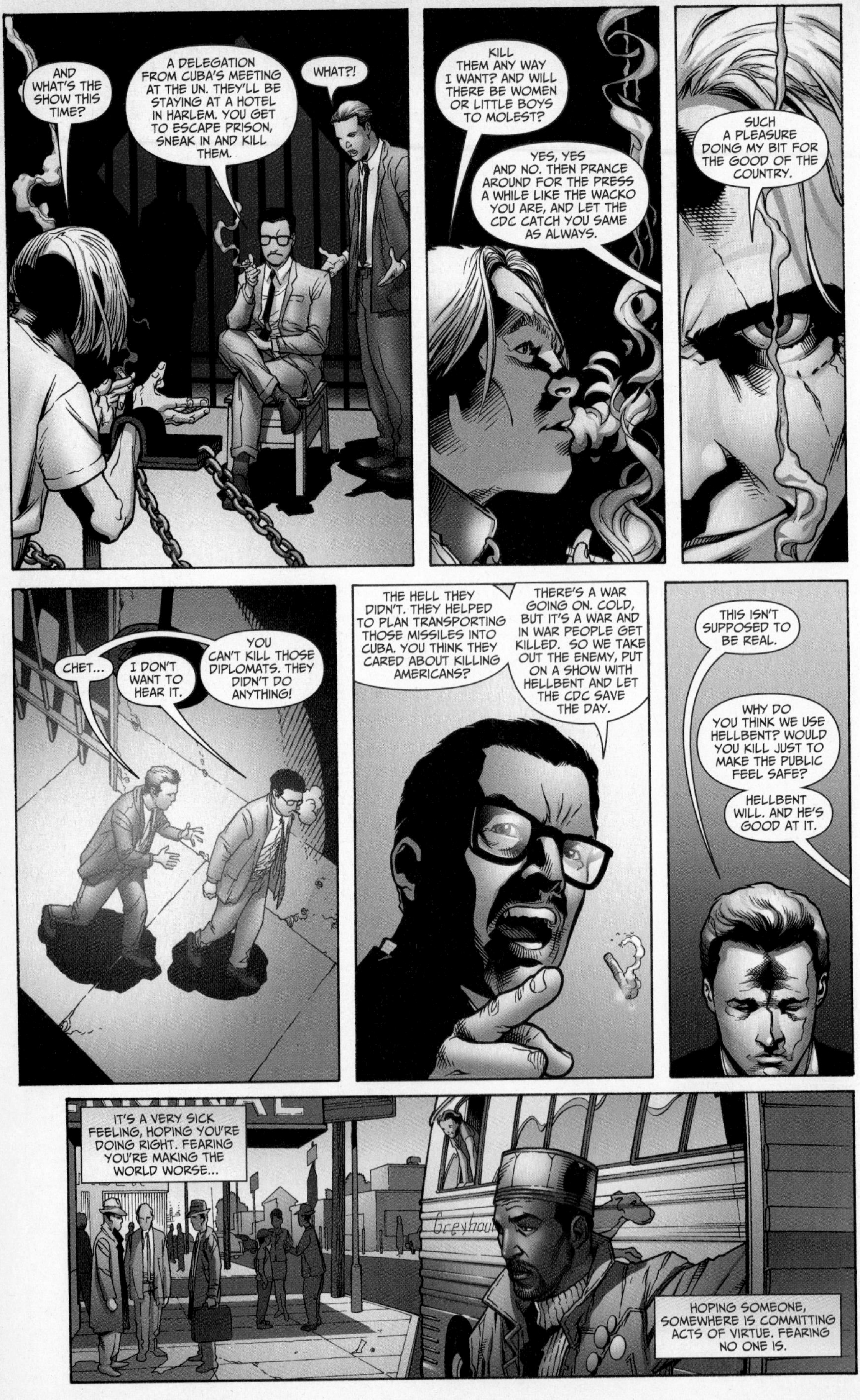

AND WHAT'S THE SHOW THIS TIME?
A DELEGATION FROM CUBA'S MEETING AT THE UN. THEY'LL BE STAYING AT A HOTEL IN HARLEM. YOU GET TO ESCAPE PRISON, SNEAK IN AND KILL THEM.
WHAT?!
KILL THEM ANY WAY I WANT? AND WILL THERE BE WOMEN OR LITTLE BOYS TO MOLEST?
YES, YES AND NO. THEN PRANCE AROUND FOR THE PRESS A WHILE LIKE THE WACKO YOU ARE, AND LET THE CDC CATCH YOU SAME AS ALWAYS.
SUCH A PLEASURE DOING MY BIT FOR THE GOOD OF THE COUNTRY.
CHET...
I DON'T WANT TO HEAR IT.
YOU CAN'T KILL THOSE DIPLOMATS. THEY DIDN'T DO ANYTHING!
THE HELL THEY DIDN'T. THEY HELPED TO PLAN TRANSPORTING THOSE MISSILES INTO CUBA. YOU THINK THEY CARED ABOUT KILLING AMERICANS?
THERE'S A WAR GOING ON. COLD, BUT IT'S A WAR AND IN WAR PEOPLE GET KILLED. SO WE TAKE OUT THE ENEMY, PUT ON A SHOW WITH HELLBENT AND LET THE CDC SAVE THE DAY.
THIS ISN'T SUPPOSED TO BE REAL.
WHY DO YOU THINK WE USE HELLBENT? WOULD YOU KILL JUST TO MAKE THE PUBLIC FEEL SAFE?
HELLBENT WILL. AND HE'S GOOD AT IT.
IT'S A VERY SICK FEELING, HOPING YOU'RE DOING RIGHT. FEARING YOU'RE MAKING THE WORLD WORSE...
Greyhound
HOPING SOMEONE, SOMEWHERE IS COMMITTING ACTS OF VIRTUE. FEARING NO ONE IS.

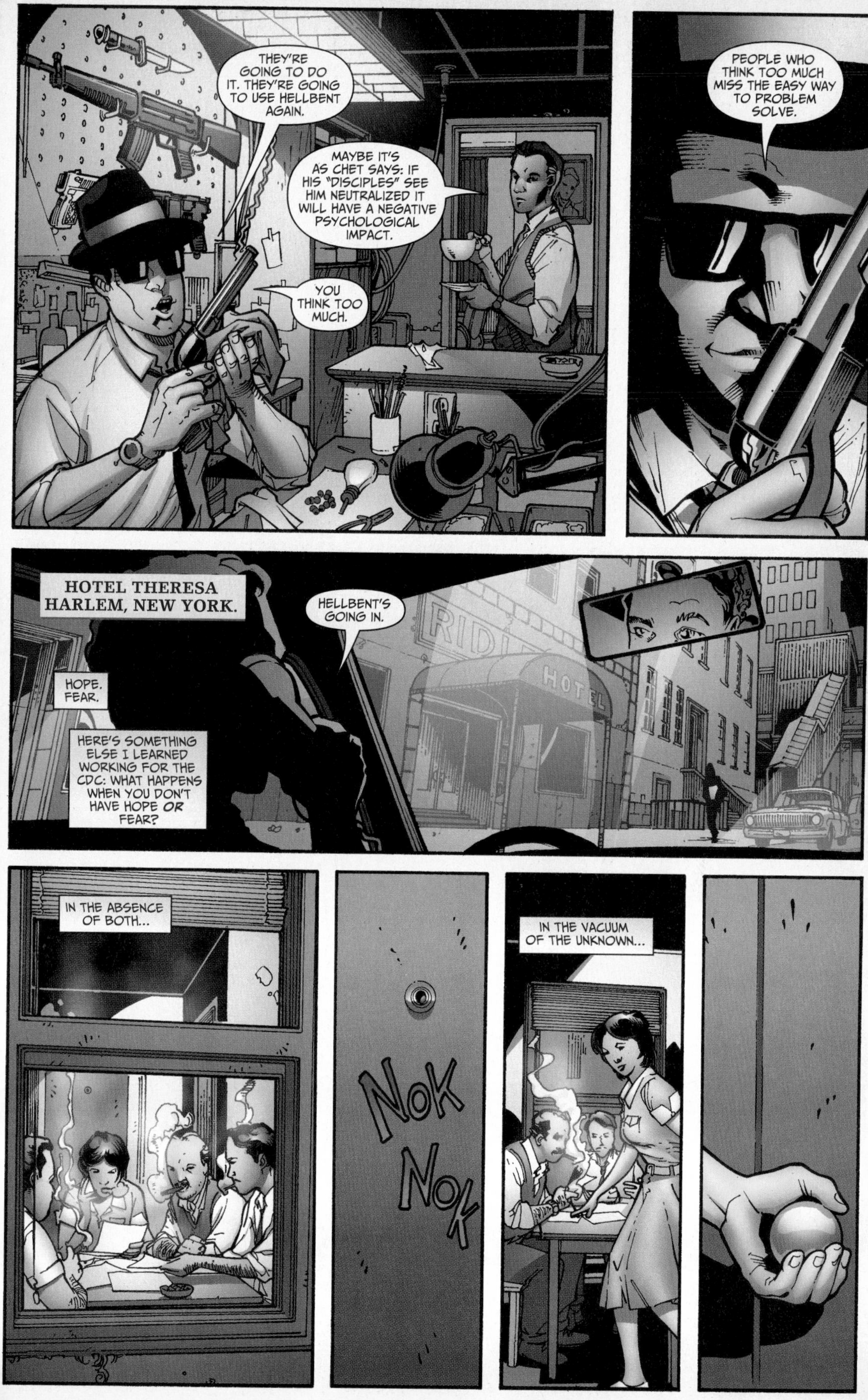
THEY'RE GOING TO DO IT. THEY'RE GOING TO USE HELLBENT AGAIN.
MAYBE IT'S AS CHET SAYS: IF HIS "DISCIPLES" SEE HIM NEUTRALIZED IT WILL HAVE A NEGATIVE PSYCHOLOGICAL IMPACT.
YOU THINK TOO MUCH.
PEOPLE WHO THINK TOO MUCH MISS THE EASY WAY TO PROBLEM SOLVE.
HOTEL THERESA
HARLEM, NEW YORK.
HELLBENT'S GOING IN.
HOTEL
HOPE. FEAR.
HERE'S SOMETHING ELSE I LEARNED WORKING FOR THE CDC: WHAT HAPPENS WHEN YOU DON'T HAVE HOPE *OR* FEAR?
IN THE ABSENCE OF BOTH...
NOK NOK
IN THE VACUUM OF THE UNKNOWN...

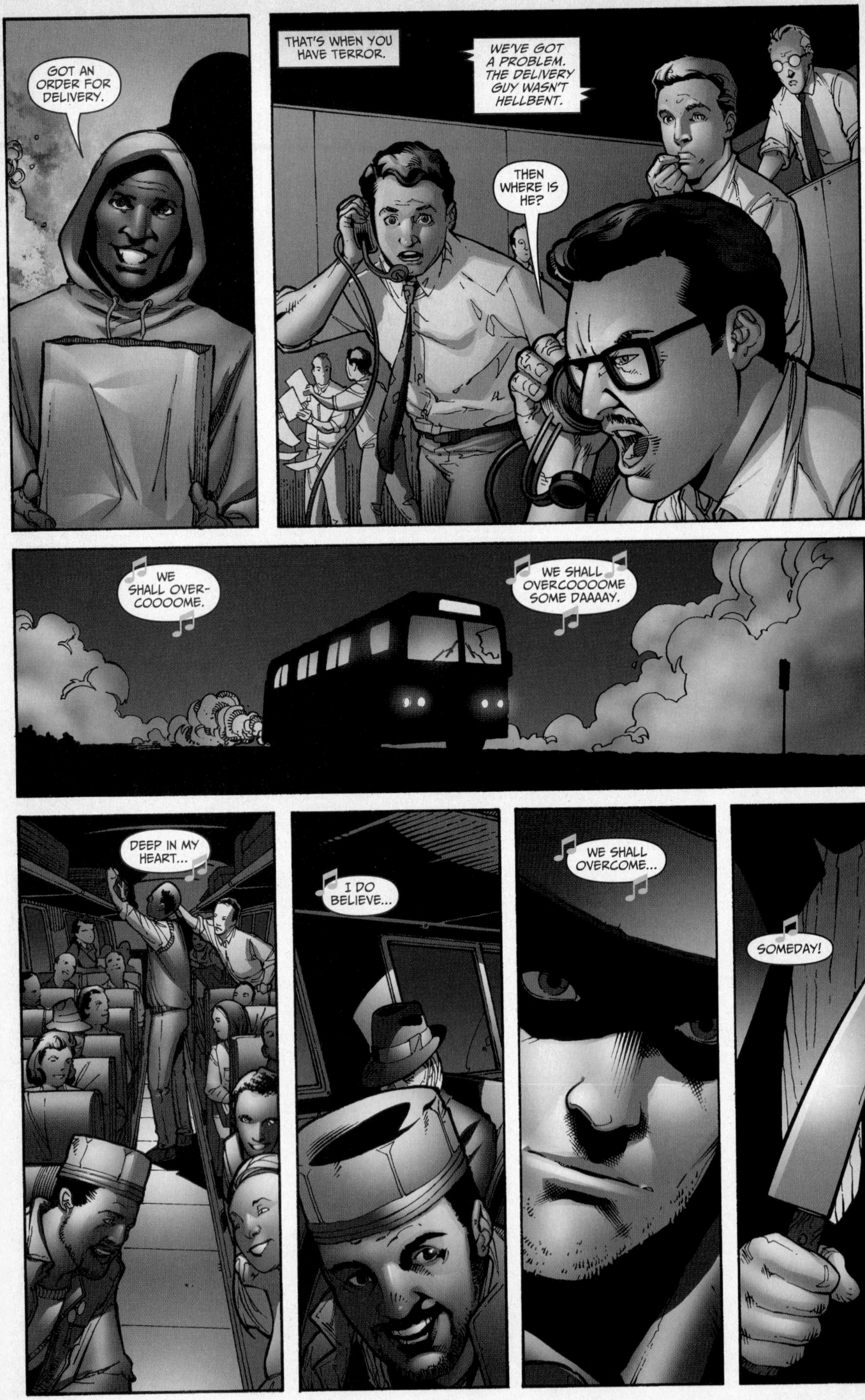
GOT AN ORDER FOR DELIVERY.
THAT'S WHEN YOU HAVE TERROR.
WE'VE GOT A PROBLEM. THE DELIVERY GUY WASN'T HELLBENT.
THEN WHERE IS HE?
WE SHALL OVER-COOOOME.
WE SHALL OVERCOOOOME SOME DAAAAY.
DEEP IN MY HEART...
I DO BELIEVE...
WE SHALL OVERCOME...
SOMEDAY!

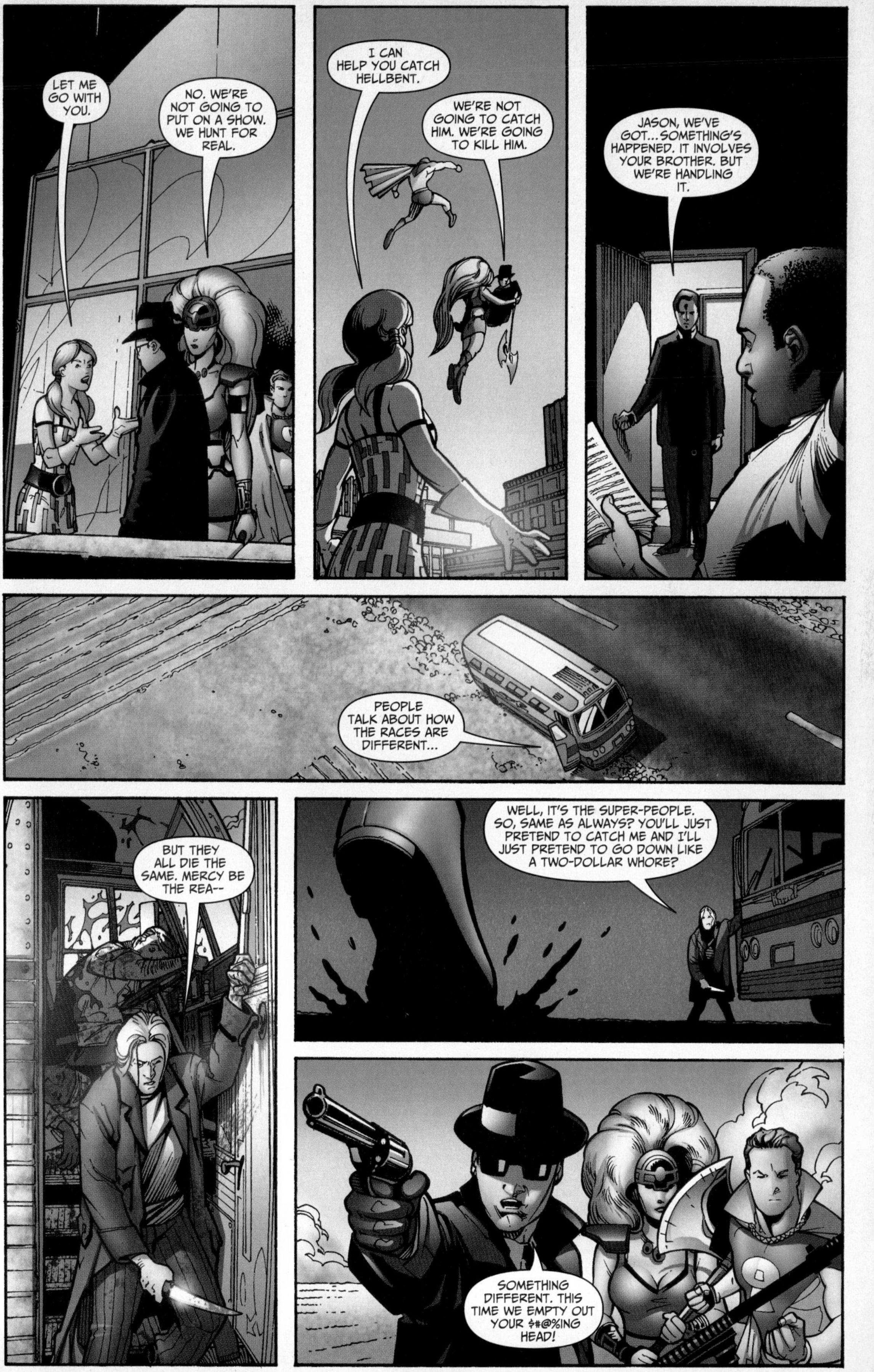

LET ME GO WITH YOU.
NO. WE'RE NOT GOING TO PUT ON A SHOW. WE HUNT FOR REAL.
I CAN HELP YOU CATCH HELLBENT.
WE'RE NOT GOING TO CATCH HIM. WE'RE GOING TO KILL HIM.
JASON, WE'VE GOT...SOMETHING'S HAPPENED. IT INVOLVES YOUR BROTHER. BUT WE'RE HANDLING IT.
PEOPLE TALK ABOUT HOW THE RACES ARE DIFFERENT...
BUT THEY ALL DIE THE SAME. MERCY BE THE REA--
WELL, IT'S THE SUPER-PEOPLE. SO, SAME AS ALWAYS? YOU'LL JUST PRETEND TO CATCH ME AND I'LL JUST PRETEND TO GO DOWN LIKE A TWO-DOLLAR WHORE?
SOMETHING DIFFERENT. THIS TIME WE EMPTY OUT YOUR $#@%ING HEAD!

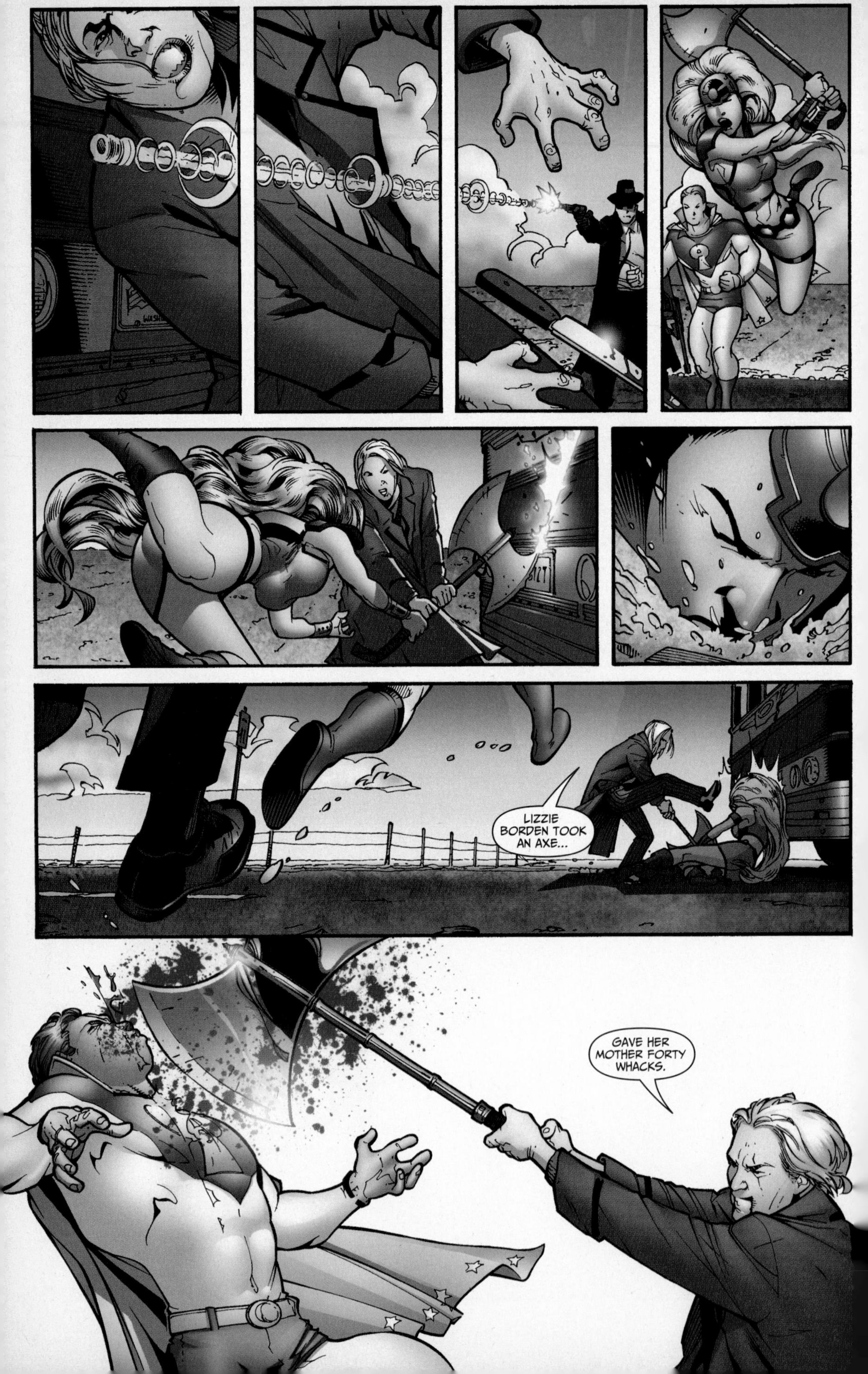
LIZZIE BORDEN TOOK AN AXE...
GAVE HER MOTHER FORTY WHACKS.

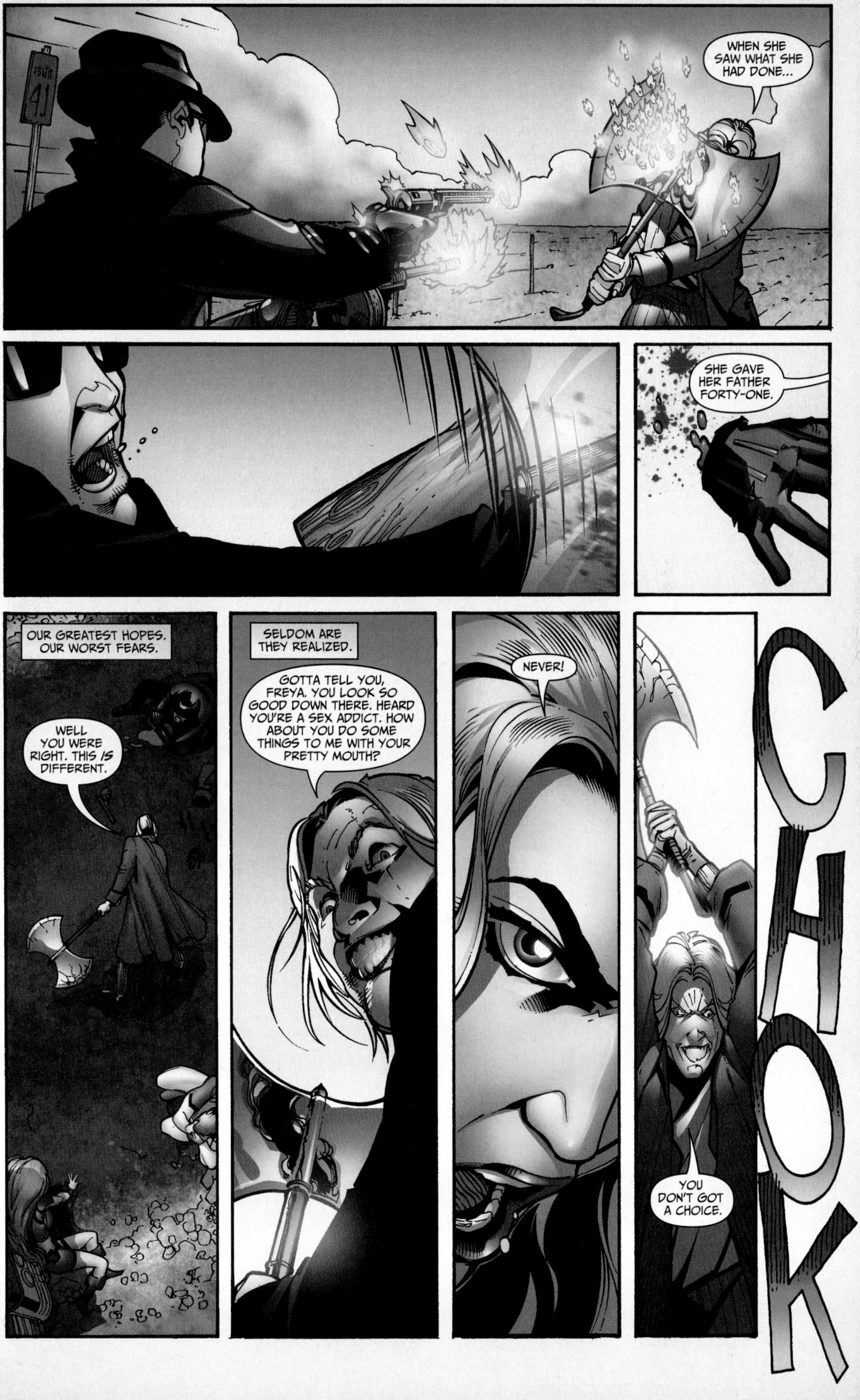
WHEN SHE SAW WHAT SHE HAD DONE...
41
SHE GAVE HER FATHER FORTY-ONE.
OUR GREATEST HOPES. OUR WORST FEARS.
WELL YOU WERE RIGHT. THIS *IS* DIFFERENT.
SELDOM ARE THEY REALIZED.
GOTTA TELL YOU, FREYA. YOU LOOK SO GOOD DOWN THERE. HEARD YOU'RE A SEX ADDICT. HOW ABOUT YOU DO SOME THINGS TO ME WITH YOUR PRETTY MOUTH?
NEVER!
YOU DON'T GOT A CHOICE.
CHOK

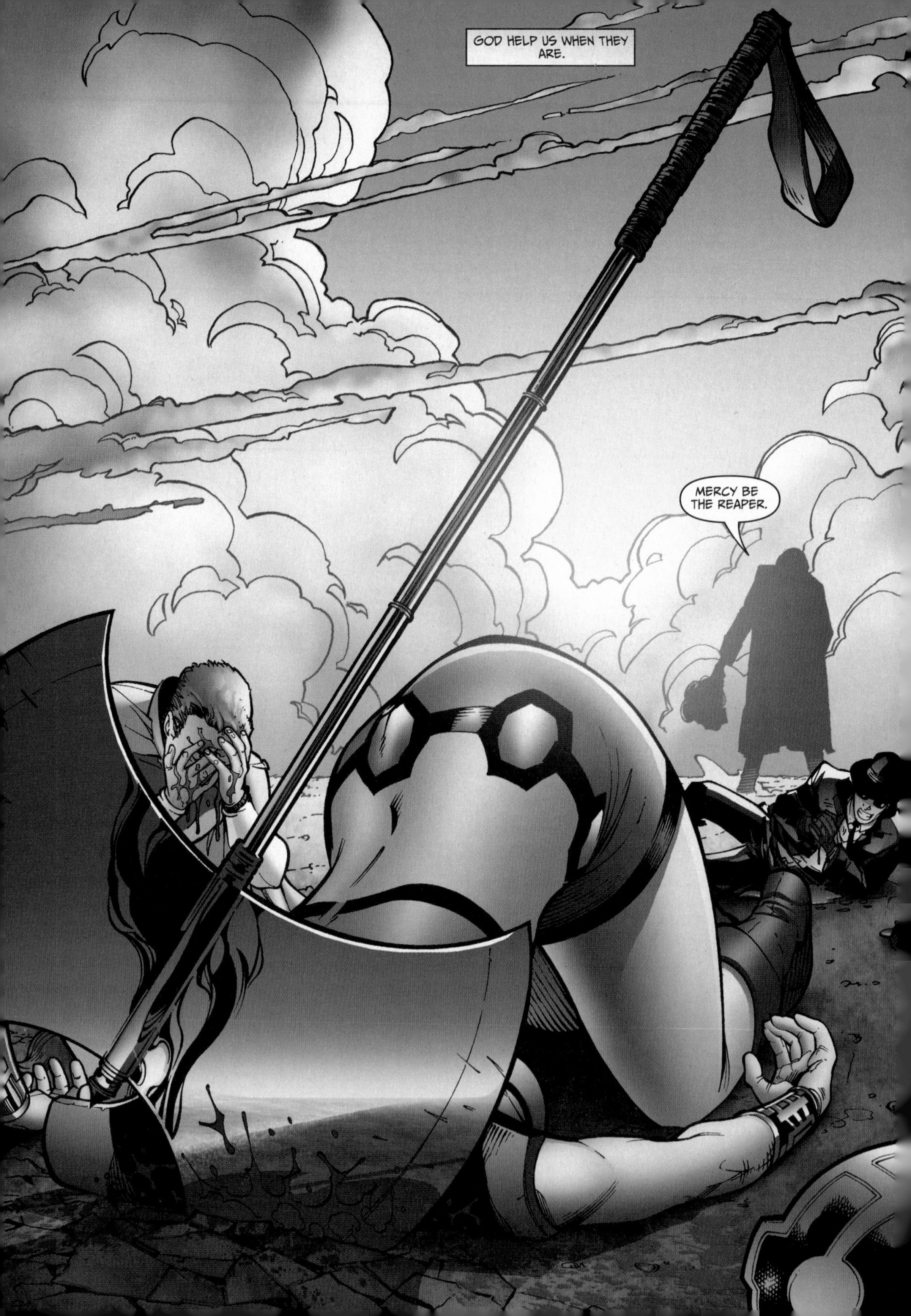
GOD HELP US WHEN THEY ARE.
MERCY BE THE REAPER.

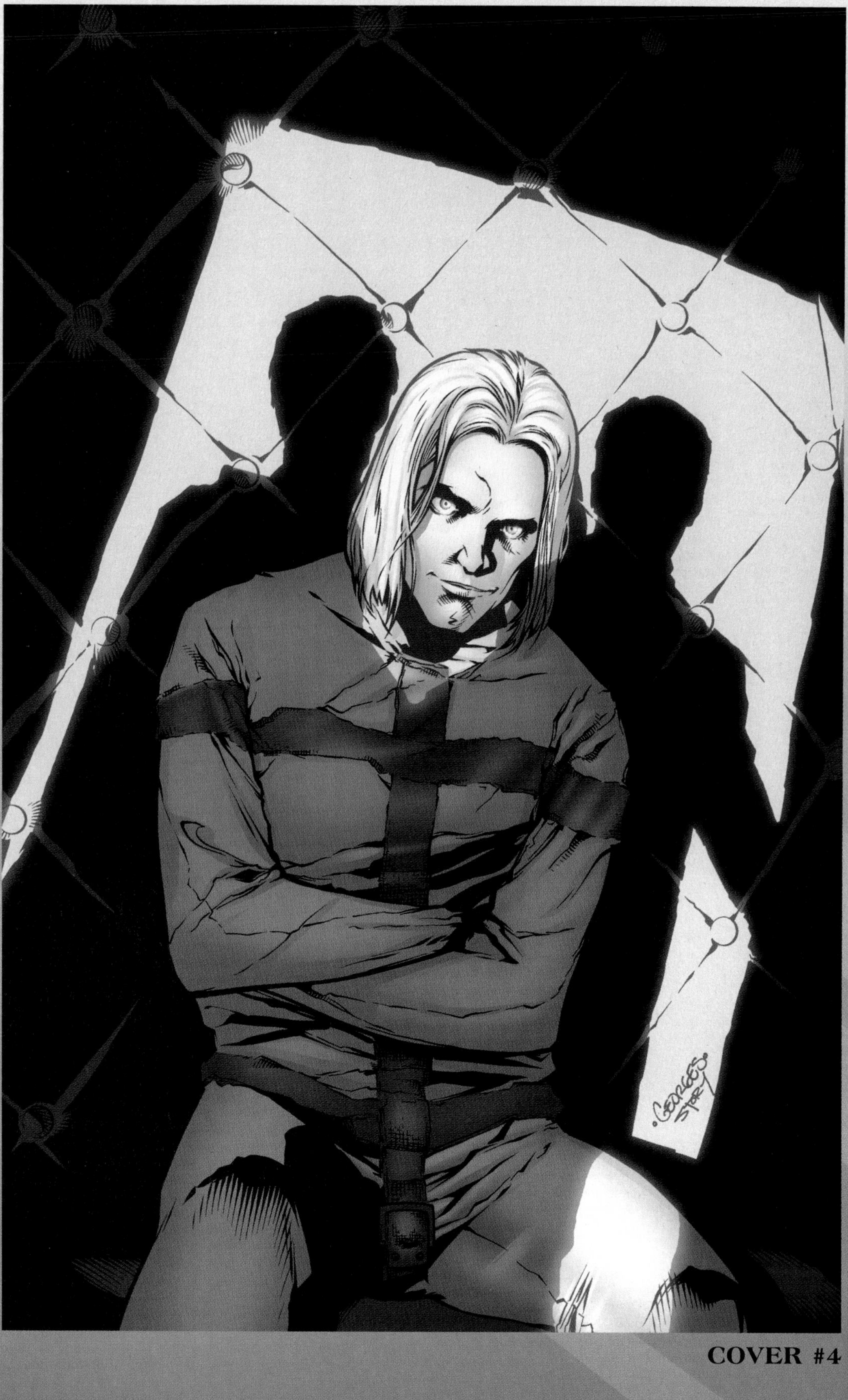

COVER #4

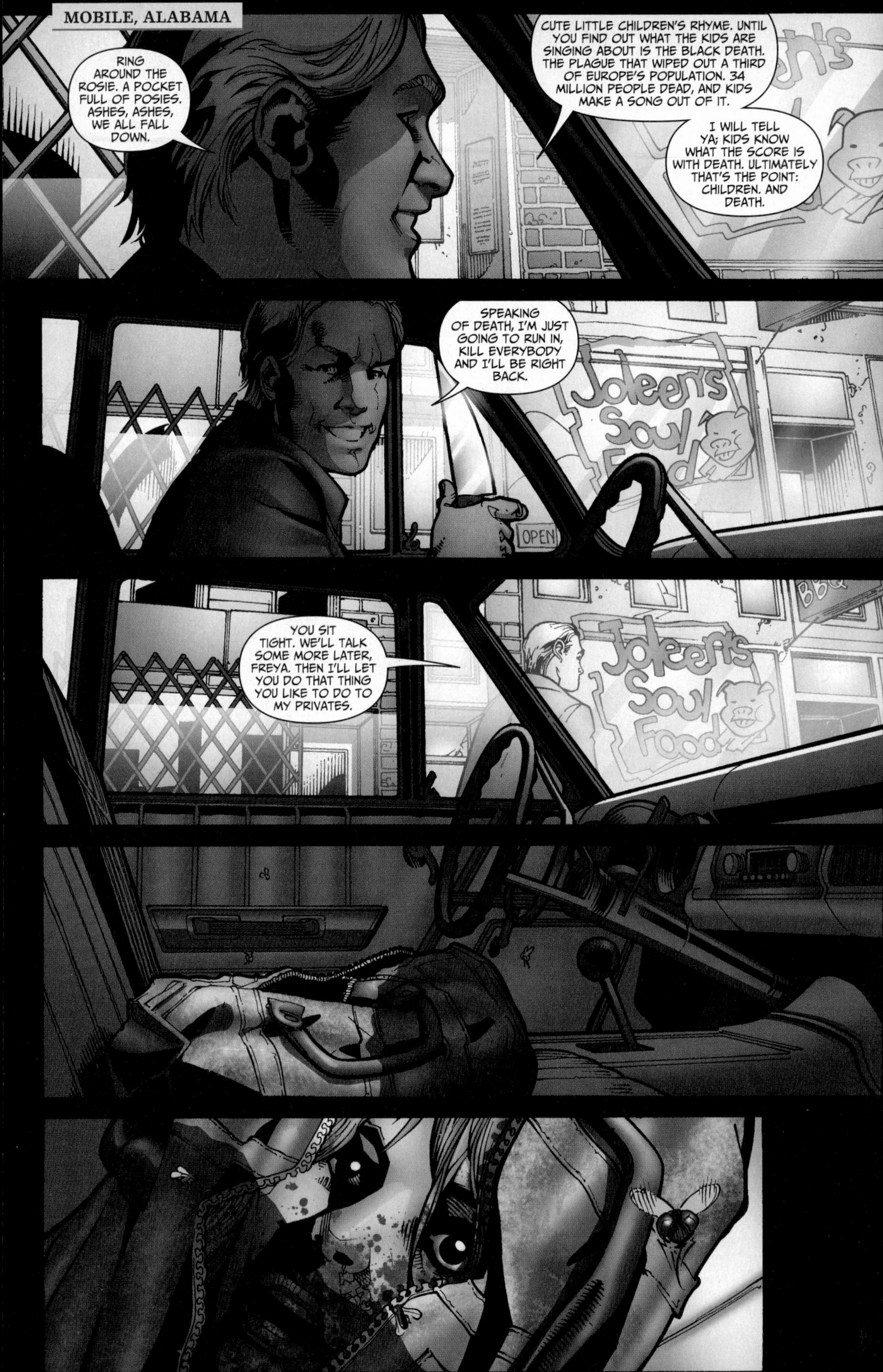
MOBILE, ALABAMA
RING AROUND THE ROSIE. A POCKET FULL OF POSIES. ASHES, ASHES, WE ALL FALL DOWN.
CUTE LITTLE CHILDREN'S RHYME. UNTIL YOU FIND OUT WHAT THE KIDS ARE SINGING ABOUT IS THE BLACK DEATH. THE PLAGUE THAT WIPED OUT A THIRD OF EUROPE'S POPULATION. 34 MILLION PEOPLE DEAD, AND KIDS MAKE A SONG OUT OF IT.
I WILL TELL YA; KIDS KNOW WHAT THE SCORE IS WITH DEATH. ULTIMATELY THAT'S THE POINT: CHILDREN. AND DEATH.
SPEAKING OF DEATH, I'M JUST GOING TO RUN IN, KILL EVERYBODY AND I'LL BE RIGHT BACK.
Joleen's Soul Food
OPEN
YOU SIT TIGHT. WE'LL TALK SOME MORE LATER, FREYA. THEN I'LL LET YOU DO THAT THING YOU LIKE TO DO TO MY PRIVATES.
BBQ
Joleen's Soul Food

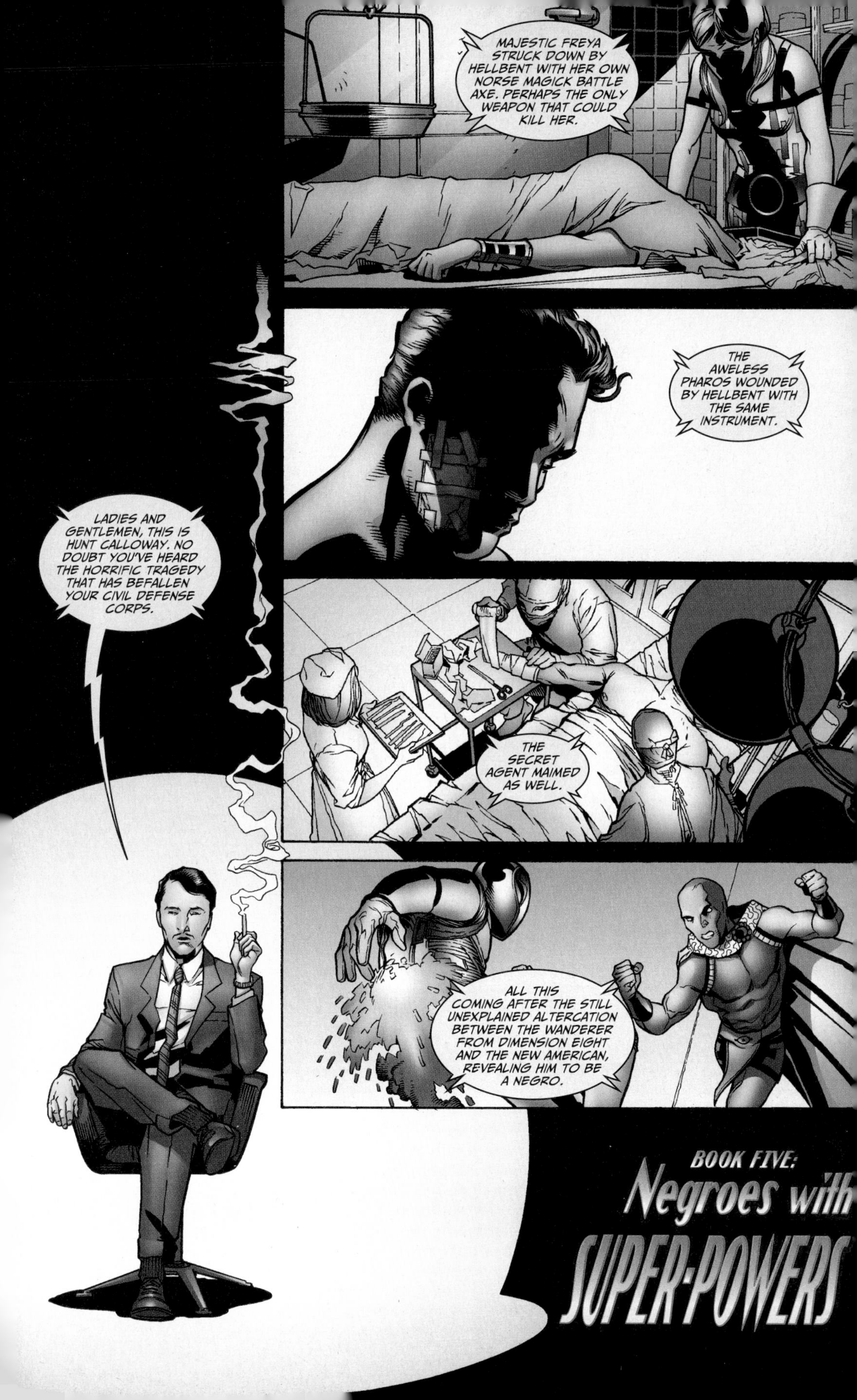
LADIES AND GENTLEMEN, THIS IS HUNT CALLOWAY. NO DOUBT YOU'VE HEARD THE HORRIFIC TRAGEDY THAT HAS BEFALLEN YOUR CIVIL DEFENSE CORPS.
MAJESTIC FREYA STRUCK DOWN BY HELLBENT WITH HER OWN NORSE MAGICK BATTLE AXE. PERHAPS THE ONLY WEAPON THAT COULD KILL HER.
THE AWELESS PHAROS WOUNDED BY HELLBENT WITH THE SAME INSTRUMENT.
THE SECRET AGENT MAIMED AS WELL.
ALL THIS COMING AFTER THE STILL UNEXPLAINED ALTERCATION BETWEEN THE WANDERER FROM DIMENSION EIGHT AND THE NEW AMERICAN, REVEALING HIM TO BE A NEGRO.
BOOK FIVE:
Negroes with
SUPER-POWERS

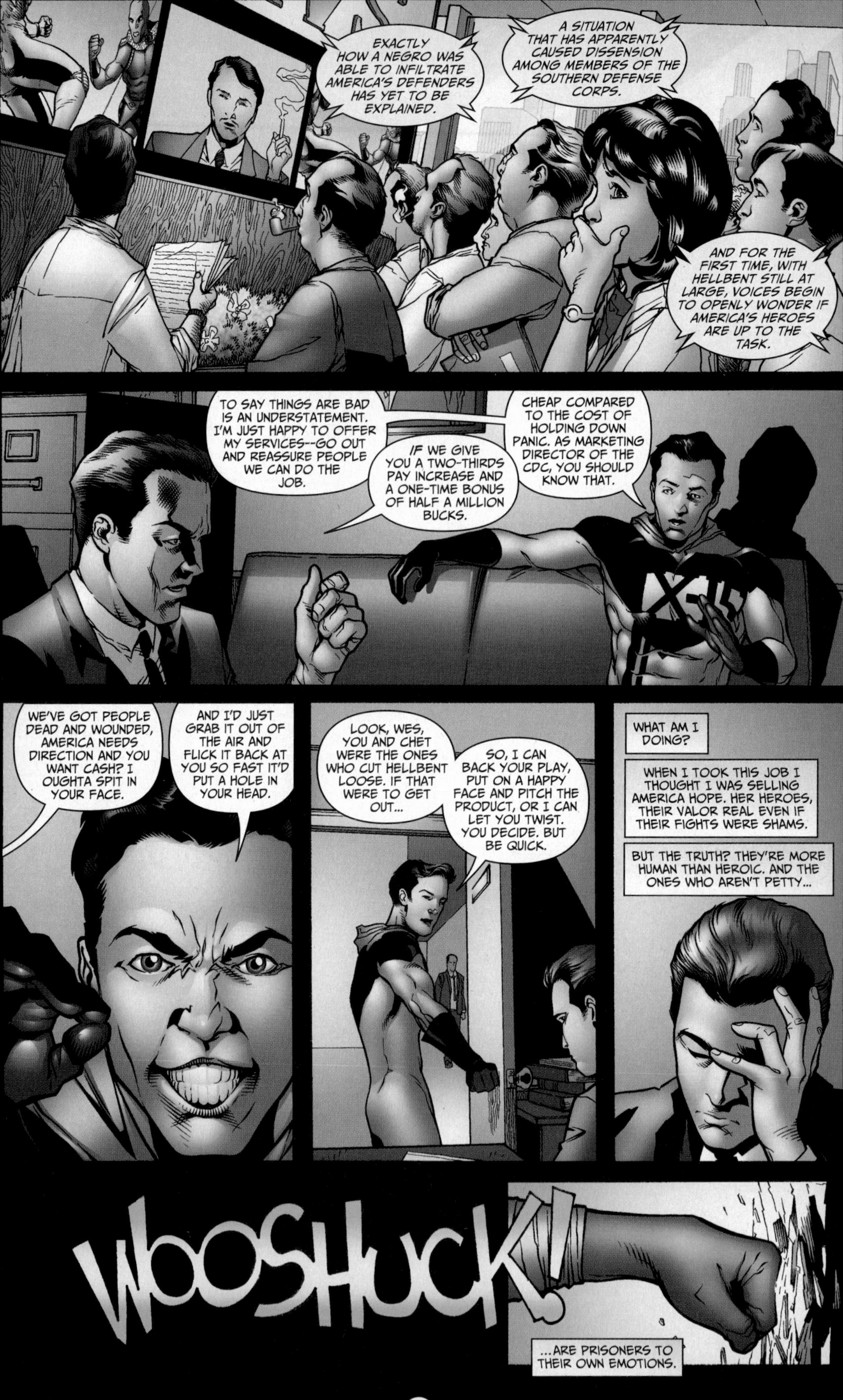
EXACTLY HOW A NEGRO WAS ABLE TO INFILTRATE AMERICA'S DEFENDERS HAS YET TO BE EXPLAINED.
A SITUATION THAT HAS APPARENTLY CAUSED DISSENSION AMONG MEMBERS OF THE SOUTHERN DEFENSE CORPS.
AND FOR THE FIRST TIME, WITH HELLBENT STILL AT LARGE, VOICES BEGIN TO OPENLY WONDER IF AMERICA'S HEROES ARE UP TO THE TASK.
TO SAY THINGS ARE BAD IS AN UNDERSTATEMENT. I'M JUST HAPPY TO OFFER MY SERVICES--GO OUT AND REASSURE PEOPLE WE CAN DO THE JOB.
IF WE GIVE YOU A TWO-THIRDS PAY INCREASE AND A ONE-TIME BONUS OF HALF A MILLION BUCKS.
CHEAP COMPARED TO THE COST OF HOLDING DOWN PANIC. AS MARKETING DIRECTOR OF THE CDC, YOU SHOULD KNOW THAT.
WE'VE GOT PEOPLE DEAD AND WOUNDED, AMERICA NEEDS DIRECTION AND YOU WANT CASH? I OUGHTA SPIT IN YOUR FACE.
AND I'D JUST GRAB IT OUT OF THE AIR AND FLICK IT BACK AT YOU SO FAST IT'D PUT A HOLE IN YOUR HEAD.
LOOK, WES, YOU AND CHET WERE THE ONES WHO CUT HELLBENT LOOSE. IF THAT WERE TO GET OUT...
SO, I CAN BACK YOUR PLAY, PUT ON A HAPPY FACE AND PITCH THE PRODUCT, OR I CAN LET YOU TWIST. YOU DECIDE. BUT BE QUICK.
WHAT AM I DOING?
WHEN I TOOK THIS JOB I THOUGHT I WAS SELLING AMERICA HOPE. HER HEROES, THEIR VALOR REAL EVEN IF THEIR FIGHTS WERE SHAMS.
BUT THE TRUTH? THEY'RE MORE HUMAN THAN HEROIC. AND THE ONES WHO AREN'T PETTY...
WOOSHUCK!
...ARE PRISONERS TO THEIR OWN EMOTIONS.

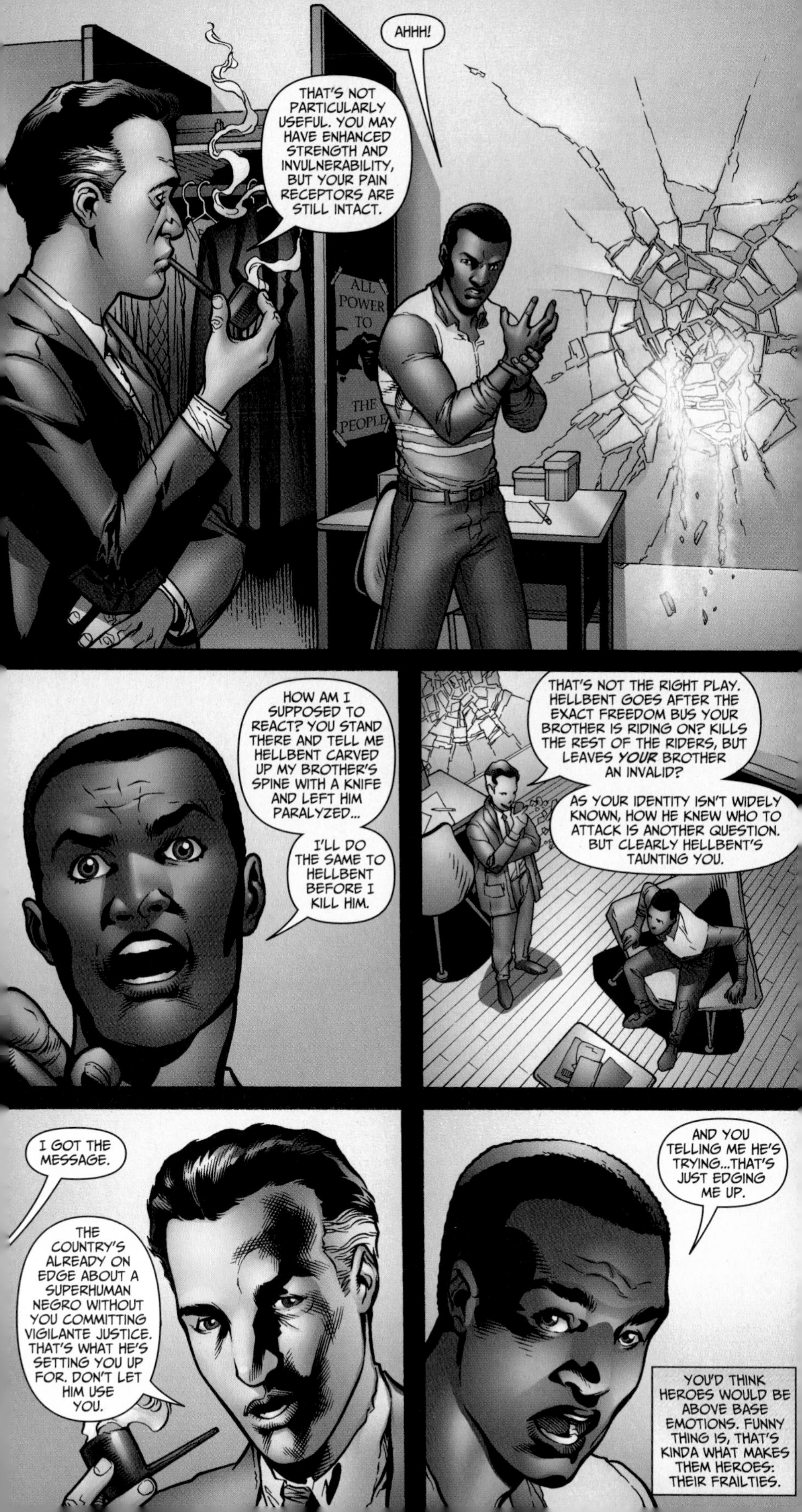
AHHH!
THAT'S NOT PARTICULARLY USEFUL. YOU MAY HAVE ENHANCED STRENGTH AND INVULNERABILITY, BUT YOUR PAIN RECEPTORS ARE STILL INTACT.
ALL POWER TO THE PEOPLE
HOW AM I SUPPOSED TO REACT? YOU STAND THERE AND TELL ME HELLBENT CARVED UP MY BROTHER'S SPINE WITH A KNIFE AND LEFT HIM PARALYZED...
I'LL DO THE SAME TO HELLBENT BEFORE I KILL HIM.
THAT'S NOT THE RIGHT PLAY. HELLBENT GOES AFTER THE EXACT FREEDOM BUS YOUR BROTHER IS RIDING ON? KILLS THE REST OF THE RIDERS, BUT LEAVES *YOUR* BROTHER AN INVALID?
AS YOUR IDENTITY ISN'T WIDELY KNOWN, HOW HE KNEW WHO TO ATTACK IS ANOTHER QUESTION. BUT CLEARLY HELLBENT'S TAUNTING YOU.
I GOT THE MESSAGE.
THE COUNTRY'S ALREADY ON EDGE ABOUT A SUPERHUMAN NEGRO WITHOUT YOU COMMITTING VIGILANTE JUSTICE. THAT'S WHAT HE'S SETTING YOU UP FOR. DON'T LET HIM USE YOU.
AND YOU TELLING ME HE'S TRYING...THAT'S JUST EDGING ME UP.
YOU'D THINK HEROES WOULD BE ABOVE BASE EMOTIONS. FUNNY THING IS, THAT'S KINDA WHAT MAKES THEM HEROES: THEIR FRAILTIES.

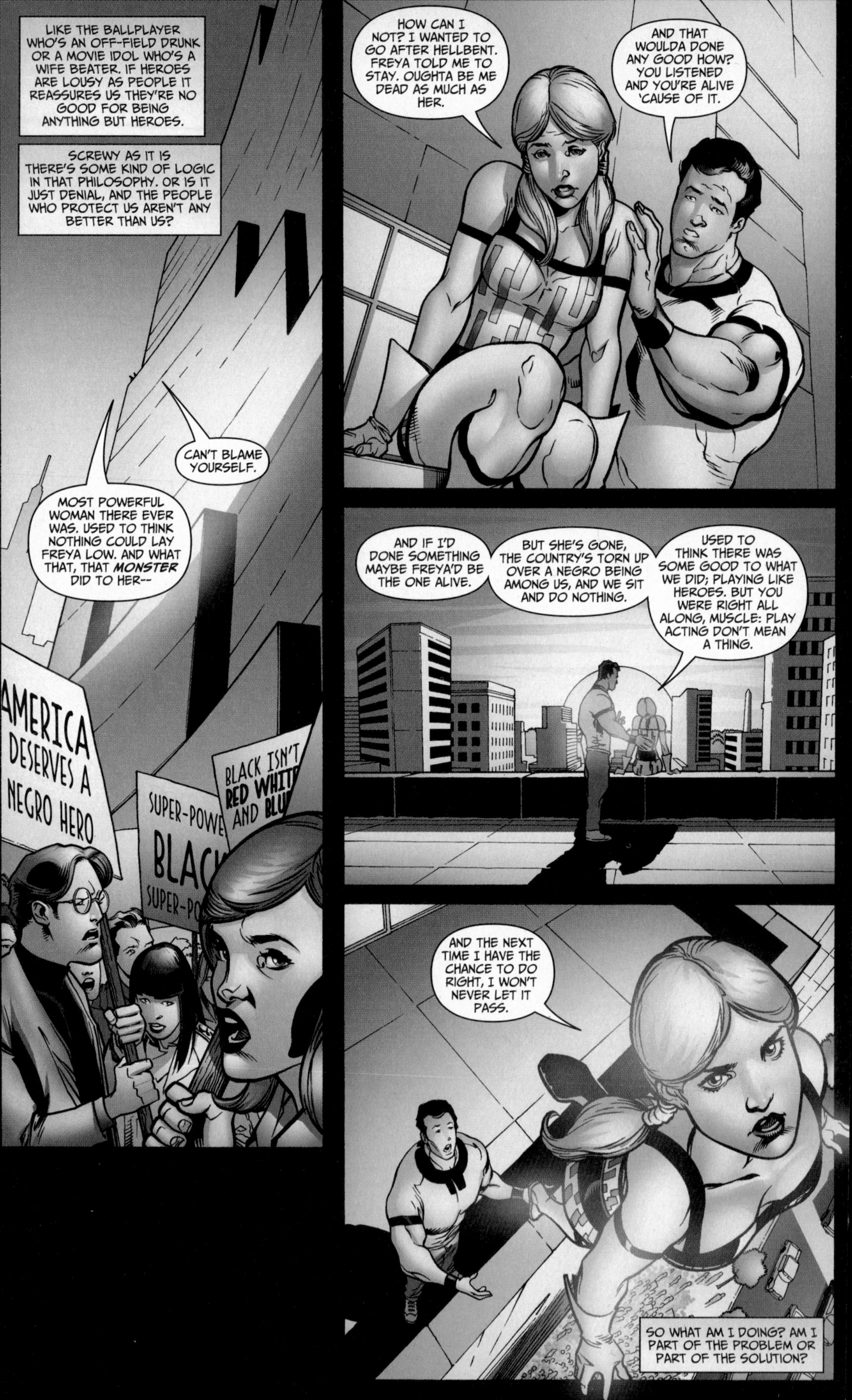

LIKE THE BALLPLAYER WHO'S AN OFF-FIELD DRUNK OR A MOVIE IDOL WHO'S A WIFE BEATER. IF HEROES ARE LOUSY AS PEOPLE IT REASSURES US THEY'RE NO GOOD FOR BEING ANYTHING BUT HEROES.
SCREWY AS IT IS THERE'S SOME KIND OF LOGIC IN THAT PHILOSOPHY. OR IS IT JUST DENIAL, AND THE PEOPLE WHO PROTECT US AREN'T ANY BETTER THAN US?
MOST POWERFUL WOMAN THERE EVER WAS. USED TO THINK NOTHING COULD LAY FREYA LOW. AND WHAT THAT, THAT *MONSTER* DID TO HER--
CAN'T BLAME YOURSELF.
AMERICA DESERVES A NEGRO HERO
BLACK ISN'T
HOW CAN I NOT? I WANTED TO GO AFTER HELLBENT. FREYA TOLD ME TO STAY. OUGHTA BE ME DEAD AS MUCH AS HER.
AND THAT WOULDA DONE ANY GOOD HOW? YOU LISTENED AND YOU'RE ALIVE 'CAUSE OF IT.
AND IF I'D DONE SOMETHING MAYBE FREYA'D BE THE ONE ALIVE.
BUT SHE'S GONE, THE COUNTRY'S TORN UP OVER A NEGRO BEING AMONG US, AND WE SIT AND DO NOTHING.
USED TO THINK THERE WAS SOME GOOD TO WHAT WE DID; PLAYING LIKE HEROES. BUT YOU WERE RIGHT ALL ALONG, MUSCLE: PLAY ACTING DON'T MEAN A THING.
AND THE NEXT TIME I HAVE THE CHANCE TO DO RIGHT, I WON'T NEVER LET IT PASS.
SO WHAT AM I DOING? AM I PART OF THE PROBLEM OR PART OF THE SOLUTION?

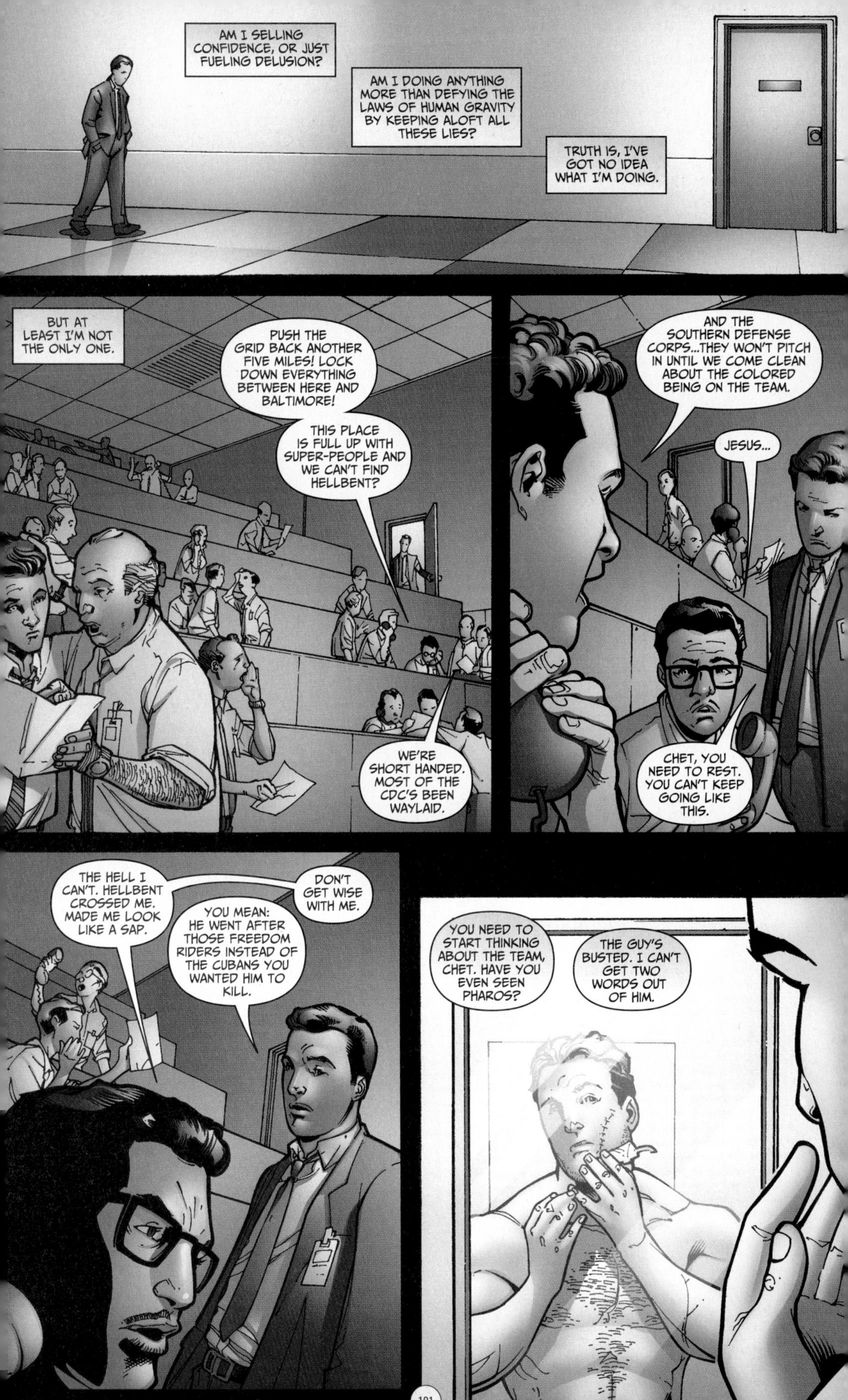
AM I SELLING CONFIDENCE, OR JUST FUELING DELUSION?
AM I DOING ANYTHING MORE THAN DEFYING THE LAWS OF HUMAN GRAVITY BY KEEPING ALOFT ALL THESE LIES?
TRUTH IS, I'VE GOT NO IDEA WHAT I'M DOING.
BUT AT LEAST I'M NOT THE ONLY ONE.
PUSH THE GRID BACK ANOTHER FIVE MILES! LOCK DOWN EVERYTHING BETWEEN HERE AND BALTIMORE!
THIS PLACE IS FULL UP WITH SUPER-PEOPLE AND WE CAN'T FIND HELLBENT?
WE'RE SHORT HANDED. MOST OF THE CDC'S BEEN WAYLAID.
AND THE SOUTHERN DEFENSE CORPS...THEY WON'T PITCH IN UNTIL WE COME CLEAN ABOUT THE COLORED BEING ON THE TEAM.
JESUS...
CHET, YOU NEED TO REST. YOU CAN'T KEEP GOING LIKE THIS.
THE HELL I CAN'T. HELLBENT CROSSED ME. MADE ME LOOK LIKE A SAP.
DON'T GET WISE WITH ME.
YOU MEAN: HE WENT AFTER THOSE FREEDOM RIDERS INSTEAD OF THE CUBANS YOU WANTED HIM TO KILL.
YOU NEED TO START THINKING ABOUT THE TEAM, CHET. HAVE YOU EVEN SEEN PHAROS?
THE GUY'S BUSTED. I CAN'T GET TWO WORDS OUT OF HIM.

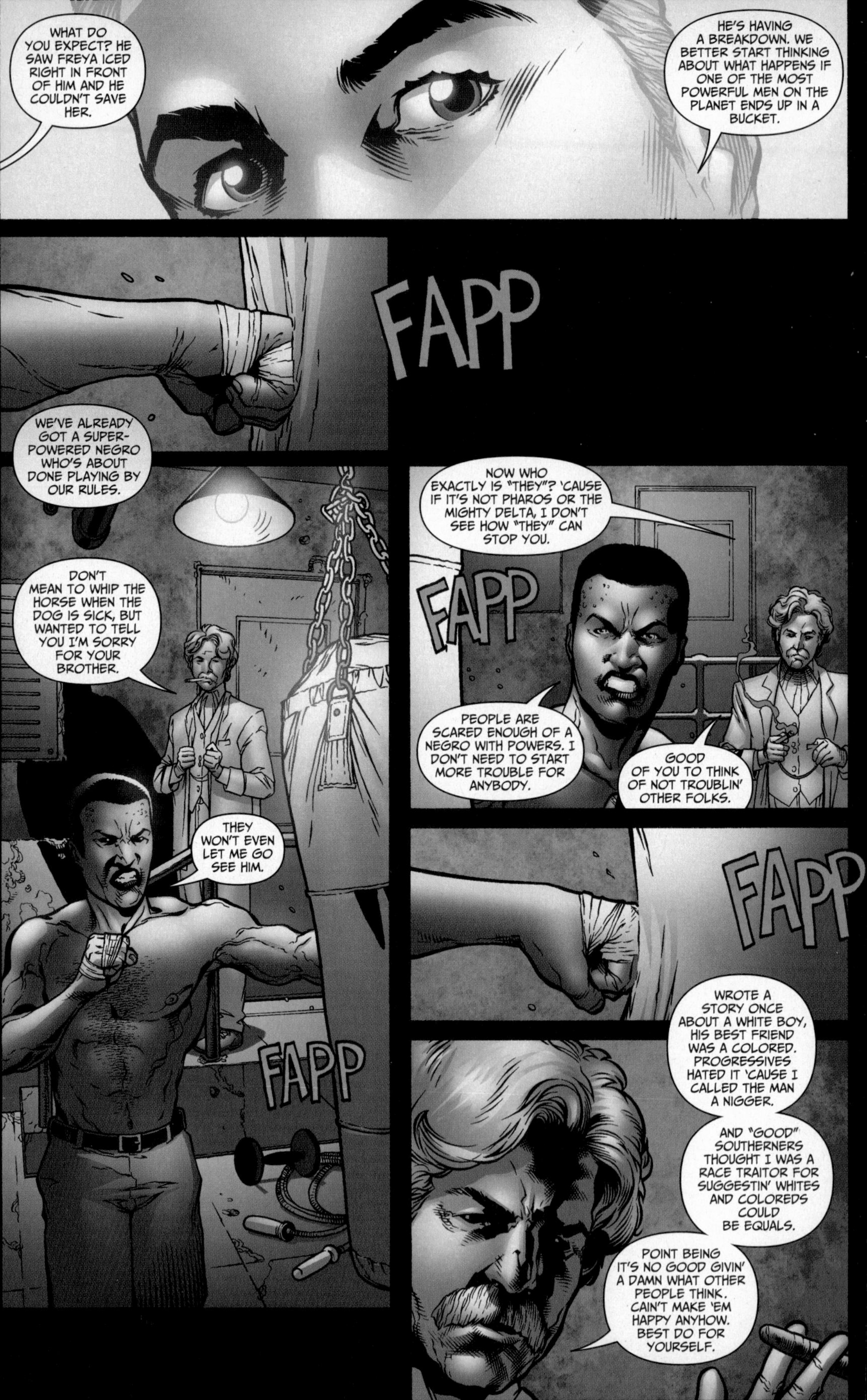

WHAT DO YOU EXPECT? HE SAW FREYA ICED RIGHT IN FRONT OF HIM AND HE COULDN'T SAVE HER.
HE'S HAVING A BREAKDOWN. WE BETTER START THINKING ABOUT WHAT HAPPENS IF ONE OF THE MOST POWERFUL MEN ON THE PLANET ENDS UP IN A BUCKET.
FAPP
WE'VE ALREADY GOT A SUPER-POWERED NEGRO WHO'S ABOUT DONE PLAYING BY OUR RULES.
DON'T MEAN TO WHIP THE HORSE WHEN THE DOG IS SICK, BUT WANTED TO TELL YOU I'M SORRY FOR YOUR BROTHER.
THEY WON'T EVEN LET ME GO SEE HIM.
FAPP
NOW WHO EXACTLY IS "THEY"? 'CAUSE IF IT'S NOT PHAROS OR THE MIGHTY DELTA, I DON'T SEE HOW "THEY" CAN STOP YOU.
FAPP
PEOPLE ARE SCARED ENOUGH OF A NEGRO WITH POWERS. I DON'T NEED TO START MORE TROUBLE FOR ANYBODY.
GOOD OF YOU TO THINK OF NOT TROUBLIN' OTHER FOLKS.
FAPP
WROTE A STORY ONCE ABOUT A WHITE BOY, HIS BEST FRIEND WAS A COLORED. PROGRESSIVES HATED IT 'CAUSE I CALLED THE MAN A NIGGER.
AND "GOOD" SOUTHERNERS THOUGHT I WAS A RACE TRAITOR FOR SUGGESTIN' WHITES AND COLOREDS COULD BE EQUALS.
POINT BEING IT'S NO GOOD GIVIN' A DAMN WHAT OTHER PEOPLE THINK. CAIN'T MAKE 'EM HAPPY ANYHOW. BEST DO FOR YOURSELF.

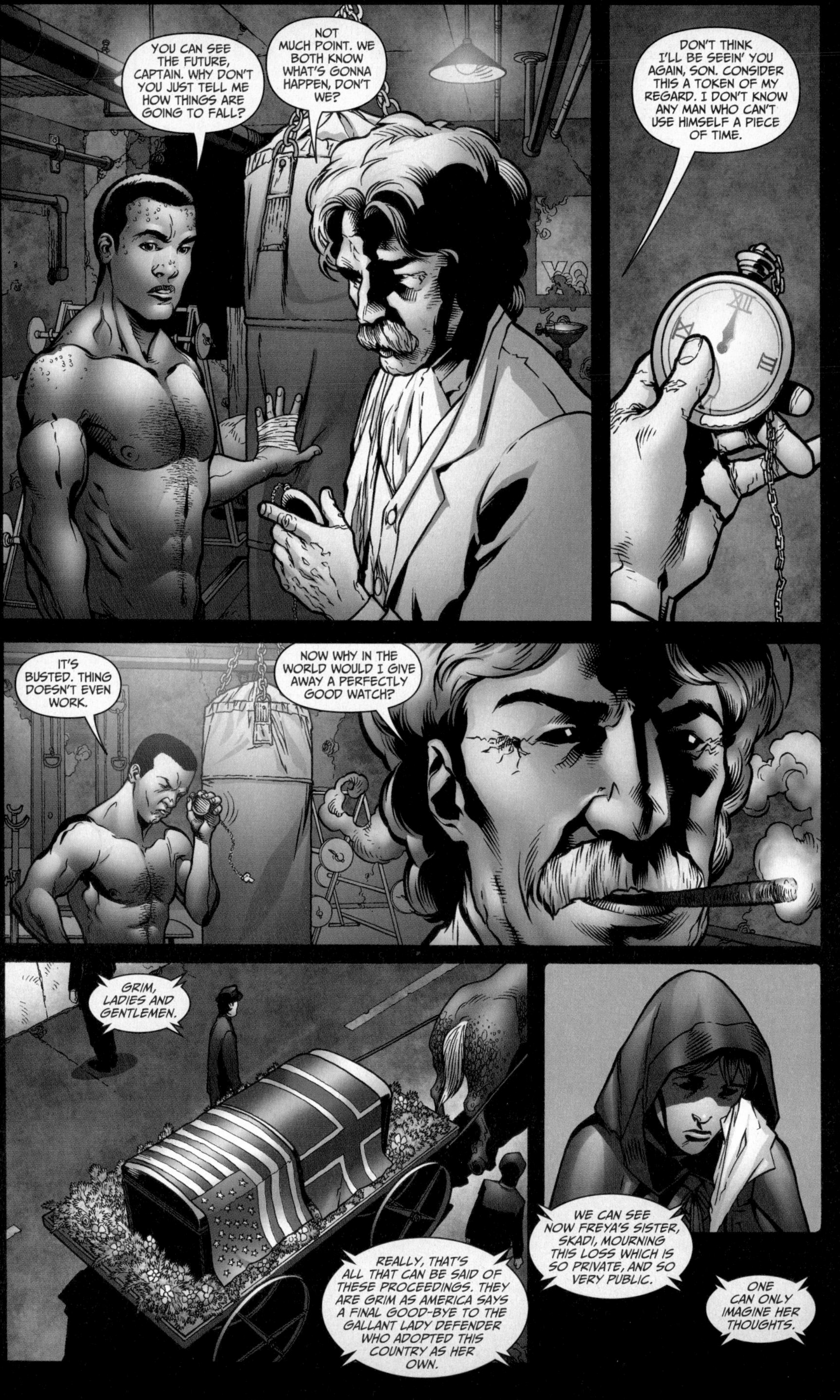
YOU CAN SEE THE FUTURE, CAPTAIN. WHY DON'T YOU JUST TELL ME HOW THINGS ARE GOING TO FALL?
NOT MUCH POINT. WE BOTH KNOW WHAT'S GONNA HAPPEN, DON'T WE?
DON'T THINK I'LL BE SEEIN' YOU AGAIN, SON. CONSIDER THIS A TOKEN OF MY REGARD. I DON'T KNOW ANY MAN WHO CAN'T USE HIMSELF A PIECE OF TIME.
IT'S BUSTED. THING DOESN'T EVEN WORK.
NOW WHY IN THE WORLD WOULD I GIVE AWAY A PERFECTLY GOOD WATCH?
GRIM, LADIES AND GENTLEMEN.
REALLY, THAT'S ALL THAT CAN BE SAID OF THESE PROCEEDINGS. THEY ARE GRIM AS AMERICA SAYS A FINAL GOOD-BYE TO THE GALLANT LADY DEFENDER WHO ADOPTED THIS COUNTRY AS HER OWN.
WE CAN SEE NOW FREYA'S SISTER, SKADI, MOURNING THIS LOSS WHICH IS SO PRIVATE, AND SO VERY PUBLIC.
ONE CAN ONLY IMAGINE HER THOUGHTS.

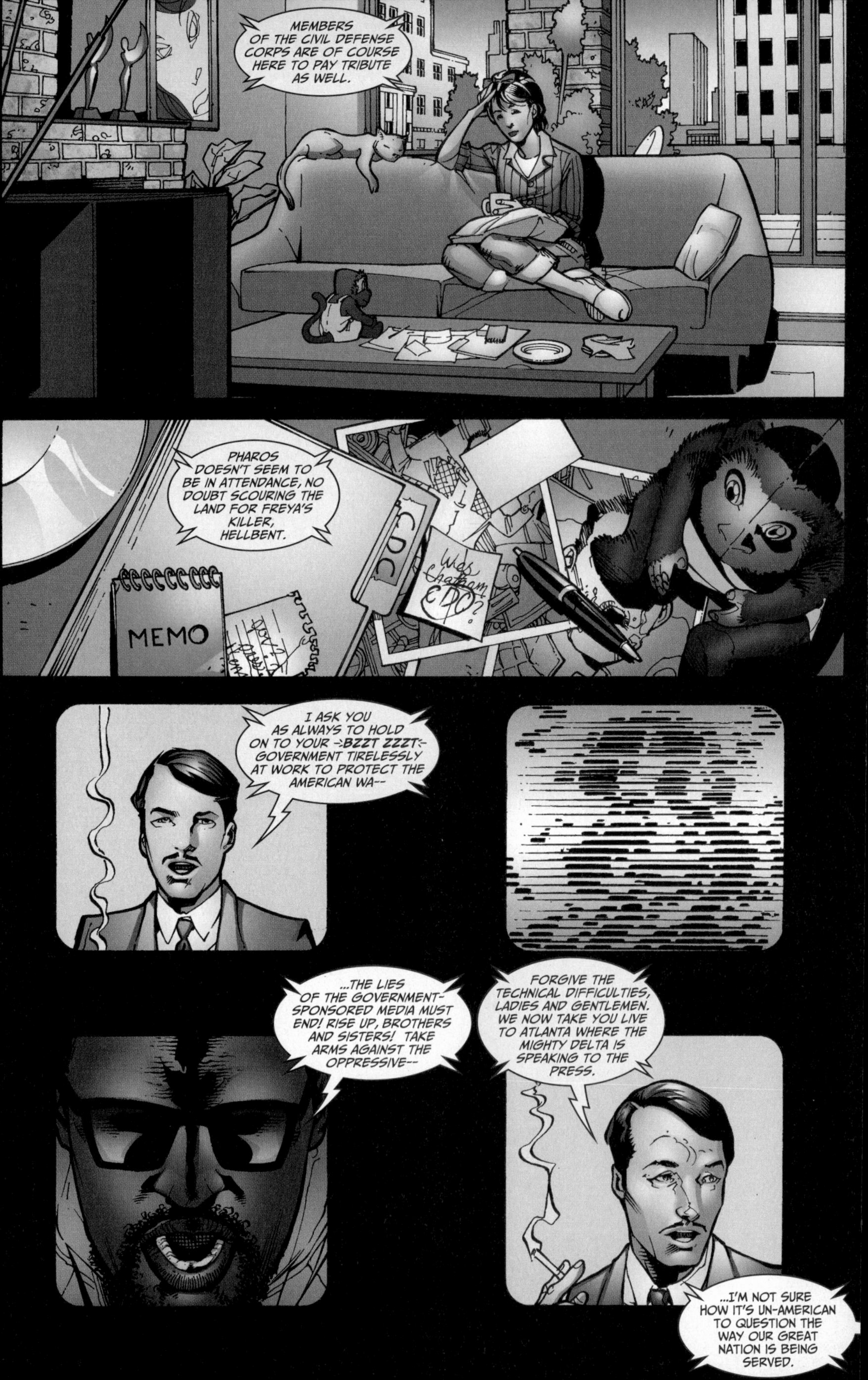
MEMBERS OF THE CIVIL DEFENSE CORPS ARE OF COURSE HERE TO PAY TRIBUTE AS WELL.
PHAROS DOESN'T SEEM TO BE IN ATTENDANCE, NO DOUBT SCOURING THE LAND FOR FREYA'S KILLER, HELLBENT.
CDC
Was Chatham CDC?
MEMO
I ASK YOU AS ALWAYS TO HOLD ON TO YOUR ->BZZT ZZZT<- GOVERNMENT TIRELESSLY AT WORK TO PROTECT THE AMERICAN WA--
...THE LIES OF THE GOVERNMENT-SPONSORED MEDIA MUST END! RISE UP, BROTHERS AND SISTERS! TAKE ARMS AGAINST THE OPPRESSIVE--
FORGIVE THE TECHNICAL DIFFICULTIES, LADIES AND GENTLEMEN. WE NOW TAKE YOU LIVE TO ATLANTA WHERE THE MIGHTY DELTA IS SPEAKING TO THE PRESS.
...I'M NOT SURE HOW IT'S UN-AMERICAN TO QUESTION THE WAY OUR GREAT NATION IS BEING SERVED.

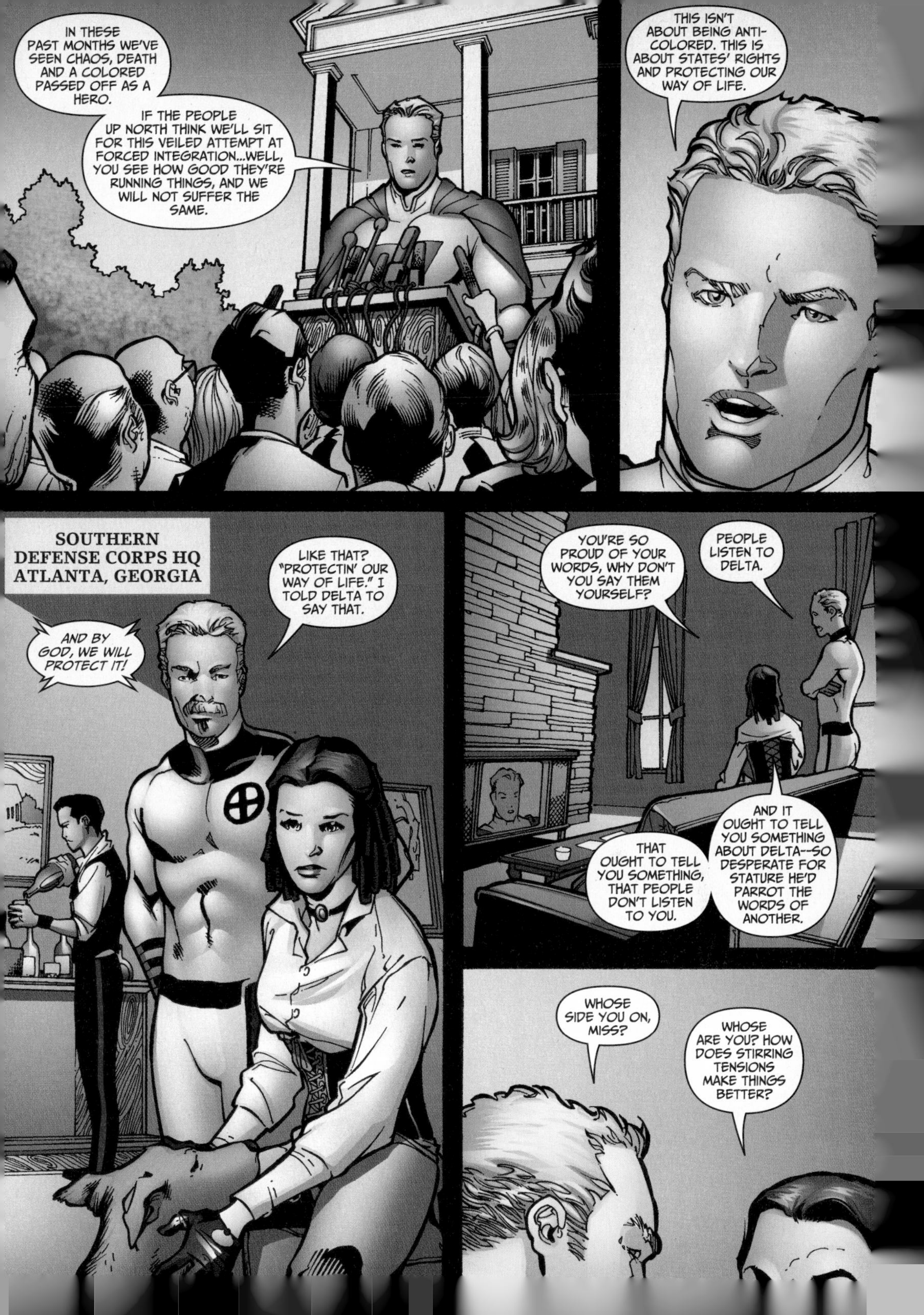
IN THESE PAST MONTHS WE'VE SEEN CHAOS, DEATH AND A COLORED PASSED OFF AS A HERO.
IF THE PEOPLE UP NORTH THINK WE'LL SIT FOR THIS VEILED ATTEMPT AT FORCED INTEGRATION...WELL, YOU SEE HOW GOOD THEY'RE RUNNING THINGS, AND WE WILL NOT SUFFER THE SAME.
THIS ISN'T ABOUT BEING ANTI-COLORED. THIS IS ABOUT STATES' RIGHTS AND PROTECTING OUR WAY OF LIFE.
SOUTHERN DEFENSE CORPS HQ ATLANTA, GEORGIA
AND BY GOD, WE WILL PROTECT IT!
LIKE THAT? "PROTECTIN' OUR WAY OF LIFE." I TOLD DELTA TO SAY THAT.
YOU'RE SO PROUD OF YOUR WORDS, WHY DON'T YOU SAY THEM YOURSELF?
PEOPLE LISTEN TO DELTA.
THAT OUGHT TO TELL YOU SOMETHING, THAT PEOPLE DON'T LISTEN TO YOU.
AND IT OUGHT TO TELL YOU SOMETHING ABOUT DELTA--SO DESPERATE FOR STATURE HE'D PARROT THE WORDS OF ANOTHER.
WHOSE SIDE YOU ON, MISS?
WHOSE ARE YOU? HOW DOES STIRRING TENSIONS MAKE THINGS BETTER?

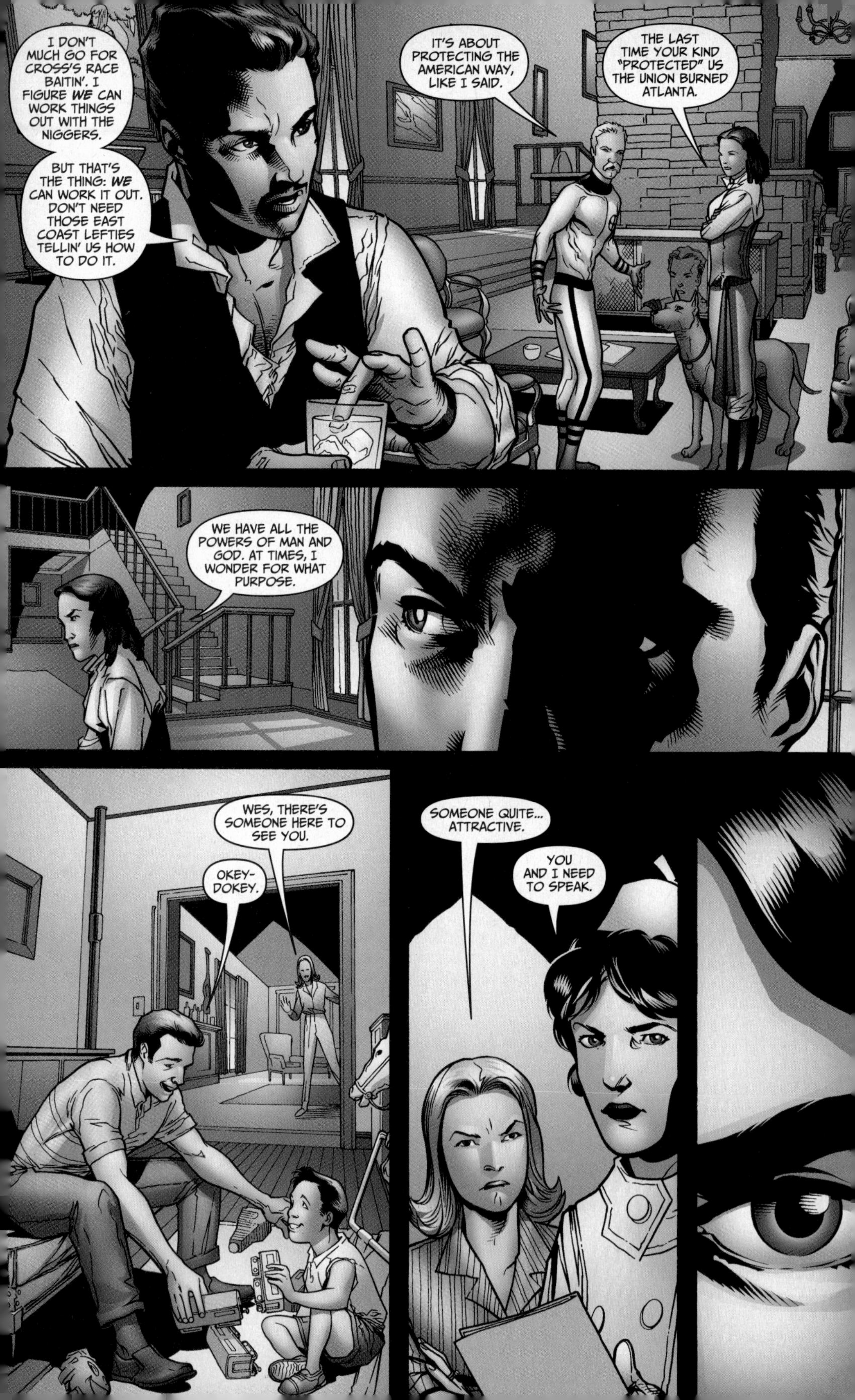
I DON'T MUCH GO FOR CROSS'S RACE BAITIN'. I FIGURE *WE* CAN WORK THINGS OUT WITH THE NIGGERS.
BUT THAT'S THE THING: *WE* CAN WORK IT OUT. DON'T NEED THOSE EAST COAST LEFTIES TELLIN' US HOW TO DO IT.
IT'S ABOUT PROTECTING THE AMERICAN WAY, LIKE I SAID.
THE LAST TIME YOUR KIND "PROTECTED" US THE UNION BURNED ATLANTA.
WE HAVE ALL THE POWERS OF MAN AND GOD. AT TIMES, I WONDER FOR WHAT PURPOSE.
WES, THERE'S SOMEONE HERE TO SEE YOU.
OKEY-DOKEY.
SOMEONE QUITE... ATTRACTIVE.
YOU AND I NEED TO SPEAK.

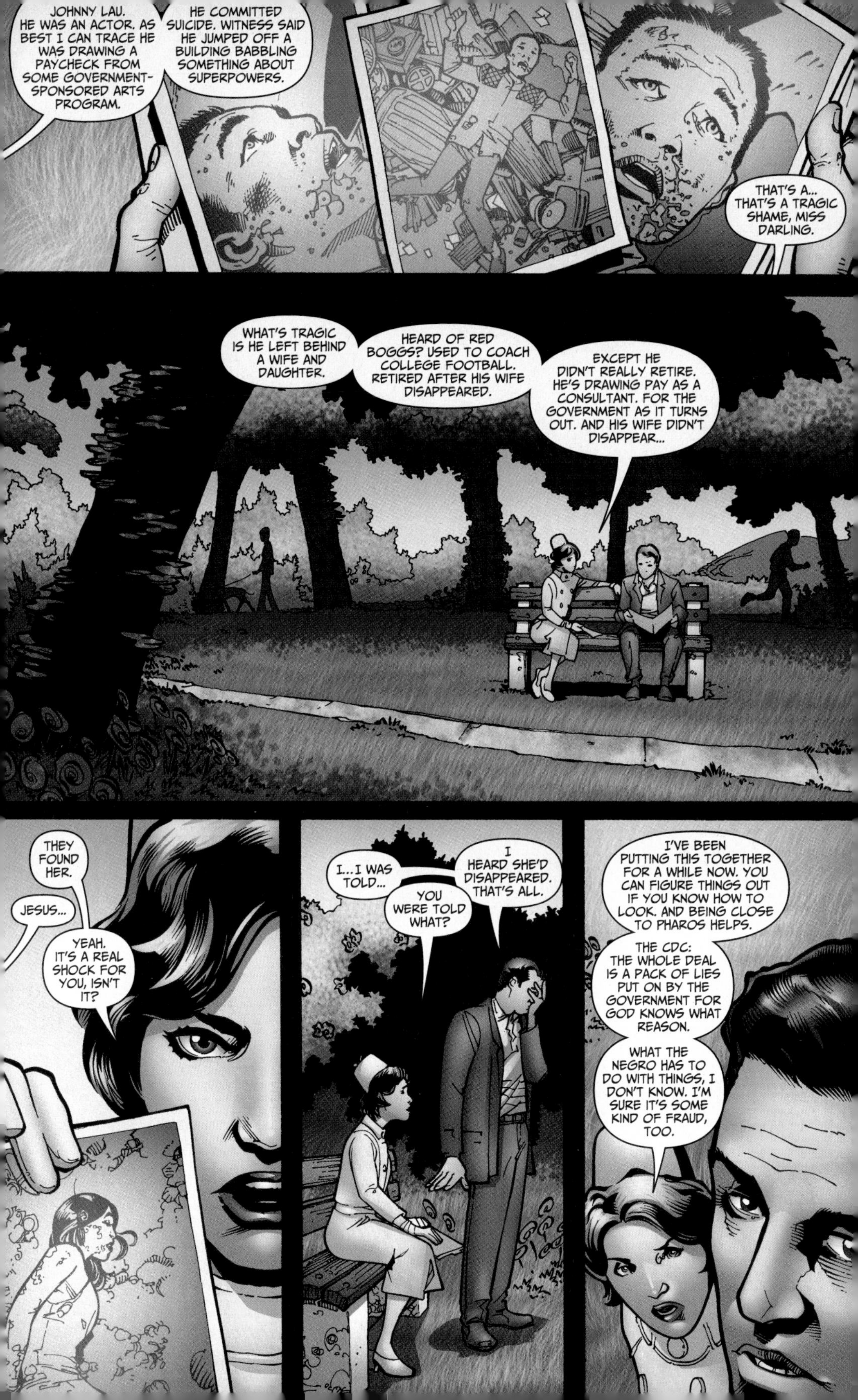
JOHNNY LAU. HE WAS AN ACTOR. AS BEST I CAN TRACE HE WAS DRAWING A PAYCHECK FROM SOME GOVERNMENT-SPONSORED ARTS PROGRAM.
HE COMMITTED SUICIDE. WITNESS SAID HE JUMPED OFF A BUILDING BABBLING SOMETHING ABOUT SUPERPOWERS.
THAT'S A... THAT'S A TRAGIC SHAME, MISS DARLING.
WHAT'S TRAGIC IS HE LEFT BEHIND A WIFE AND DAUGHTER.
HEARD OF RED BOGGS? USED TO COACH COLLEGE FOOTBALL. RETIRED AFTER HIS WIFE DISAPPEARED.
EXCEPT HE DIDN'T REALLY RETIRE. HE'S DRAWING PAY AS A CONSULTANT. FOR THE GOVERNMENT AS IT TURNS OUT. AND HIS WIFE DIDN'T DISAPPEAR...
THEY FOUND HER.
JESUS...
YEAH. IT'S A REAL SHOCK FOR YOU, ISN'T IT?
I...I WAS TOLD...
YOU WERE TOLD WHAT?
I HEARD SHE'D DISAPPEARED. THAT'S ALL.
I'VE BEEN PUTTING THIS TOGETHER FOR A WHILE NOW. YOU CAN FIGURE THINGS OUT IF YOU KNOW HOW TO LOOK. AND BEING CLOSE TO PHAROS HELPS.
THE CDC: THE WHOLE DEAL IS A PACK OF LIES PUT ON BY THE GOVERNMENT FOR GOD KNOWS WHAT REASON.
WHAT THE NEGRO HAS TO DO WITH THINGS, I DON'T KNOW. I'M SURE IT'S SOME KIND OF FRAUD, TOO.

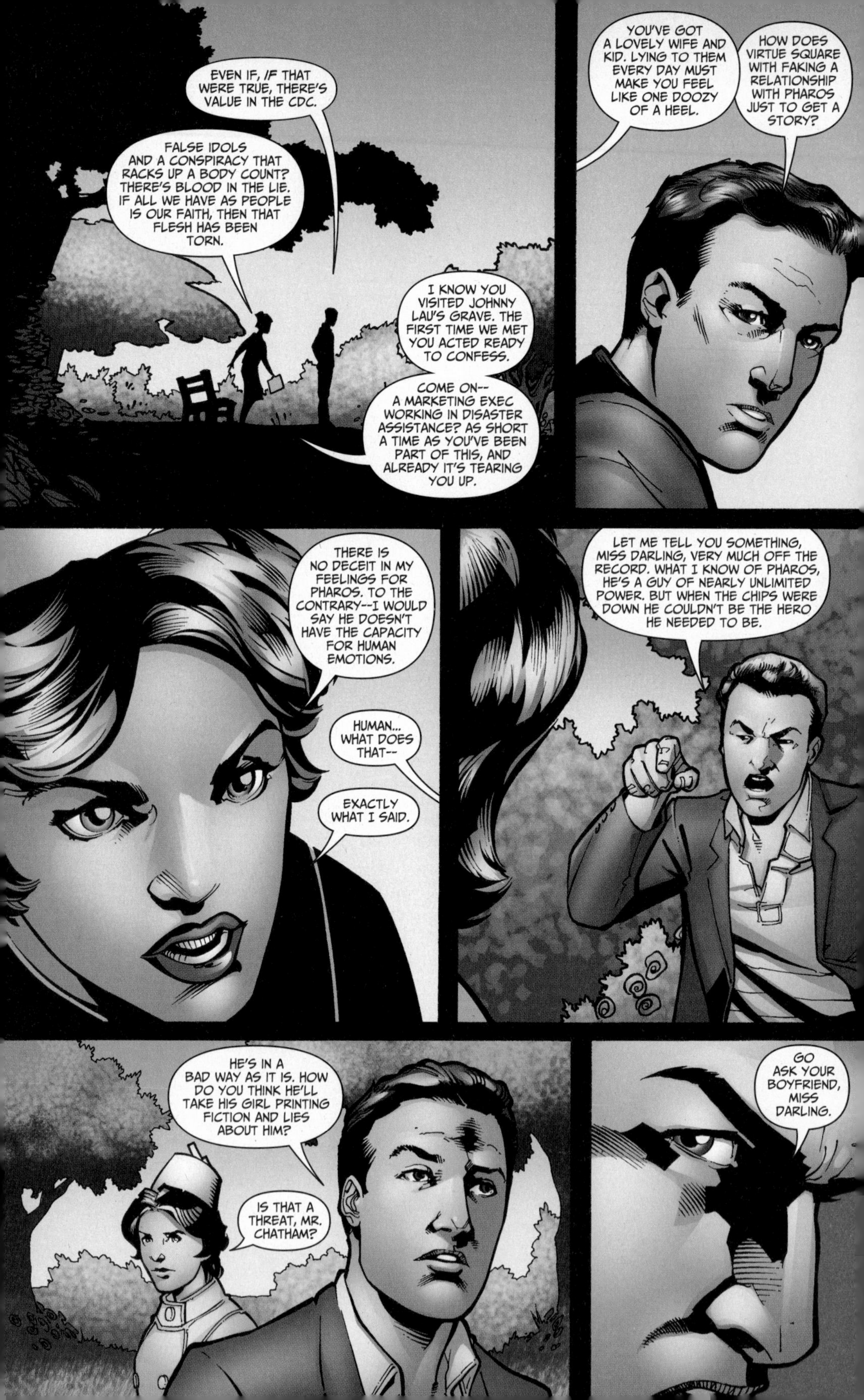
EVEN IF, IF THAT WERE TRUE, THERE'S VALUE IN THE CDC.
FALSE IDOLS AND A CONSPIRACY THAT RACKS UP A BODY COUNT? THERE'S BLOOD IN THE LIE. IF ALL WE HAVE AS PEOPLE IS OUR FAITH, THEN THAT FLESH HAS BEEN TORN.
I KNOW YOU VISITED JOHNNY LAU'S GRAVE. THE FIRST TIME WE MET YOU ACTED READY TO CONFESS.
COME ON-- A MARKETING EXEC WORKING IN DISASTER ASSISTANCE? AS SHORT A TIME AS YOU'VE BEEN PART OF THIS, AND ALREADY IT'S TEARING YOU UP.
YOU'VE GOT A LOVELY WIFE AND KID. LYING TO THEM EVERY DAY MUST MAKE YOU FEEL LIKE ONE DOOZY OF A HEEL.
HOW DOES VIRTUE SQUARE WITH FAKING A RELATIONSHIP WITH PHAROS JUST TO GET A STORY?
THERE IS NO DECEIT IN MY FEELINGS FOR PHAROS. TO THE CONTRARY--I WOULD SAY HE DOESN'T HAVE THE CAPACITY FOR HUMAN EMOTIONS.
HUMAN... WHAT DOES THAT--
EXACTLY WHAT I SAID.
LET ME TELL YOU SOMETHING, MISS DARLING, VERY MUCH OFF THE RECORD. WHAT I KNOW OF PHAROS, HE'S A GUY OF NEARLY UNLIMITED POWER. BUT WHEN THE CHIPS WERE DOWN HE COULDN'T BE THE HERO HE NEEDED TO BE.
HE'S IN A BAD WAY AS IT IS. HOW DO YOU THINK HE'LL TAKE HIS GIRL PRINTING FICTION AND LIES ABOUT HIM?
IS THAT A THREAT, MR. CHATHAM?
GO ASK YOUR BOYFRIEND, MISS DARLING.

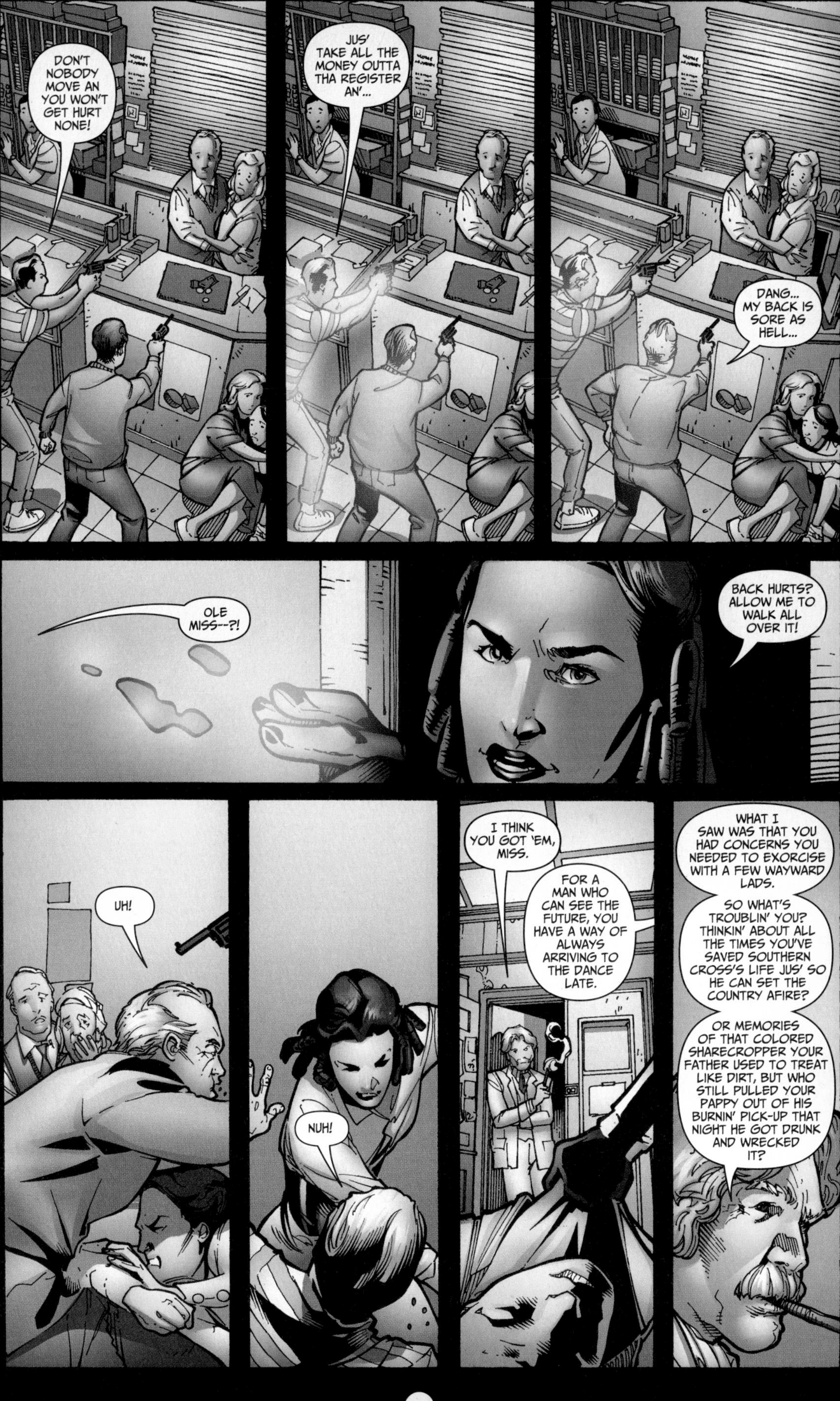
DON'T NOBODY MOVE AN YOU WON'T GET HURT NONE!
JUS' TAKE ALL THE MONEY OUTTA THA REGISTER AN'...
DANG... MY BACK IS SORE AS HELL...
OLE MISS--?!
BACK HURTS? ALLOW ME TO WALK ALL OVER IT!
UH!
NUH!
I THINK YOU GOT 'EM, MISS.
FOR A MAN WHO CAN SEE THE FUTURE, YOU HAVE A WAY OF ALWAYS ARRIVING TO THE DANCE LATE.
WHAT I SAW WAS THAT YOU HAD CONCERNS YOU NEEDED TO EXORCISE WITH A FEW WAYWARD LADS.
SO WHAT'S TROUBLIN' YOU? THINKIN' ABOUT ALL THE TIMES YOU'VE SAVED SOUTHERN CROSS'S LIFE JUS' SO HE CAN SET THE COUNTRY AFIRE?
OR MEMORIES OF THAT COLORED SHARECROPPER YOUR FATHER USED TO TREAT LIKE DIRT, BUT WHO STILL PULLED YOUR PAPPY OUT OF HIS BURNIN' PICK-UP THAT NIGHT HE GOT DRUNK AND WRECKED IT?

DUH!

CALL THE POLICE.

THINK A DOCTOR'S WHAT THEY NEED.

LET 'EM BLEED.

FIRST WE THOUGHT IT WAS SOME KLAN BOYS, GOT CARRIED AWAY.

THEN WE SAW THIS AND...WELL, WE KNEW THINGS WAS BAD. FIGURE WE OUGHTA CALL THE FEDS.

IT'S...IT'S HELLBENT WHO DONE THIS.

WHAT IN TARNATION FOR?

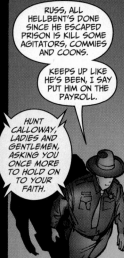

RUSS, ALL HELLBENT'S DONE SINCE HE ESCAPED PRISON IS KILL SOME AGITATORS, COMMIES AND COONS.

KEEPS UP LIKE HE'S BEEN, I SAY PUT HIM ON THE PAYROLL.

HUNT CALLOWAY, LADIES AND GENTLEMEN, ASKING YOU ONCE MORE TO HOLD ON TO YOUR FAITH.

YES, HELLBENT HAS STRUCK AGAIN. BUT KNOW THAT YOUR LAW ENFORCEMENT OFFICIALS ARE DOING ALL THEY CAN TO APPREHEND HIM.

REST ASSURED THAT YOUR GOVERNMENT-- BZZT ZZT-EVER VIGILANT-ZZZ BZZT-

DO NOT BELIEVE THE LIES OF THE OPPRESSORS! THIS IS ROBERT WILLIAMS AND RADIO FREE DIXIE COMING TO YOU FROM OUR ASYLUM IN CUBA!

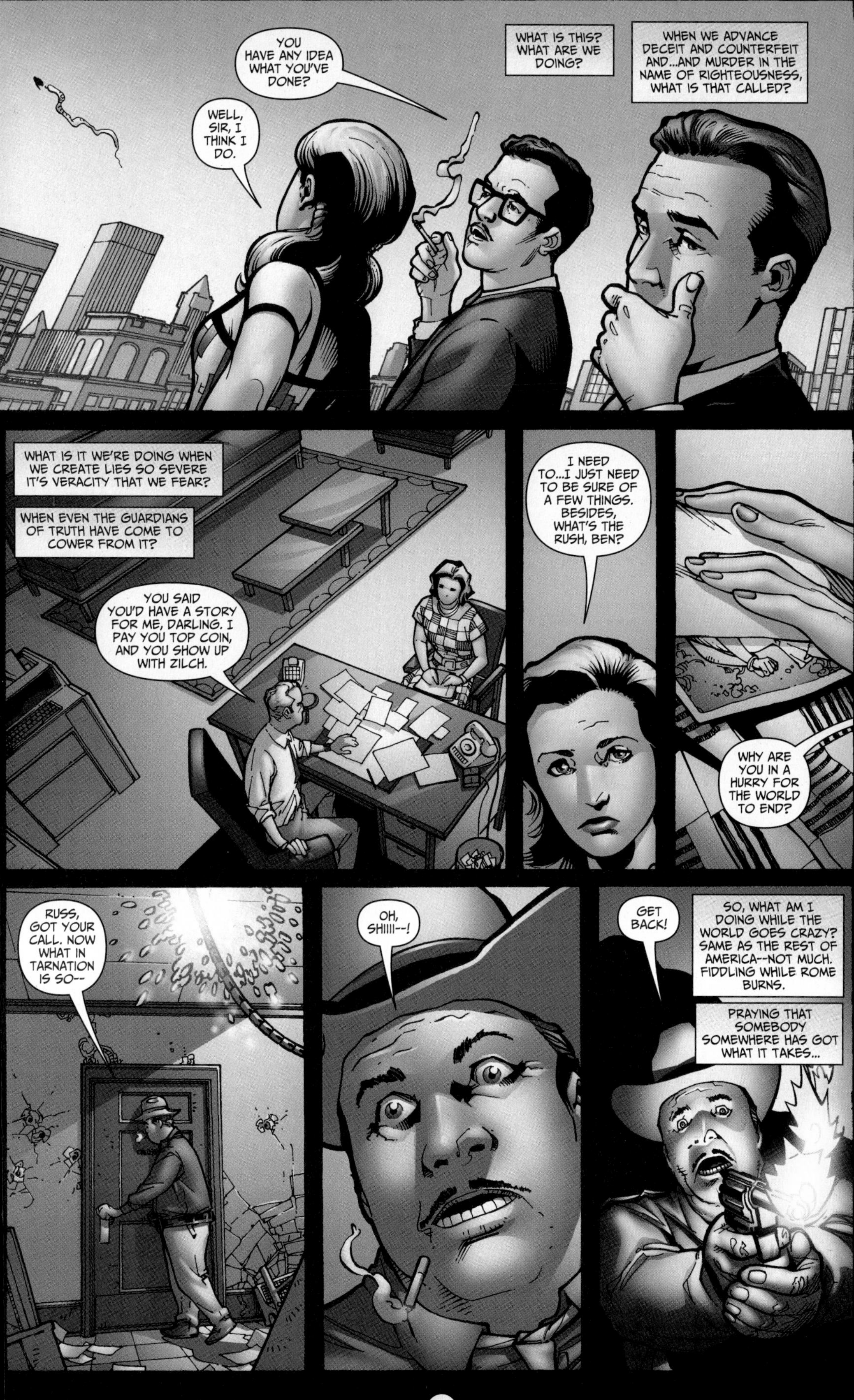
YOU HAVE ANY IDEA WHAT YOU'VE DONE?
WELL, SIR, I THINK I DO.
WHAT IS THIS? WHAT ARE WE DOING?
WHEN WE ADVANCE DECEIT AND COUNTERFEIT AND...AND MURDER IN THE NAME OF RIGHTEOUSNESS, WHAT IS THAT CALLED?
WHAT IS IT WE'RE DOING WHEN WE CREATE LIES SO SEVERE IT'S VERACITY THAT WE FEAR?
WHEN EVEN THE GUARDIANS OF TRUTH HAVE COME TO COWER FROM IT?
YOU SAID YOU'D HAVE A STORY FOR ME, DARLING. I PAY YOU TOP COIN, AND YOU SHOW UP WITH ZILCH.
I NEED TO...I JUST NEED TO BE SURE OF A FEW THINGS. BESIDES, WHAT'S THE RUSH, BEN?
WHY ARE YOU IN A HURRY FOR THE WORLD TO END?
RUSS, GOT YOUR CALL. NOW WHAT IN TARNATION IS SO--
OH, SHIIII--!
GET BACK!
SO, WHAT AM I DOING WHILE THE WORLD GOES CRAZY? SAME AS THE REST OF AMERICA--NOT MUCH. FIDDLING WHILE ROME BURNS.
PRAYING THAT SOMEBODY SOMEWHERE HAS GOT WHAT IT TAKES...

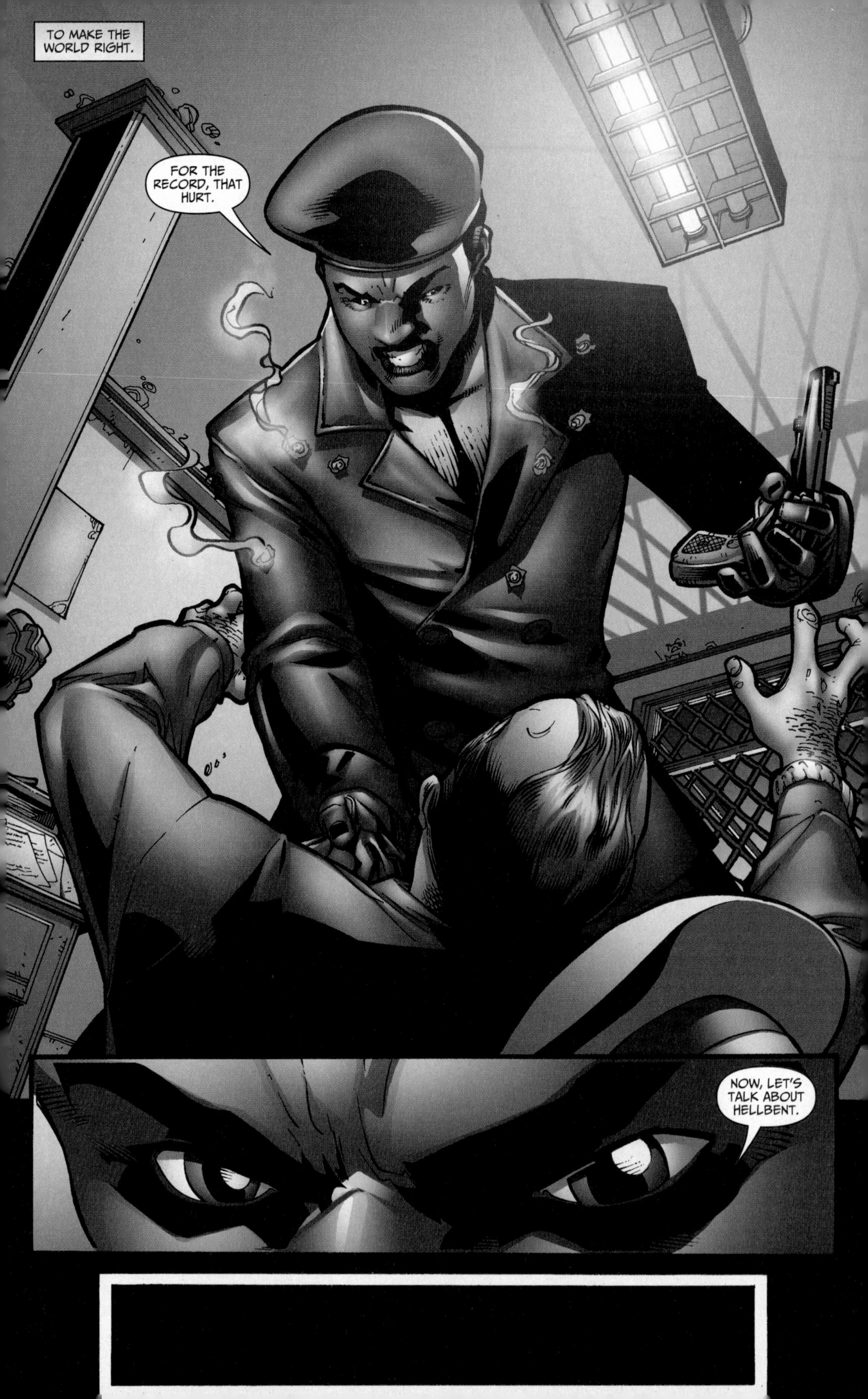
TO MAKE THE WORLD RIGHT.
FOR THE RECORD, THAT HURT.
NOW, LET'S TALK ABOUT HELLBENT.

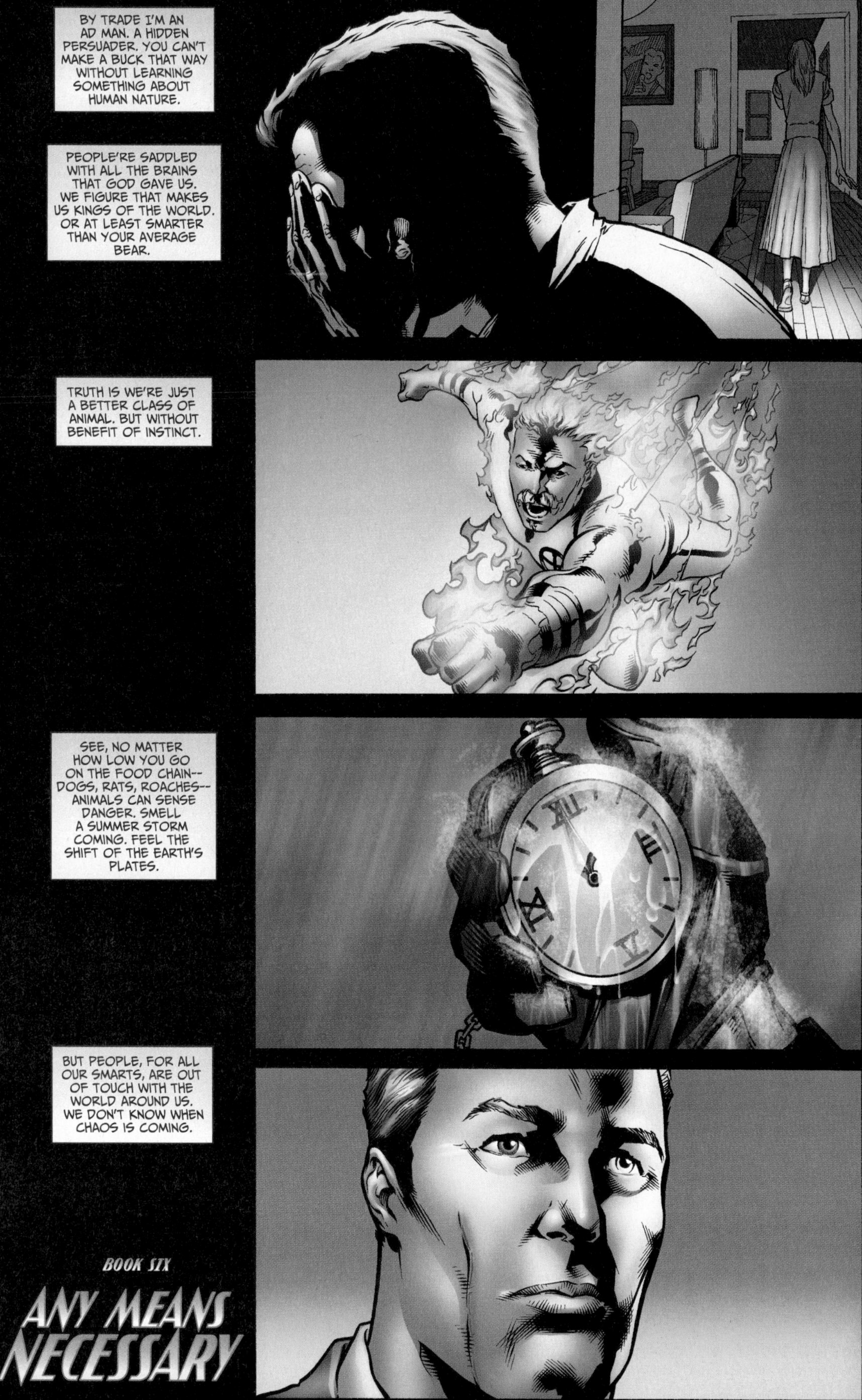
BY TRADE I'M AN AD MAN. A HIDDEN PERSUADER. YOU CAN'T MAKE A BUCK THAT WAY WITHOUT LEARNING SOMETHING ABOUT HUMAN NATURE.
PEOPLE'RE SADDLED WITH ALL THE BRAINS THAT GOD GAVE US. WE FIGURE THAT MAKES US KINGS OF THE WORLD. OR AT LEAST SMARTER THAN YOUR AVERAGE BEAR.
TRUTH IS WE'RE JUST A BETTER CLASS OF ANIMAL. BUT WITHOUT BENEFIT OF INSTINCT.
SEE, NO MATTER HOW LOW YOU GO ON THE FOOD CHAIN--DOGS, RATS, ROACHES--ANIMALS CAN SENSE DANGER. SMELL A SUMMER STORM COMING. FEEL THE SHIFT OF THE EARTH'S PLATES.
BUT PEOPLE, FOR ALL OUR SMARTS, ARE OUT OF TOUCH WITH THE WORLD AROUND US. WE DON'T KNOW WHEN CHAOS IS COMING.
BOOK SIX
ANY MEANS NECESSARY

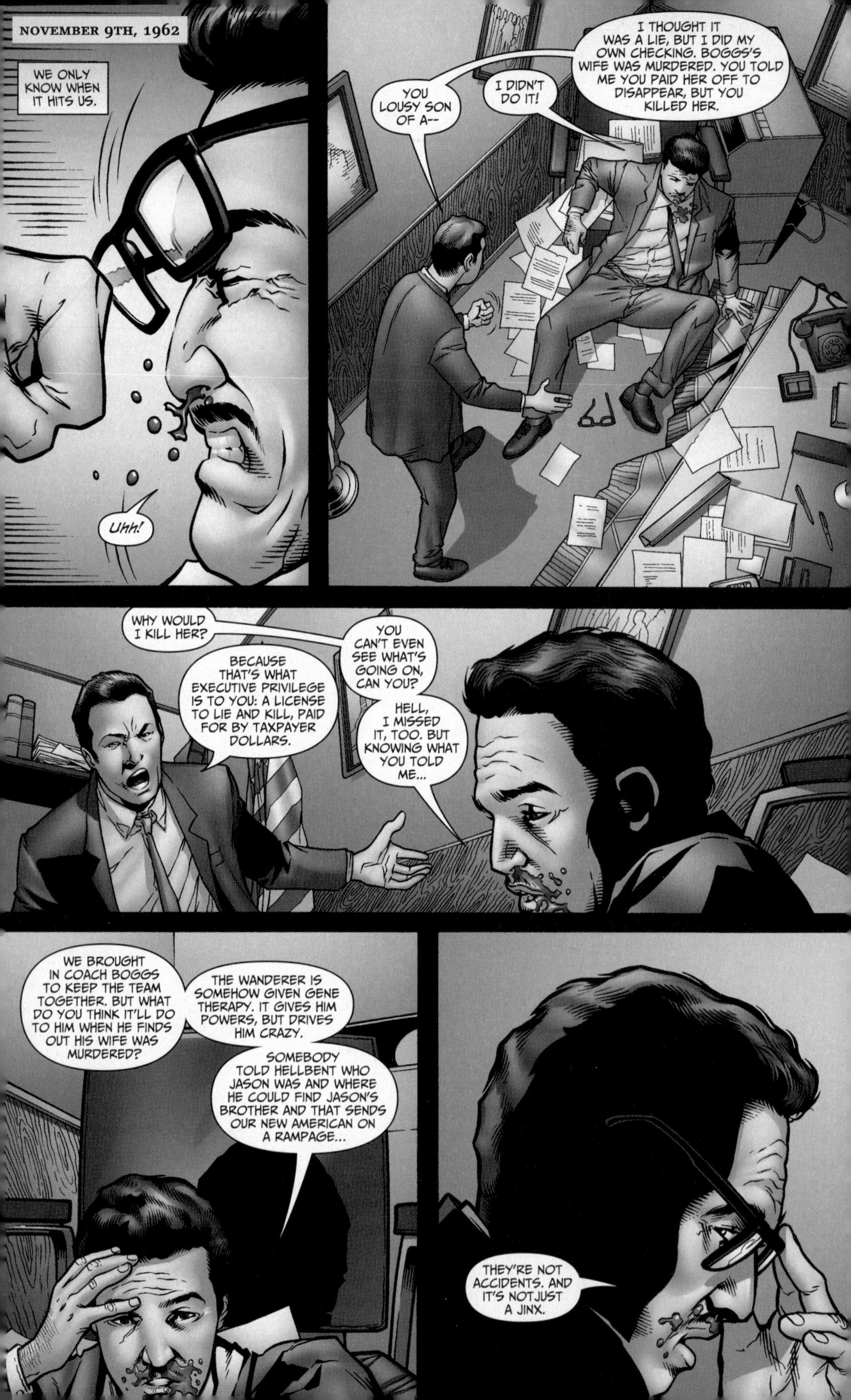
NOVEMBER 9TH, 1962
WE ONLY KNOW WHEN IT HITS US.
Uhh!
YOU LOUSY SON OF A--
I DIDN'T DO IT!
I THOUGHT IT WAS A LIE, BUT I DID MY OWN CHECKING. BOGGS'S WIFE WAS MURDERED. YOU TOLD ME YOU PAID HER OFF TO DISAPPEAR, BUT YOU KILLED HER.
WHY WOULD I KILL HER?
BECAUSE THAT'S WHAT EXECUTIVE PRIVILEGE IS TO YOU: A LICENSE TO LIE AND KILL, PAID FOR BY TAXPAYER DOLLARS.
YOU CAN'T EVEN SEE WHAT'S GOING ON, CAN YOU?
HELL, I MISSED IT, TOO. BUT KNOWING WHAT YOU TOLD ME...
WE BROUGHT IN COACH BOGGS TO KEEP THE TEAM TOGETHER. BUT WHAT DO YOU THINK IT'LL DO TO HIM WHEN HE FINDS OUT HIS WIFE WAS MURDERED?
THE WANDERER IS SOMEHOW GIVEN GENE THERAPY. IT GIVES HIM POWERS, BUT DRIVES HIM CRAZY.
SOMEBODY TOLD HELLBENT WHO JASON WAS AND WHERE HE COULD FIND JASON'S BROTHER AND THAT SENDS OUR NEW AMERICAN ON A RAMPAGE...
THEY'RE NOT ACCIDENTS. AND IT'S NOTJUST A JINX.

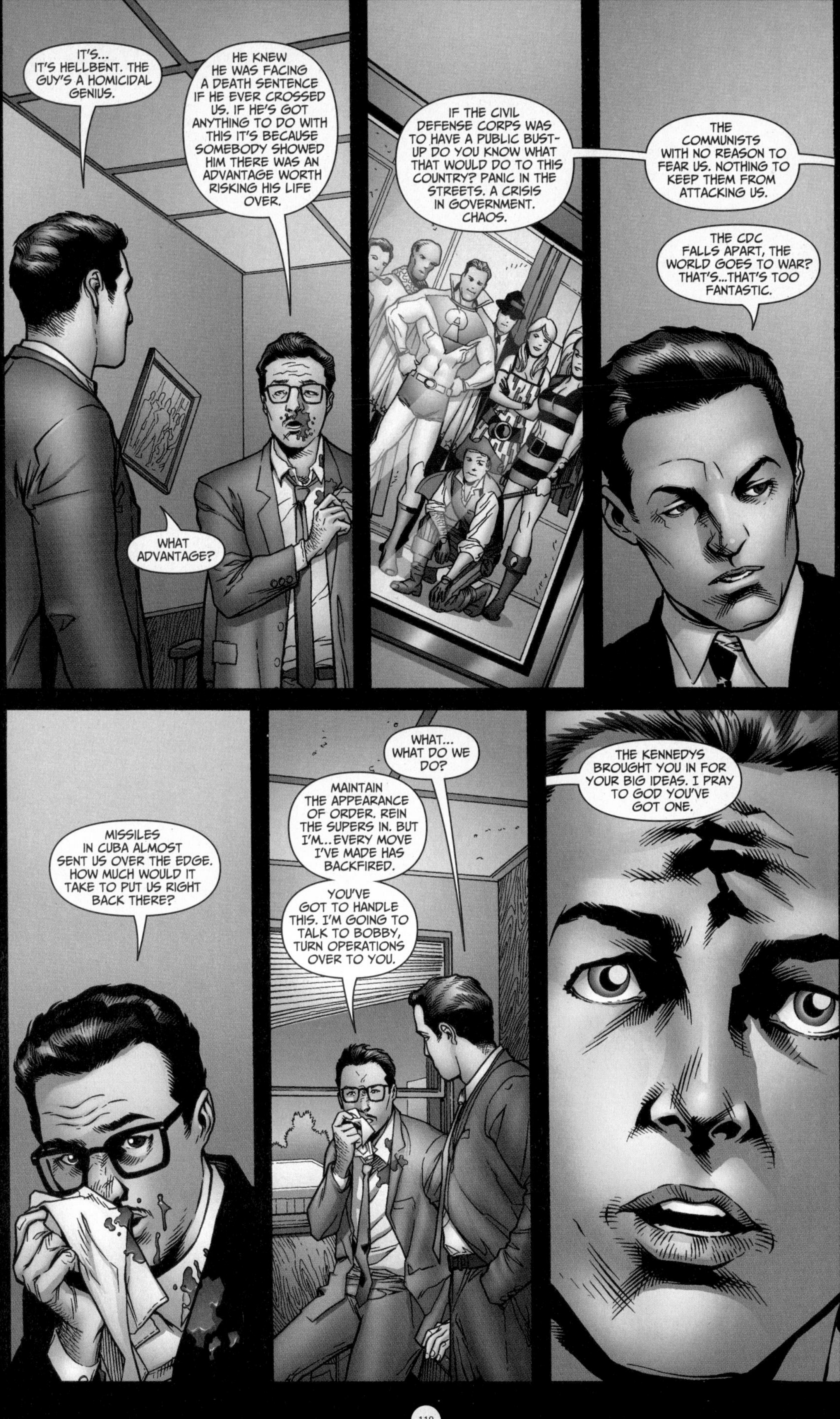
IT'S... IT'S HELLBENT. THE GUY'S A HOMICIDAL GENIUS.
HE KNEW HE WAS FACING A DEATH SENTENCE IF HE EVER CROSSED US. IF HE'S GOT ANYTHING TO DO WITH THIS IT'S BECAUSE SOMEBODY SHOWED HIM THERE WAS AN ADVANTAGE WORTH RISKING HIS LIFE OVER.
WHAT ADVANTAGE?
IF THE CIVIL DEFENSE CORPS WAS TO HAVE A PUBLIC BUST-UP DO YOU KNOW WHAT THAT WOULD DO TO THIS COUNTRY? PANIC IN THE STREETS. A CRISIS IN GOVERNMENT. CHAOS.
THE COMMUNISTS WITH NO REASON TO FEAR US. NOTHING TO KEEP THEM FROM ATTACKING US.
THE CDC FALLS APART, THE WORLD GOES TO WAR? THAT'S...THAT'S TOO FANTASTIC.
MISSILES IN CUBA ALMOST SENT US OVER THE EDGE. HOW MUCH WOULD IT TAKE TO PUT US RIGHT BACK THERE?
WHAT... WHAT DO WE DO?
MAINTAIN THE APPEARANCE OF ORDER. REIN THE SUPERS IN. BUT I'M...EVERY MOVE I'VE MADE HAS BACKFIRED.
YOU'VE GOT TO HANDLE THIS. I'M GOING TO TALK TO BOBBY, TURN OPERATIONS OVER TO YOU.
THE KENNEDYS BROUGHT YOU IN FOR YOUR BIG IDEAS. I PRAY TO GOD YOU'VE GOT ONE.

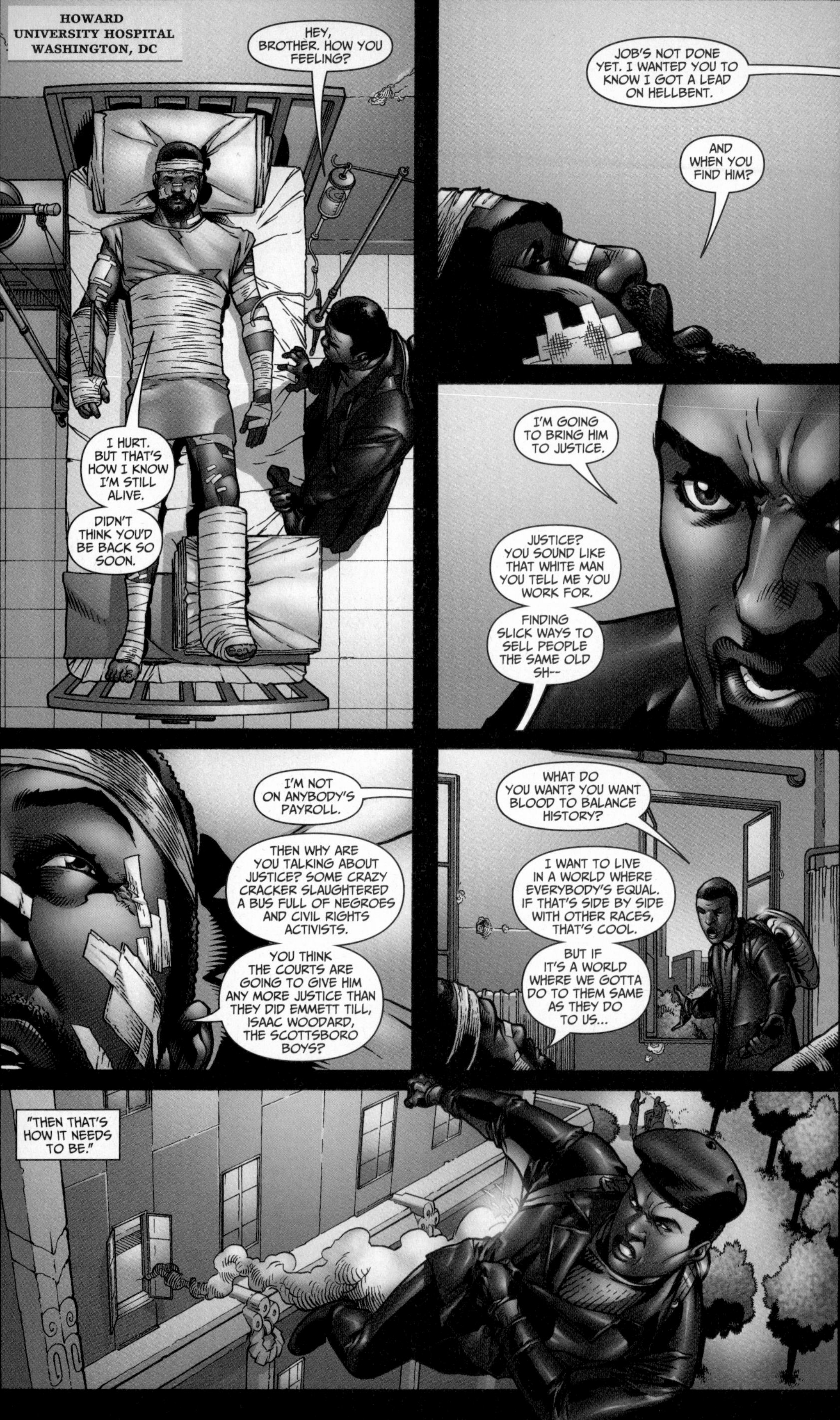
HOWARD UNIVERSITY HOSPITAL WASHINGTON, DC
HEY, BROTHER. HOW YOU FEELING?
I HURT. BUT THAT'S HOW I KNOW I'M STILL ALIVE.
DIDN'T THINK YOU'D BE BACK SO SOON.
JOB'S NOT DONE YET. I WANTED YOU TO KNOW I GOT A LEAD ON HELLBENT.
AND WHEN YOU FIND HIM?
I'M GOING TO BRING HIM TO JUSTICE.
JUSTICE? YOU SOUND LIKE THAT WHITE MAN YOU TELL ME YOU WORK FOR.
FINDING SLICK WAYS TO SELL PEOPLE THE SAME OLD SH--
I'M NOT ON ANYBODY'S PAYROLL.
THEN WHY ARE YOU TALKING ABOUT JUSTICE? SOME CRAZY CRACKER SLAUGHTERED A BUS FULL OF NEGROES AND CIVIL RIGHTS ACTIVISTS.
YOU THINK THE COURTS ARE GOING TO GIVE HIM ANY MORE JUSTICE THAN THEY DID EMMETT TILL, ISAAC WOODARD, THE SCOTTSBORO BOYS?
WHAT DO YOU WANT? YOU WANT BLOOD TO BALANCE HISTORY?
I WANT TO LIVE IN A WORLD WHERE EVERYBODY'S EQUAL. IF THAT'S SIDE BY SIDE WITH OTHER RACES, THAT'S COOL.
BUT IF IT'S A WORLD WHERE WE GOTTA DO TO THEM SAME AS THEY DO TO US...
"THEN THAT'S HOW IT NEEDS TO BE."

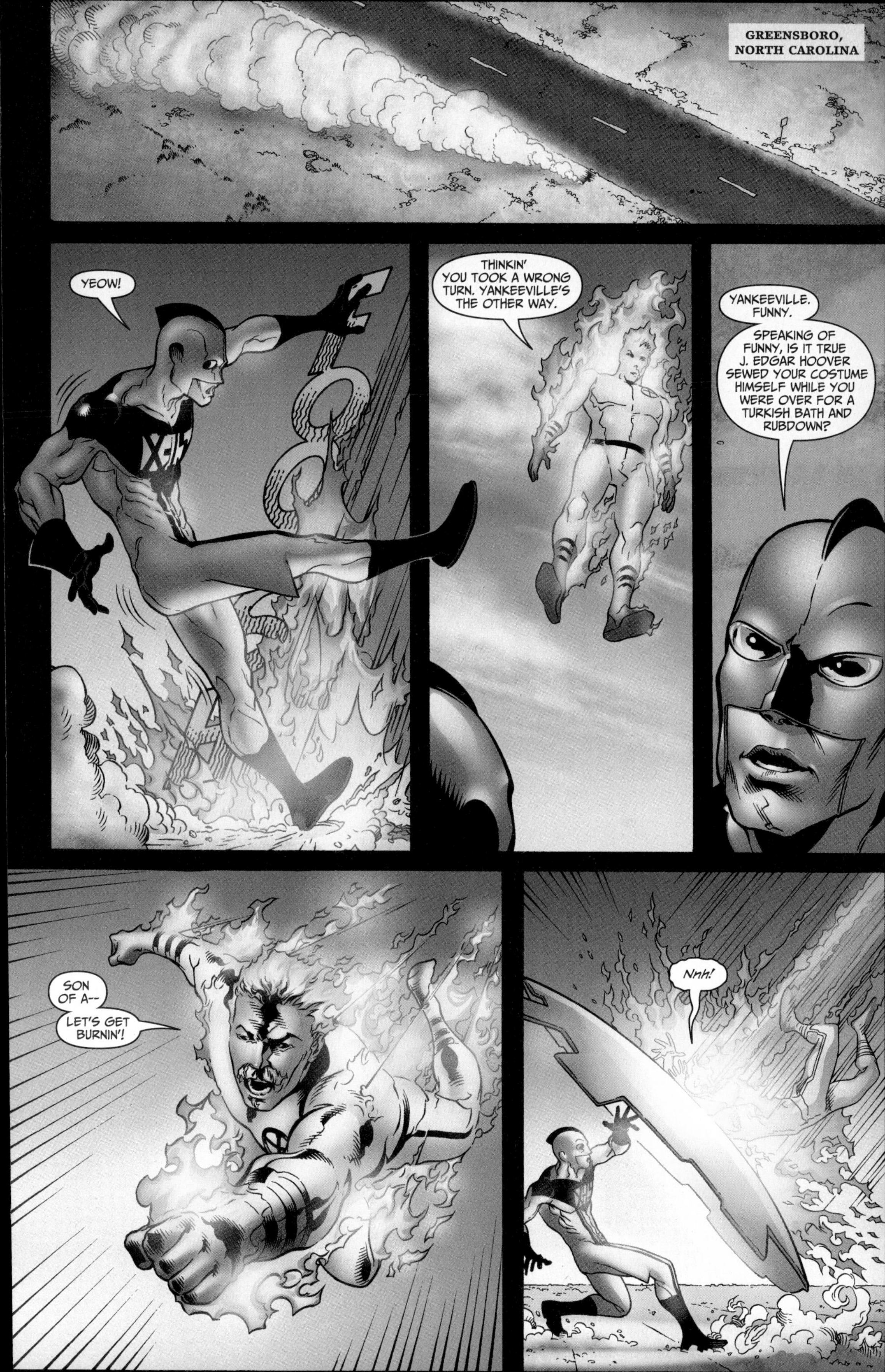
GREENSBORO, NORTH CAROLINA
YEOW!
THINKIN' YOU TOOK A WRONG TURN. YANKEEVILLE'S THE OTHER WAY.
YANKEEVILLE. FUNNY.
SPEAKING OF FUNNY, IS IT TRUE J. EDGAR HOOVER SEWED YOUR COSTUME HIMSELF WHILE YOU WERE OVER FOR A TURKISH BATH AND RUBDOWN?
SON OF A--
LET'S GET BURNIN'!
Nnh!

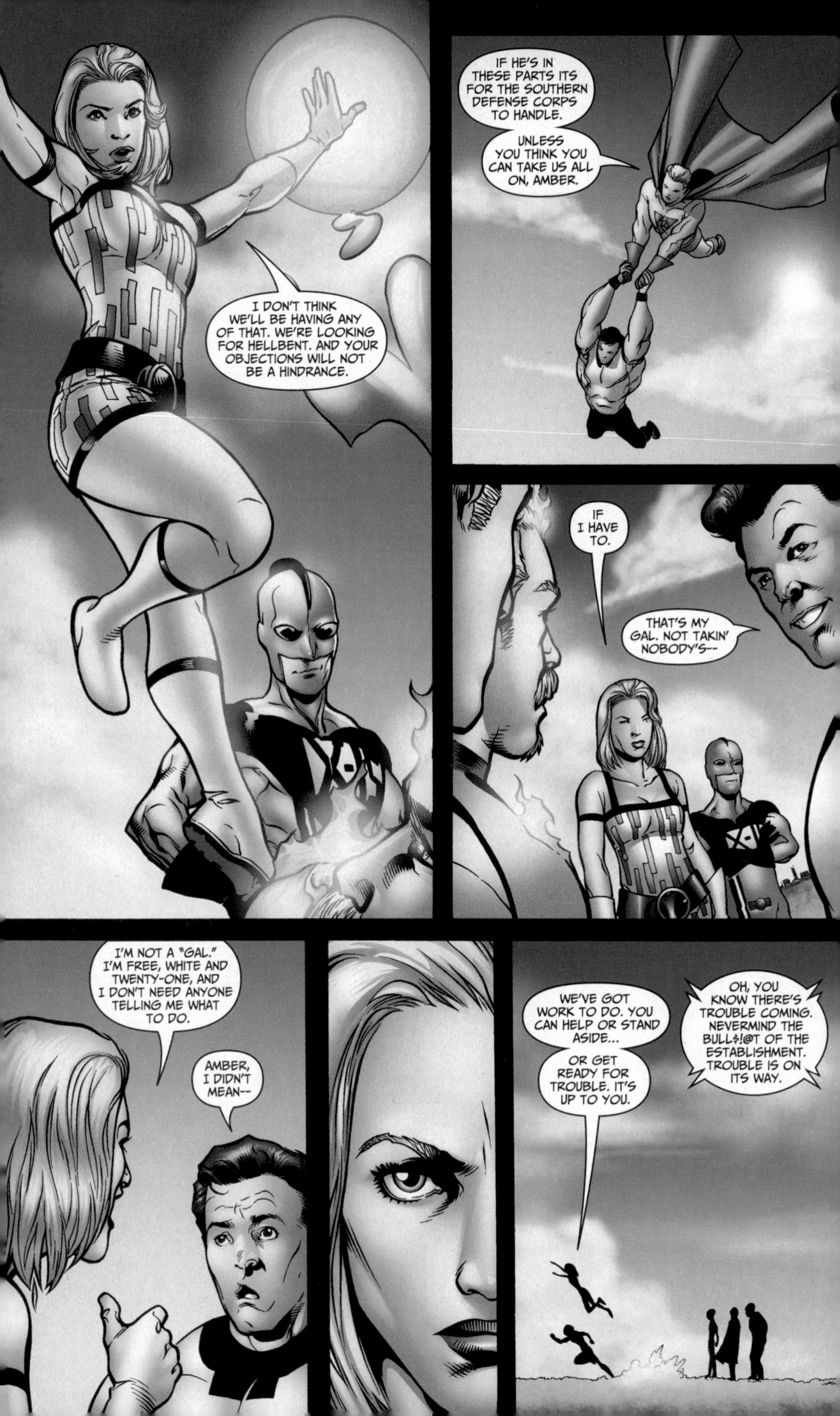
I DON'T THINK WE'LL BE HAVING ANY OF THAT. WE'RE LOOKING FOR HELLBENT. AND YOUR OBJECTIONS WILL NOT BE A HINDRANCE.
IF HE'S IN THESE PARTS ITS FOR THE SOUTHERN DEFENSE CORPS TO HANDLE.
UNLESS YOU THINK YOU CAN TAKE US ALL ON, AMBER.
IF I HAVE TO.
THAT'S MY GAL. NOT TAKIN' NOBODY'S--
I'M NOT A "GAL." I'M FREE, WHITE AND TWENTY-ONE, AND I DON'T NEED ANYONE TELLING ME WHAT TO DO.
AMBER, I DIDN'T MEAN--
WE'VE GOT WORK TO DO. YOU CAN HELP OR STAND ASIDE...
OR GET READY FOR TROUBLE. IT'S UP TO YOU.
OH, YOU KNOW THERE'S TROUBLE COMING. NEVERMIND THE BULL$!@T OF THE ESTABLISHMENT. TROUBLE IS ON ITS WAY.

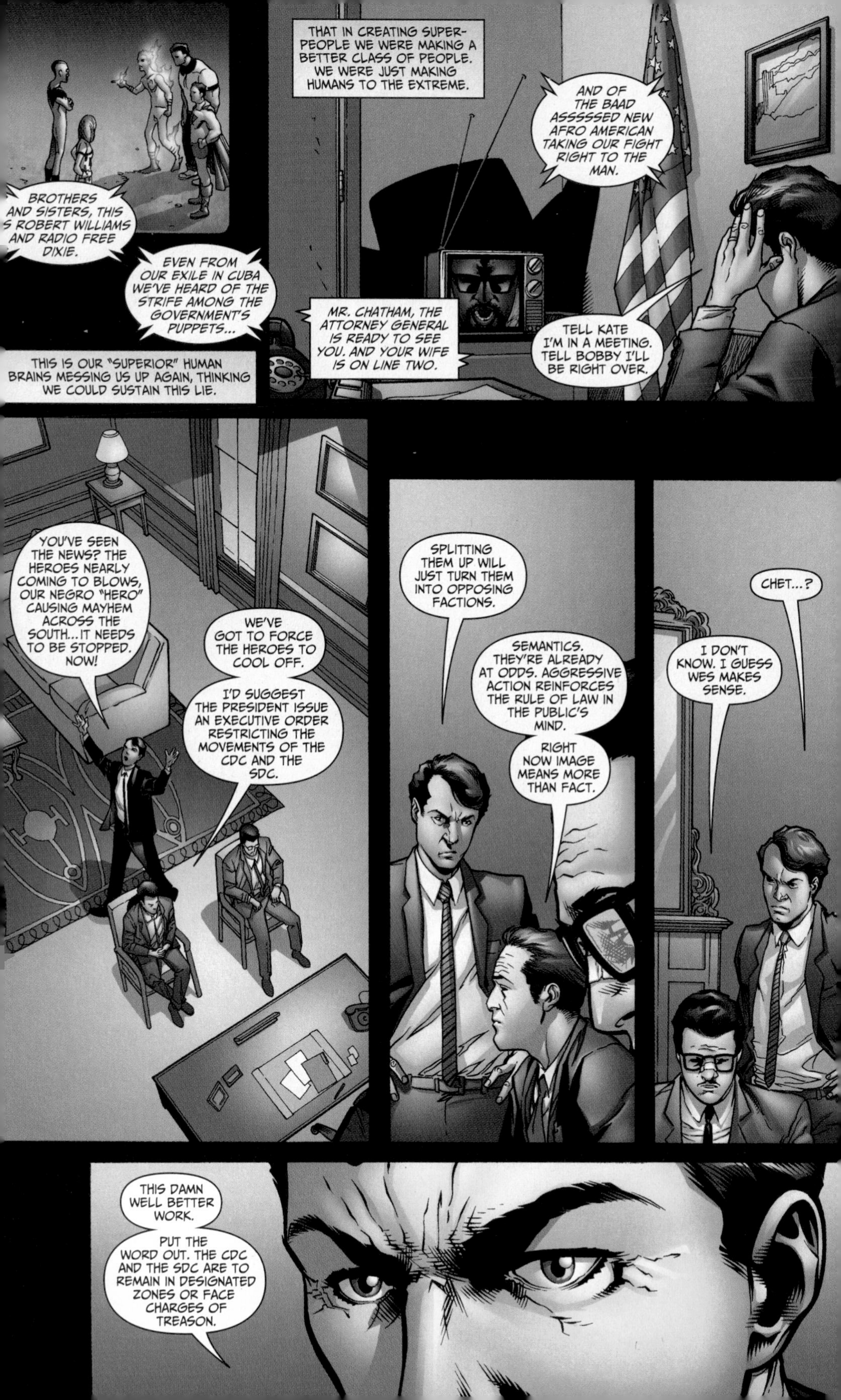

BROTHERS AND SISTERS, THIS IS ROBERT WILLIAMS AND RADIO FREE DIXIE.
EVEN FROM OUR EXILE IN CUBA WE'VE HEARD OF THE STRIFE AMONG THE GOVERNMENT'S PUPPETS...
THIS IS OUR "SUPERIOR" HUMAN BRAINS MESSING US UP AGAIN, THINKING WE COULD SUSTAIN THIS LIE.
THAT IN CREATING SUPER-PEOPLE WE WERE MAKING A BETTER CLASS OF PEOPLE. WE WERE JUST MAKING HUMANS TO THE EXTREME.
AND OF THE BAAD ASSSSSED NEW AFRO AMERICAN TAKING OUR FIGHT RIGHT TO THE MAN.
MR. CHATHAM, THE ATTORNEY GENERAL IS READY TO SEE YOU. AND YOUR WIFE IS ON LINE TWO.
TELL KATE I'M IN A MEETING. TELL BOBBY I'LL BE RIGHT OVER.
YOU'VE SEEN THE NEWS? THE HEROES NEARLY COMING TO BLOWS, OUR NEGRO "HERO" CAUSING MAYHEM ACROSS THE SOUTH...IT NEEDS TO BE STOPPED. NOW!
WE'VE GOT TO FORCE THE HEROES TO COOL OFF.
I'D SUGGEST THE PRESIDENT ISSUE AN EXECUTIVE ORDER RESTRICTING THE MOVEMENTS OF THE CDC AND THE SDC.
SPLITTING THEM UP WILL JUST TURN THEM INTO OPPOSING FACTIONS.
SEMANTICS. THEY'RE ALREADY AT ODDS. AGGRESSIVE ACTION REINFORCES THE RULE OF LAW IN THE PUBLIC'S MIND.
RIGHT NOW IMAGE MEANS MORE THAN FACT.
CHET...?
I DON'T KNOW. I GUESS WES MAKES SENSE.
THIS DAMN WELL BETTER WORK.
PUT THE WORD OUT. THE CDC AND THE SDC ARE TO REMAIN IN DESIGNATED ZONES OR FACE CHARGES OF TREASON.

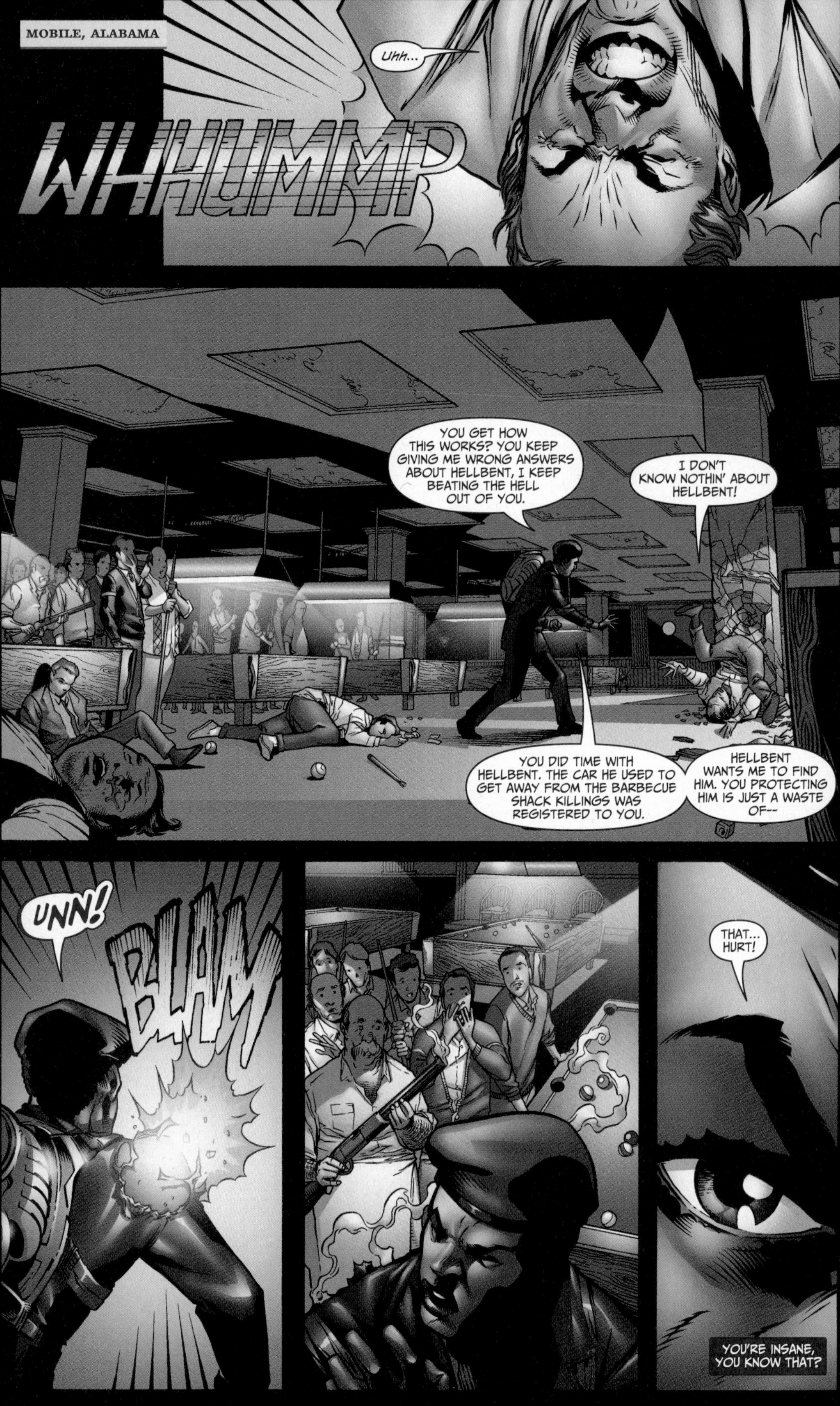

MOBILE, ALABAMA
Uhh...
WHHUMMP
YOU GET HOW THIS WORKS? YOU KEEP GIVING ME WRONG ANSWERS ABOUT HELLBENT, I KEEP BEATING THE HELL OUT OF YOU.
I DON'T KNOW NOTHIN' ABOUT HELLBENT!
YOU DID TIME WITH HELLBENT. THE CAR HE USED TO GET AWAY FROM THE BARBECUE SHACK KILLINGS WAS REGISTERED TO YOU.
HELLBENT WANTS ME TO FIND HIM. YOU PROTECTING HIM IS JUST A WASTE OF--
UNN!
BLAM
THAT... HURT!
YOU'RE INSANE, YOU KNOW THAT?

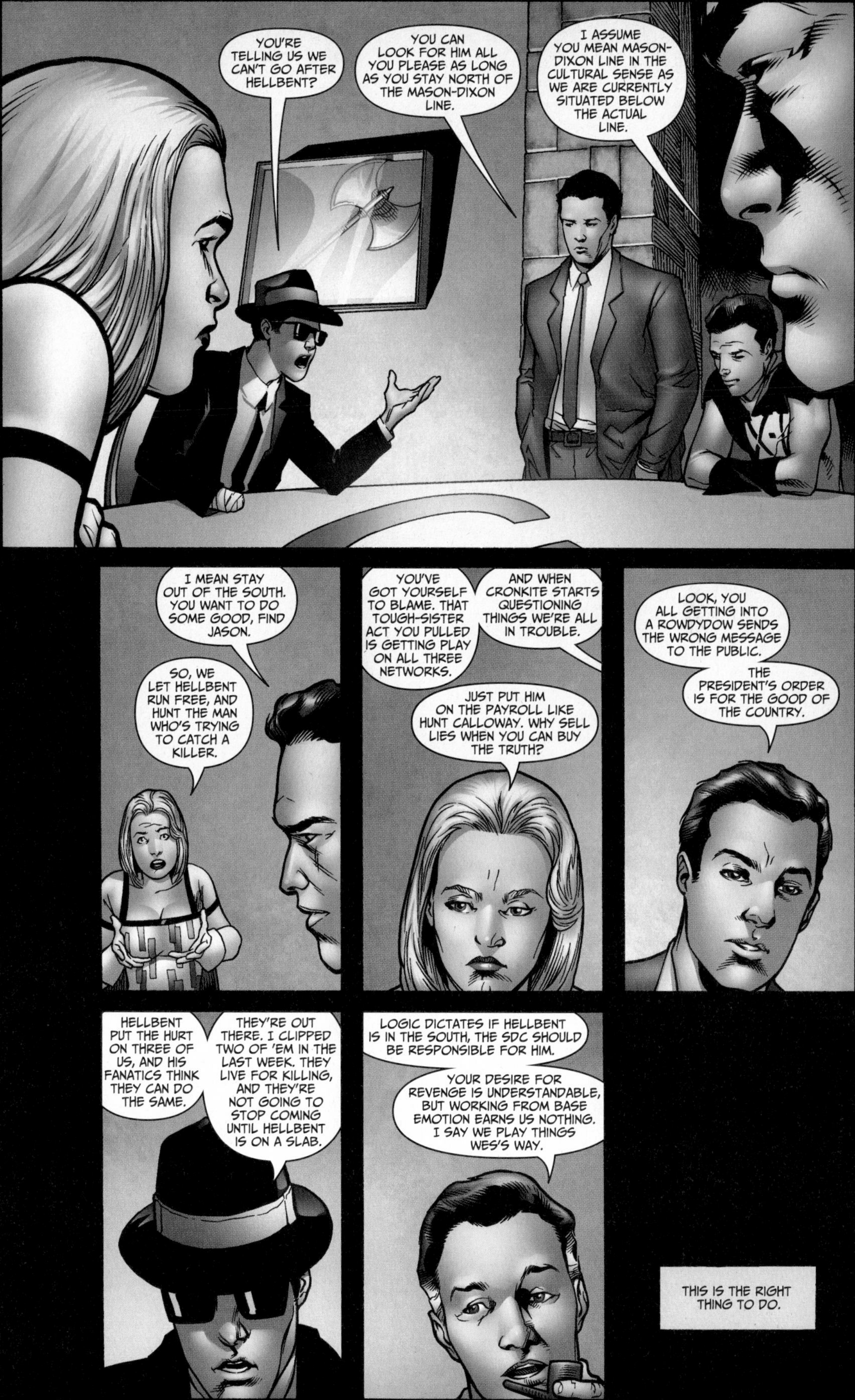
YOU'RE TELLING US WE CAN'T GO AFTER HELLBENT?
YOU CAN LOOK FOR HIM ALL YOU PLEASE AS LONG AS YOU STAY NORTH OF THE MASON-DIXON LINE.
I ASSUME YOU MEAN MASON-DIXON LINE IN THE CULTURAL SENSE AS WE ARE CURRENTLY SITUATED BELOW THE ACTUAL LINE.
I MEAN STAY OUT OF THE SOUTH. YOU WANT TO DO SOME GOOD, FIND JASON.
SO, WE LET HELLBENT RUN FREE, AND HUNT THE MAN WHO'S TRYING TO CATCH A KILLER.
YOU'VE GOT YOURSELF TO BLAME. THAT TOUGH-SISTER ACT YOU PULLED IS GETTING PLAY ON ALL THREE NETWORKS.
AND WHEN CRONKITE STARTS QUESTIONING THINGS WE'RE ALL IN TROUBLE.
JUST PUT HIM ON THE PAYROLL LIKE HUNT CALLOWAY. WHY SELL LIES WHEN YOU CAN BUY THE TRUTH?
LOOK, YOU ALL GETTING INTO A ROWDYDOW SENDS THE WRONG MESSAGE TO THE PUBLIC.
THE PRESIDENT'S ORDER IS FOR THE GOOD OF THE COUNTRY.
HELLBENT PUT THE HURT ON THREE OF US, AND HIS FANATICS THINK THEY CAN DO THE SAME.
THEY'RE OUT THERE. I CLIPPED TWO OF 'EM IN THE LAST WEEK. THEY LIVE FOR KILLING, AND THEY'RE NOT GOING TO STOP COMING UNTIL HELLBENT IS ON A SLAB.
LOGIC DICTATES IF HELLBENT IS IN THE SOUTH, THE SDC SHOULD BE RESPONSIBLE FOR HIM.
YOUR DESIRE FOR REVENGE IS UNDERSTANDABLE, BUT WORKING FROM BASE EMOTION EARNS US NOTHING. I SAY WE PLAY THINGS WES'S WAY.
THIS IS THE RIGHT THING TO DO.

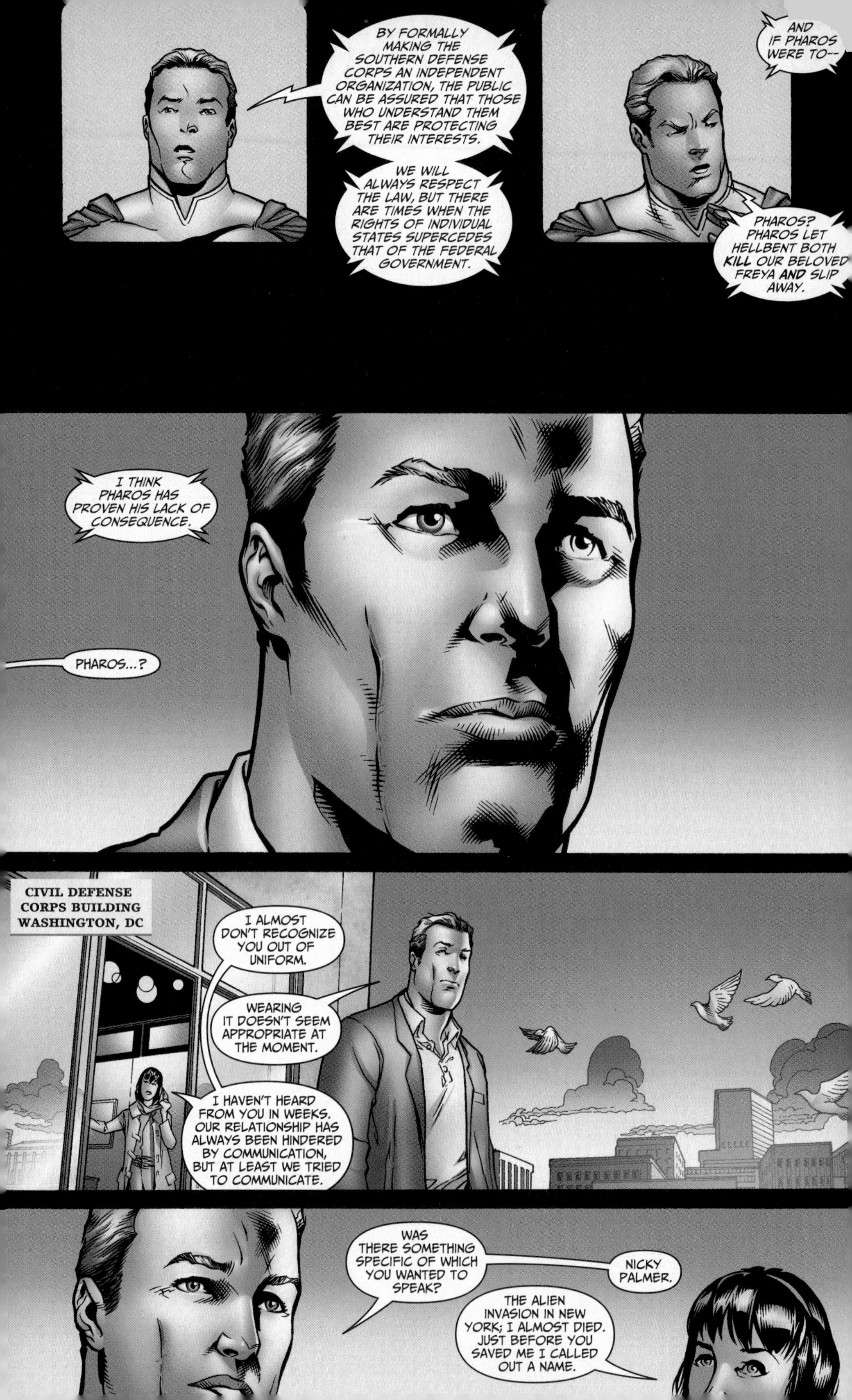
BY FORMALLY MAKING THE SOUTHERN DEFENSE CORPS AN INDEPENDENT ORGANIZATION, THE PUBLIC CAN BE ASSURED THAT THOSE WHO UNDERSTAND THEM BEST ARE PROTECTING THEIR INTERESTS.
WE WILL ALWAYS RESPECT THE LAW, BUT THERE ARE TIMES WHEN THE RIGHTS OF INDIVIDUAL STATES SUPERCEDES THAT OF THE FEDERAL GOVERNMENT.
AND IF PHAROS WERE TO--
PHAROS? PHAROS LET HELLBENT BOTH KILL OUR BELOVED FREYA AND SLIP AWAY.
I THINK PHAROS HAS PROVEN HIS LACK OF CONSEQUENCE.
PHAROS...?
CIVIL DEFENSE CORPS BUILDING WASHINGTON, DC
I ALMOST DON'T RECOGNIZE YOU OUT OF UNIFORM.
WEARING IT DOESN'T SEEM APPROPRIATE AT THE MOMENT.
I HAVEN'T HEARD FROM YOU IN WEEKS. OUR RELATIONSHIP HAS ALWAYS BEEN HINDERED BY COMMUNICATION, BUT AT LEAST WE TRIED TO COMMUNICATE.
WAS THERE SOMETHING SPECIFIC OF WHICH YOU WANTED TO SPEAK?
THE ALIEN INVASION IN NEW YORK; I ALMOST DIED. JUST BEFORE YOU SAVED ME I CALLED OUT A NAME.
NICKY PALMER.

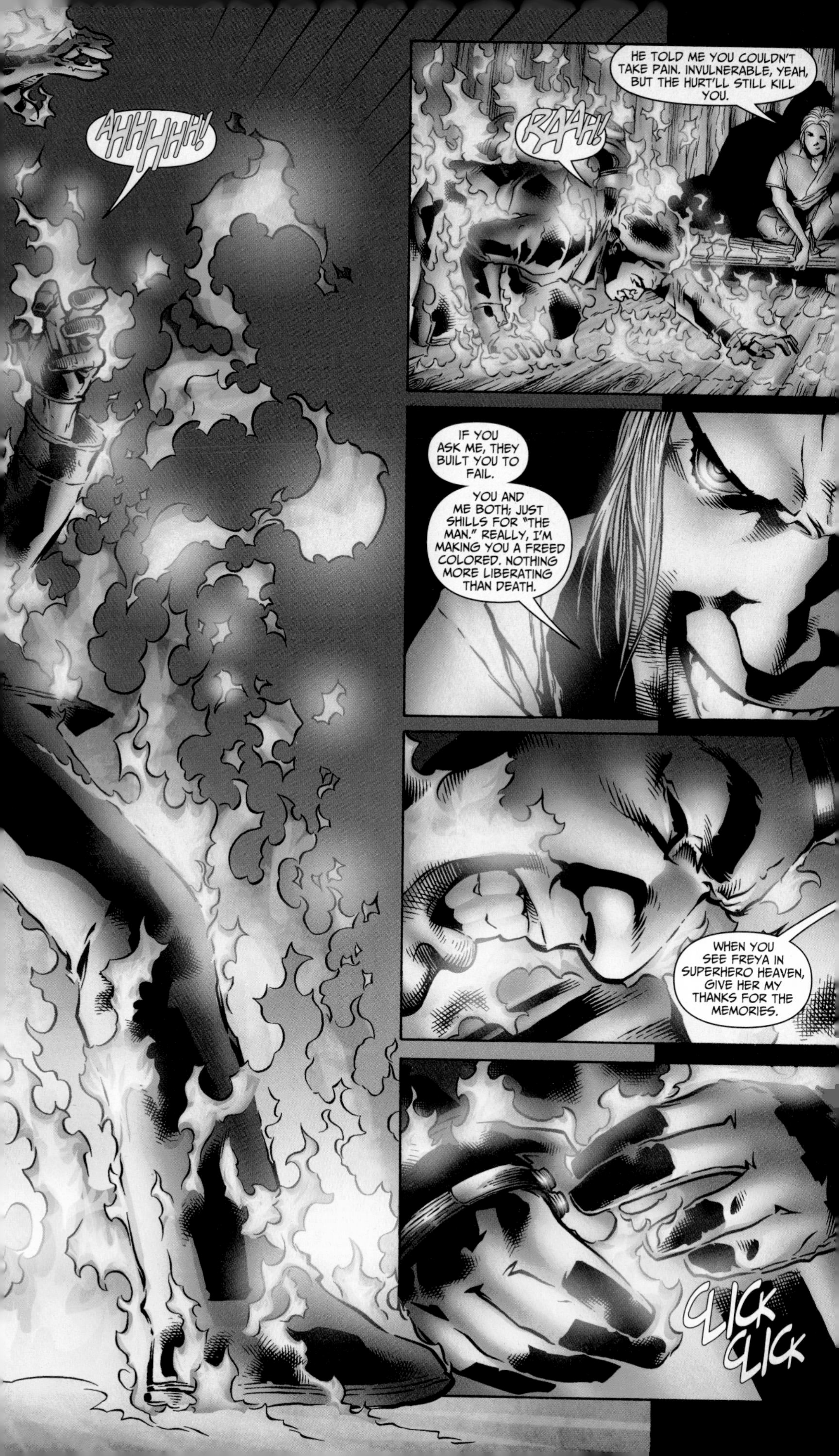
AHHHHH!
RAAH!
HE TOLD ME YOU COULDN'T TAKE PAIN. INVULNERABLE, YEAH, BUT THE HURT'LL STILL KILL YOU.
IF YOU ASK ME, THEY BUILT YOU TO FAIL.
YOU AND ME BOTH; JUST SHILLS FOR "THE MAN." REALLY, I'M MAKING YOU A FREED COLORED. NOTHING MORE LIBERATING THAN DEATH.
WHEN YOU SEE FREYA IN SUPERHERO HEAVEN, GIVE HER MY THANKS FOR THE MEMORIES.
CLICK CLICK

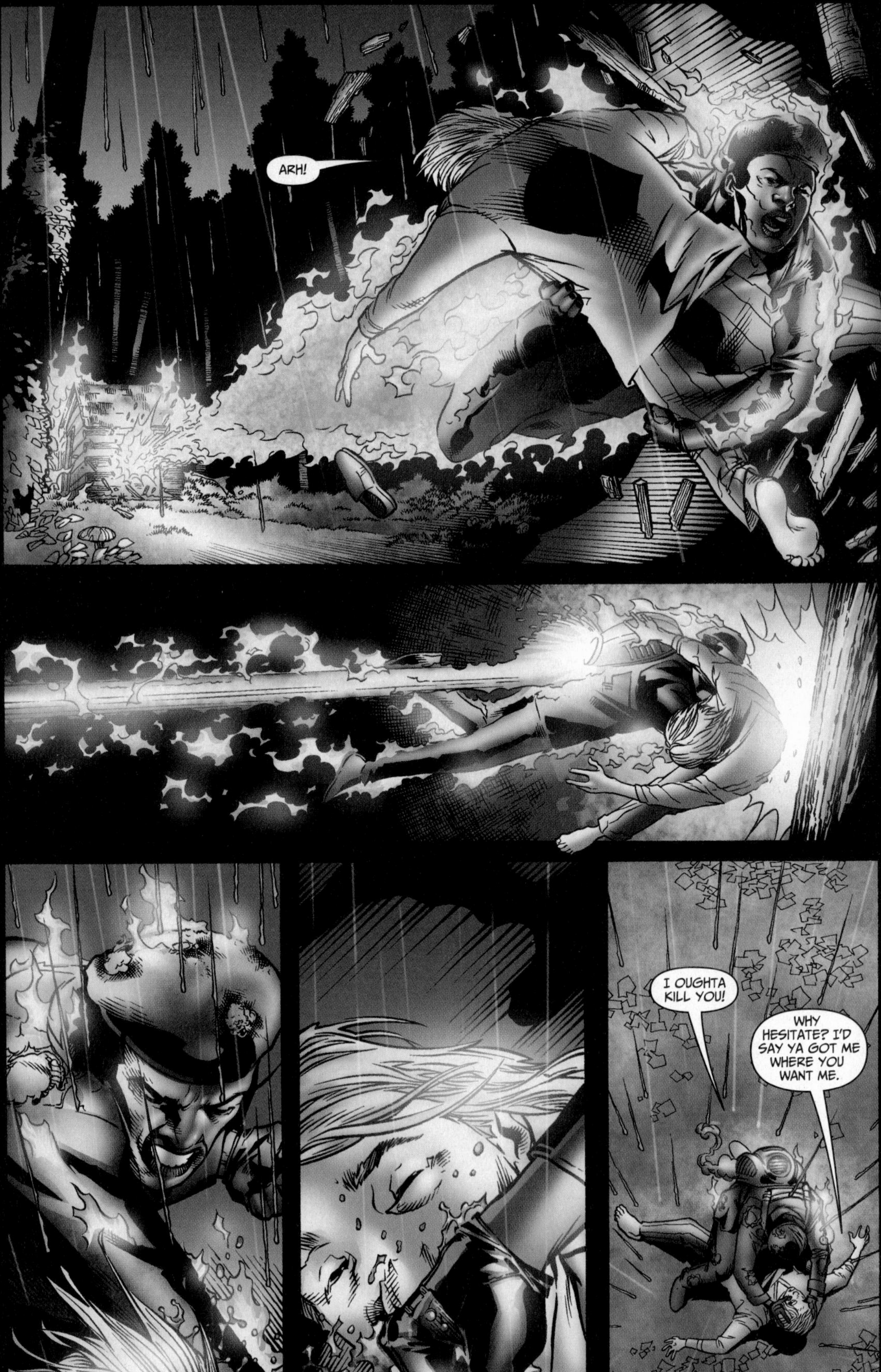
ARH!
I OUGHTA KILL YOU!
WHY HESITATE? I'D SAY YA GOT ME WHERE YOU WANT ME.

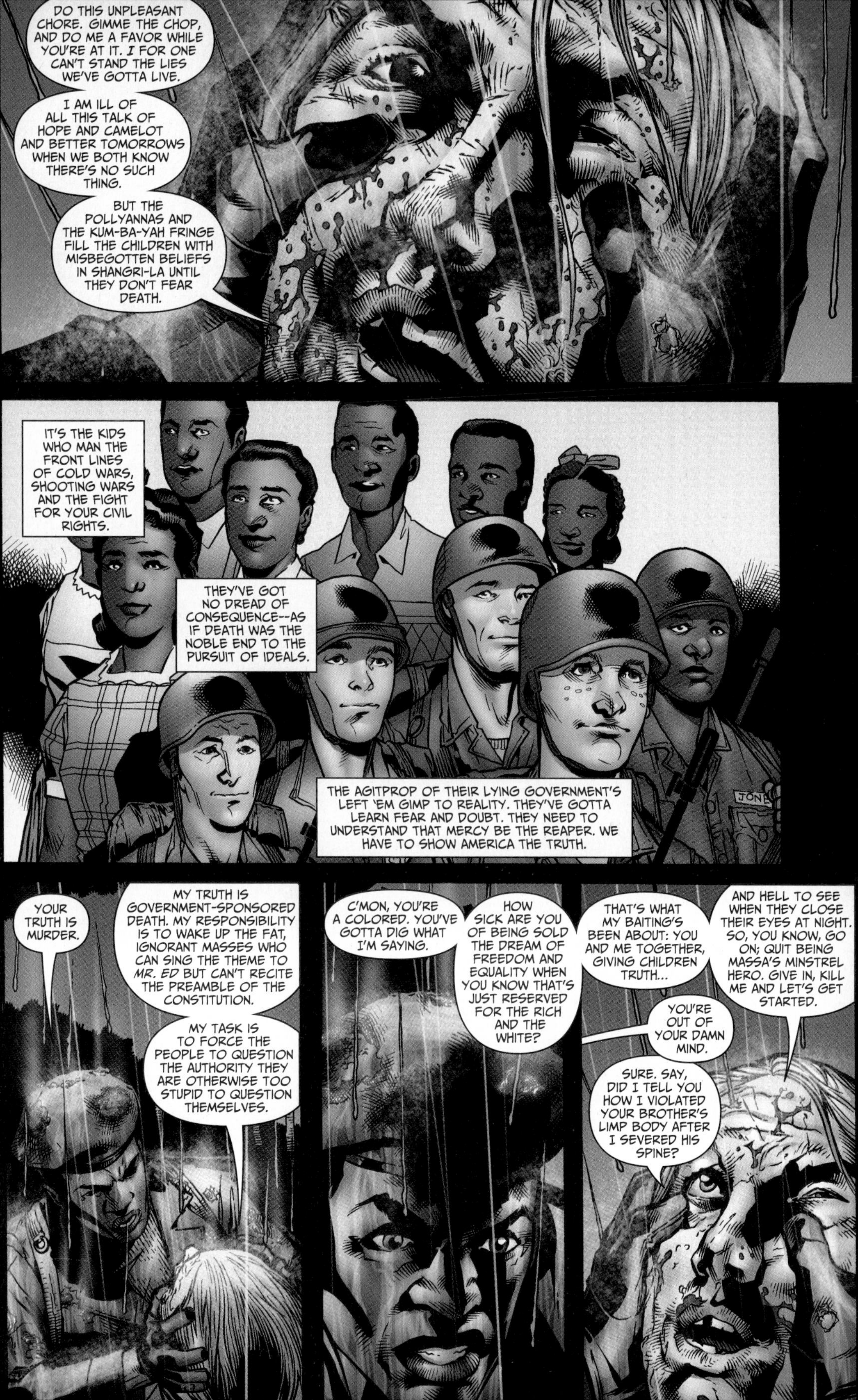

DO THIS UNPLEASANT CHORE. GIMME THE CHOP, AND DO ME A FAVOR WHILE YOU'RE AT IT. I FOR ONE CAN'T STAND THE LIES WE'VE GOTTA LIVE.
I AM ILL OF ALL THIS TALK OF HOPE AND CAMELOT AND BETTER TOMORROWS WHEN WE BOTH KNOW THERE'S NO SUCH THING.
BUT THE POLLYANNAS AND THE KUM-BA-YAH FRINGE FILL THE CHILDREN WITH MISBEGOTTEN BELIEFS IN SHANGRI-LA UNTIL THEY DON'T FEAR DEATH.
IT'S THE KIDS WHO MAN THE FRONT LINES OF COLD WARS, SHOOTING WARS AND THE FIGHT FOR YOUR CIVIL RIGHTS.
THEY'VE GOT NO DREAD OF CONSEQUENCE--AS IF DEATH WAS THE NOBLE END TO THE PURSUIT OF IDEALS.
THE AGITPROP OF THEIR LYING GOVERNMENT'S LEFT 'EM GIMP TO REALITY. THEY'VE GOTTA LEARN FEAR AND DOUBT. THEY NEED TO UNDERSTAND THAT MERCY BE THE REAPER. WE HAVE TO SHOW AMERICA THE TRUTH.
JONE
YOUR TRUTH IS MURDER.
MY TRUTH IS GOVERNMENT-SPONSORED DEATH. MY RESPONSIBILITY IS TO WAKE UP THE FAT, IGNORANT MASSES WHO CAN SING THE THEME TO MR. ED BUT CAN'T RECITE THE PREAMBLE OF THE CONSTITUTION.
MY TASK IS TO FORCE THE PEOPLE TO QUESTION THE AUTHORITY THEY ARE OTHERWISE TOO STUPID TO QUESTION THEMSELVES.
C'MON, YOU'RE A COLORED. YOU'VE GOTTA DIG WHAT I'M SAYING.
HOW SICK ARE YOU OF BEING SOLD THE DREAM OF FREEDOM AND EQUALITY WHEN YOU KNOW THAT'S JUST RESERVED FOR THE RICH AND THE WHITE?
THAT'S WHAT MY BAITING'S BEEN ABOUT: YOU AND ME TOGETHER, GIVING CHILDREN TRUTH...
AND HELL TO SEE WHEN THEY CLOSE THEIR EYES AT NIGHT. SO, YOU KNOW, GO ON; QUIT BEING MASSA'S MINSTREL HERO. GIVE IN, KILL ME AND LET'S GET STARTED.
YOU'RE OUT OF YOUR DAMN MIND.
SURE. SAY, DID I TELL YOU HOW I VIOLATED YOUR BROTHER'S LIMP BODY AFTER I SEVERED HIS SPINE?

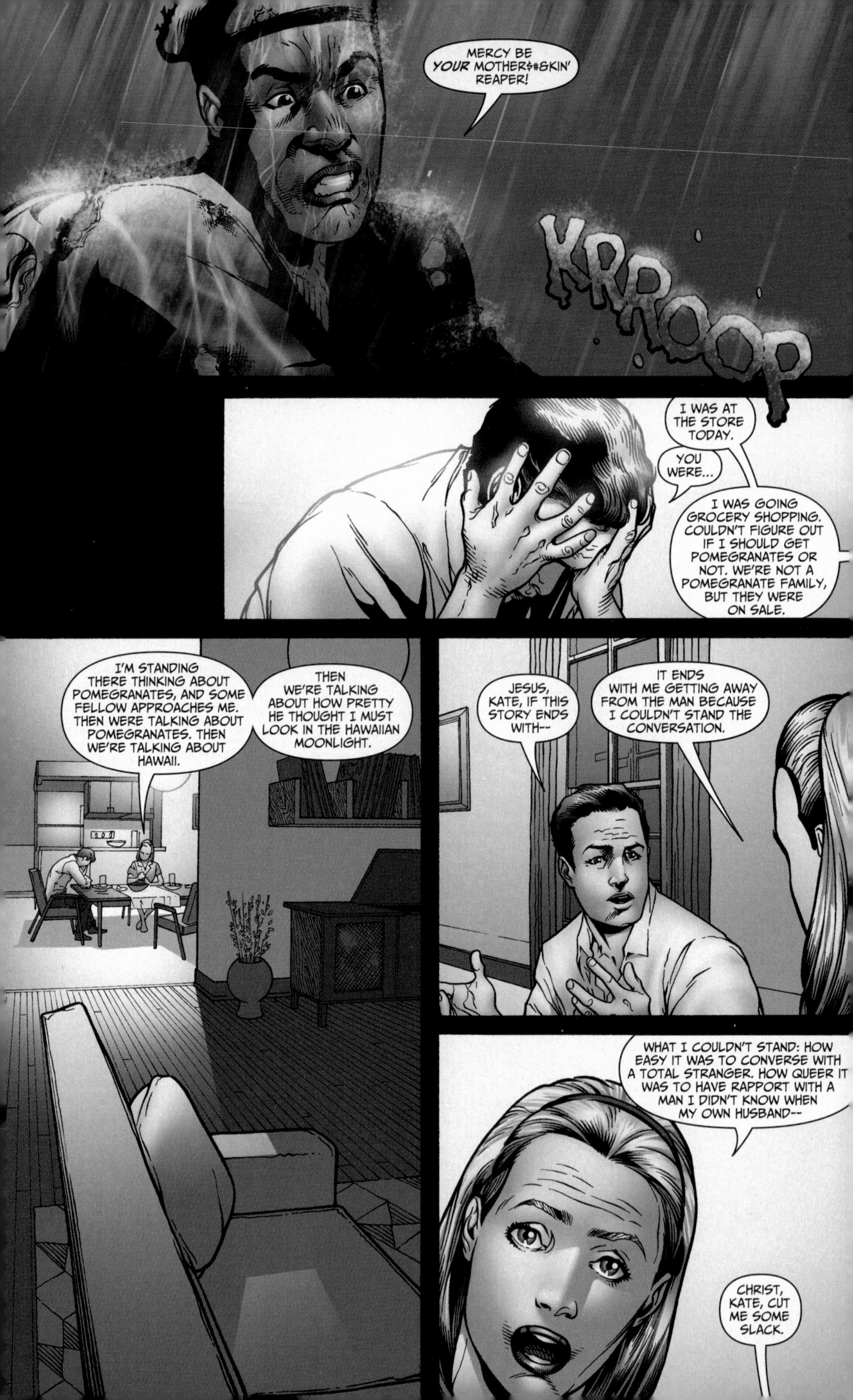
MERCY BE YOUR MOTHER$#&KIN' REAPER!
KRROOOP
I WAS AT THE STORE TODAY.
YOU WERE...
I WAS GOING GROCERY SHOPPING. COULDN'T FIGURE OUT IF I SHOULD GET POMEGRANATES OR NOT. WE'RE NOT A POMEGRANATE FAMILY, BUT THEY WERE ON SALE.
I'M STANDING THERE THINKING ABOUT POMEGRANATES, AND SOME FELLOW APPROACHES ME. THEN WERE TALKING ABOUT POMEGRANATES. THEN WE'RE TALKING ABOUT HAWAII.
THEN WE'RE TALKING ABOUT HOW PRETTY HE THOUGHT I MUST LOOK IN THE HAWAIIAN MOONLIGHT.
JESUS, KATE, IF THIS STORY ENDS WITH--
IT ENDS WITH ME GETTING AWAY FROM THE MAN BECAUSE I COULDN'T STAND THE CONVERSATION.
WHAT I COULDN'T STAND: HOW EASY IT WAS TO CONVERSE WITH A TOTAL STRANGER. HOW QUEER IT WAS TO HAVE RAPPORT WITH A MAN I DIDN'T KNOW WHEN MY OWN HUSBAND--
CHRIST, KATE, CUT ME SOME SLACK.

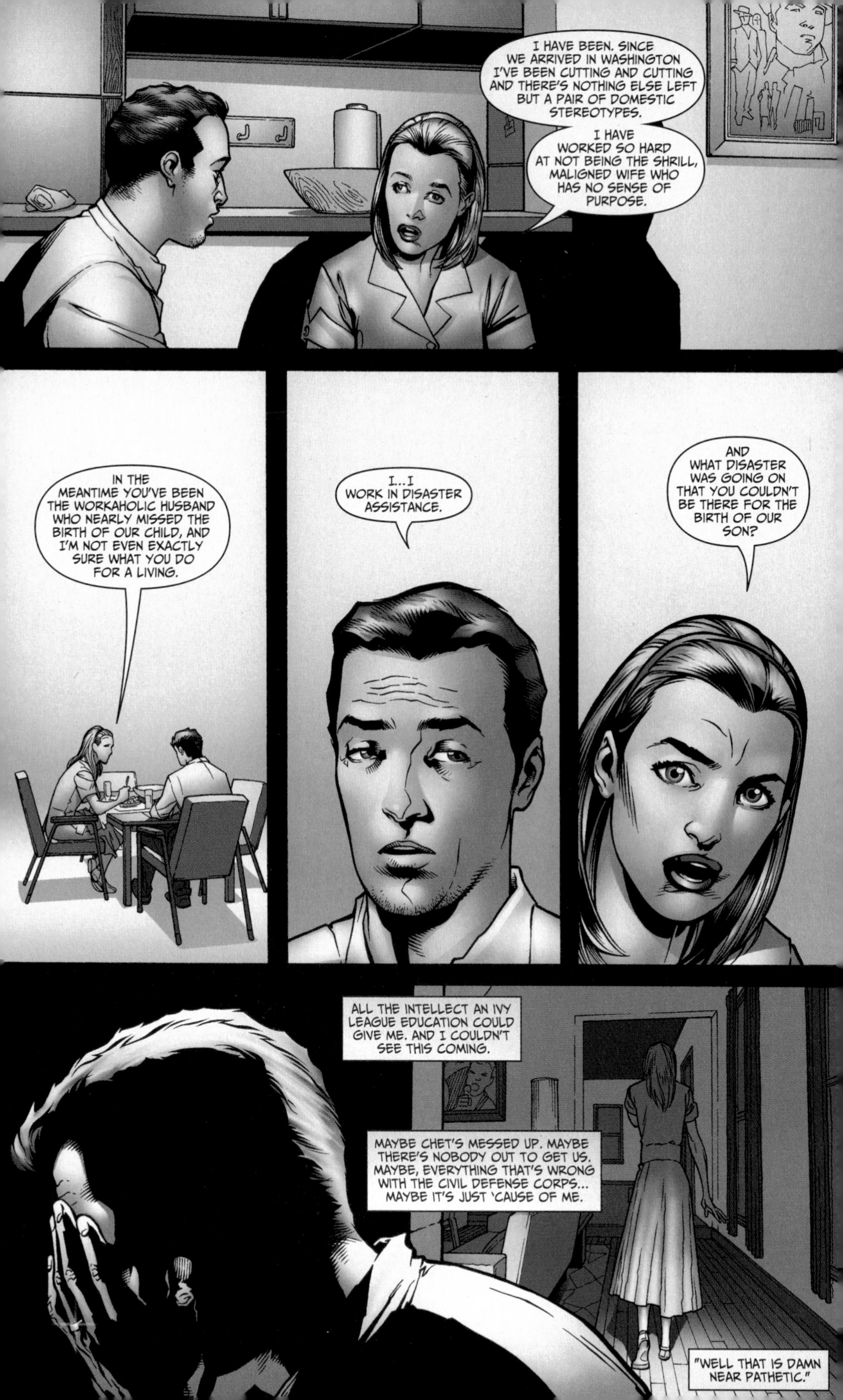
I HAVE BEEN. SINCE WE ARRIVED IN WASHINGTON I'VE BEEN CUTTING AND CUTTING AND THERE'S NOTHING ELSE LEFT BUT A PAIR OF DOMESTIC STEREOTYPES.
I HAVE WORKED SO HARD AT NOT BEING THE SHRILL, MALIGNED WIFE WHO HAS NO SENSE OF PURPOSE.
IN THE MEANTIME YOU'VE BEEN THE WORKAHOLIC HUSBAND WHO NEARLY MISSED THE BIRTH OF OUR CHILD, AND I'M NOT EVEN EXACTLY SURE WHAT YOU DO FOR A LIVING.
I...I WORK IN DISASTER ASSISTANCE.
AND WHAT DISASTER WAS GOING ON THAT YOU COULDN'T BE THERE FOR THE BIRTH OF OUR SON?
ALL THE INTELLECT AN IVY LEAGUE EDUCATION COULD GIVE ME. AND I COULDN'T SEE THIS COMING.
MAYBE CHET'S MESSED UP. MAYBE THERE'S NOBODY OUT TO GET US. MAYBE, EVERYTHING THAT'S WRONG WITH THE CIVIL DEFENSE CORPS... MAYBE IT'S JUST 'CAUSE OF ME.
"WELL THAT IS DAMN NEAR PATHETIC."

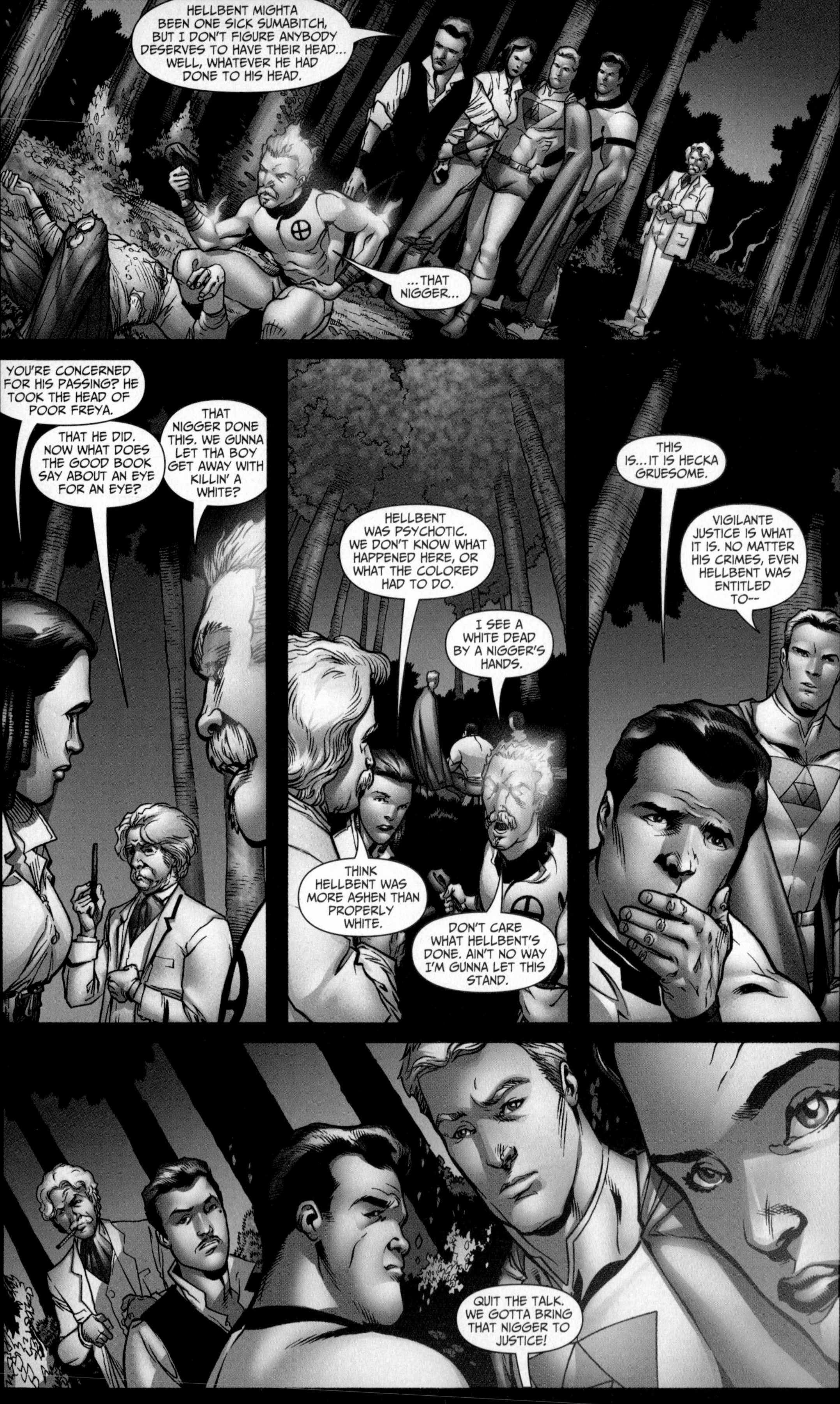
HELLBENT MIGHTA BEEN ONE SICK SUMABITCH, BUT I DON'T FIGURE ANYBODY DESERVES TO HAVE THEIR HEAD... WELL, WHATEVER HE HAD DONE TO HIS HEAD.
...THAT NIGGER...
YOU'RE CONCERNED FOR HIS PASSING? HE TOOK THE HEAD OF POOR FREYA.
THAT HE DID. NOW WHAT DOES THE GOOD BOOK SAY ABOUT AN EYE FOR AN EYE?
THAT NIGGER DONE THIS. WE GUNNA LET THA BOY GET AWAY WITH KILLIN' A WHITE?
HELLBENT WAS PSYCHOTIC. WE DON'T KNOW WHAT HAPPENED HERE, OR WHAT THE COLORED HAD TO DO.
I SEE A WHITE DEAD BY A NIGGER'S HANDS.
THINK HELLBENT WAS MORE ASHEN THAN PROPERLY WHITE.
DON'T CARE WHAT HELLBENT'S DONE. AIN'T NO WAY I'M GUNNA LET THIS STAND.
THIS IS...IT IS HECKA GRUESOME.
VIGILANTE JUSTICE IS WHAT IT IS. NO MATTER HIS CRIMES, EVEN HELLBENT WAS ENTITLED TO--
QUIT THE TALK. WE GOTTA BRING THAT NIGGER TO JUSTICE!

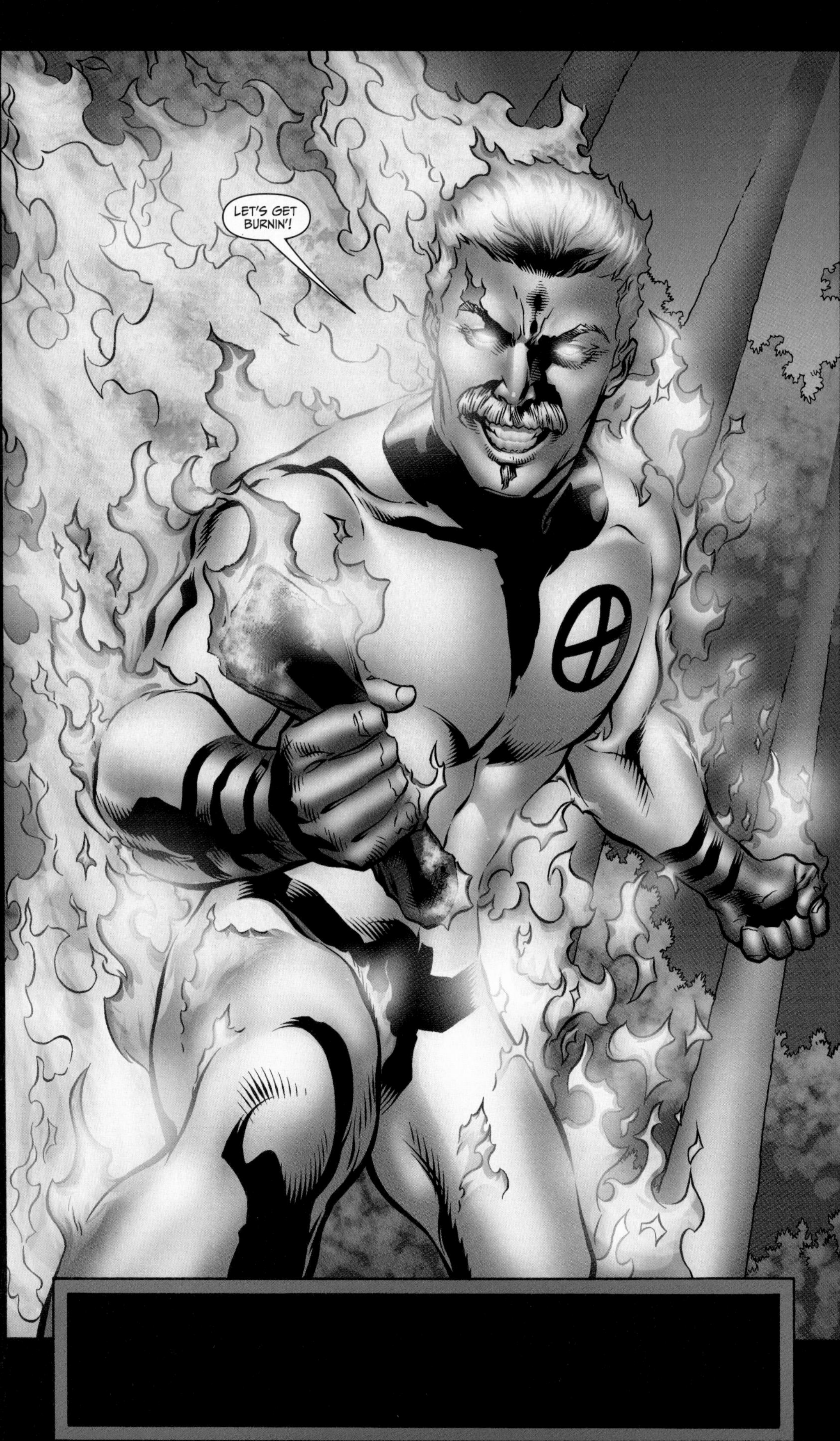
LET'S GET BURNIN'!

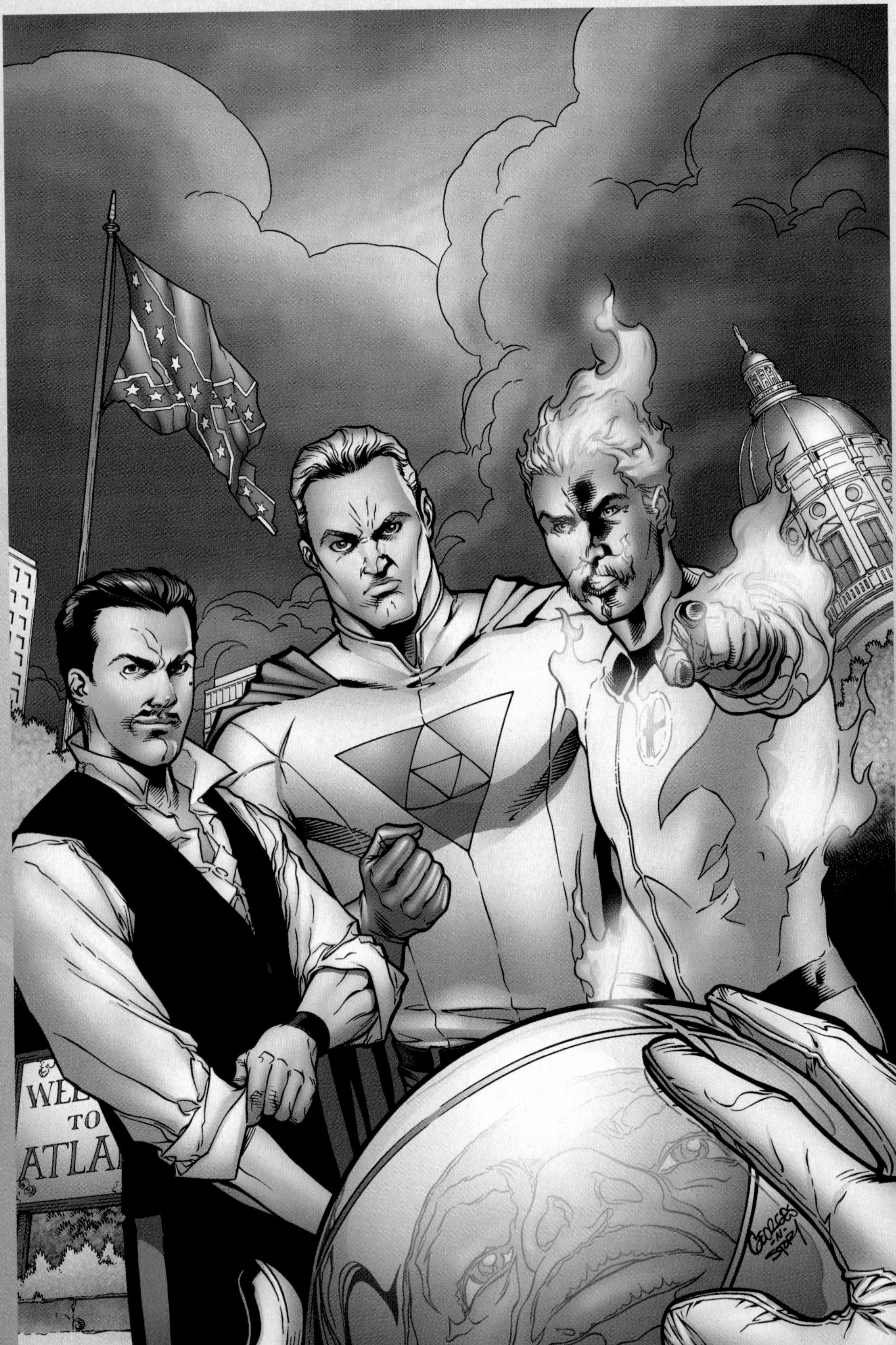
WEL
TO
ATLA

COVER #6

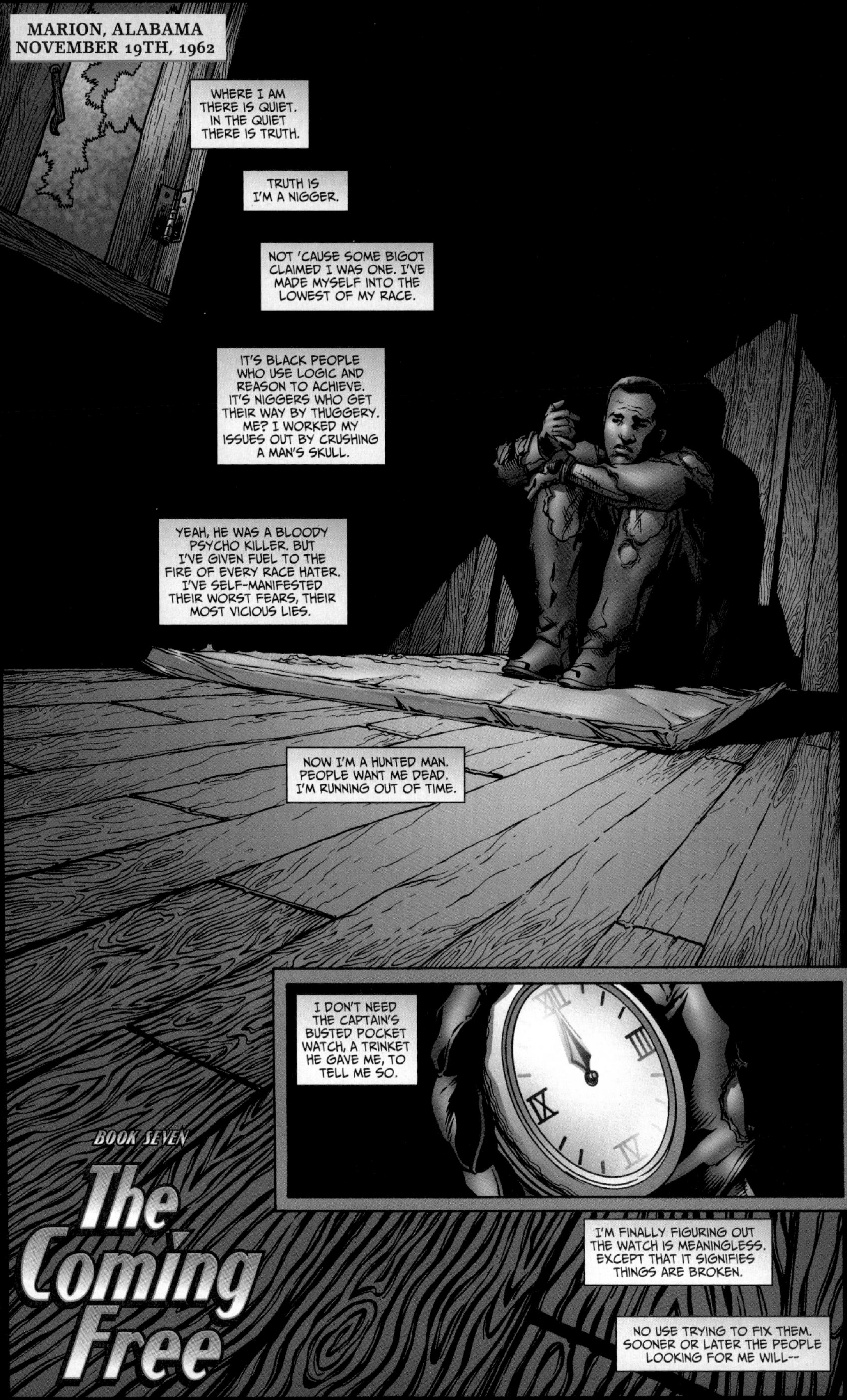
MARION, ALABAMA
NOVEMBER 19TH, 1962
WHERE I AM THERE IS QUIET. IN THE QUIET THERE IS TRUTH.
TRUTH IS I'M A NIGGER.
NOT 'CAUSE SOME BIGOT CLAIMED I WAS ONE. I'VE MADE MYSELF INTO THE LOWEST OF MY RACE.
IT'S BLACK PEOPLE WHO USE LOGIC AND REASON TO ACHIEVE. IT'S NIGGERS WHO GET THEIR WAY BY THUGGERY. ME? I WORKED MY ISSUES OUT BY CRUSHING A MAN'S SKULL.
YEAH, HE WAS A BLOODY PSYCHO KILLER. BUT I'VE GIVEN FUEL TO THE FIRE OF EVERY RACE HATER. I'VE SELF-MANIFESTED THEIR WORST FEARS, THEIR MOST VICIOUS LIES.
NOW I'M A HUNTED MAN. PEOPLE WANT ME DEAD. I'M RUNNING OUT OF TIME.
I DON'T NEED THE CAPTAIN'S BUSTED POCKET WATCH, A TRINKET HE GAVE ME, TO TELL ME SO.
BOOK SEVEN
The Coming Free
I'M FINALLY FIGURING OUT THE WATCH IS MEANINGLESS. EXCEPT THAT IT SIGNIFIES THINGS ARE BROKEN.
NO USE TRYING TO FIX THEM. SOONER OR LATER THE PEOPLE LOOKING FOR ME WILL--

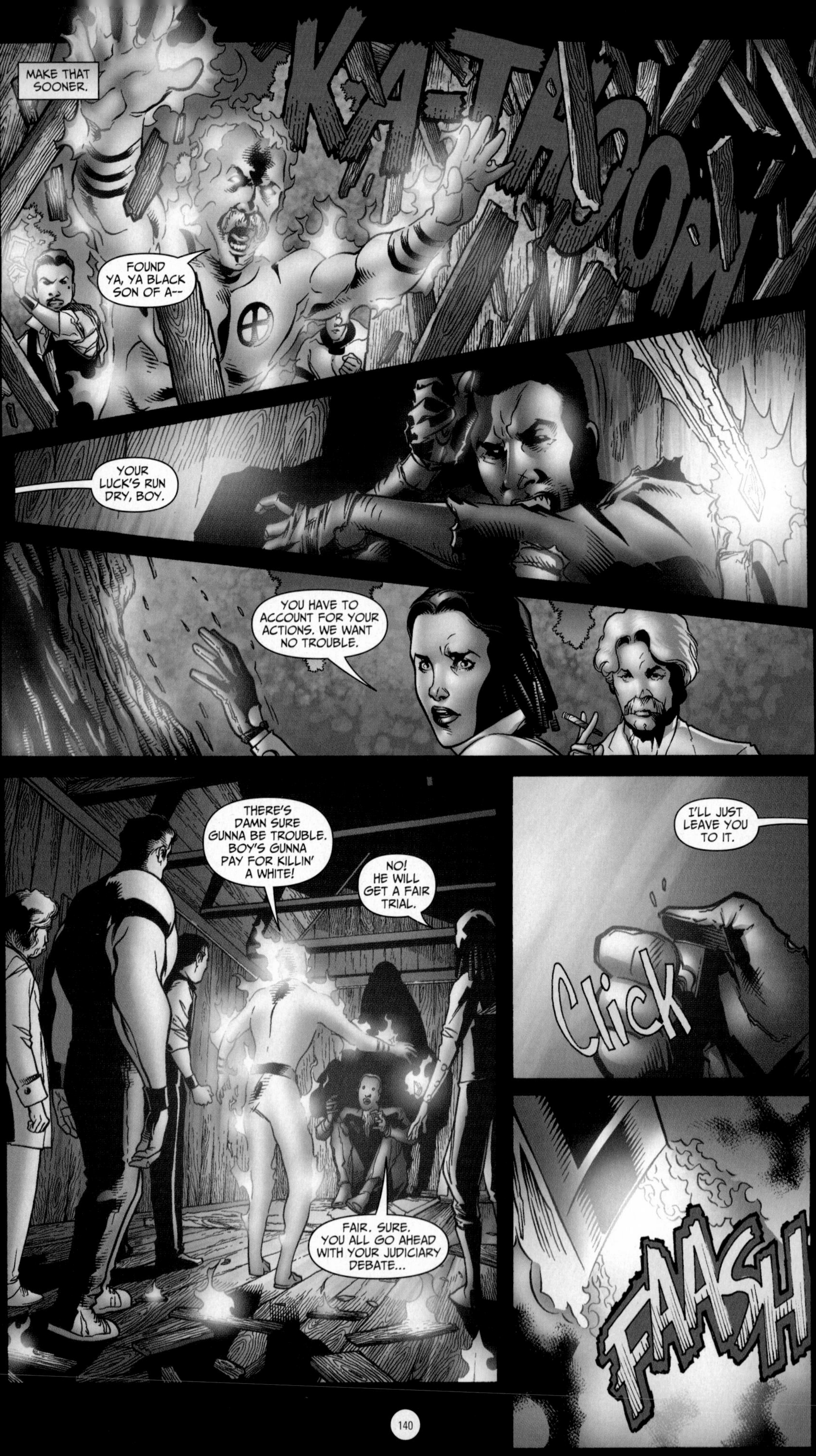
MAKE THAT SOONER.
KA-TA-BOOM
FOUND YA, YA BLACK SON OF A--
YOUR LUCK'S RUN DRY, BOY.
YOU HAVE TO ACCOUNT FOR YOUR ACTIONS. WE WANT NO TROUBLE.
THERE'S DAMN SURE GUNNA BE TROUBLE. BOY'S GUNNA PAY FOR KILLIN' A WHITE!
NO! HE WILL GET A FAIR TRIAL.
FAIR. SURE. YOU ALL GO AHEAD WITH YOUR JUDICIARY DEBATE...
I'LL JUST LEAVE YOU TO IT.
CLICK
FAASH

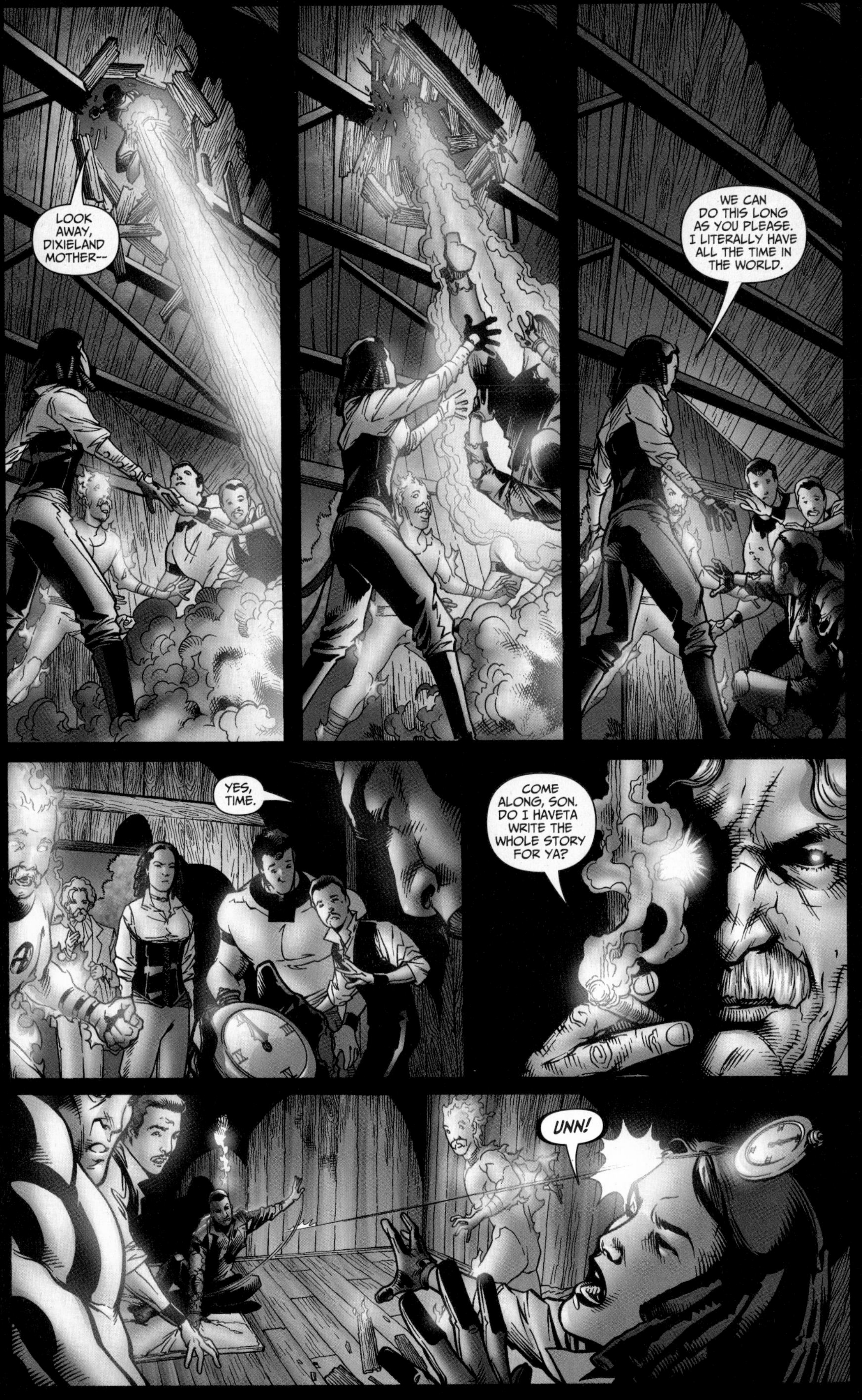
LOOK AWAY, DIXIELAND MOTHER--
WE CAN DO THIS LONG AS YOU PLEASE. I LITERALLY HAVE ALL THE TIME IN THE WORLD.
YES, TIME.
COME ALONG, SON. DO I HAVETA WRITE THE WHOLE STORY FOR YA?
UNN!

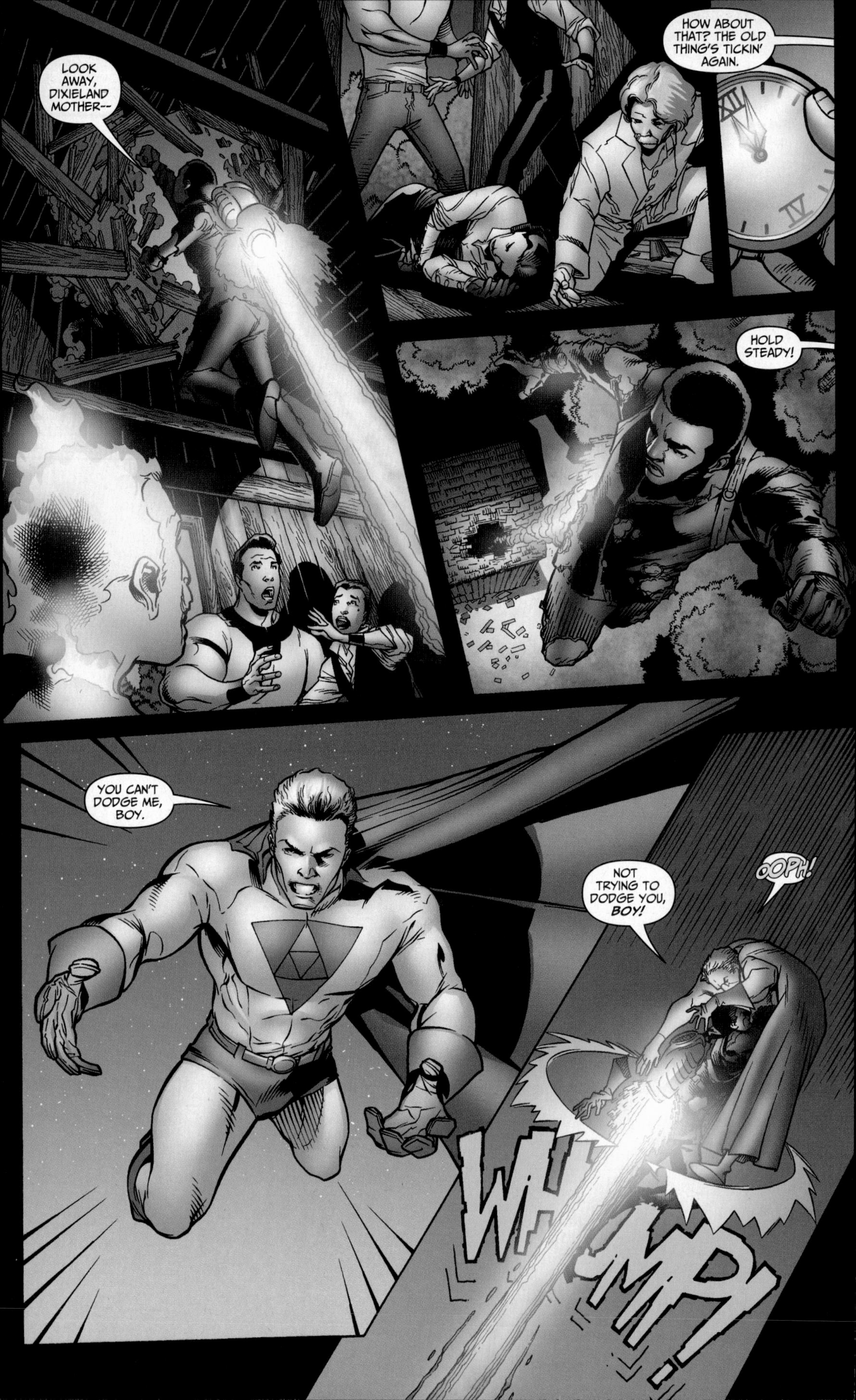
LOOK AWAY, DIXIELAND MOTHER--
HOW ABOUT THAT? THE OLD THING'S TICKIN' AGAIN.
HOLD STEADY!
YOU CAN'T DODGE ME, BOY.
NOT TRYING TO DODGE YOU, BOY!
OOPH!
WHUMP!

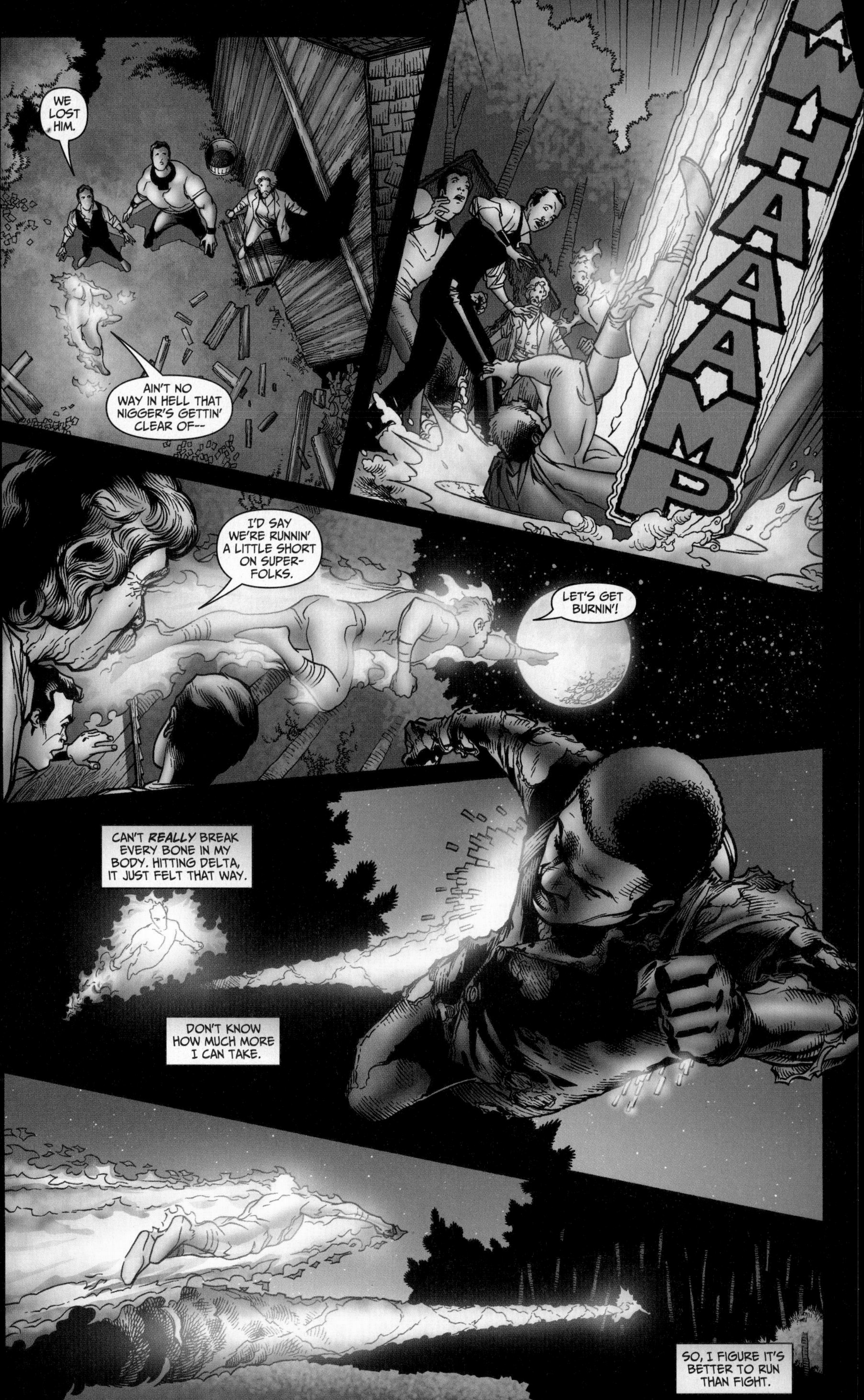
WE LOST HIM.
AIN'T NO WAY IN HELL THAT NIGGER'S GETTIN' CLEAR OF--
WHAAAAMP
I'D SAY WE'RE RUNNIN' A LITTLE SHORT ON SUPER-FOLKS.
LET'S GET BURNIN'!
CAN'T REALLY BREAK EVERY BONE IN MY BODY. HITTING DELTA, IT JUST FELT THAT WAY.
DON'T KNOW HOW MUCH MORE I CAN TAKE.
SO, I FIGURE IT'S BETTER TO RUN THAN FIGHT.

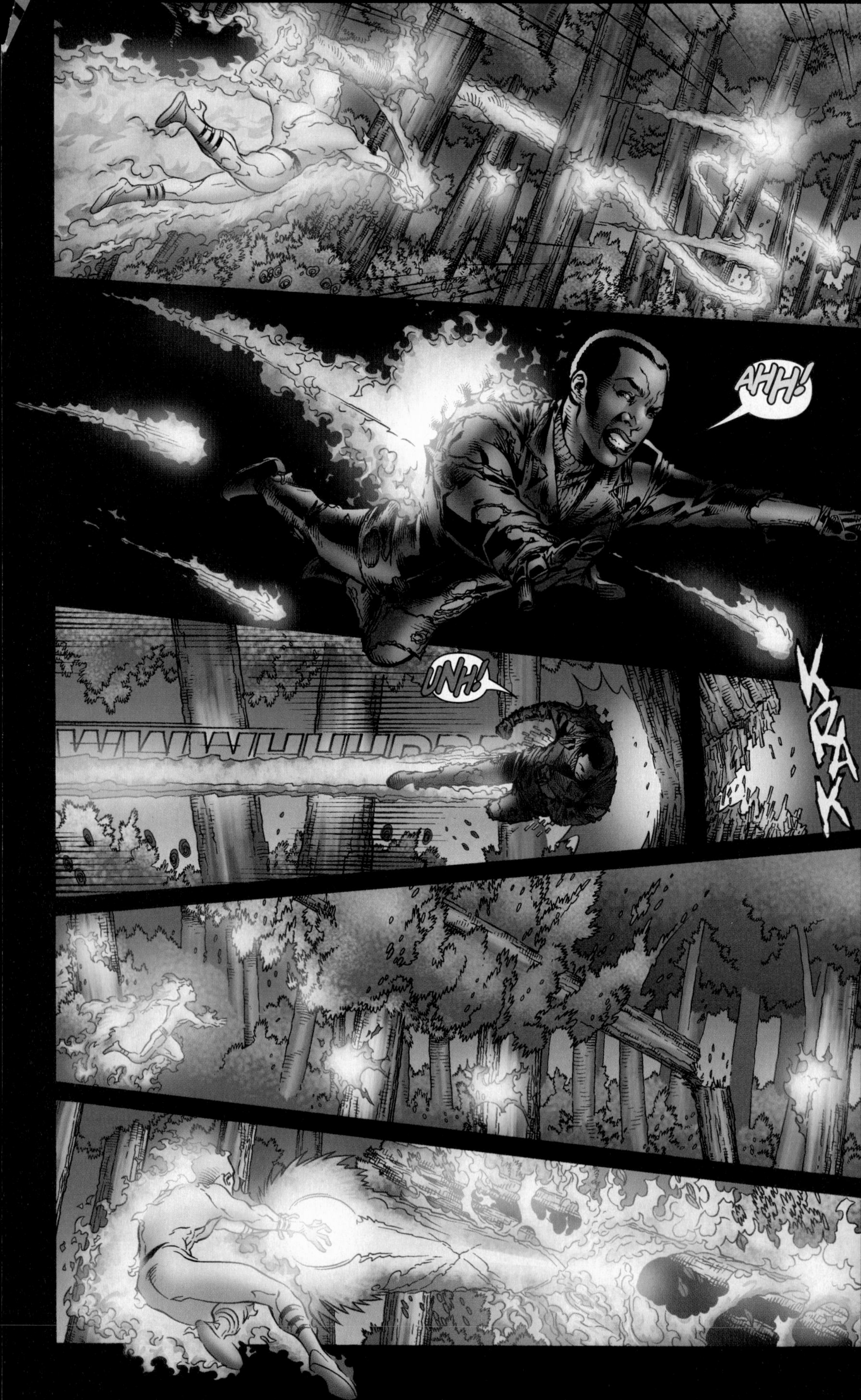

AHH!
UNH!
KRAK

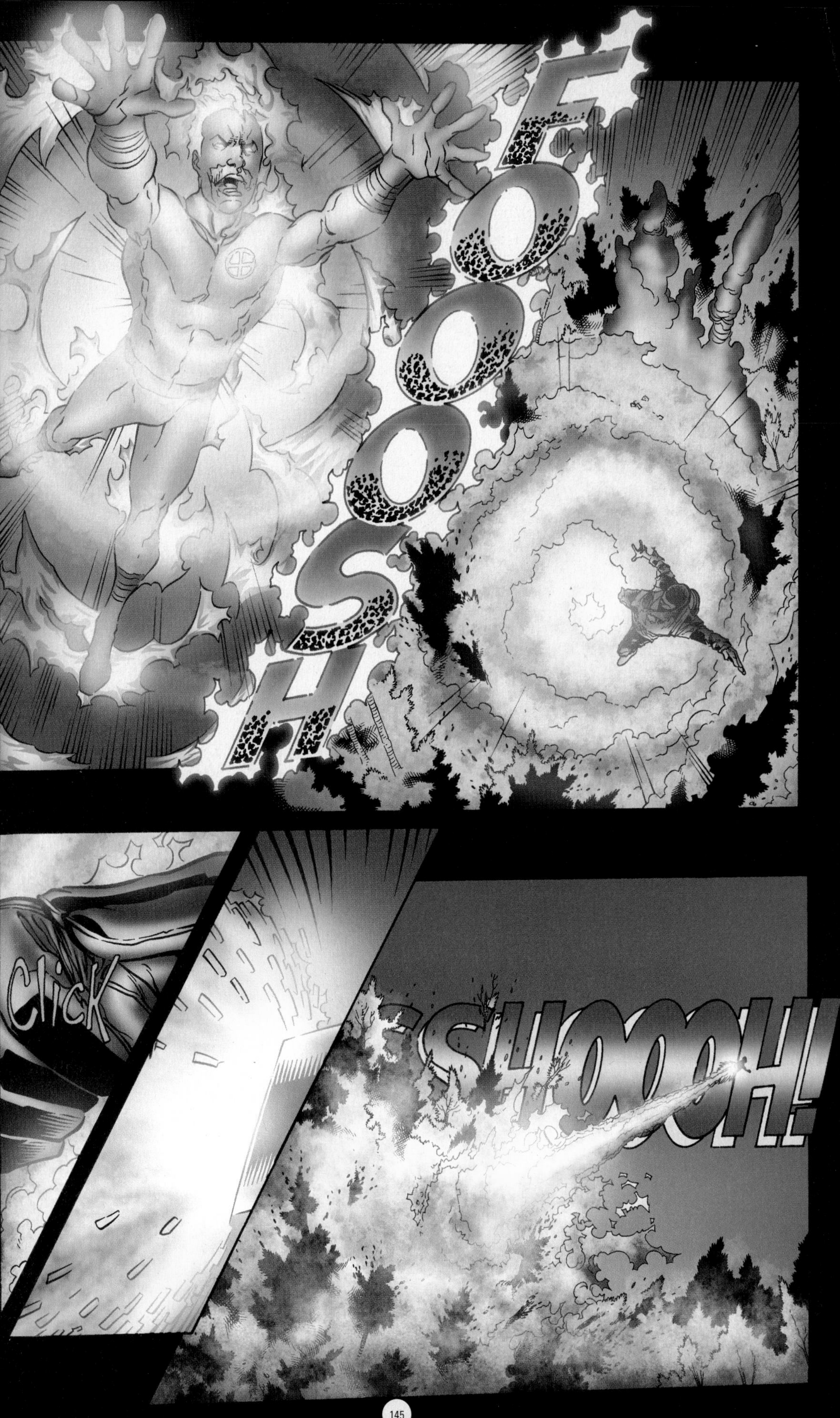
FOOOSH
CLICK
FSHOOOOH!

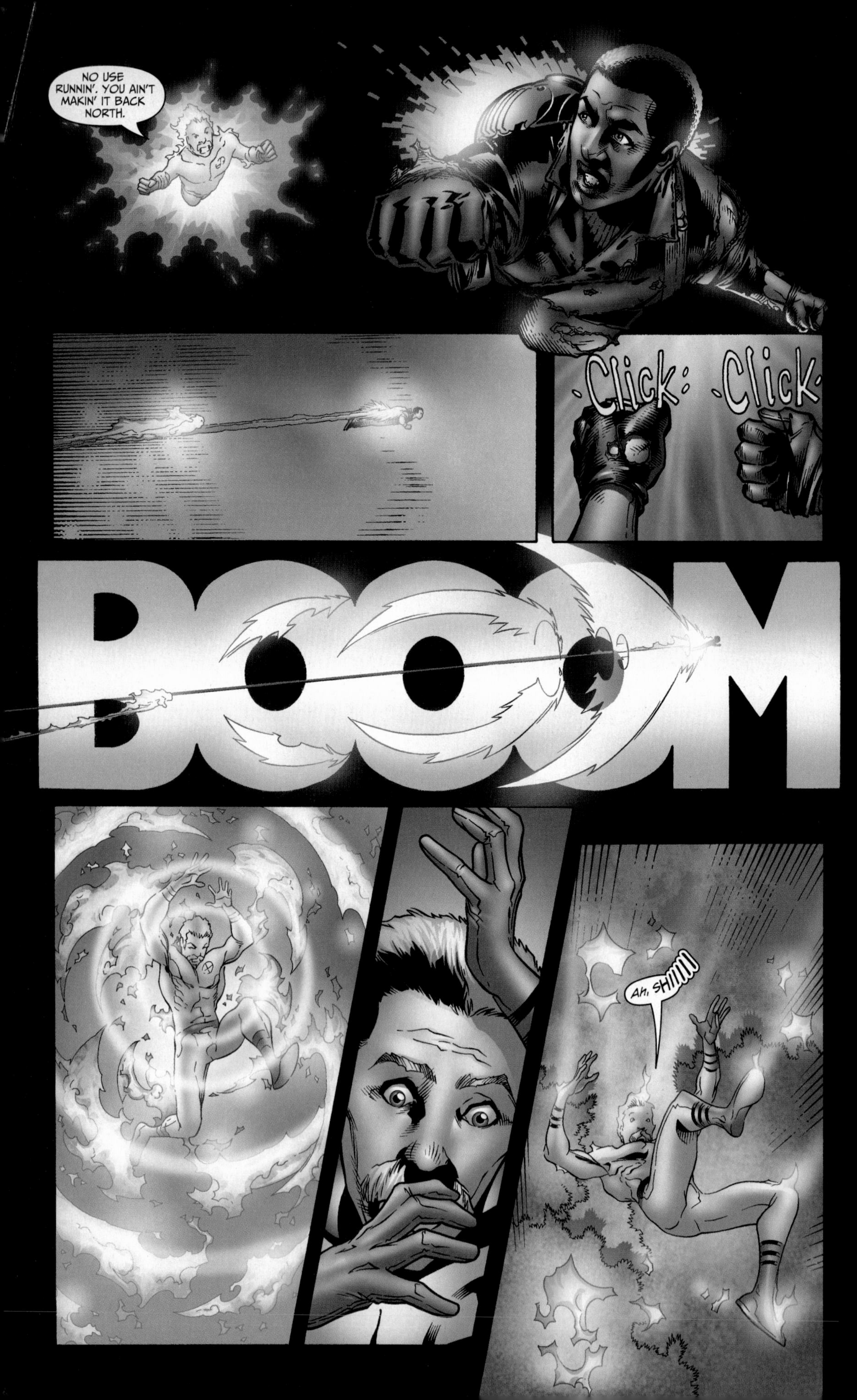
NO USE RUNNIN'. YOU AIN'T MAKIN' IT BACK NORTH.
CLICK: CLICK
BOOOOM
AH, SHIIIII

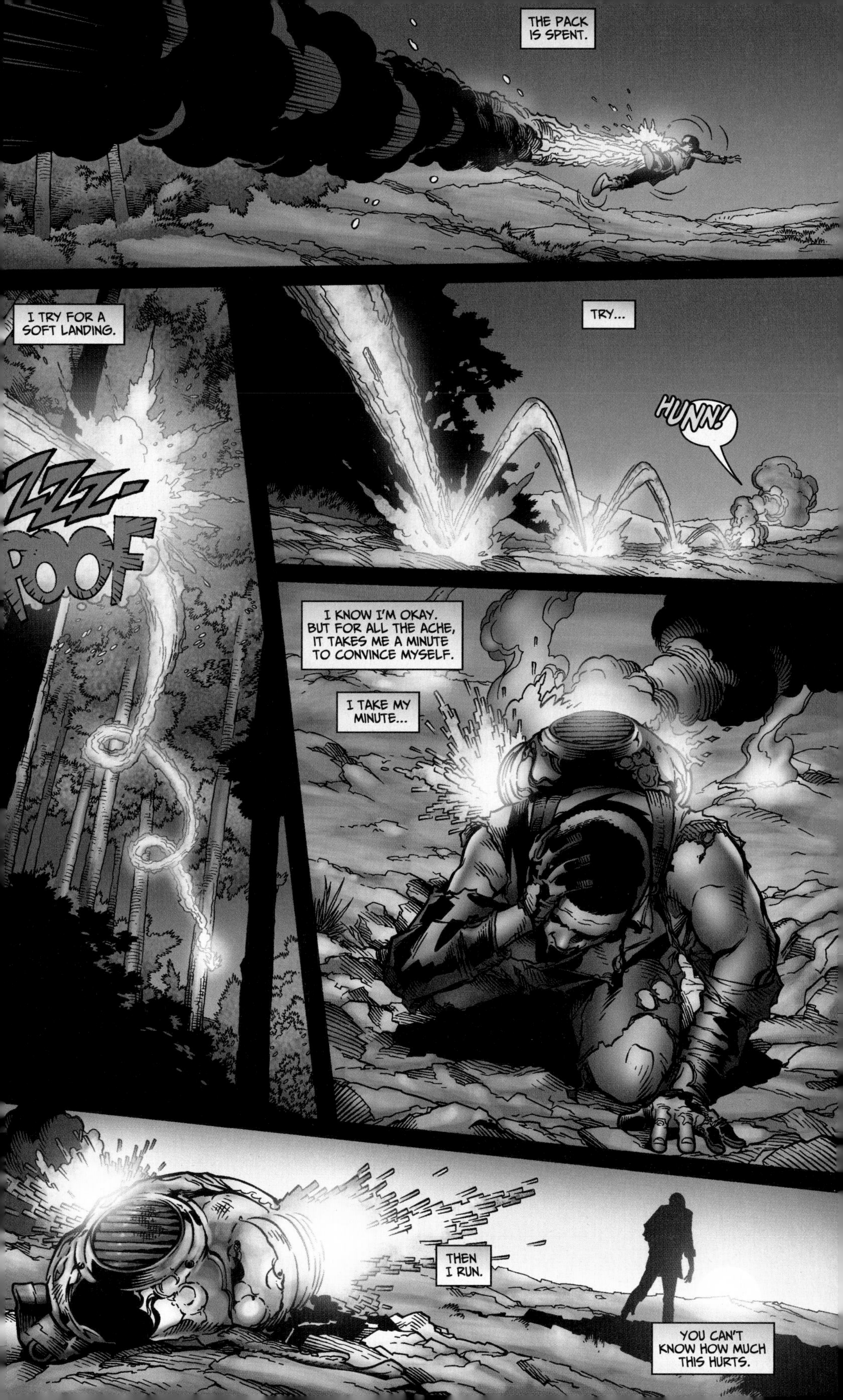
THE PACK IS SPENT.
I TRY FOR A SOFT LANDING.
ZZZZ-POOF
TRY...
HUNN!
I KNOW I'M OKAY. BUT FOR ALL THE ACHE, IT TAKES ME A MINUTE TO CONVINCE MYSELF.
I TAKE MY MINUTE...
THEN I RUN.
YOU CAN'T KNOW HOW MUCH THIS HURTS.

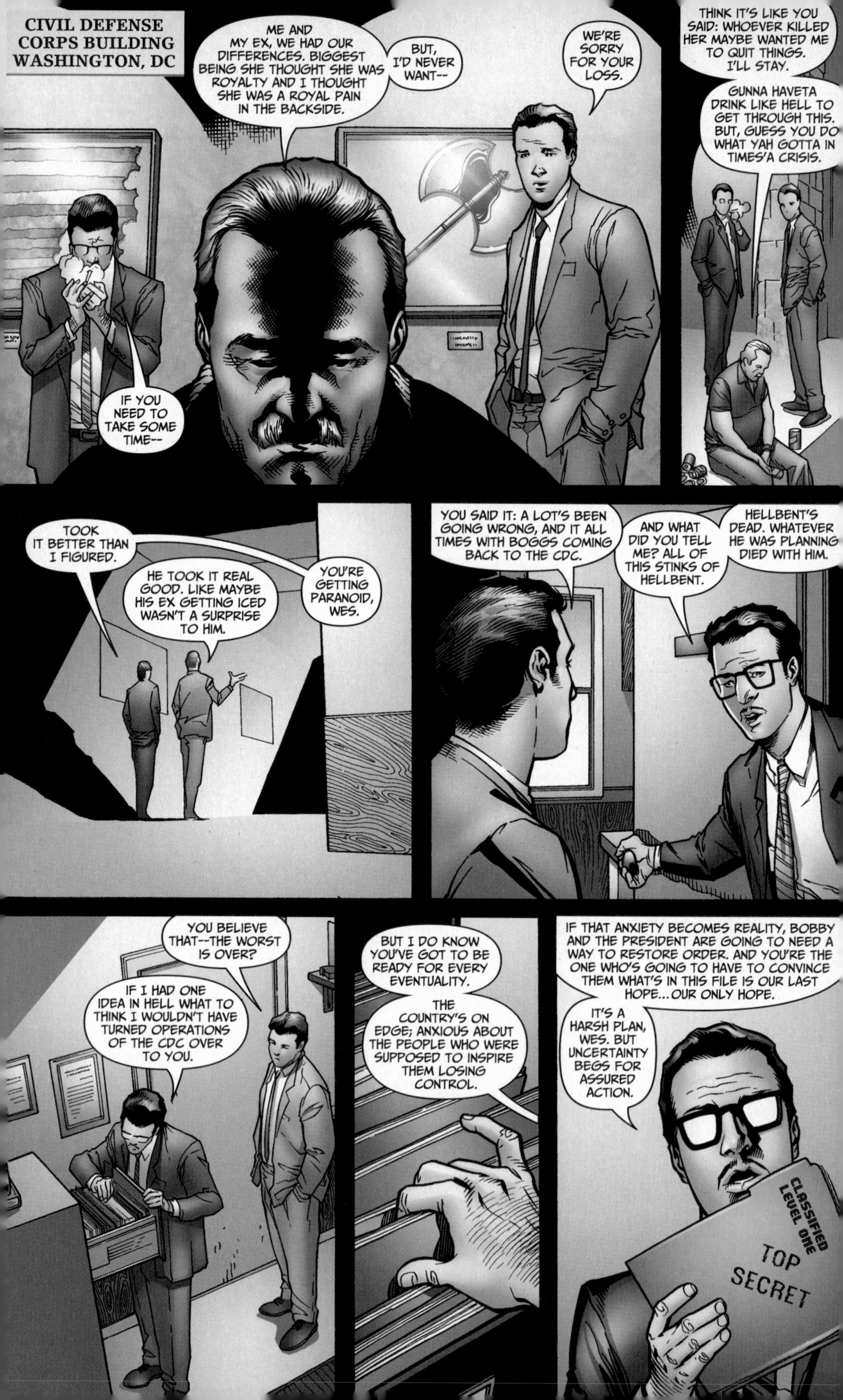
CIVIL DEFENSE CORPS BUILDING WASHINGTON, DC
ME AND MY EX, WE HAD OUR DIFFERENCES. BIGGEST BEING SHE THOUGHT SHE WAS ROYALTY AND I THOUGHT SHE WAS A ROYAL PAIN IN THE BACKSIDE.
BUT, I'D NEVER WANT--
IF YOU NEED TO TAKE SOME TIME--
WE'RE SORRY FOR YOUR LOSS.
THINK IT'S LIKE YOU SAID: WHOEVER KILLED HER MAYBE WANTED ME TO QUIT THINGS. I'LL STAY.
GUNNA HAVETA DRINK LIKE HELL TO GET THROUGH THIS. BUT, GUESS YOU DO WHAT YAH GOTTA IN TIMES'A CRISIS.
TOOK IT BETTER THAN I FIGURED.
HE TOOK IT REAL GOOD. LIKE MAYBE HIS EX GETTING ICED WASN'T A SURPRISE TO HIM.
YOU'RE GETTING PARANOID, WES.
YOU SAID IT: A LOT'S BEEN GOING WRONG, AND IT ALL TIMES WITH BOGGS COMING BACK TO THE CDC.
AND WHAT DID YOU TELL ME? ALL OF THIS STINKS OF HELLBENT.
HELLBENT'S DEAD. WHATEVER HE WAS PLANNING DIED WITH HIM.
YOU BELIEVE THAT--THE WORST IS OVER?
IF I HAD ONE IDEA IN HELL WHAT TO THINK I WOULDN'T HAVE TURNED OPERATIONS OF THE CDC OVER TO YOU.
BUT I DO KNOW YOU'VE GOT TO BE READY FOR EVERY EVENTUALITY.
THE COUNTRY'S ON EDGE; ANXIOUS ABOUT THE PEOPLE WHO WERE SUPPOSED TO INSPIRE THEM LOSING CONTROL.
IF THAT ANXIETY BECOMES REALITY, BOBBY AND THE PRESIDENT ARE GOING TO NEED A WAY TO RESTORE ORDER. AND YOU'RE THE ONE WHO'S GOING TO HAVE TO CONVINCE THEM WHAT'S IN THIS FILE IS OUR LAST HOPE...OUR ONLY HOPE.
IT'S A HARSH PLAN, WES. BUT UNCERTAINTY BEGS FOR ASSURED ACTION.
CLASSIFIED LEVEL ONE
TOP SECRET

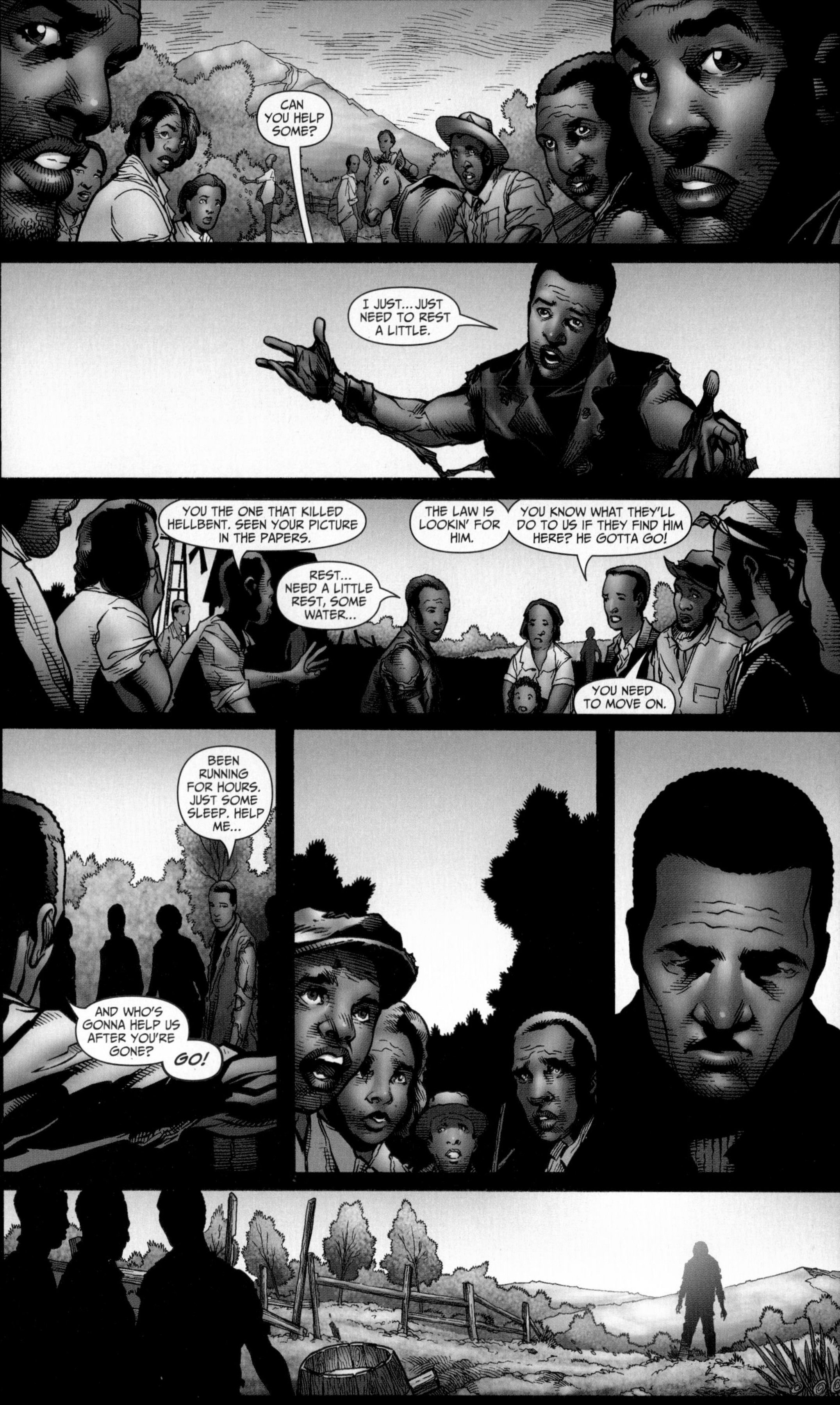
CAN YOU HELP SOME?
I JUST... JUST NEED TO REST A LITTLE.
YOU THE ONE THAT KILLED HELLBENT. SEEN YOUR PICTURE IN THE PAPERS.
REST... NEED A LITTLE REST, SOME WATER...
THE LAW IS LOOKIN' FOR HIM.
YOU KNOW WHAT THEY'LL DO TO US IF THEY FIND HIM HERE? HE GOTTA GO!
YOU NEED TO MOVE ON.
BEEN RUNNING FOR HOURS. JUST SOME SLEEP. HELP ME...
AND WHO'S GONNA HELP US AFTER YOU'RE GONE?
GO!

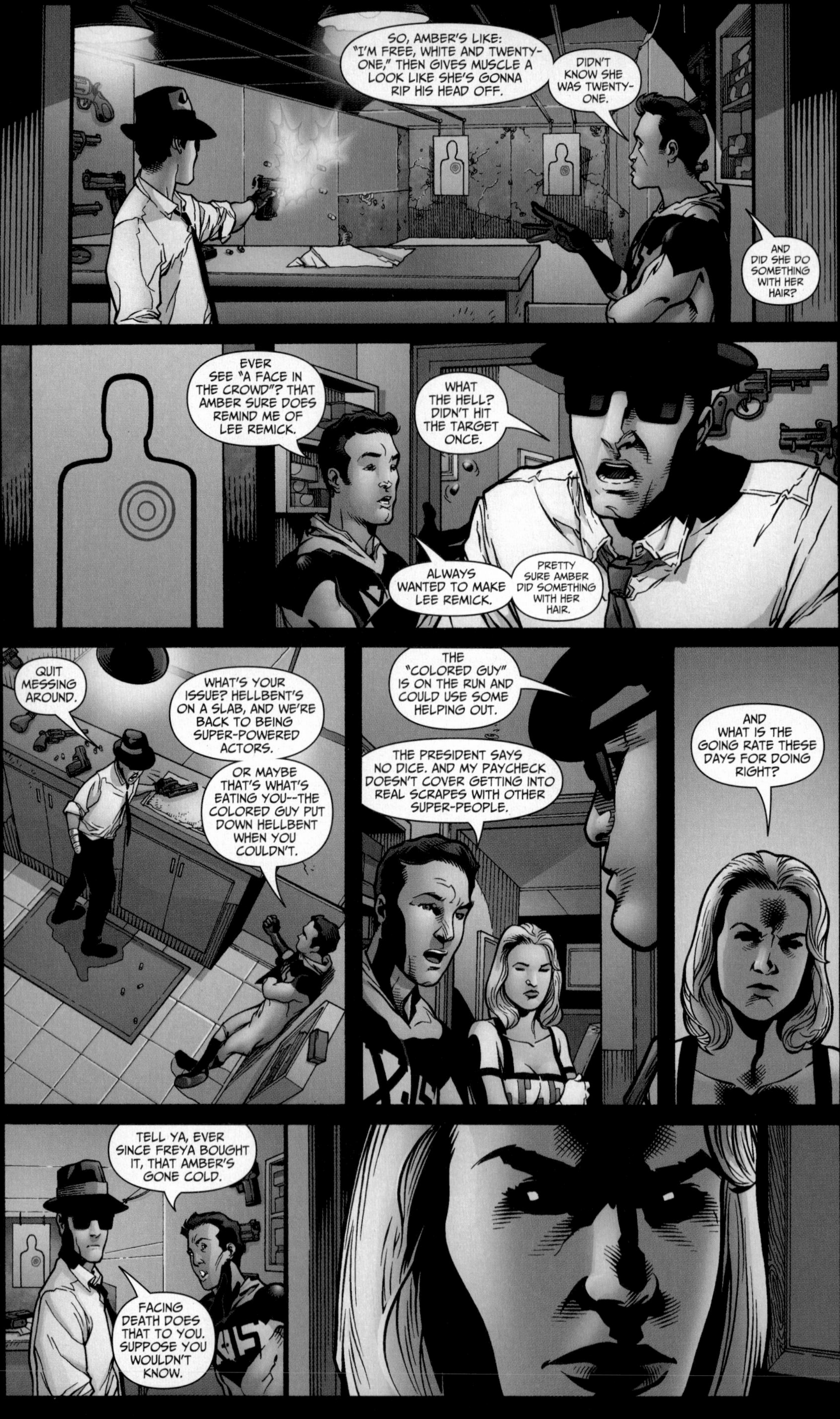
SO, AMBER'S LIKE: "I'M FREE, WHITE AND TWENTY-ONE," THEN GIVES MUSCLE A LOOK LIKE SHE'S GONNA RIP HIS HEAD OFF.
DIDN'T KNOW SHE WAS TWENTY-ONE.
AND DID SHE DO SOMETHING WITH HER HAIR?
EVER SEE "A FACE IN THE CROWD"? THAT AMBER SURE DOES REMIND ME OF LEE REMICK.
WHAT THE HELL? DIDN'T HIT THE TARGET ONCE.
ALWAYS WANTED TO MAKE LEE REMICK.
PRETTY SURE AMBER DID SOMETHING WITH HER HAIR.
QUIT MESSING AROUND.
WHAT'S YOUR ISSUE? HELLBENT'S ON A SLAB, AND WE'RE BACK TO BEING SUPER-POWERED ACTORS.
OR MAYBE THAT'S WHAT'S EATING YOU--THE COLORED GUY PUT DOWN HELLBENT WHEN YOU COULDN'T.
THE "COLORED GUY" IS ON THE RUN AND COULD USE SOME HELPING OUT.
THE PRESIDENT SAYS NO DICE. AND MY PAYCHECK DOESN'T COVER GETTING INTO REAL SCRAPES WITH OTHER SUPER-PEOPLE.
AND WHAT IS THE GOING RATE THESE DAYS FOR DOING RIGHT?
TELL YA, EVER SINCE FREYA BOUGHT IT, THAT AMBER'S GONE COLD.
FACING DEATH DOES THAT TO YOU. SUPPOSE YOU WOULDN'T KNOW.

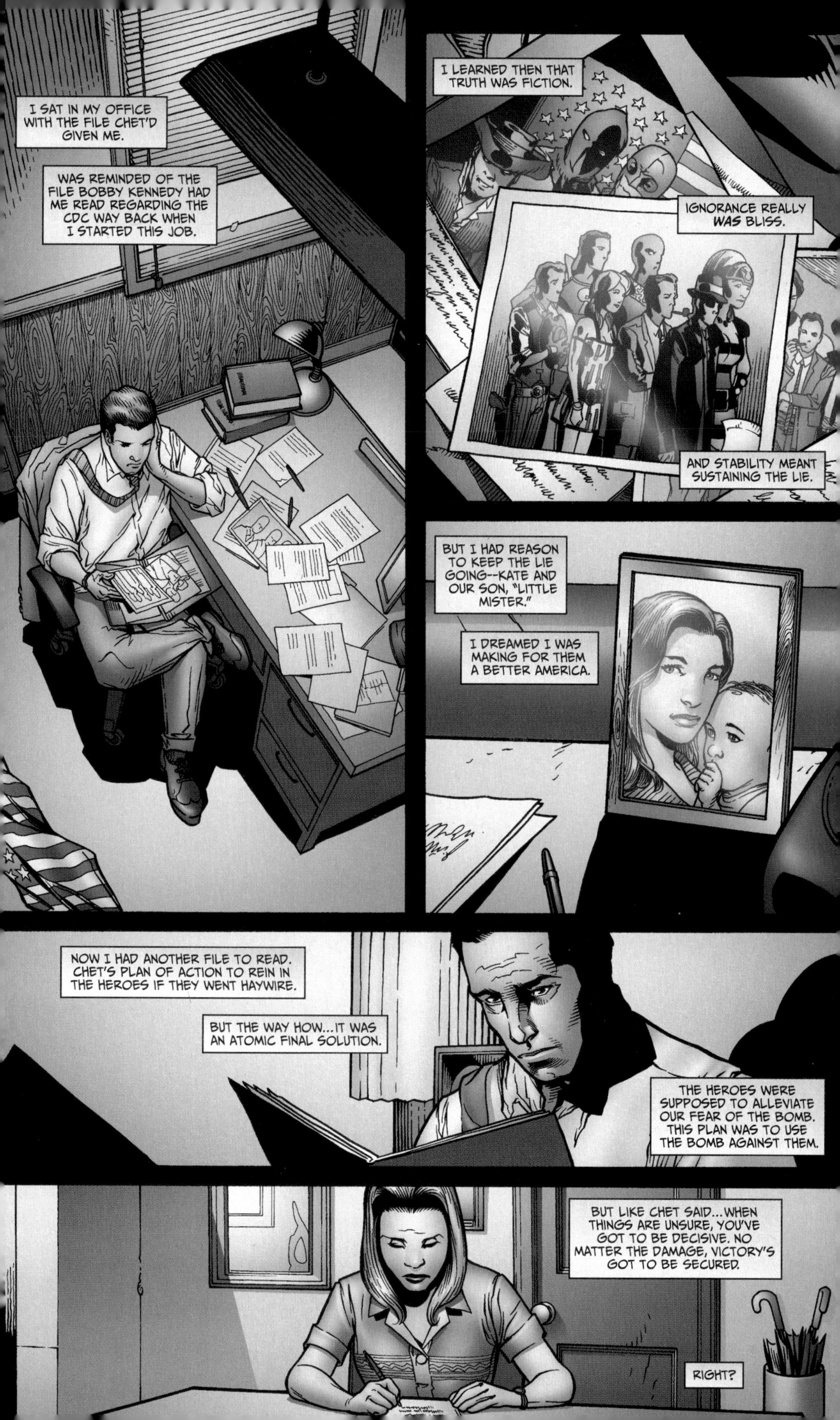
I SAT IN MY OFFICE WITH THE FILE CHET'D GIVEN ME.
WAS REMINDED OF THE FILE BOBBY KENNEDY HAD ME READ REGARDING THE CDC WAY BACK WHEN I STARTED THIS JOB.
I LEARNED THEN THAT TRUTH WAS FICTION.
IGNORANCE REALLY WAS BLISS.
AND STABILITY MEANT SUSTAINING THE LIE.
BUT I HAD REASON TO KEEP THE LIE GOING--KATE AND OUR SON, "LITTLE MISTER."
I DREAMED I WAS MAKING FOR THEM A BETTER AMERICA.
NOW I HAD ANOTHER FILE TO READ. CHET'S PLAN OF ACTION TO REIN IN THE HEROES IF THEY WENT HAYWIRE.
BUT THE WAY HOW...IT WAS AN ATOMIC FINAL SOLUTION.
THE HEROES WERE SUPPOSED TO ALLEVIATE OUR FEAR OF THE BOMB. THIS PLAN WAS TO USE THE BOMB AGAINST THEM.
BUT LIKE CHET SAID...WHEN THINGS ARE UNSURE, YOU'VE GOT TO BE DECISIVE. NO MATTER THE DAMAGE, VICTORY'S GOT TO BE SECURED.
RIGHT?

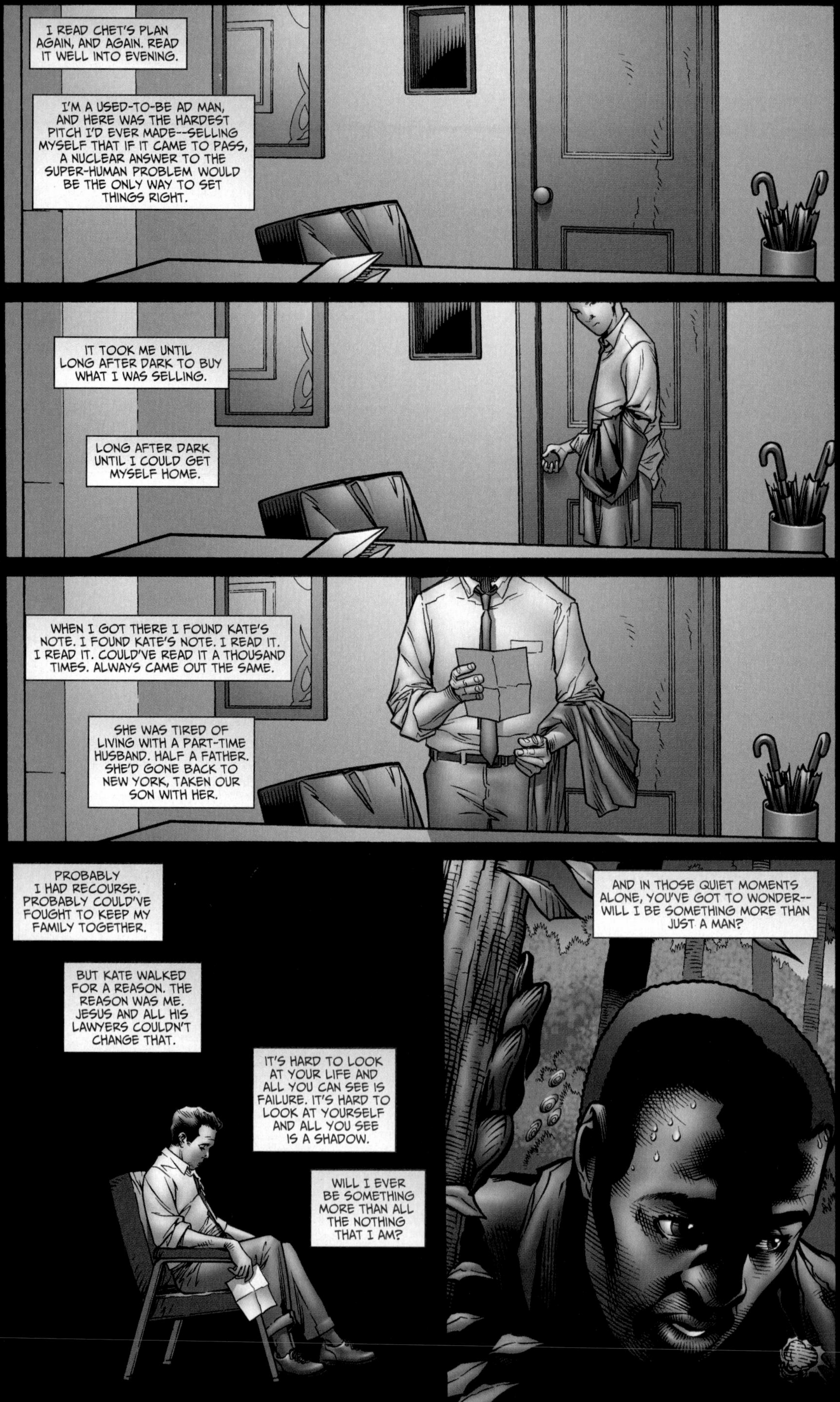
I READ CHET'S PLAN AGAIN, AND AGAIN. READ IT WELL INTO EVENING.
I'M A USED-TO-BE AD MAN, AND HERE WAS THE HARDEST PITCH I'D EVER MADE--SELLING MYSELF THAT IF IT CAME TO PASS, A NUCLEAR ANSWER TO THE SUPER-HUMAN PROBLEM WOULD BE THE ONLY WAY TO SET THINGS RIGHT.
IT TOOK ME UNTIL LONG AFTER DARK TO BUY WHAT I WAS SELLING.
LONG AFTER DARK UNTIL I COULD GET MYSELF HOME.
WHEN I GOT THERE I FOUND KATE'S NOTE. I FOUND KATE'S NOTE. I READ IT. I READ IT. COULD'VE READ IT A THOUSAND TIMES. ALWAYS CAME OUT THE SAME.
SHE WAS TIRED OF LIVING WITH A PART-TIME HUSBAND. HALF A FATHER. SHE'D GONE BACK TO NEW YORK, TAKEN OUR SON WITH HER.
PROBABLY I HAD RECOURSE. PROBABLY COULD'VE FOUGHT TO KEEP MY FAMILY TOGETHER.
BUT KATE WALKED FOR A REASON. THE REASON WAS ME. JESUS AND ALL HIS LAWYERS COULDN'T CHANGE THAT.
IT'S HARD TO LOOK AT YOUR LIFE AND ALL YOU CAN SEE IS FAILURE. IT'S HARD TO LOOK AT YOURSELF AND ALL YOU SEE IS A SHADOW.
WILL I EVER BE SOMETHING MORE THAN ALL THE NOTHING THAT I AM?
AND IN THOSE QUIET MOMENTS ALONE, YOU'VE GOT TO WONDER-- WILL I BE SOMETHING MORE THAN JUST A MAN?

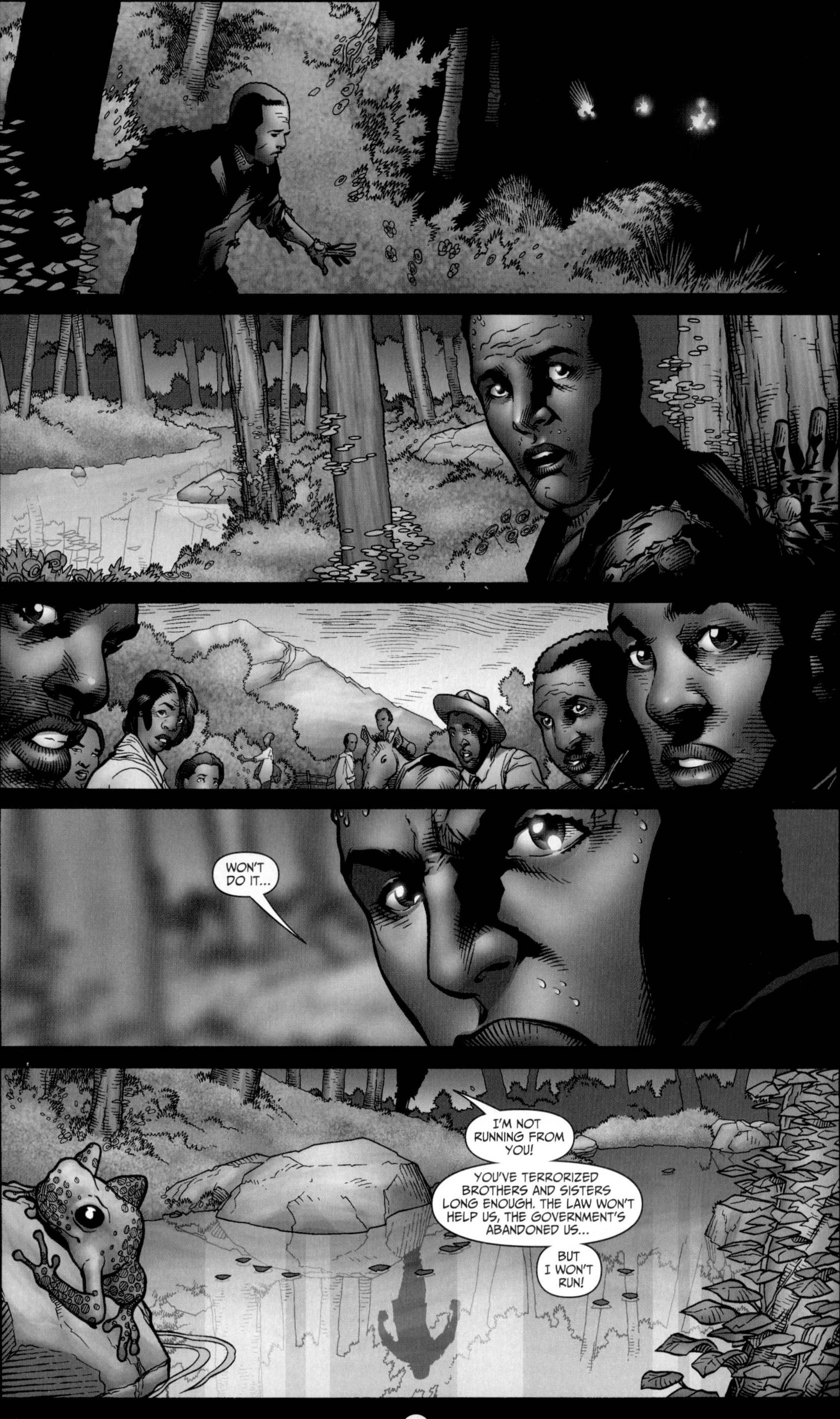
WON'T DO IT...
I'M NOT RUNNING FROM YOU!
YOU'VE TERRORIZED BROTHERS AND SISTERS LONG ENOUGH. THE LAW WON'T HELP US, THE GOVERNMENT'S ABANDONED US...
BUT I WON'T RUN!

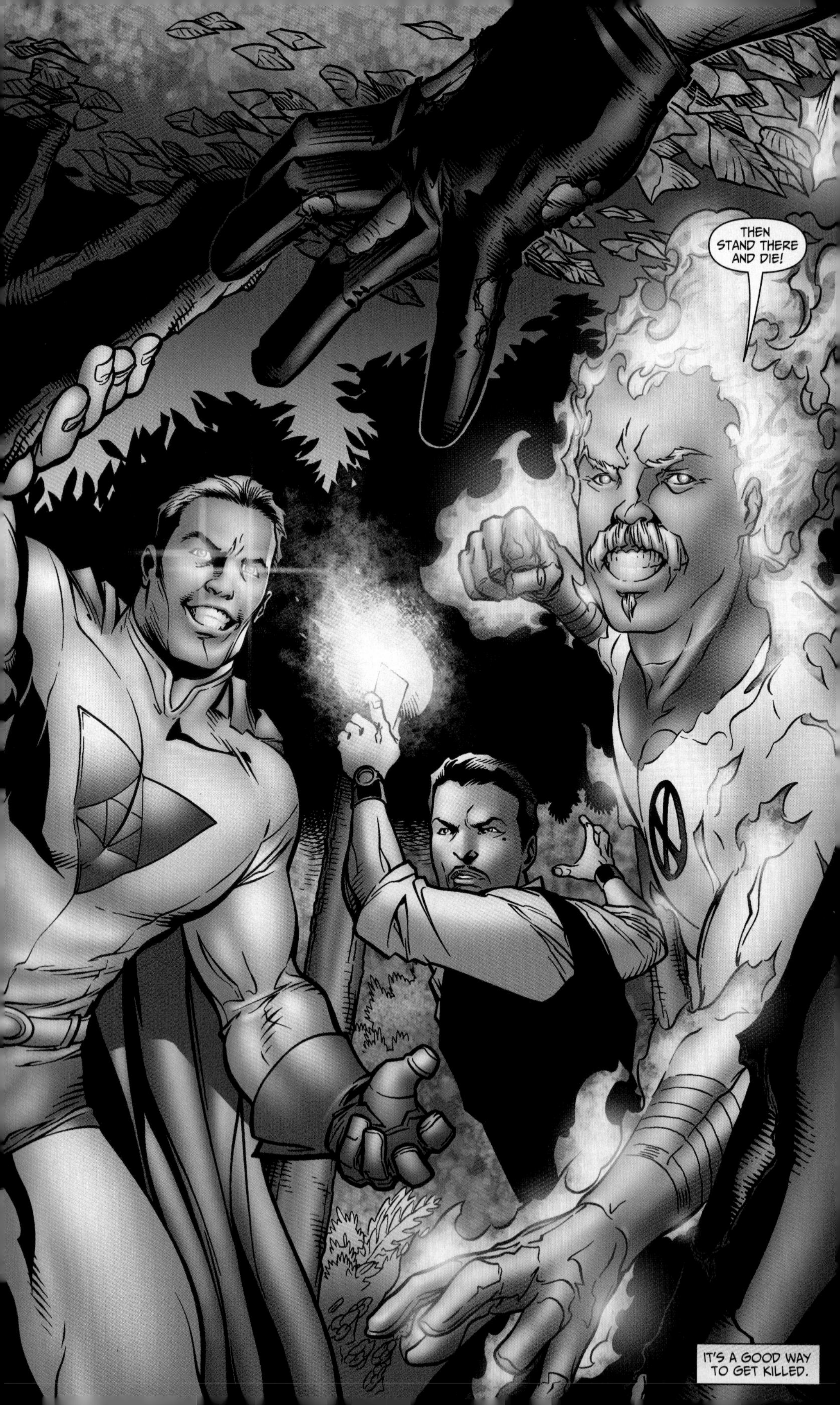
THEN STAND THERE AND DIE!
IT'S A GOOD WAY TO GET KILLED.

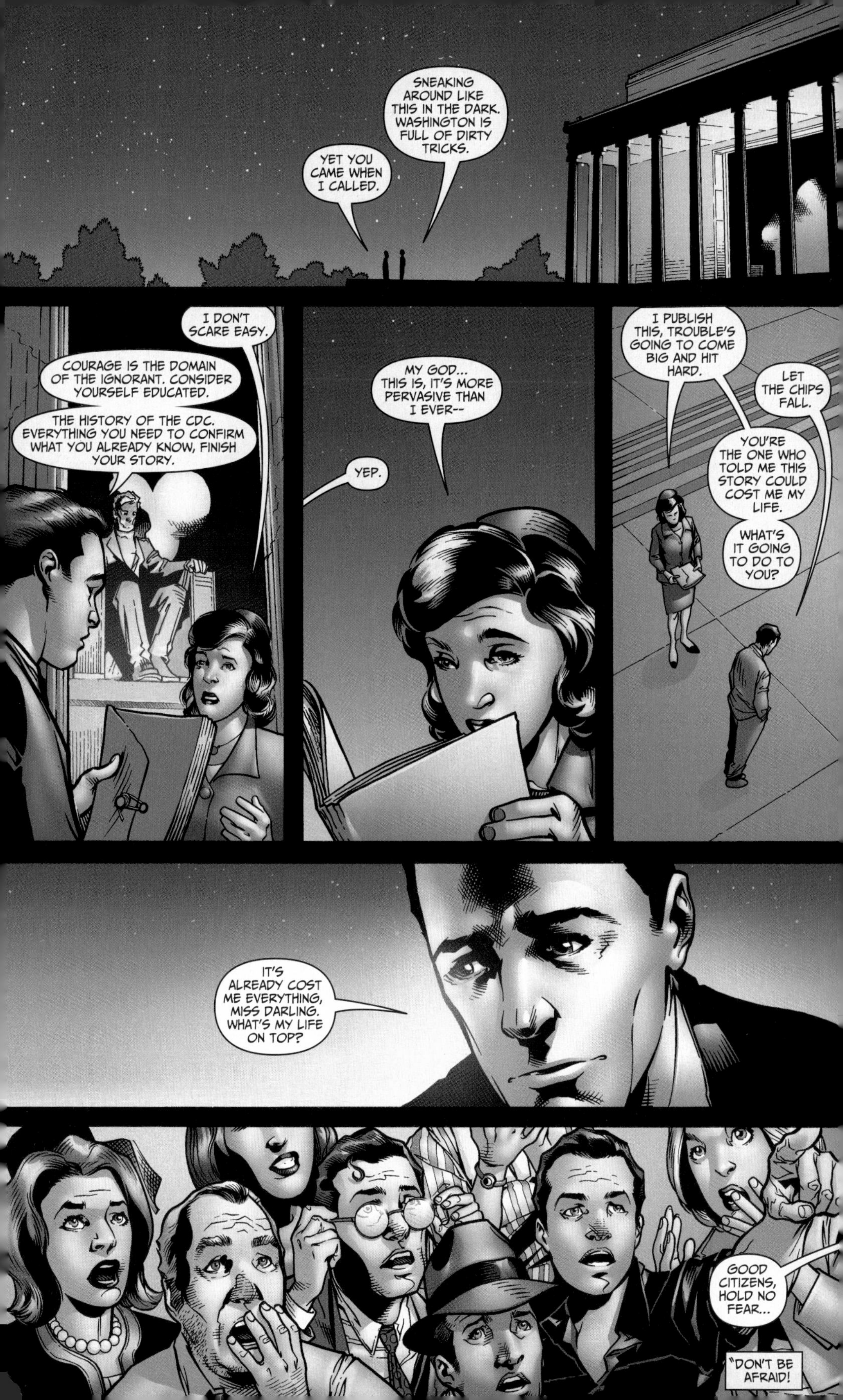
SNEAKING AROUND LIKE THIS IN THE DARK. WASHINGTON IS FULL OF DIRTY TRICKS.
YET YOU CAME WHEN I CALLED.
I DON'T SCARE EASY.
COURAGE IS THE DOMAIN OF THE IGNORANT. CONSIDER YOURSELF EDUCATED.
THE HISTORY OF THE CDC. EVERYTHING YOU NEED TO CONFIRM WHAT YOU ALREADY KNOW, FINISH YOUR STORY.
MY GOD... THIS IS, IT'S MORE PERVASIVE THAN I EVER--
YEP.
I PUBLISH THIS, TROUBLE'S GOING TO COME BIG AND HIT HARD.
LET THE CHIPS FALL.
YOU'RE THE ONE WHO TOLD ME THIS STORY COULD COST ME MY LIFE.
WHAT'S IT GOING TO DO TO YOU?
IT'S ALREADY COST ME EVERYTHING, MISS DARLING. WHAT'S MY LIFE ON TOP?
GOOD CITIZENS, HOLD NO FEAR...
"DON'T BE AFRAID!

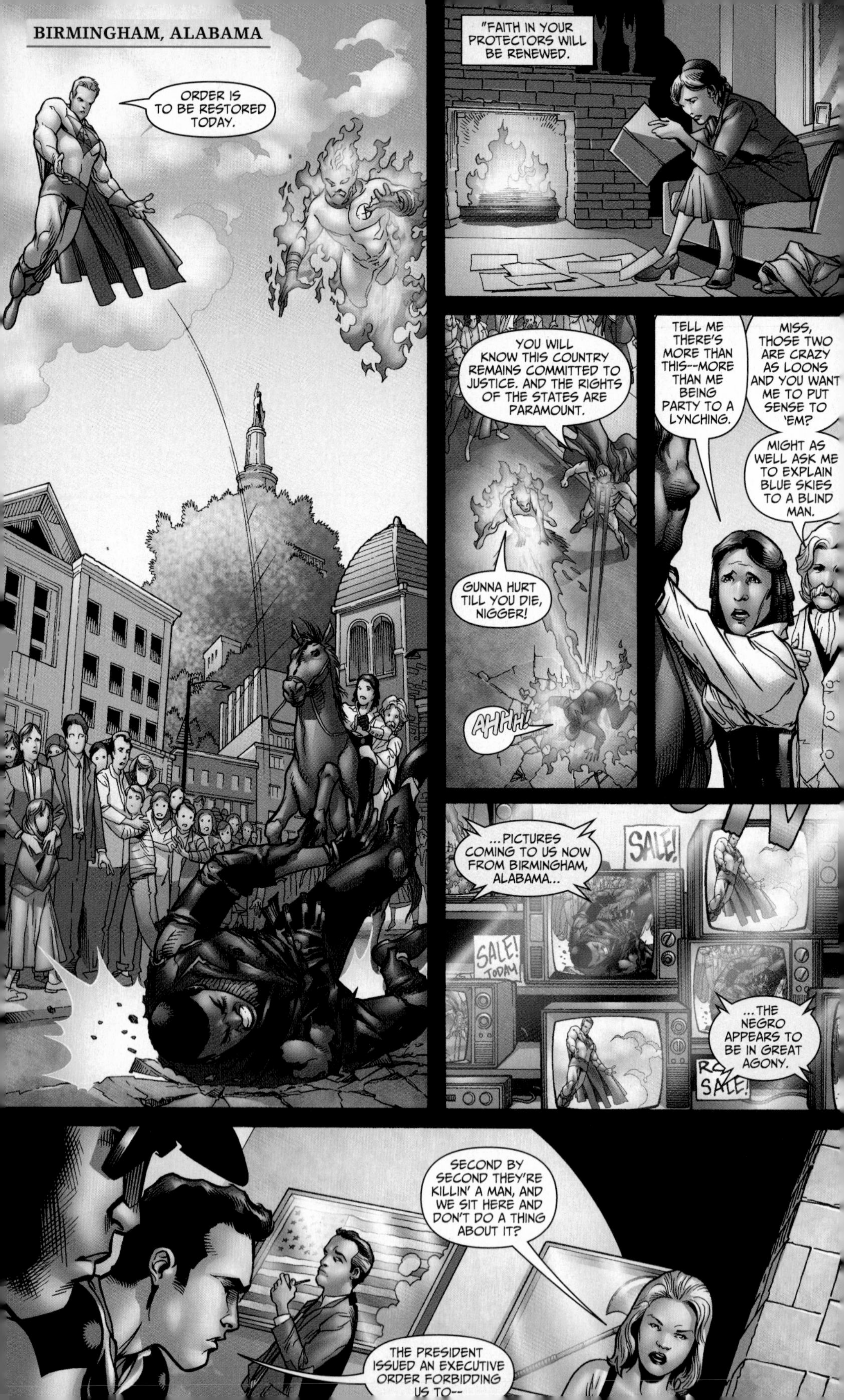
BIRMINGHAM, ALABAMA
ORDER IS TO BE RESTORED TODAY.
"FAITH IN YOUR PROTECTORS WILL BE RENEWED.
YOU WILL KNOW THIS COUNTRY REMAINS COMMITTED TO JUSTICE. AND THE RIGHTS OF THE STATES ARE PARAMOUNT.
GUNNA HURT TILL YOU DIE, NIGGER!
AHHH!
TELL ME THERE'S MORE THAN THIS--MORE THAN ME BEING PARTY TO A LYNCHING.
MISS, THOSE TWO ARE CRAZY AS LOONS AND YOU WANT ME TO PUT SENSE TO 'EM?
MIGHT AS WELL ASK ME TO EXPLAIN BLUE SKIES TO A BLIND MAN.
...PICTURES COMING TO US NOW FROM BIRMINGHAM, ALABAMA...
SALE!
SALE! TODAY
...THE NEGRO APPEARS TO BE IN GREAT AGONY.
SALE!
SECOND BY SECOND THEY'RE KILLIN' A MAN, AND WE SIT HERE AND DON'T DO A THING ABOUT IT?
THE PRESIDENT ISSUED AN EXECUTIVE ORDER FORBIDDING US TO--

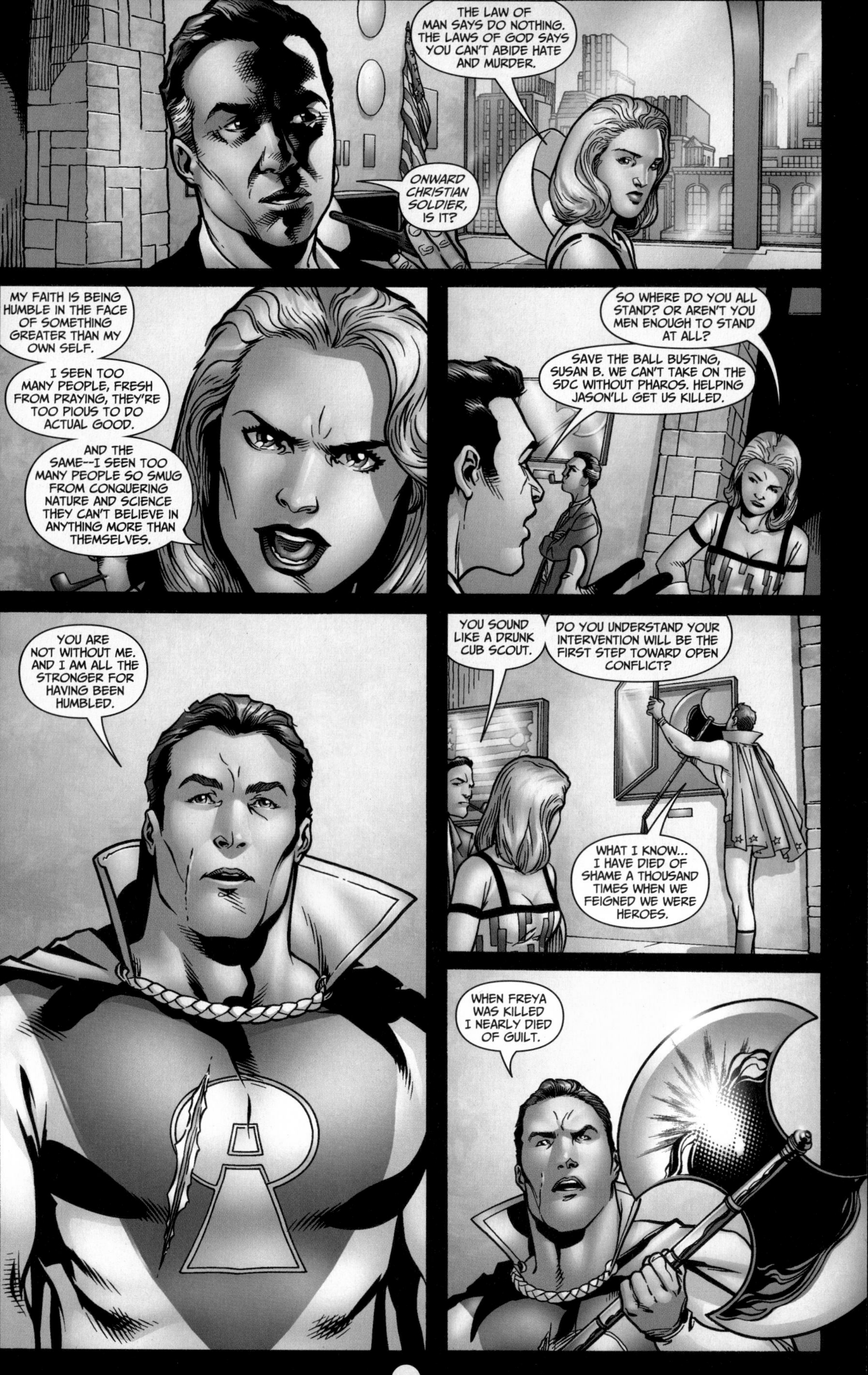
THE LAW OF MAN SAYS DO NOTHING. THE LAWS OF GOD SAYS YOU CAN'T ABIDE HATE AND MURDER.
ONWARD CHRISTIAN SOLDIER, IS IT?
MY FAITH IS BEING HUMBLE IN THE FACE OF SOMETHING GREATER THAN MY OWN SELF.
I SEEN TOO MANY PEOPLE, FRESH FROM PRAYING, THEY'RE TOO PIOUS TO DO ACTUAL GOOD.
AND THE SAME--I SEEN TOO MANY PEOPLE SO SMUG FROM CONQUERING NATURE AND SCIENCE THEY CAN'T BELIEVE IN ANYTHING MORE THAN THEMSELVES.
SO WHERE DO YOU ALL STAND? OR AREN'T YOU MEN ENOUGH TO STAND AT ALL?
SAVE THE BALL BUSTING, SUSAN B. WE CAN'T TAKE ON THE SDC WITHOUT PHAROS. HELPING JASON'LL GET US KILLED.
YOU ARE NOT WITHOUT ME. AND I AM ALL THE STRONGER FOR HAVING BEEN HUMBLED.
YOU SOUND LIKE A DRUNK CUB SCOUT.
DO YOU UNDERSTAND YOUR INTERVENTION WILL BE THE FIRST STEP TOWARD OPEN CONFLICT?
WHAT I KNOW... I HAVE DIED OF SHAME A THOUSAND TIMES WHEN WE FEIGNED WE WERE HEROES.
WHEN FREYA WAS KILLED I NEARLY DIED OF GUILT.

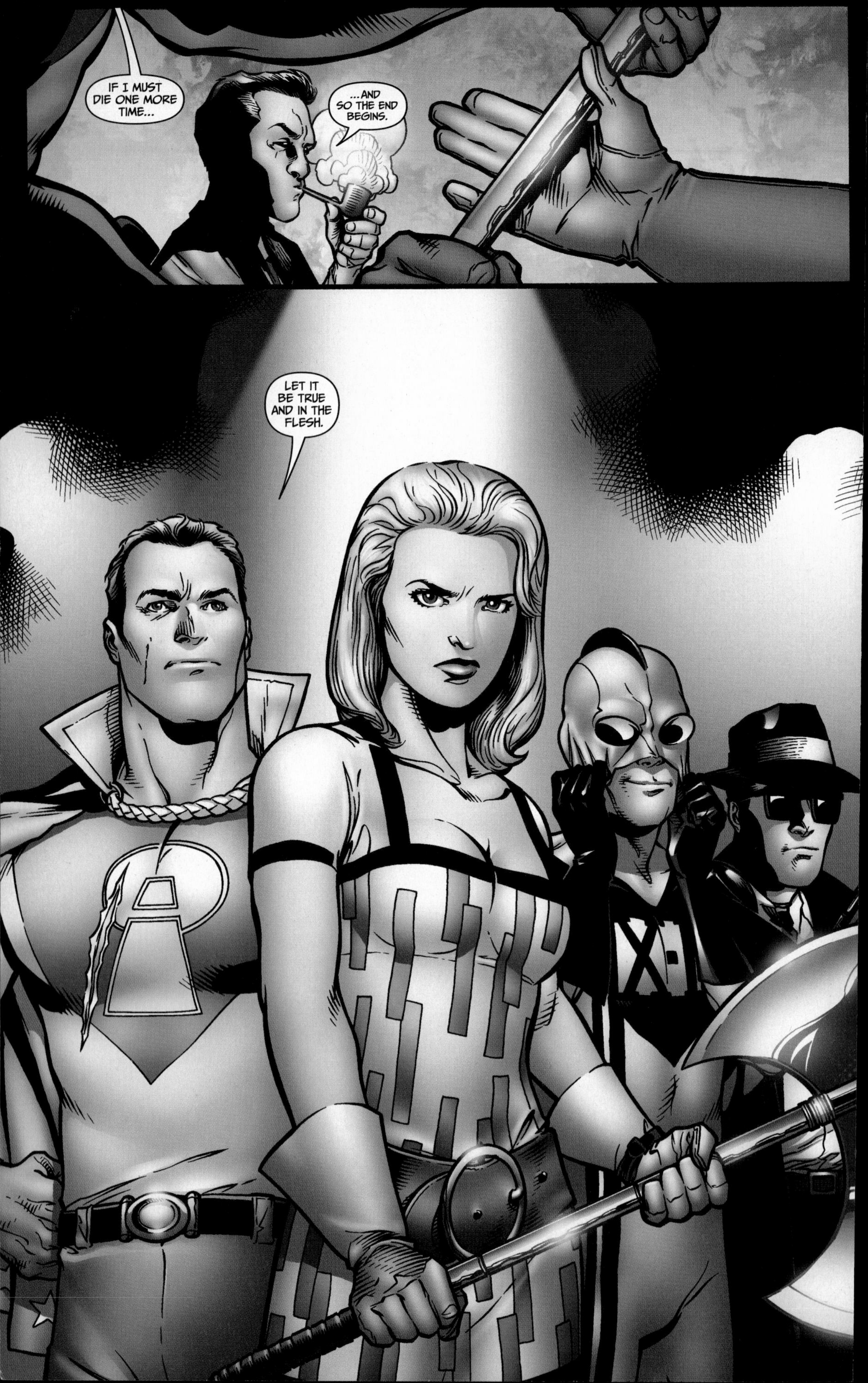
IF I MUST DIE ONE MORE TIME...
...AND SO THE END BEGINS.
LET IT BE TRUE AND IN THE FLESH.

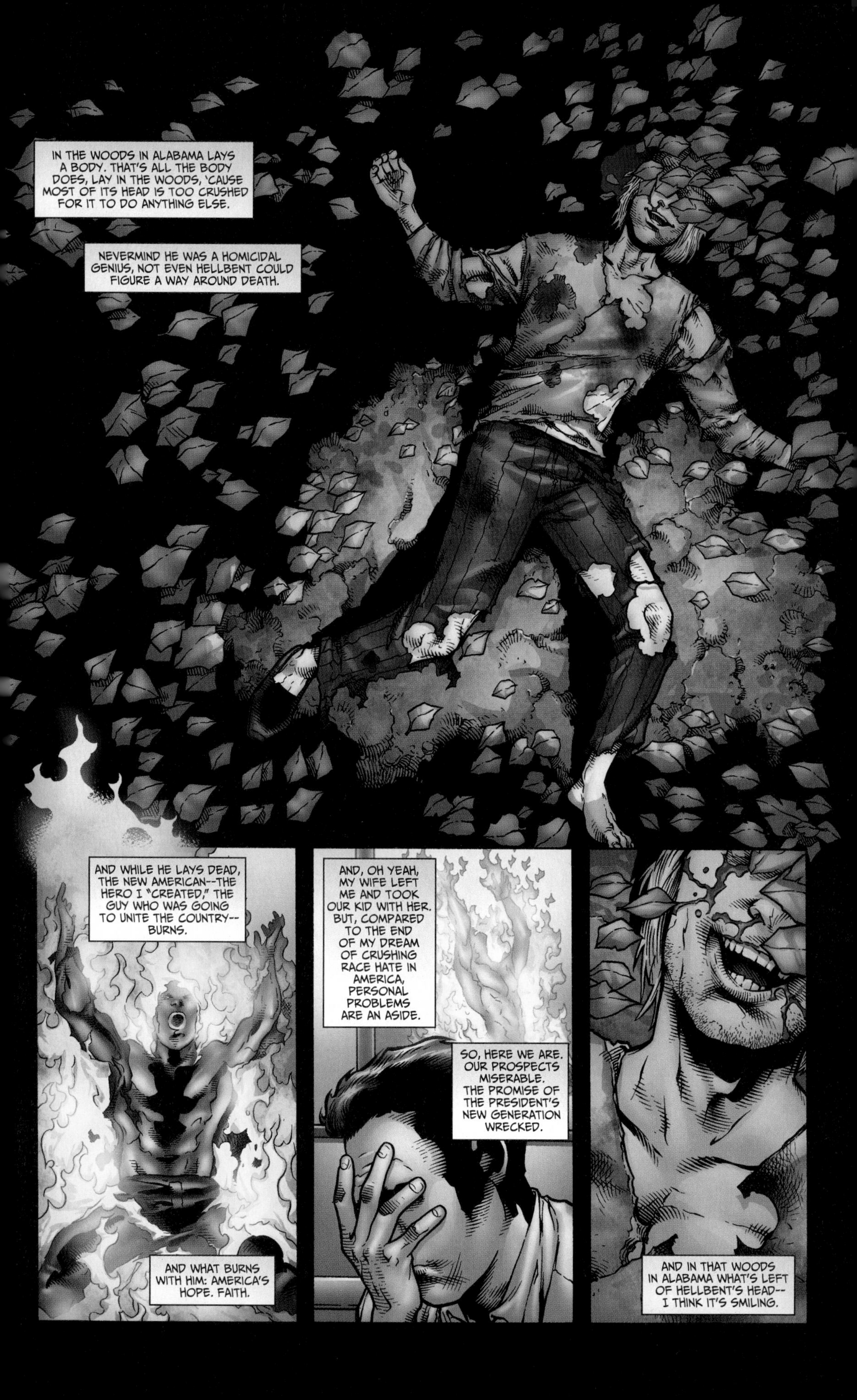
IN THE WOODS IN ALABAMA LAYS A BODY. THAT'S ALL THE BODY DOES, LAY IN THE WOODS, 'CAUSE MOST OF ITS HEAD IS TOO CRUSHED FOR IT TO DO ANYTHING ELSE.
NEVERMIND HE WAS A HOMICIDAL GENIUS, NOT EVEN HELLBENT COULD FIGURE A WAY AROUND DEATH.
AND WHILE HE LAYS DEAD, THE NEW AMERICAN--THE HERO I "CREATED," THE GUY WHO WAS GOING TO UNITE THE COUNTRY--BURNS.
AND WHAT BURNS WITH HIM: AMERICA'S HOPE. FAITH.
AND, OH YEAH, MY WIFE LEFT ME AND TOOK OUR KID WITH HER. BUT, COMPARED TO THE END OF MY DREAM OF CRUSHING RACE HATE IN AMERICA, PERSONAL PROBLEMS ARE AN ASIDE.
SO, HERE WE ARE. OUR PROSPECTS MISERABLE. THE PROMISE OF THE PRESIDENT'S NEW GENERATION WRECKED.
AND IN THAT WOODS IN ALABAMA WHAT'S LEFT OF HELLBENT'S HEAD--I THINK IT'S SMILING.

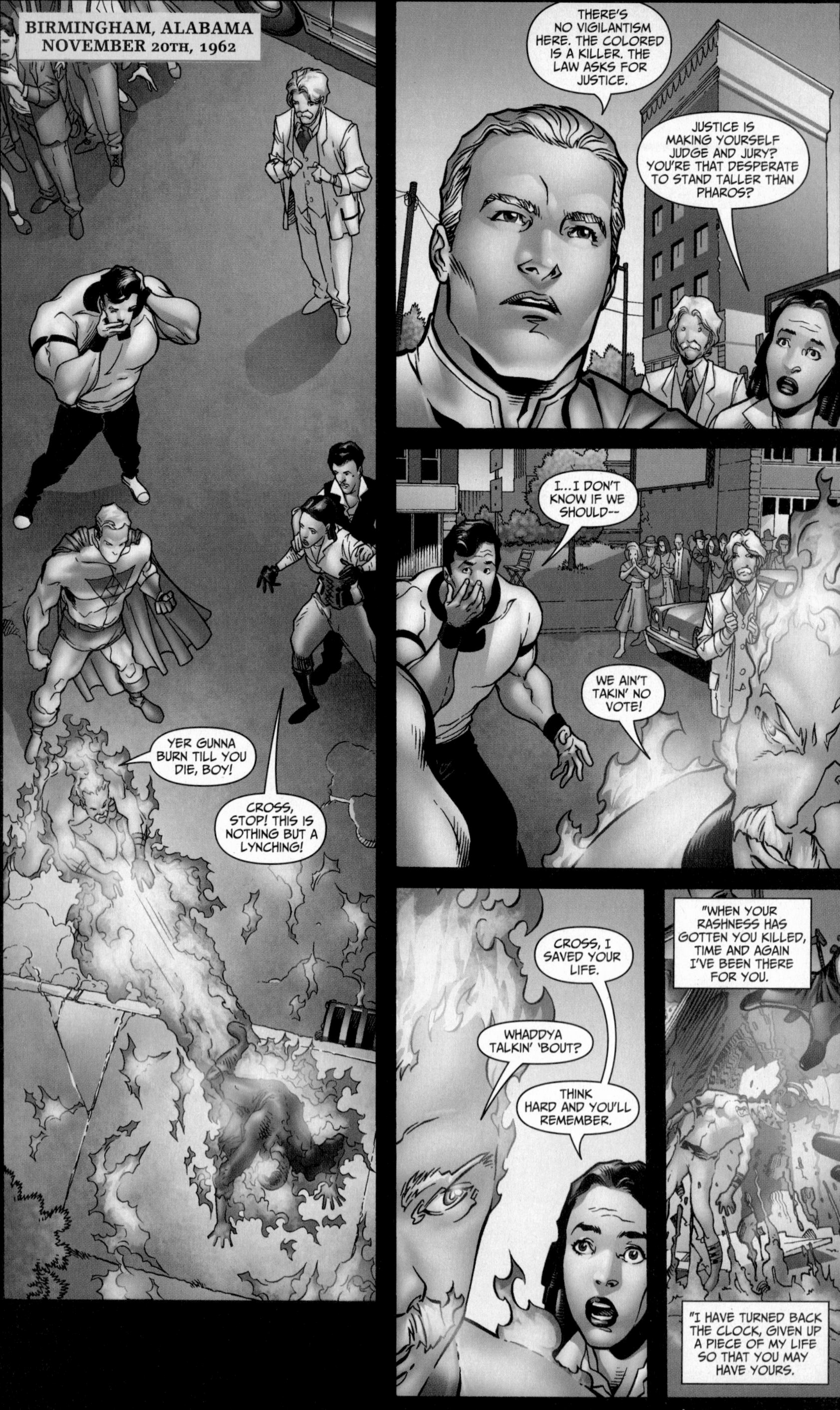
BIRMINGHAM, ALABAMA
NOVEMBER 20TH, 1962
YER GUNNA BURN TILL YOU DIE, BOY!
CROSS, STOP! THIS IS NOTHING BUT A LYNCHING!
THERE'S NO VIGILANTISM HERE. THE COLORED IS A KILLER. THE LAW ASKS FOR JUSTICE.
JUSTICE IS MAKING YOURSELF JUDGE AND JURY? YOU'RE THAT DESPERATE TO STAND TALLER THAN PHAROS?
I...I DON'T KNOW IF WE SHOULD--
WE AIN'T TAKIN' NO VOTE!
CROSS, I SAVED YOUR LIFE.
WHADDYA TALKIN' 'BOUT?
THINK HARD AND YOU'LL REMEMBER.
"WHEN YOUR RASHNESS HAS GOTTEN YOU KILLED, TIME AND AGAIN I'VE BEEN THERE FOR YOU.
"I HAVE TURNED BACK THE CLOCK, GIVEN UP A PIECE OF MY LIFE SO THAT YOU MAY HAVE YOURS.

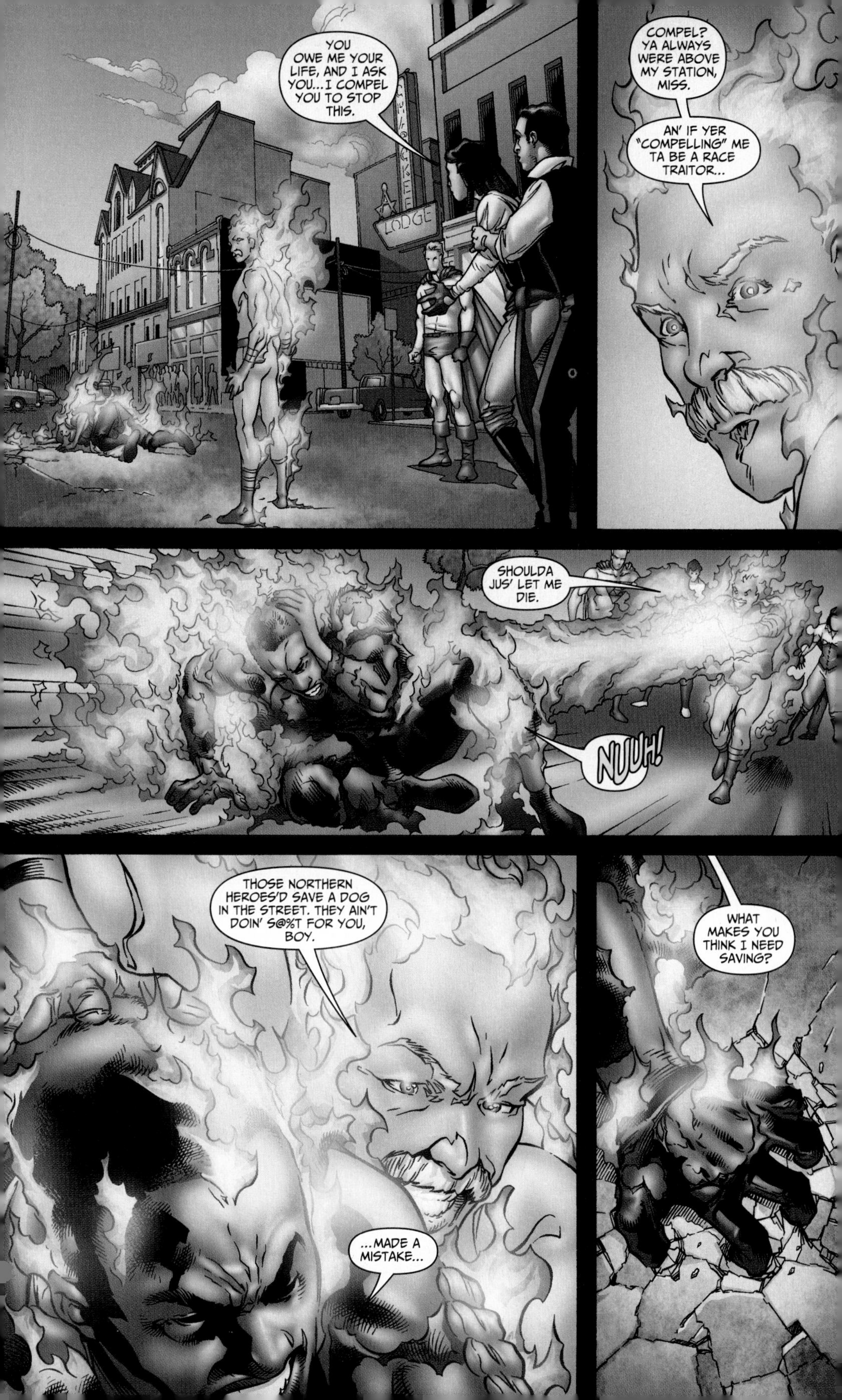
YOU OWE ME YOUR LIFE, AND I ASK YOU...I COMPEL YOU TO STOP THIS.
COMPEL? YA ALWAYS WERE ABOVE MY STATION, MISS.
AN' IF YER "COMPELLING" ME TA BE A RACE TRAITOR...
LODGE
SHOULDA JUS' LET ME DIE.
NUUH!
THOSE NORTHERN HEROES'D SAVE A DOG IN THE STREET. THEY AIN'T DOIN' S@%T FOR YOU, BOY.
...MADE A MISTAKE...
WHAT MAKES YOU THINK I NEED SAVING?

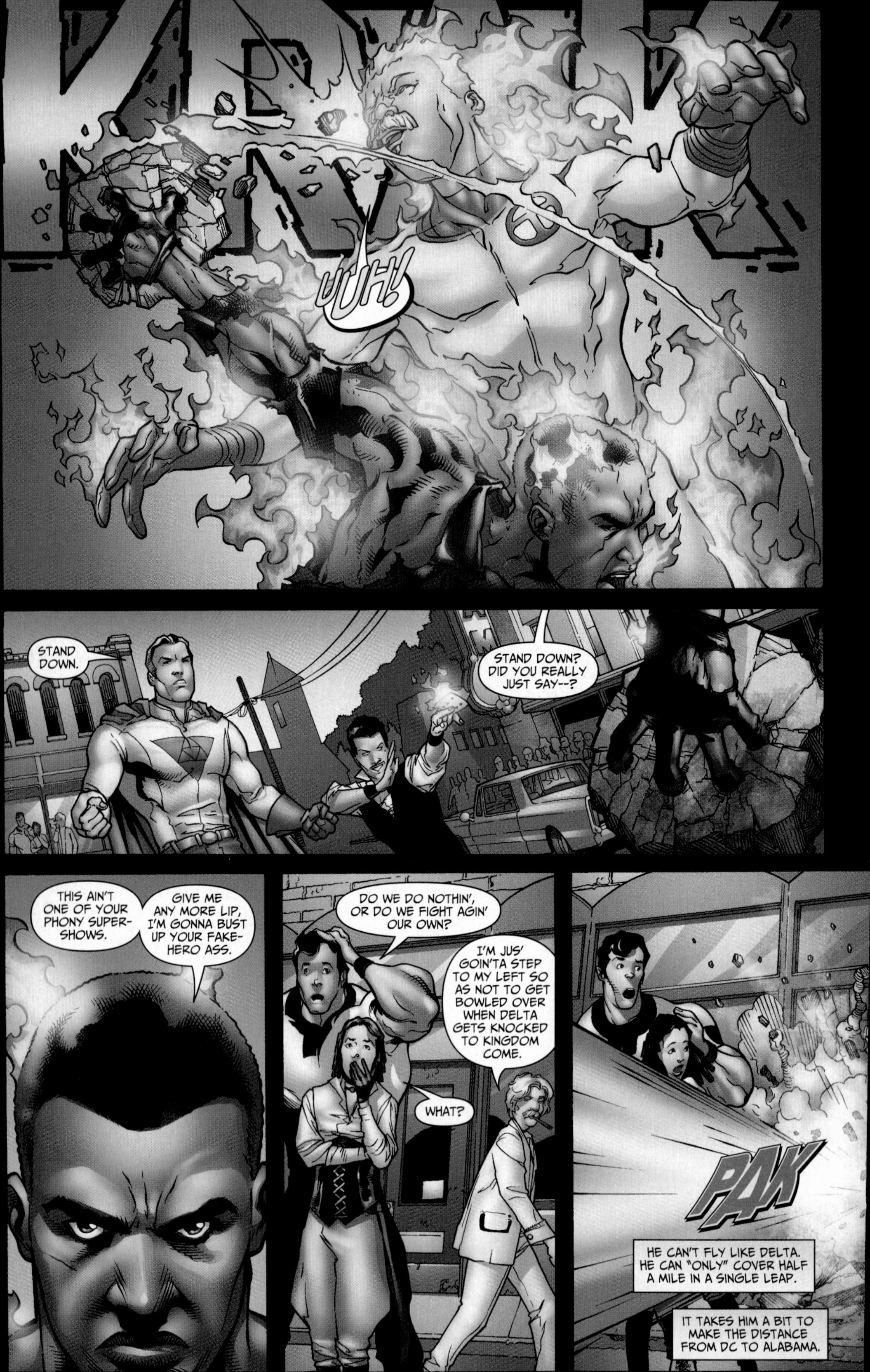
UUH!
STAND DOWN.
STAND DOWN? DID YOU REALLY JUST SAY--?
THIS AIN'T ONE OF YOUR PHONY SUPER-SHOWS.
GIVE ME ANY MORE LIP, I'M GONNA BUST UP YOUR FAKE-HERO ASS.
DO WE DO NOTHIN', OR DO WE FIGHT AGIN' OUR OWN?
I'M JUS' GOIN'TA STEP TO MY LEFT SO AS NOT TO GET BOWLED OVER WHEN DELTA GETS KNOCKED TO KINGDOM COME.
WHAT?
PAK
HE CAN'T FLY LIKE DELTA. HE CAN "ONLY" COVER HALF A MILE IN A SINGLE LEAP.
IT TAKES HIM A BIT TO MAKE THE DISTANCE FROM DC TO ALABAMA.

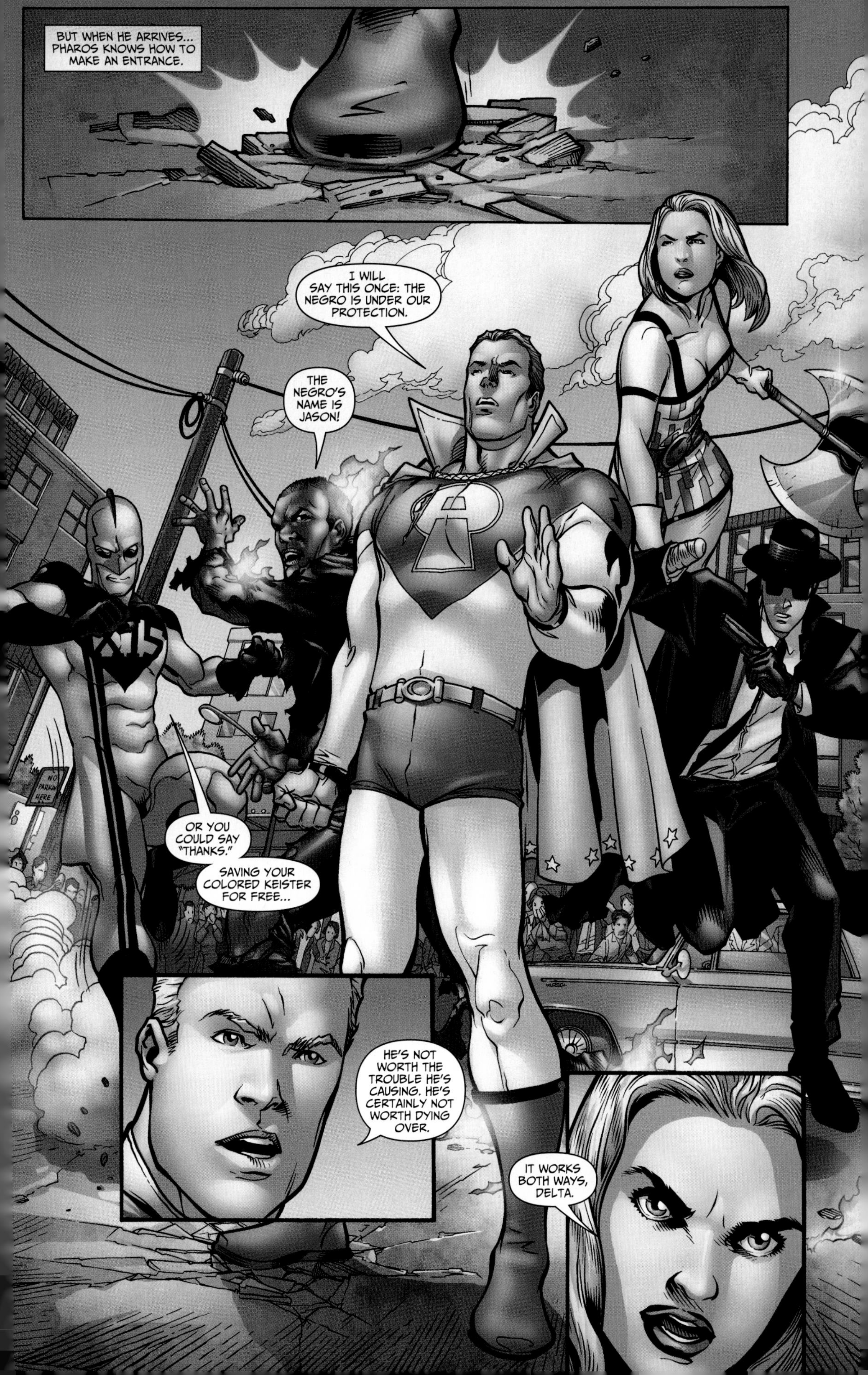
BUT WHEN HE ARRIVES... PHAROS KNOWS HOW TO MAKE AN ENTRANCE.
I WILL SAY THIS ONCE: THE NEGRO IS UNDER OUR PROTECTION.
THE NEGRO'S NAME IS JASON!
OR YOU COULD SAY "THANKS."
SAVING YOUR COLORED KEISTER FOR FREE...
NO PARKING HERE
HE'S NOT WORTH THE TROUBLE HE'S CAUSING. HE'S CERTAINLY NOT WORTH DYING OVER.
IT WORKS BOTH WAYS, DELTA.

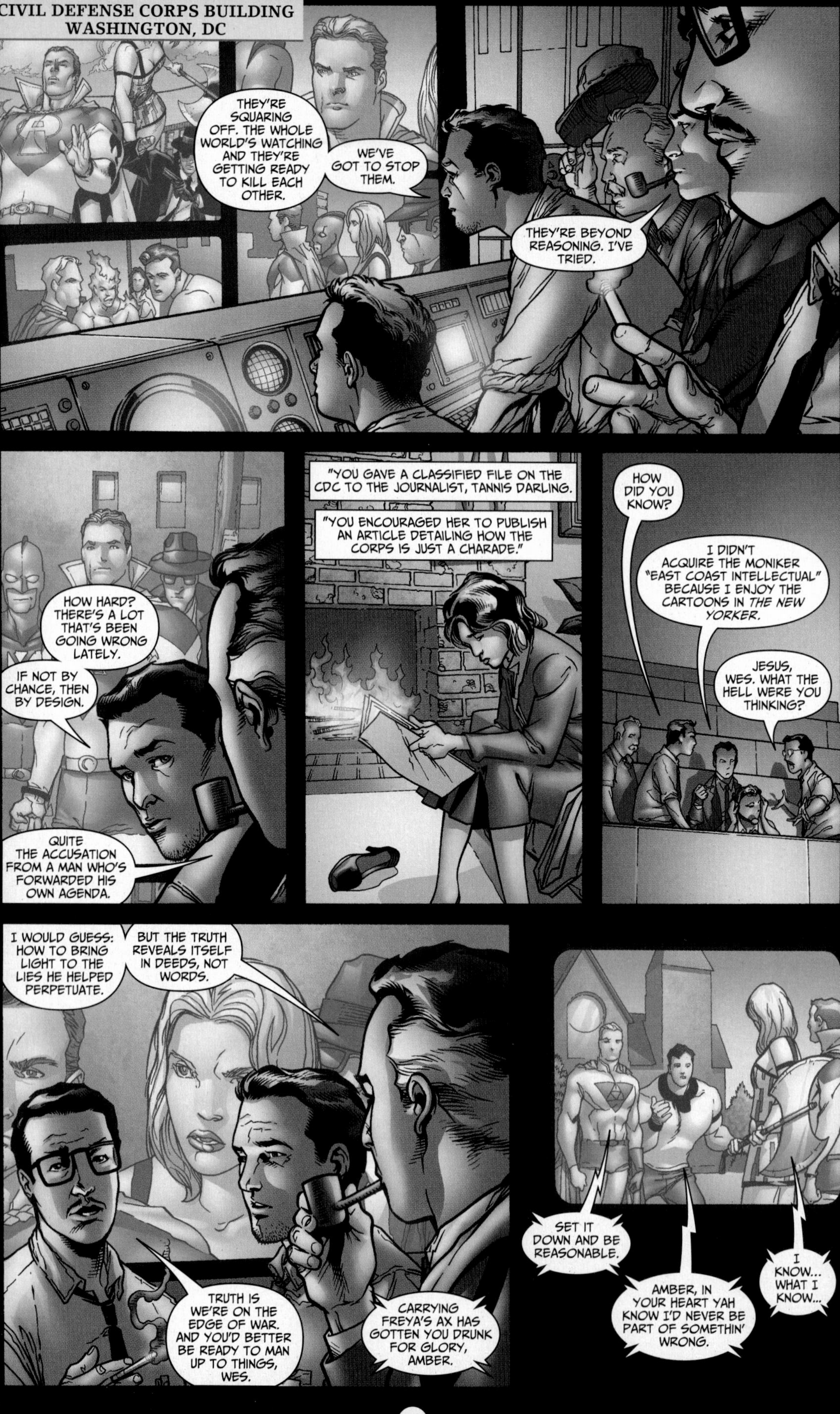
CIVIL DEFENSE CORPS BUILDING WASHINGTON, DC
THEY'RE SQUARING OFF. THE WHOLE WORLD'S WATCHING AND THEY'RE GETTING READY TO KILL EACH OTHER.
WE'VE GOT TO STOP THEM.
THEY'RE BEYOND REASONING. I'VE TRIED.
HOW HARD? THERE'S A LOT THAT'S BEEN GOING WRONG LATELY.
IF NOT BY CHANCE, THEN BY DESIGN.
QUITE THE ACCUSATION FROM A MAN WHO'S FORWARDED HIS OWN AGENDA.
"YOU GAVE A CLASSIFIED FILE ON THE CDC TO THE JOURNALIST, TANNIS DARLING.
"YOU ENCOURAGED HER TO PUBLISH AN ARTICLE DETAILING HOW THE CORPS IS JUST A CHARADE."
HOW DID YOU KNOW?
I DIDN'T ACQUIRE THE MONIKER "EAST COAST INTELLECTUAL" BECAUSE I ENJOY THE CARTOONS IN *THE NEW YORKER*.
JESUS, WES. WHAT THE HELL WERE YOU THINKING?
I WOULD GUESS: HOW TO BRING LIGHT TO THE LIES HE HELPED PERPETUATE.
BUT THE TRUTH REVEALS ITSELF IN DEEDS, NOT WORDS.
TRUTH IS WE'RE ON THE EDGE OF WAR. AND YOU'D BETTER BE READY TO MAN UP TO THINGS, WES.
CARRYING FREYA'S AX HAS GOTTEN YOU DRUNK FOR GLORY, AMBER.
SET IT DOWN AND BE REASONABLE.
AMBER, IN YOUR HEART YAH KNOW I'D NEVER BE PART OF SOMETHIN' WRONG.
I KNOW... WHAT I KNOW...

TO HELL WITH 'EM ALL! LET'S GET BURNIN'!

JASON'S FLYING PACK--YOU RECALL WHERE IT IS?

DO I...?

YOU WERE SEARCHING FOR PURPOSE. GO FIND IT.

AND RIDE TA BEAT THE DEVIL HIMSELF.

DON'T TAKE THIS WRONG-- YOU REALLY THINK A GIMP LIKE YOURSELF IS GOOD ENOUGH TO TAKE ME?

YOU'RE NOT THAT LUCKY.

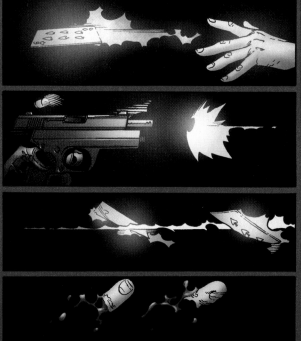

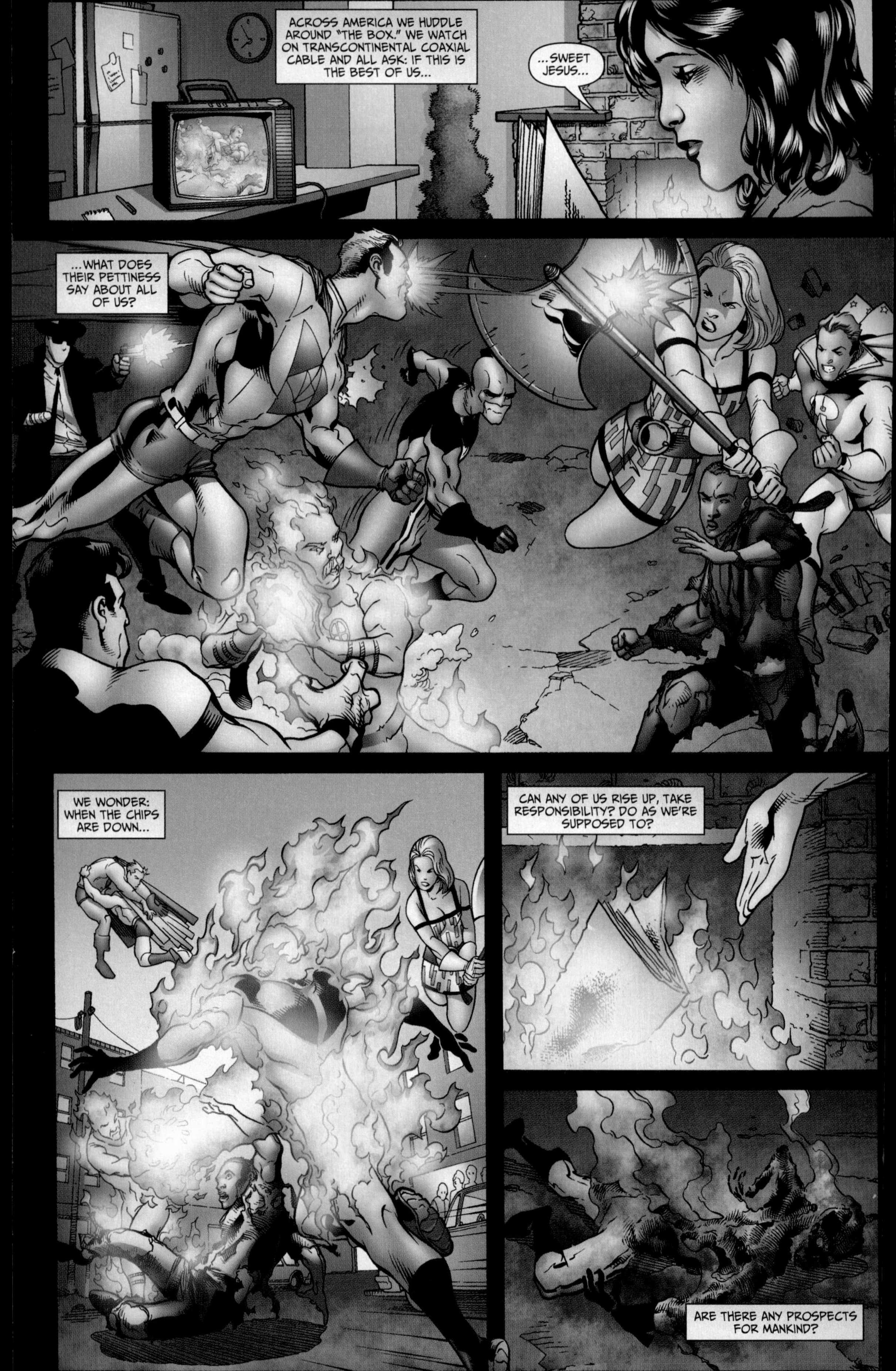
ACROSS AMERICA WE HUDDLE AROUND "THE BOX." WE WATCH ON TRANSCONTINENTAL COAXIAL CABLE AND ALL ASK: IF THIS IS THE BEST OF US...
...SWEET JESUS...
...WHAT DOES THEIR PETTINESS SAY ABOUT ALL OF US?
WE WONDER: WHEN THE CHIPS ARE DOWN...
CAN ANY OF US RISE UP, TAKE RESPONSIBILITY? DO AS WE'RE SUPPOSED TO?
ARE THERE ANY PROSPECTS FOR MANKIND?

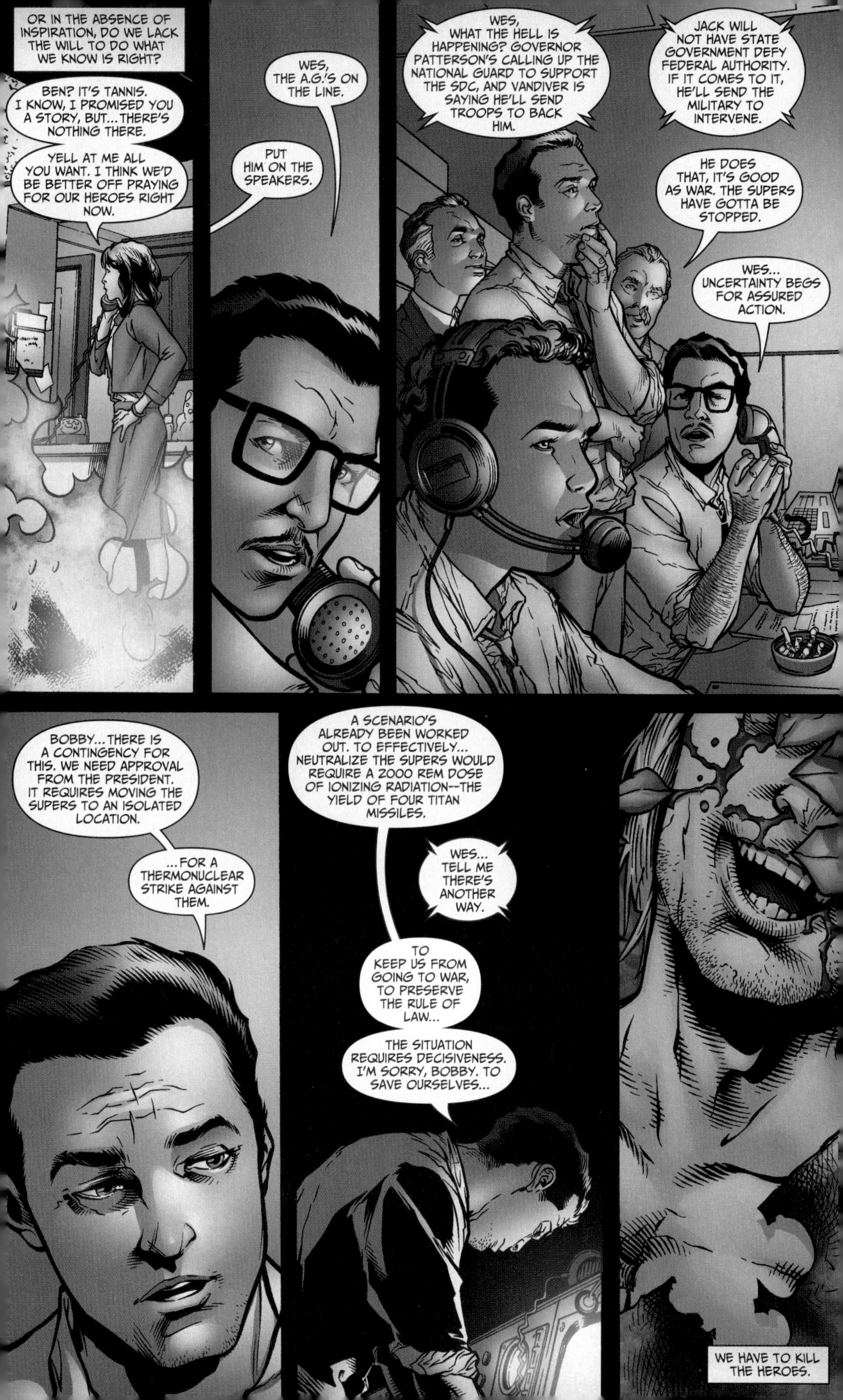
OR IN THE ABSENCE OF INSPIRATION, DO WE LACK THE WILL TO DO WHAT WE KNOW IS RIGHT?
BEN? IT'S TANNIS. I KNOW, I PROMISED YOU A STORY, BUT... THERE'S NOTHING THERE.
YELL AT ME ALL YOU WANT. I THINK WE'D BE BETTER OFF PRAYING FOR OUR HEROES RIGHT NOW.
WES, THE A.G.'S ON THE LINE.
PUT HIM ON THE SPEAKERS.
WES, WHAT THE HELL IS HAPPENING? GOVERNOR PATTERSON'S CALLING UP THE NATIONAL GUARD TO SUPPORT THE SDC, AND VANDIVER IS SAYING HE'LL SEND TROOPS TO BACK HIM.
JACK WILL NOT HAVE STATE GOVERNMENT DEFY FEDERAL AUTHORITY. IF IT COMES TO IT, HE'LL SEND THE MILITARY TO INTERVENE.
HE DOES THAT, IT'S GOOD AS WAR. THE SUPERS HAVE GOTTA BE STOPPED.
WES... UNCERTAINTY BEGS FOR ASSURED ACTION.
BOBBY... THERE IS A CONTINGENCY FOR THIS. WE NEED APPROVAL FROM THE PRESIDENT. IT REQUIRES MOVING THE SUPERS TO AN ISOLATED LOCATION.
...FOR A THERMONUCLEAR STRIKE AGAINST THEM.
A SCENARIO'S ALREADY BEEN WORKED OUT. TO EFFECTIVELY... NEUTRALIZE THE SUPERS WOULD REQUIRE A 2000 REM DOSE OF IONIZING RADIATION--THE YIELD OF FOUR TITAN MISSILES.
WES... TELL ME THERE'S ANOTHER WAY.
TO KEEP US FROM GOING TO WAR, TO PRESERVE THE RULE OF LAW...
THE SITUATION REQUIRES DECISIVENESS. I'M SORRY, BOBBY. TO SAVE OURSELVES...
WE HAVE TO KILL THE HEROES.

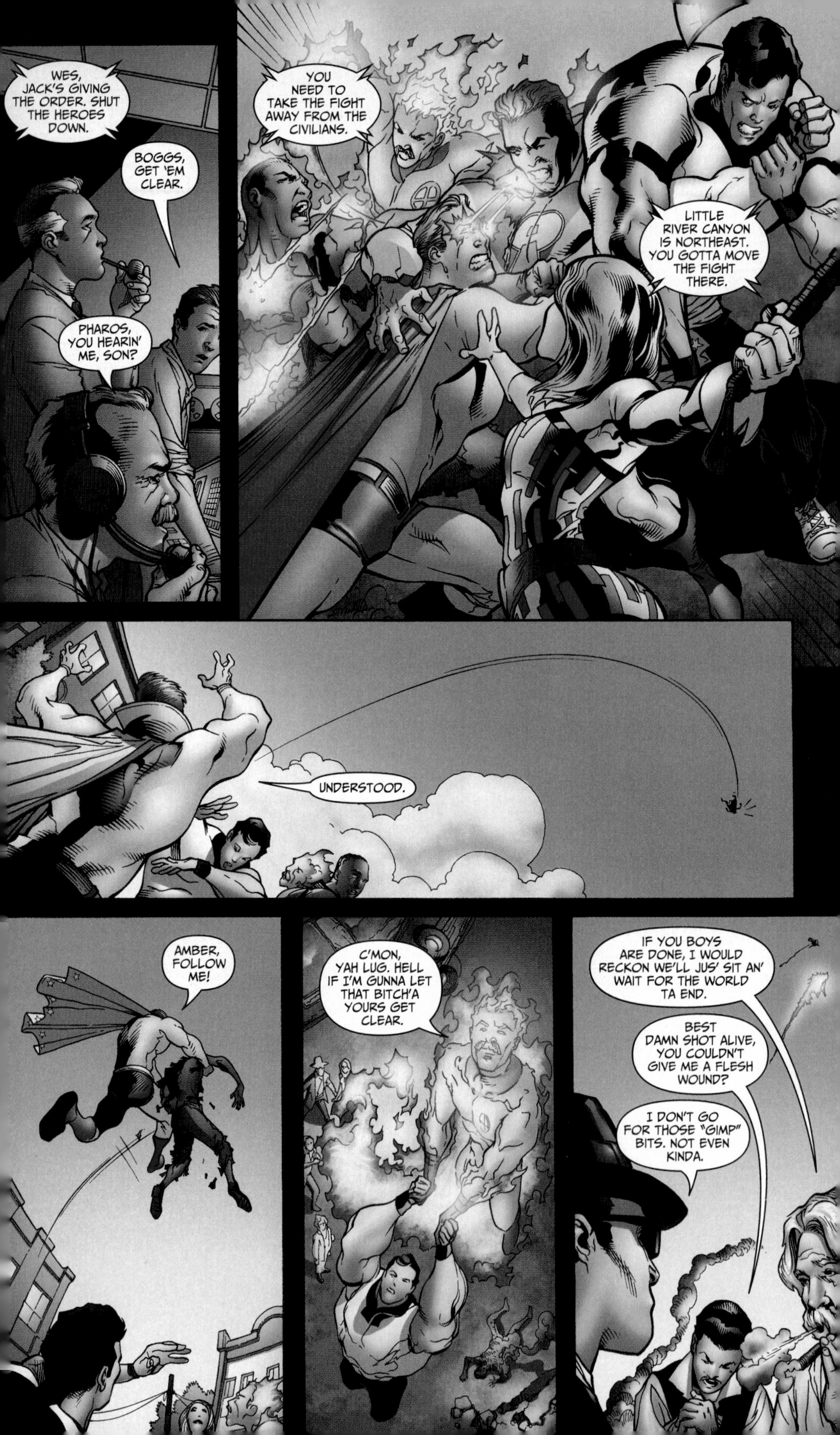
WES, JACK'S GIVING THE ORDER. SHUT THE HEROES DOWN.
BOGGS, GET 'EM CLEAR.
PHAROS, YOU HEARIN' ME, SON?
YOU NEED TO TAKE THE FIGHT AWAY FROM THE CIVILIANS.
LITTLE RIVER CANYON IS NORTHEAST. YOU GOTTA MOVE THE FIGHT THERE.
UNDERSTOOD.
AMBER, FOLLOW ME!
C'MON, YAH LUG. HELL IF I'M GUNNA LET THAT BITCH'A YOURS GET CLEAR.
IF YOU BOYS ARE DONE, I WOULD RECKON WE'LL JUS' SIT AN' WAIT FOR THE WORLD TA END.
BEST DAMN SHOT ALIVE, YOU COULDN'T GIVE ME A FLESH WOUND?
I DON'T GO FOR THOSE "GIMP" BITS. NOT EVEN KINDA.

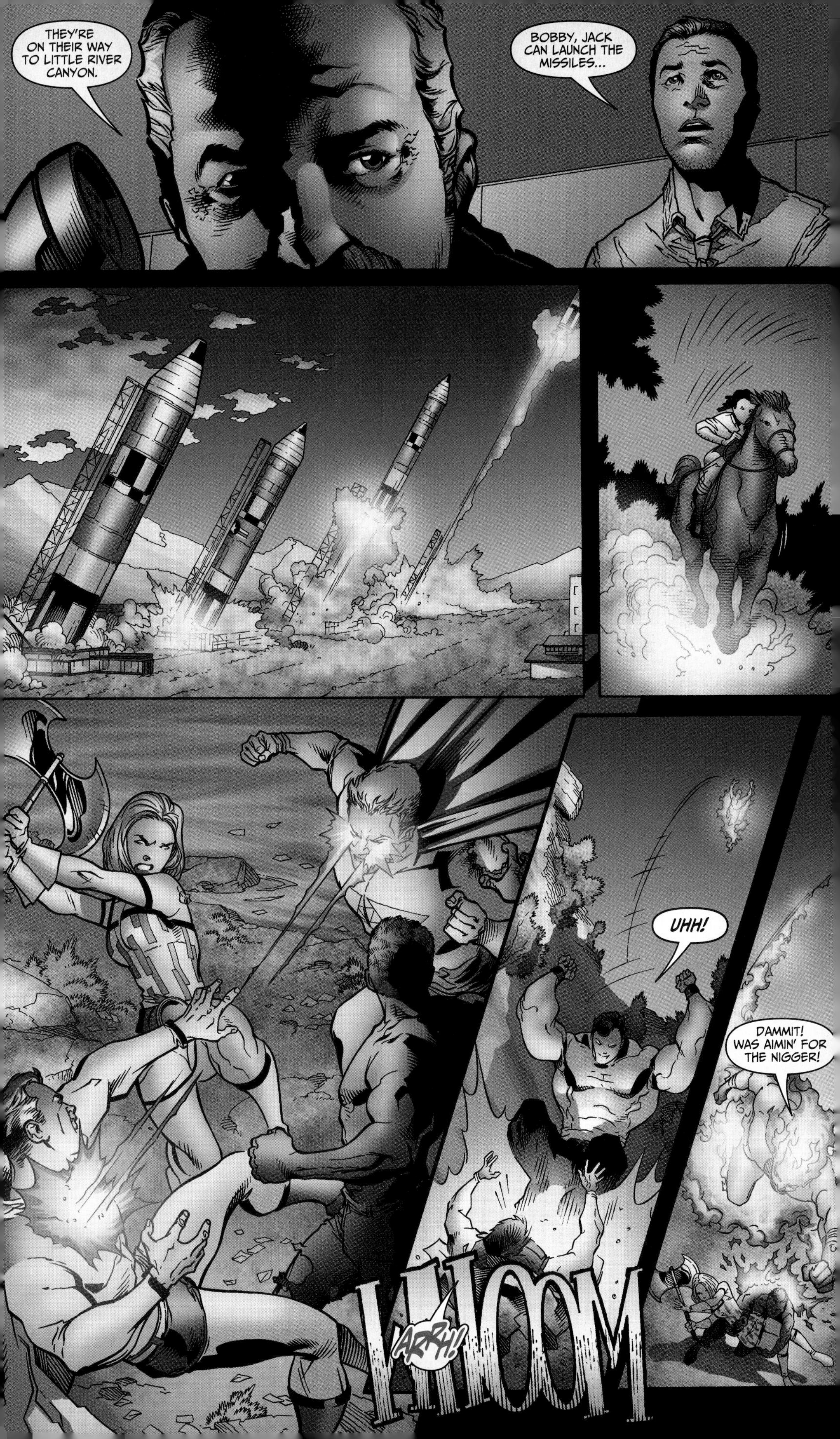
THEY'RE ON THEIR WAY TO LITTLE RIVER CANYON.
BOBBY, JACK CAN LAUNCH THE MISSILES...
UHH!
DAMMIT! WAS AIMIN' FOR THE NIGGER!
VHOOM
ARRH!

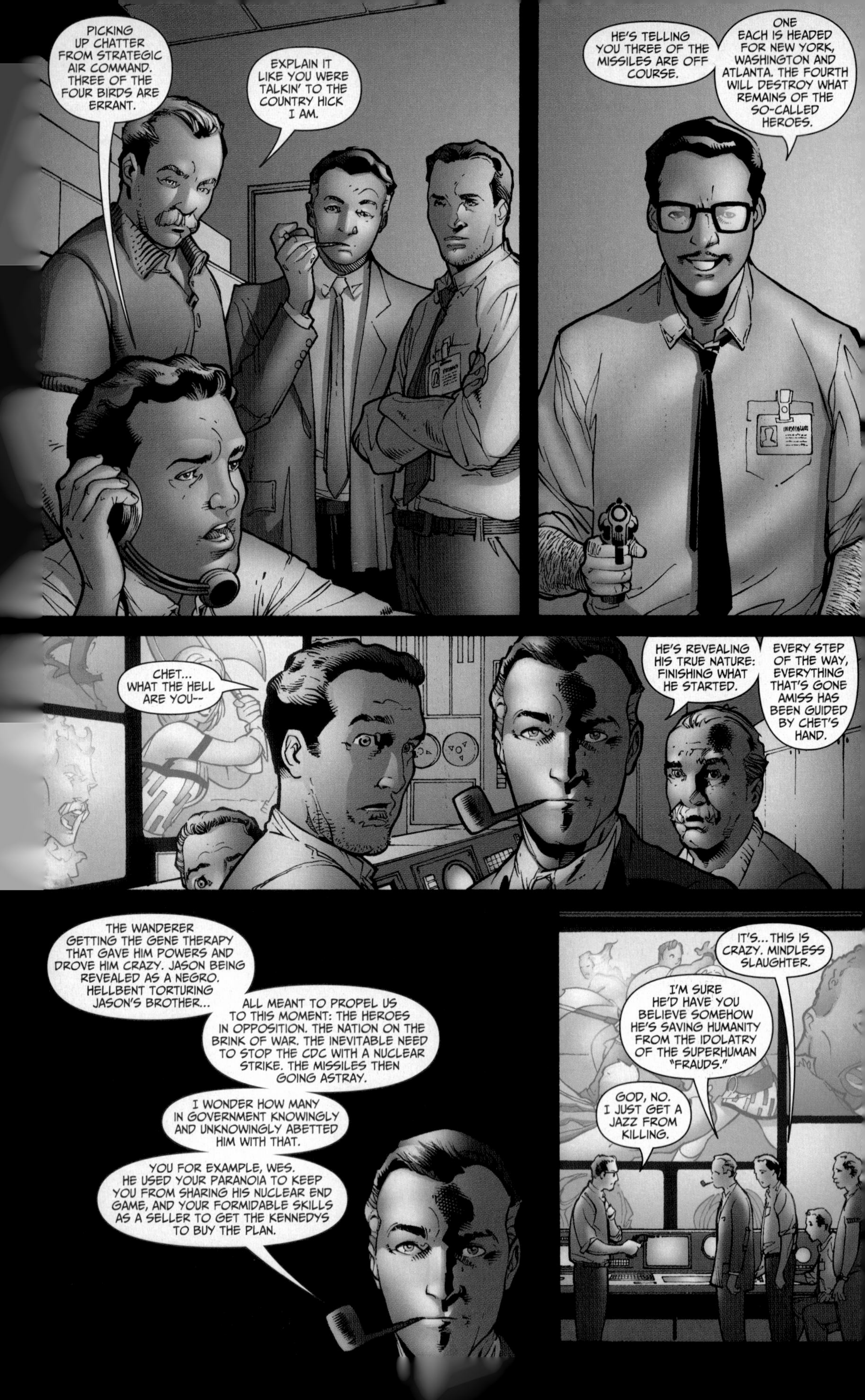
PICKING UP CHATTER FROM STRATEGIC AIR COMMAND. THREE OF THE FOUR BIRDS ARE ERRANT.
EXPLAIN IT LIKE YOU WERE TALKIN' TO THE COUNTRY HICK I AM.
HE'S TELLING YOU THREE OF THE MISSILES ARE OFF COURSE.
ONE EACH IS HEADED FOR NEW YORK, WASHINGTON AND ATLANTA. THE FOURTH WILL DESTROY WHAT REMAINS OF THE SO-CALLED HEROES.
CHET... WHAT THE HELL ARE YOU--
HE'S REVEALING HIS TRUE NATURE: FINISHING WHAT HE STARTED.
EVERY STEP OF THE WAY, EVERYTHING THAT'S GONE AMISS HAS BEEN GUIDED BY CHET'S HAND.
THE WANDERER GETTING THE GENE THERAPY THAT GAVE HIM POWERS AND DROVE HIM CRAZY. JASON BEING REVEALED AS A NEGRO. HELLBENT TORTURING JASON'S BROTHER...
ALL MEANT TO PROPEL US TO THIS MOMENT: THE HEROES IN OPPOSITION. THE NATION ON THE BRINK OF WAR. THE INEVITABLE NEED TO STOP THE CDC WITH A NUCLEAR STRIKE. THE MISSILES THEN GOING ASTRAY.
I WONDER HOW MANY IN GOVERNMENT KNOWINGLY AND UNKNOWINGLY ABETTED HIM WITH THAT.
YOU FOR EXAMPLE, WES. HE USED YOUR PARANOIA TO KEEP YOU FROM SHARING HIS NUCLEAR END GAME, AND YOUR FORMIDABLE SKILLS AS A SELLER TO GET THE KENNEDYS TO BUY THE PLAN.
IT'S... THIS IS CRAZY. MINDLESS SLAUGHTER.
I'M SURE HE'D HAVE YOU BELIEVE SOMEHOW HE'S SAVING HUMANITY FROM THE IDOLATRY OF THE SUPERHUMAN "FRAUDS."
GOD, NO. I JUST GET A JAZZ FROM KILLING.

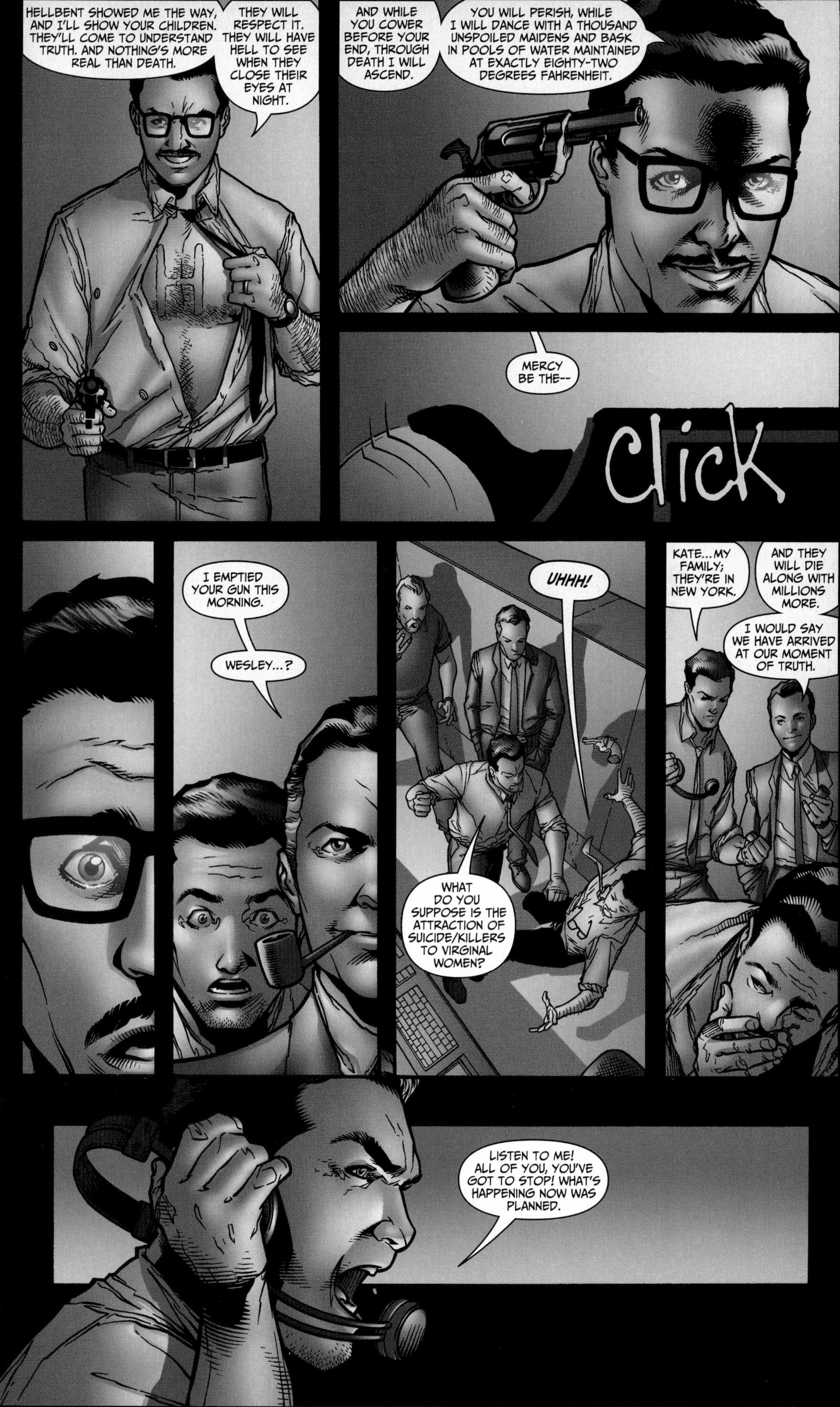

HELLBENT SHOWED ME THE WAY, AND I'LL SHOW YOUR CHILDREN. THEY'LL COME TO UNDERSTAND TRUTH. AND NOTHING'S MORE REAL THAN DEATH.
THEY WILL RESPECT IT. THEY WILL HAVE HELL TO SEE WHEN THEY CLOSE THEIR EYES AT NIGHT.
AND WHILE YOU COWER BEFORE YOUR END, THROUGH DEATH I WILL ASCEND.
YOU WILL PERISH, WHILE I WILL DANCE WITH A THOUSAND UNSPOILED MAIDENS AND BASK IN POOLS OF WATER MAINTAINED AT EXACTLY EIGHTY-TWO DEGREES FAHRENHEIT.
MERCY BE THE--
CLICK
I EMPTIED YOUR GUN THIS MORNING.
WESLEY...?
UHHH!
WHAT DO YOU SUPPOSE IS THE ATTRACTION OF SUICIDE/KILLERS TO VIRGINAL WOMEN?
KATE...MY FAMILY; THEY'RE IN NEW YORK.
AND THEY WILL DIE ALONG WITH MILLIONS MORE.
I WOULD SAY WE HAVE ARRIVED AT OUR MOMENT OF TRUTH.
LISTEN TO ME! ALL OF YOU, YOU'VE GOT TO STOP! WHAT'S HAPPENING NOW WAS PLANNED.

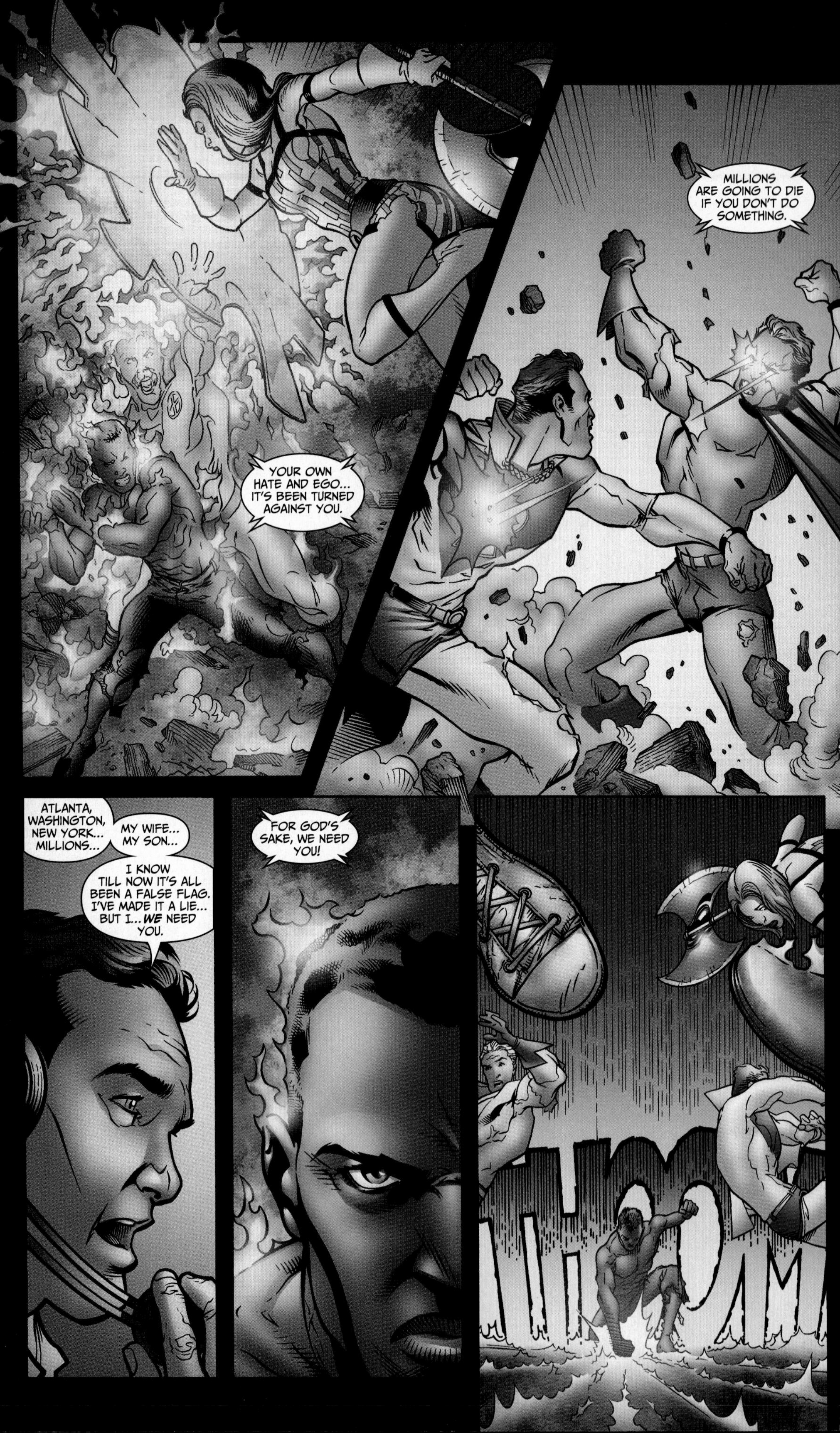
YOUR OWN HATE AND EGO... IT'S BEEN TURNED AGAINST YOU.
MILLIONS ARE GOING TO DIE IF YOU DON'T DO SOMETHING.
ATLANTA, WASHINGTON, NEW YORK... MILLIONS...
MY WIFE... MY SON...
I KNOW TILL NOW IT'S ALL BEEN A FALSE FLAG. I'VE MADE IT A LIE... BUT I... *WE* NEED YOU.
FOR GOD'S SAKE, WE NEED YOU!

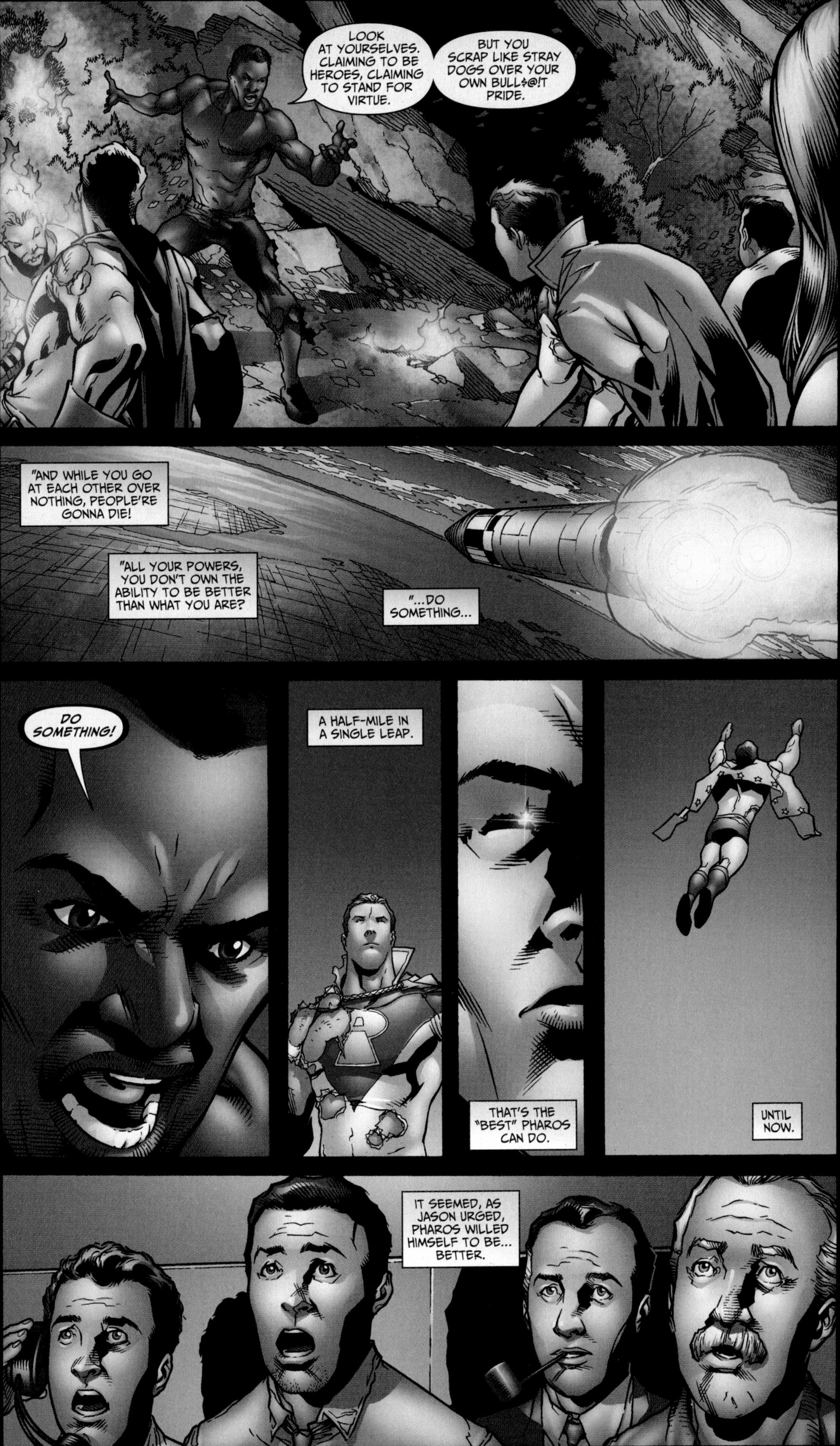
LOOK AT YOURSELVES. CLAIMING TO BE HEROES, CLAIMING TO STAND FOR VIRTUE.
BUT YOU SCRAP LIKE STRAY DOGS OVER YOUR OWN BULL$@!T PRIDE.
"AND WHILE YOU GO AT EACH OTHER OVER NOTHING, PEOPLE'RE GONNA DIE!
"ALL YOUR POWERS, YOU DON'T OWN THE ABILITY TO BE BETTER THAN WHAT YOU ARE?
"...DO SOMETHING...
DO SOMETHING!
A HALF-MILE IN A SINGLE LEAP.
THAT'S THE "BEST" PHAROS CAN DO.
UNTIL NOW.
IT SEEMED, AS JASON URGED, PHAROS WILLED HIMSELF TO BE... BETTER.

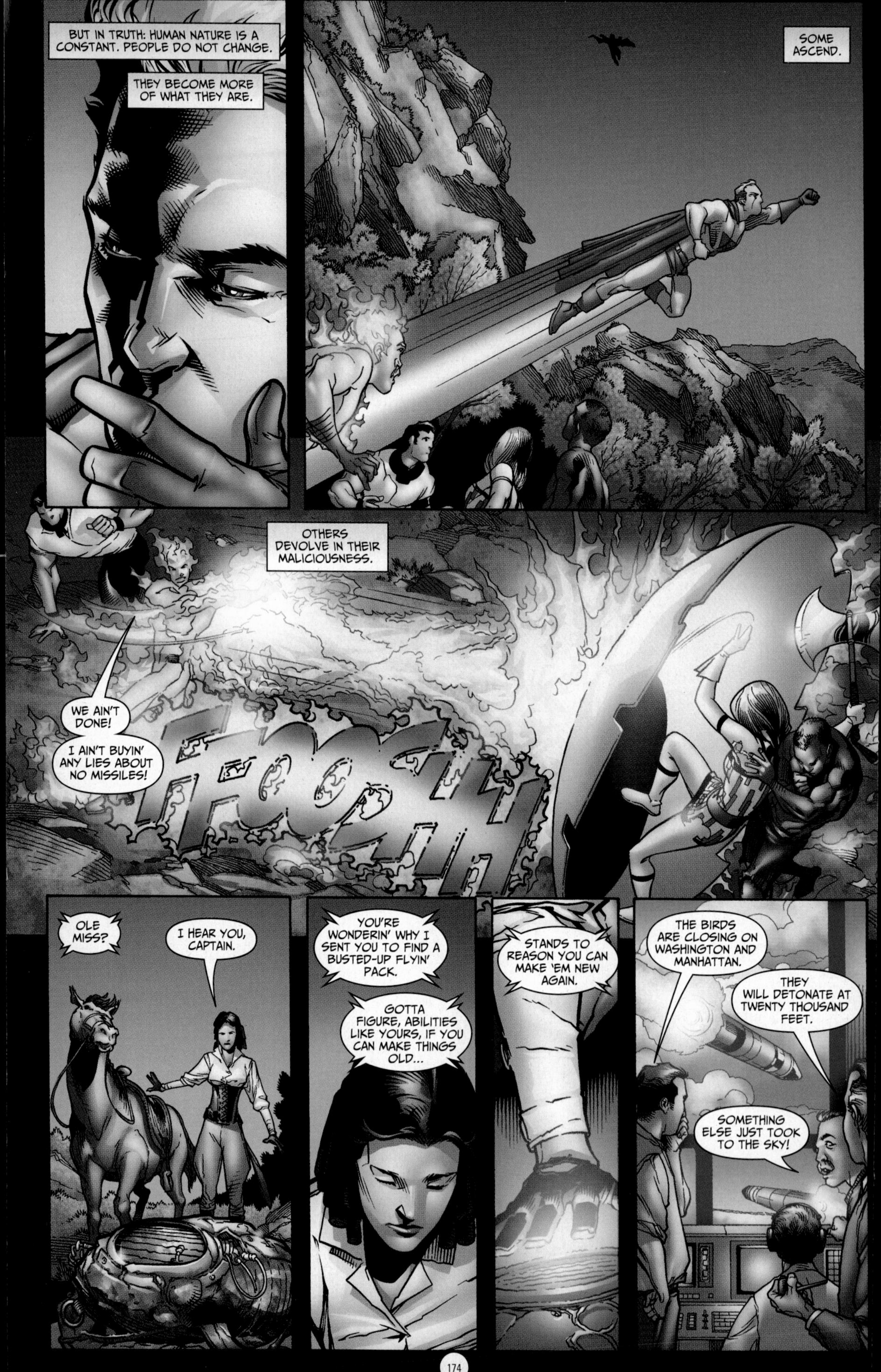

BUT IN TRUTH: HUMAN NATURE IS A CONSTANT. PEOPLE DO NOT CHANGE.
THEY BECOME MORE OF WHAT THEY ARE.
SOME ASCEND.
OTHERS DEVOLVE IN THEIR MALICIOUSNESS.
WE AIN'T DONE!
I AIN'T BUYIN' ANY LIES ABOUT NO MISSILES!
OLE MISS?
I HEAR YOU, CAPTAIN.
YOU'RE WONDERIN' WHY I SENT YOU TO FIND A BUSTED-UP FLYIN' PACK.
GOTTA FIGURE, ABILITIES LIKE YOURS, IF YOU CAN MAKE THINGS OLD...
STANDS TO REASON YOU CAN MAKE 'EM NEW AGAIN.
THE BIRDS ARE CLOSING ON WASHINGTON AND MANHATTAN.
THEY WILL DETONATE AT TWENTY THOUSAND FEET.
SOMETHING ELSE JUST TOOK TO THE SKY!

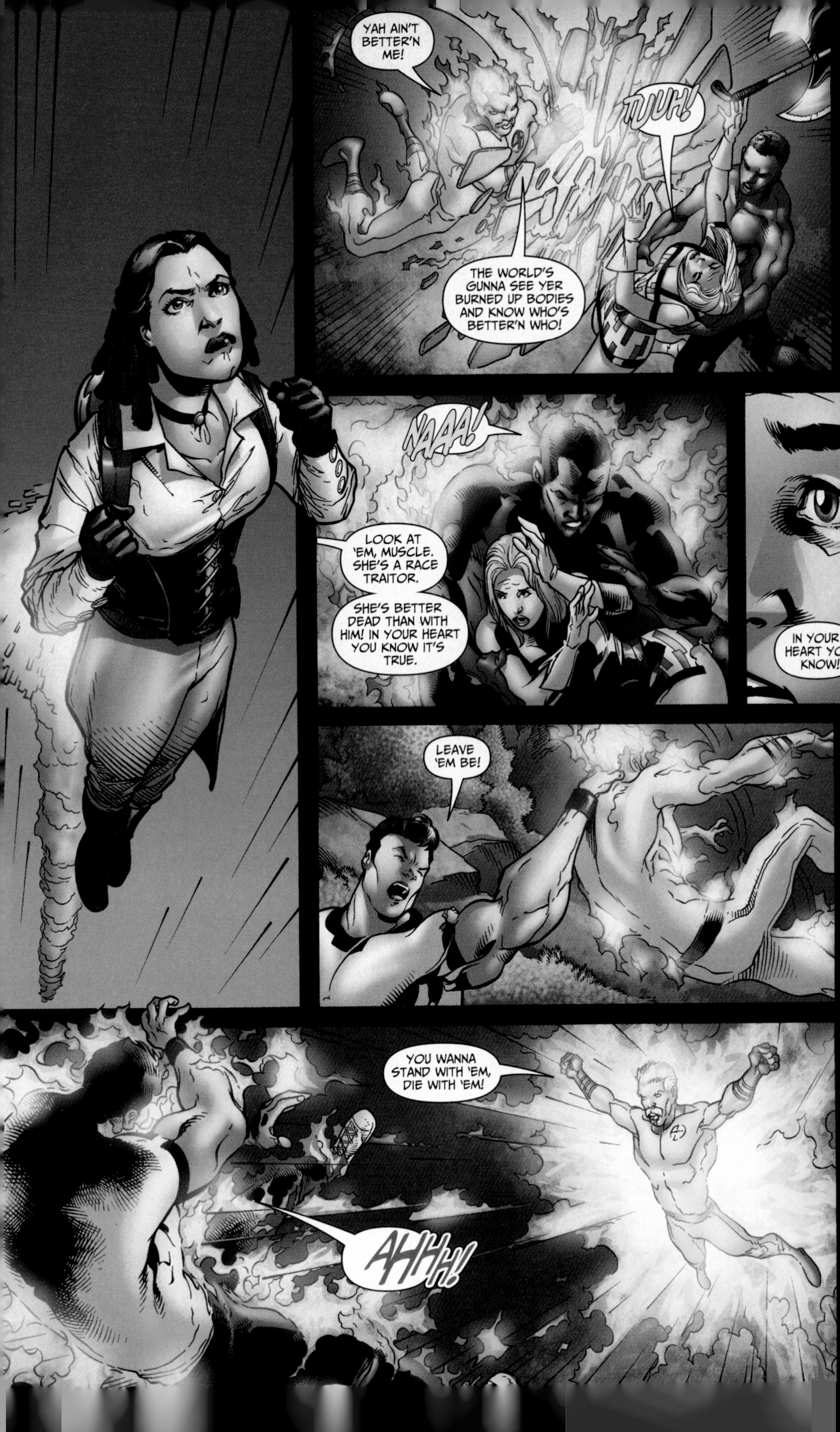
YAH AIN'T BETTER'N ME!
TUUH!
THE WORLD'S GUNNA SEE YER BURNED UP BODIES AND KNOW WHO'S BETTER'N WHO!
NAAA!
LOOK AT 'EM, MUSCLE. SHE'S A RACE TRAITOR.
SHE'S BETTER DEAD THAN WITH HIM! IN YOUR HEART YOU KNOW IT'S TRUE.
IN YOUR HEART YOU KNOW!
LEAVE 'EM BE!
YOU WANNA STAND WITH 'EM, DIE WITH 'EM!
AHHH!

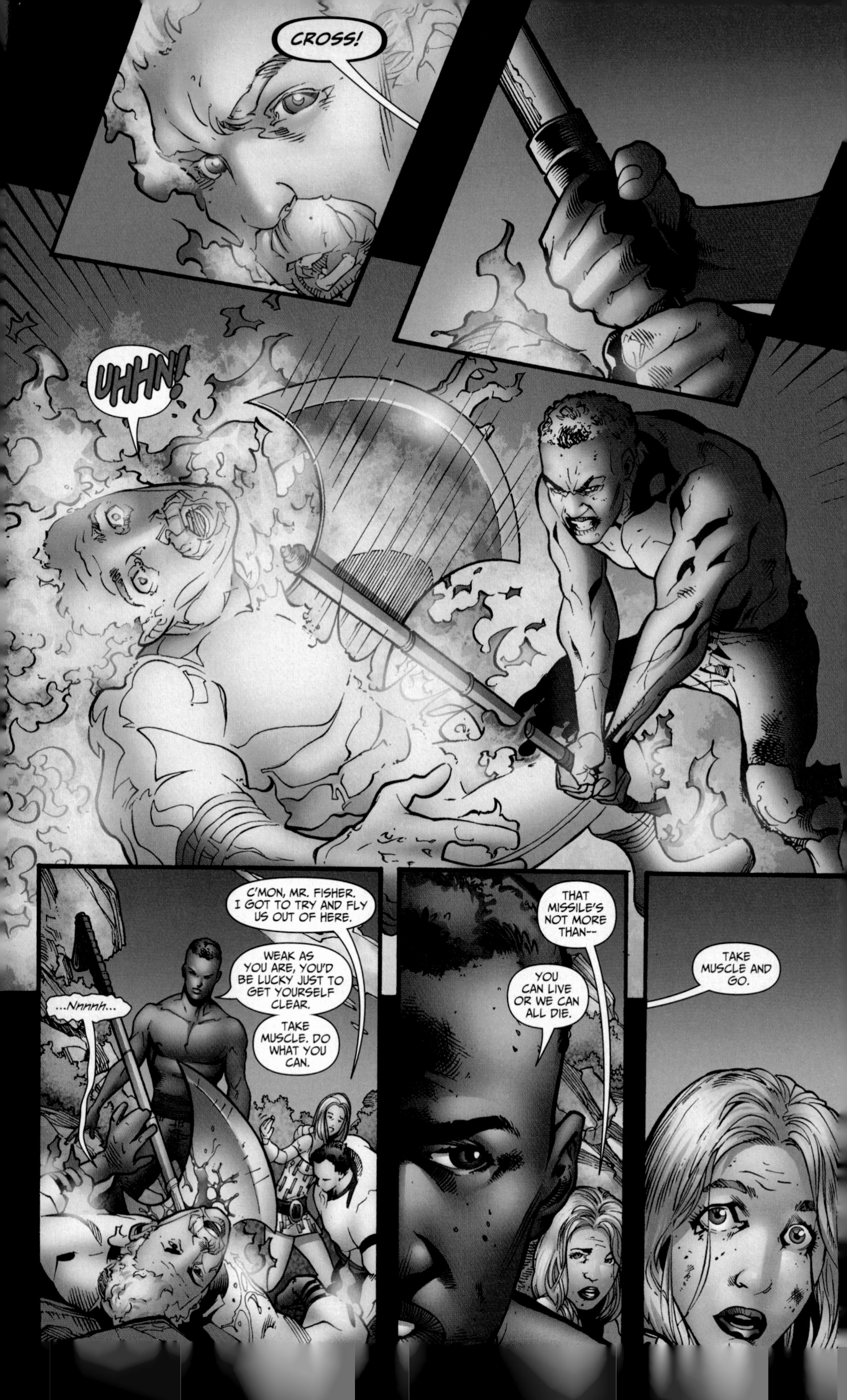
CROSS!
UHHN!
C'MON, MR. FISHER. I GOT TO TRY AND FLY US OUT OF HERE.
WEAK AS YOU ARE, YOU'D BE LUCKY JUST TO GET YOURSELF CLEAR.
TAKE MUSCLE. DO WHAT YOU CAN.
...Nnnnh...
THAT MISSILE'S NOT MORE THAN--
YOU CAN LIVE OR WE CAN ALL DIE.
TAKE MUSCLE AND GO.

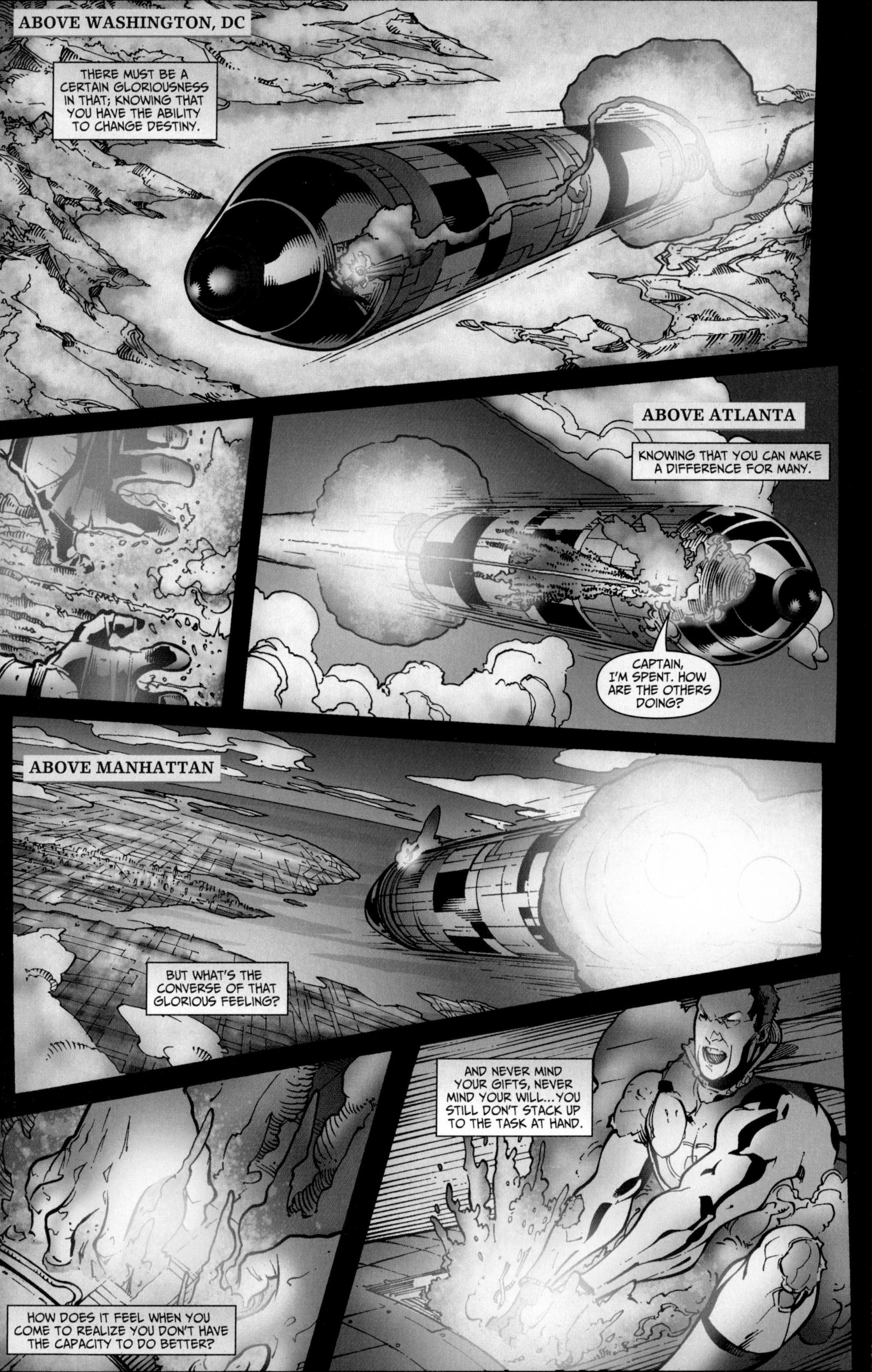
ABOVE WASHINGTON, DC
THERE MUST BE A CERTAIN GLORIOUSNESS IN THAT; KNOWING THAT YOU HAVE THE ABILITY TO CHANGE DESTINY.
ABOVE ATLANTA
KNOWING THAT YOU CAN MAKE A DIFFERENCE FOR MANY.
CAPTAIN, I'M SPENT. HOW ARE THE OTHERS DOING?
ABOVE MANHATTAN
BUT WHAT'S THE CONVERSE OF THAT GLORIOUS FEELING?
AND NEVER MIND YOUR GIFTS, NEVER MIND YOUR WILL...YOU STILL DON'T STACK UP TO THE TASK AT HAND.
HOW DOES IT FEEL WHEN YOU COME TO REALIZE YOU DON'T HAVE THE CAPACITY TO DO BETTER?

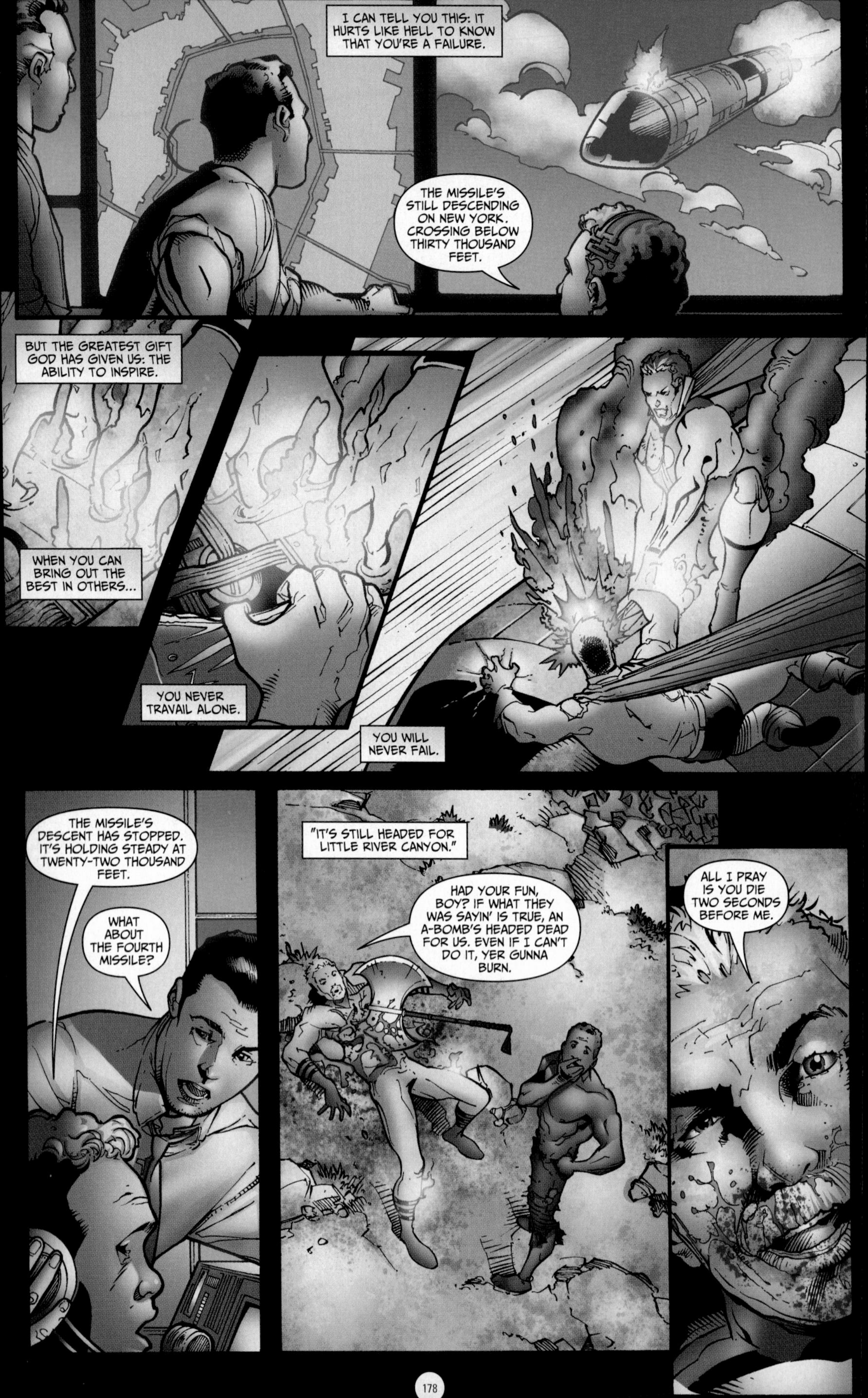
I CAN TELL YOU THIS: IT HURTS LIKE HELL TO KNOW THAT YOU'RE A FAILURE.
THE MISSILE'S STILL DESCENDING ON NEW YORK. CROSSING BELOW THIRTY THOUSAND FEET.
BUT THE GREATEST GIFT GOD HAS GIVEN US: THE ABILITY TO INSPIRE.
WHEN YOU CAN BRING OUT THE BEST IN OTHERS...
YOU NEVER TRAVAIL ALONE.
YOU WILL NEVER FAIL.
THE MISSILE'S DESCENT HAS STOPPED. IT'S HOLDING STEADY AT TWENTY-TWO THOUSAND FEET.
WHAT ABOUT THE FOURTH MISSILE?
"IT'S STILL HEADED FOR LITTLE RIVER CANYON."
HAD YOUR FUN, BOY? IF WHAT THEY WAS SAYIN' IS TRUE, AN A-BOMB'S HEADED DEAD FOR US. EVEN IF I CAN'T DO IT, YER GUNNA BURN.
ALL I PRAY IS YOU DIE TWO SECONDS BEFORE ME.

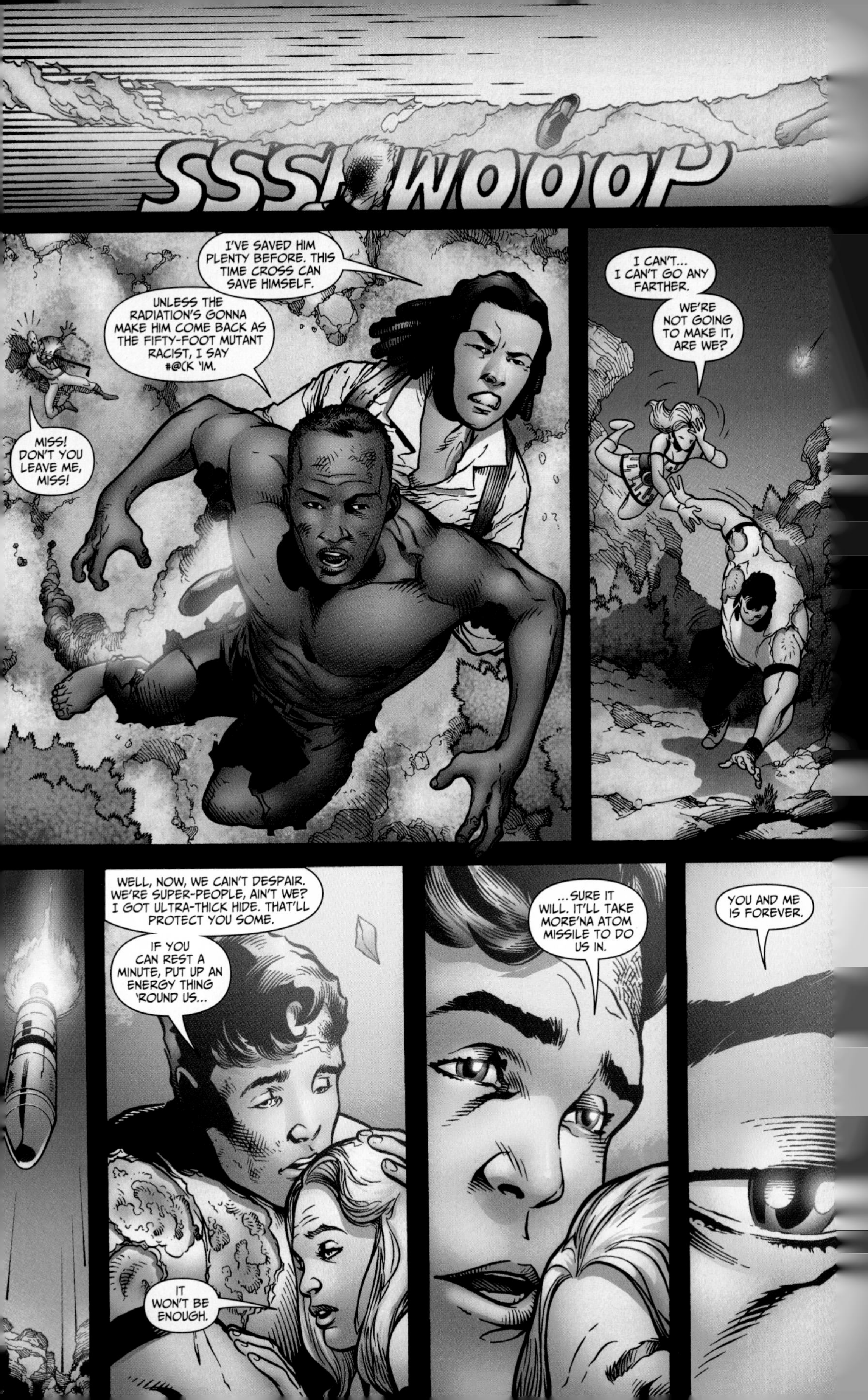
SSSHWOOOP
I'VE SAVED HIM PLENTY BEFORE. THIS TIME CROSS CAN SAVE HIMSELF.
UNLESS THE RADIATION'S GONNA MAKE HIM COME BACK AS THE FIFTY-FOOT MUTANT RACIST, I SAY #@CK 'IM.
MISS! DON'T YOU LEAVE ME, MISS!
I CAN'T... I CAN'T GO ANY FARTHER.
WE'RE NOT GOING TO MAKE IT, ARE WE?
WELL, NOW, WE CAIN'T DESPAIR. WE'RE SUPER-PEOPLE, AIN'T WE? I GOT ULTRA-THICK HIDE. THAT'LL PROTECT YOU SOME.
IF YOU CAN REST A MINUTE, PUT UP AN ENERGY THING 'ROUND US...
IT WON'T BE ENOUGH.
...SURE IT WILL. IT'LL TAKE MORE'NA ATOM MISSILE TO DO US IN.
YOU AND ME IS FOREVER.

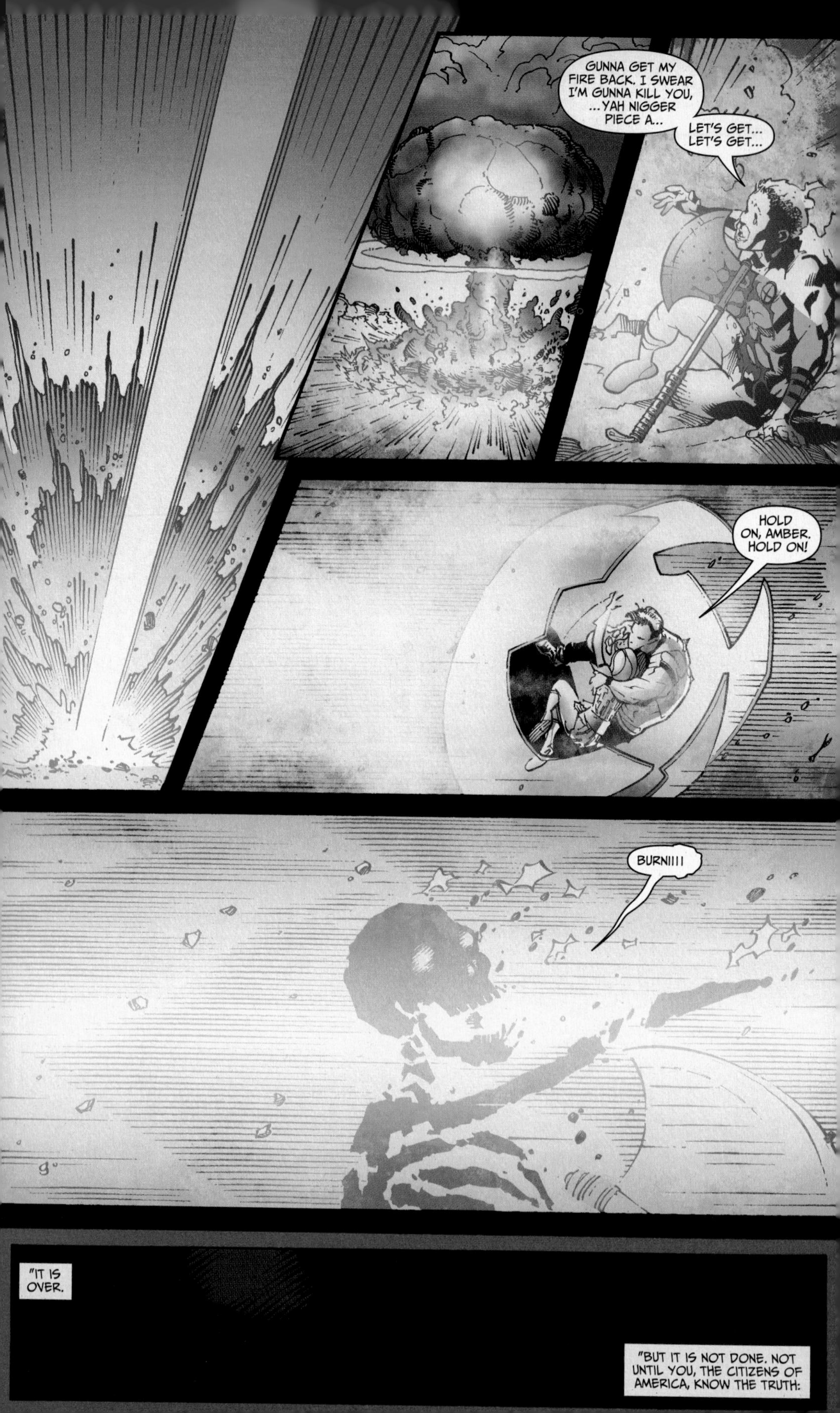
GUNNA GET MY FIRE BACK. I SWEAR I'M GUNNA KILL YOU, ...YAH NIGGER PIECE A...
LET'S GET... LET'S GET...
HOLD ON, AMBER. HOLD ON!
BURNIIII
"IT IS OVER.
"BUT IT IS NOT DONE. NOT UNTIL YOU, THE CITIZENS OF AMERICA, KNOW THE TRUTH:

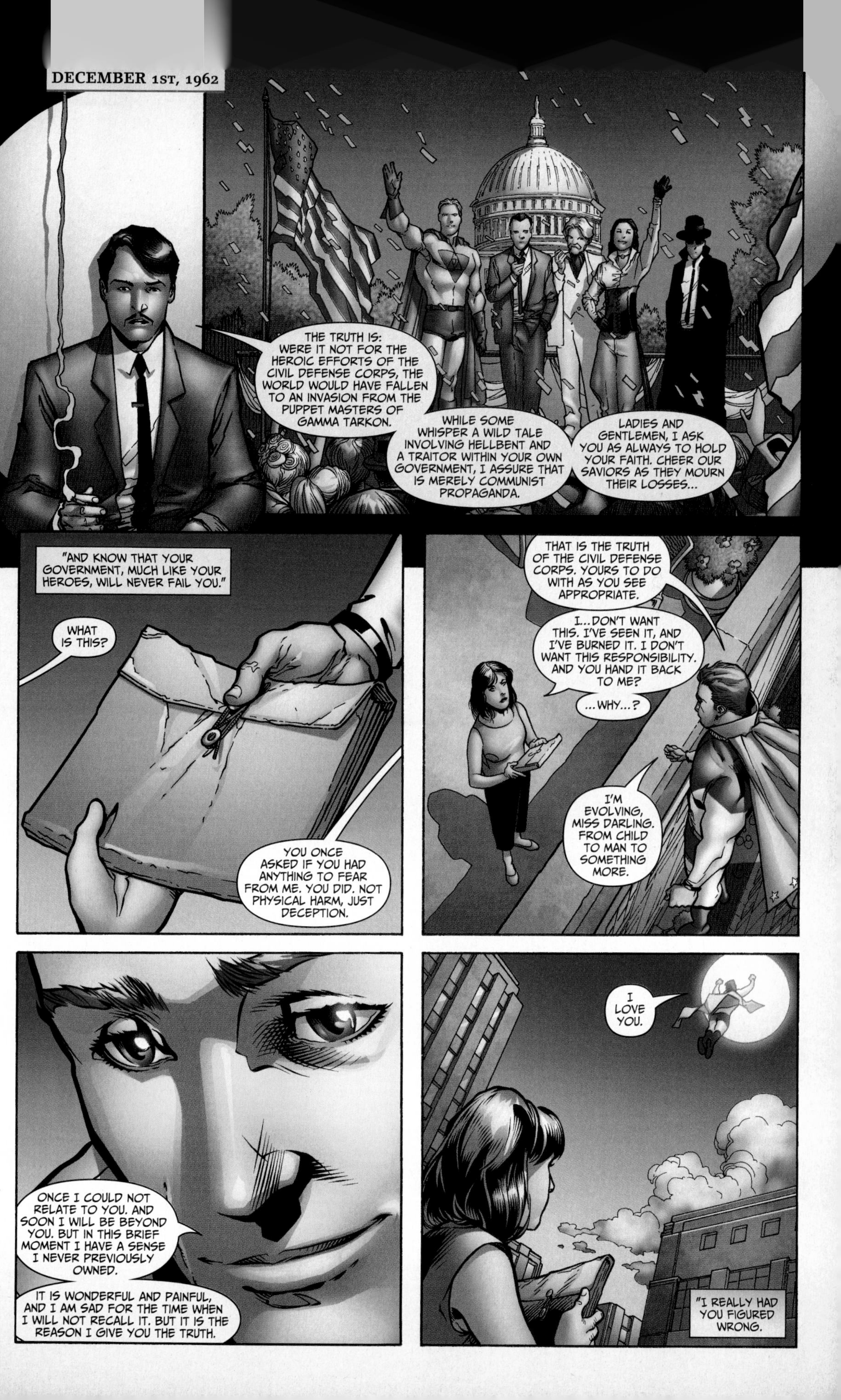
DECEMBER 1ST, 1962
THE TRUTH IS: WERE IT NOT FOR THE HEROIC EFFORTS OF THE CIVIL DEFENSE CORPS, THE WORLD WOULD HAVE FALLEN TO AN INVASION FROM THE PUPPET MASTERS OF GAMMA TARKON.
WHILE SOME WHISPER A WILD TALE INVOLVING HELLBENT AND A TRAITOR WITHIN YOUR OWN GOVERNMENT, I ASSURE THAT IS MERELY COMMUNIST PROPAGANDA.
LADIES AND GENTLEMEN, I ASK YOU AS ALWAYS TO HOLD YOUR FAITH. CHEER OUR SAVIORS AS THEY MOURN THEIR LOSSES...
"AND KNOW THAT YOUR GOVERNMENT, MUCH LIKE YOUR HEROES, WILL NEVER FAIL YOU."
WHAT IS THIS?
YOU ONCE ASKED IF YOU HAD ANYTHING TO FEAR FROM ME. YOU DID. NOT PHYSICAL HARM, JUST DECEPTION.
THAT IS THE TRUTH OF THE CIVIL DEFENSE CORPS. YOURS TO DO WITH AS YOU SEE APPROPRIATE.
I...DON'T WANT THIS. I'VE SEEN IT, AND I'VE BURNED IT. I DON'T WANT THIS RESPONSIBILITY. AND YOU HAND IT BACK TO ME?
...WHY...?
I'M EVOLVING, MISS DARLING. FROM CHILD TO MAN TO SOMETHING MORE.
ONCE I COULD NOT RELATE TO YOU. AND SOON I WILL BE BEYOND YOU. BUT IN THIS BRIEF MOMENT I HAVE A SENSE I NEVER PREVIOUSLY OWNED.
IT IS WONDERFUL AND PAINFUL, AND I AM SAD FOR THE TIME WHEN I WILL NOT RECALL IT. BUT IT IS THE REASON I GIVE YOU THE TRUTH.
I LOVE YOU.
"I REALLY HAD YOU FIGURED WRONG.

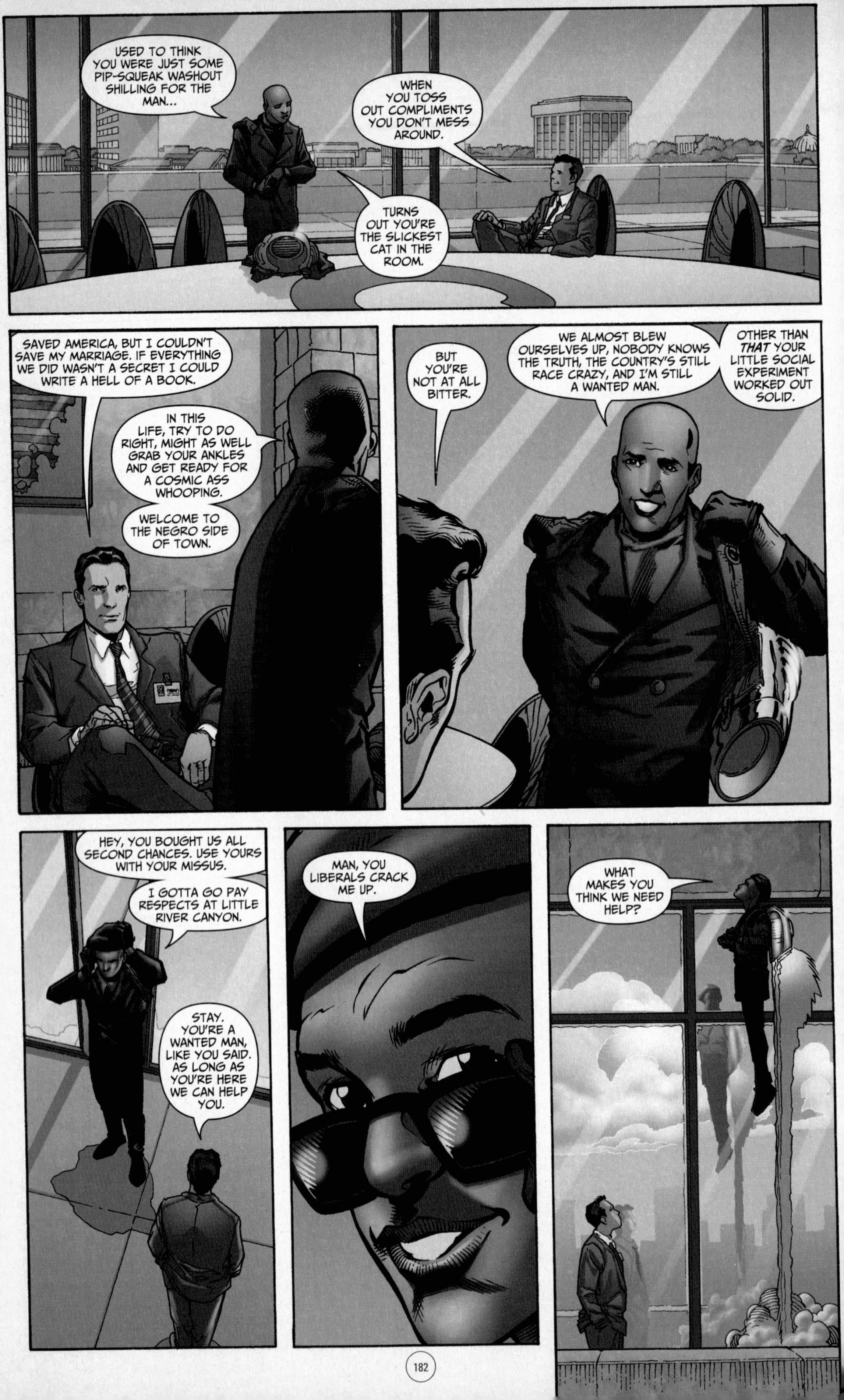
USED TO THINK YOU WERE JUST SOME PIP-SQUEAK WASHOUT SHILLING FOR THE MAN...
WHEN YOU TOSS OUT COMPLIMENTS YOU DON'T MESS AROUND.
TURNS OUT YOU'RE THE SLICKEST CAT IN THE ROOM.
SAVED AMERICA, BUT I COULDN'T SAVE MY MARRIAGE. IF EVERYTHING WE DID WASN'T A SECRET I COULD WRITE A HELL OF A BOOK.
IN THIS LIFE, TRY TO DO RIGHT, MIGHT AS WELL GRAB YOUR ANKLES AND GET READY FOR A COSMIC ASS WHOOPING.
WELCOME TO THE NEGRO SIDE OF TOWN.
BUT YOU'RE NOT AT ALL BITTER.
WE ALMOST BLEW OURSELVES UP, NOBODY KNOWS THE TRUTH, THE COUNTRY'S STILL RACE CRAZY, AND I'M STILL A WANTED MAN.
OTHER THAN THAT YOUR LITTLE SOCIAL EXPERIMENT WORKED OUT SOLID.
HEY, YOU BOUGHT US ALL SECOND CHANCES. USE YOURS WITH YOUR MISSUS.
I GOTTA GO PAY RESPECTS AT LITTLE RIVER CANYON.
STAY. YOU'RE A WANTED MAN, LIKE YOU SAID. AS LONG AS YOU'RE HERE WE CAN HELP YOU.
MAN, YOU LIBERALS CRACK ME UP.
WHAT MAKES YOU THINK WE NEED HELP?

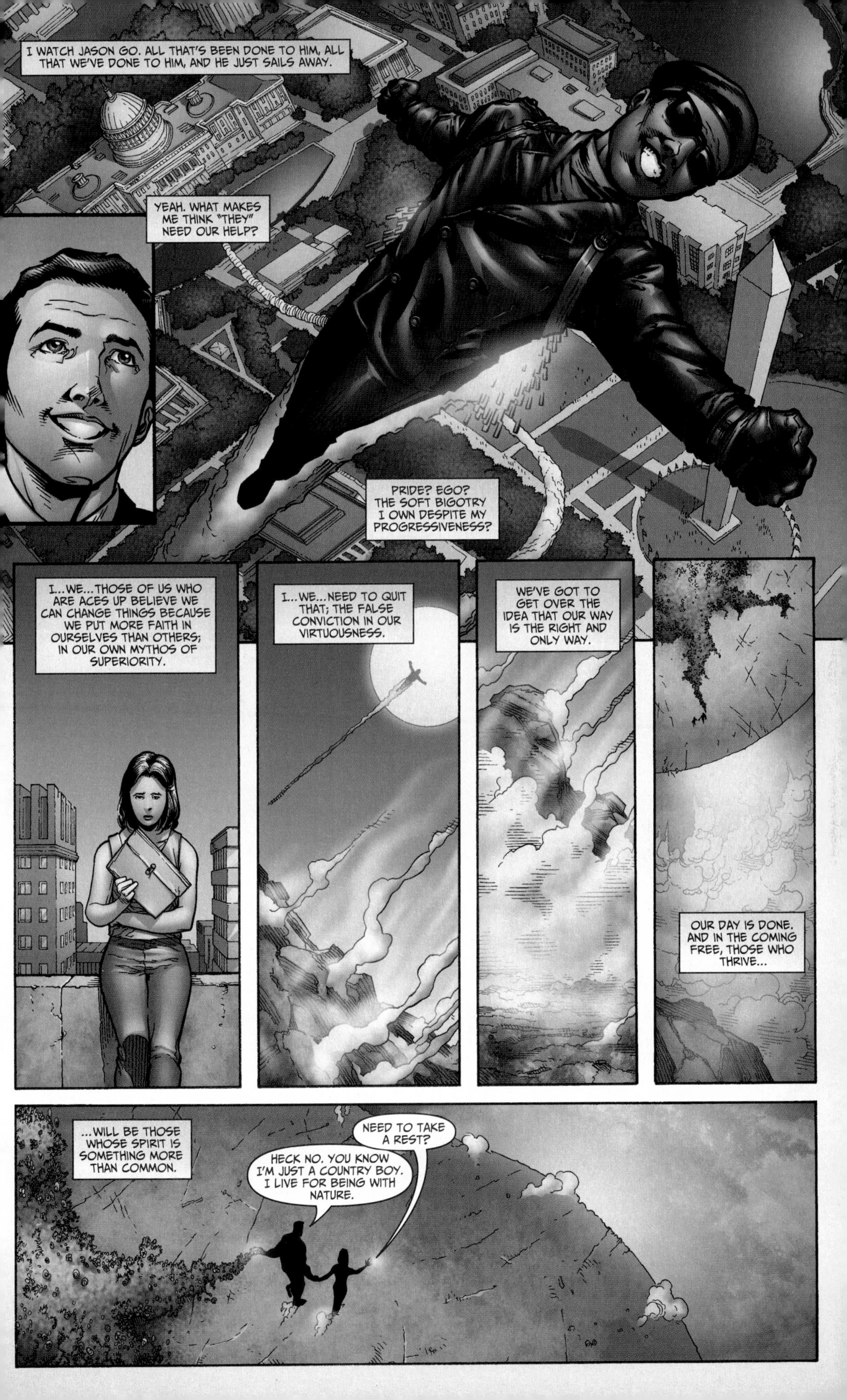
I WATCH JASON GO. ALL THAT'S BEEN DONE TO HIM, ALL THAT WE'VE DONE TO HIM, AND HE JUST SAILS AWAY.
YEAH. WHAT MAKES ME THINK "THEY" NEED OUR HELP?
PRIDE? EGO? THE SOFT BIGOTRY I OWN DESPITE MY PROGRESSIVENESS?
I...WE...THOSE OF US WHO ARE ACES UP BELIEVE WE CAN CHANGE THINGS BECAUSE WE PUT MORE FAITH IN OURSELVES THAN OTHERS; IN OUR OWN MYTHOS OF SUPERIORITY.
I...WE...NEED TO QUIT THAT; THE FALSE CONVICTION IN OUR VIRTUOUSNESS.
WE'VE GOT TO GET OVER THE IDEA THAT OUR WAY IS THE RIGHT AND ONLY WAY.
OUR DAY IS DONE. AND IN THE COMING FREE, THOSE WHO THRIVE...
...WILL BE THOSE WHOSE SPIRIT IS SOMETHING MORE THAN COMMON.
NEED TO TAKE A REST?
HECK NO. YOU KNOW I'M JUST A COUNTRY BOY. I LIVE FOR BEING WITH NATURE.

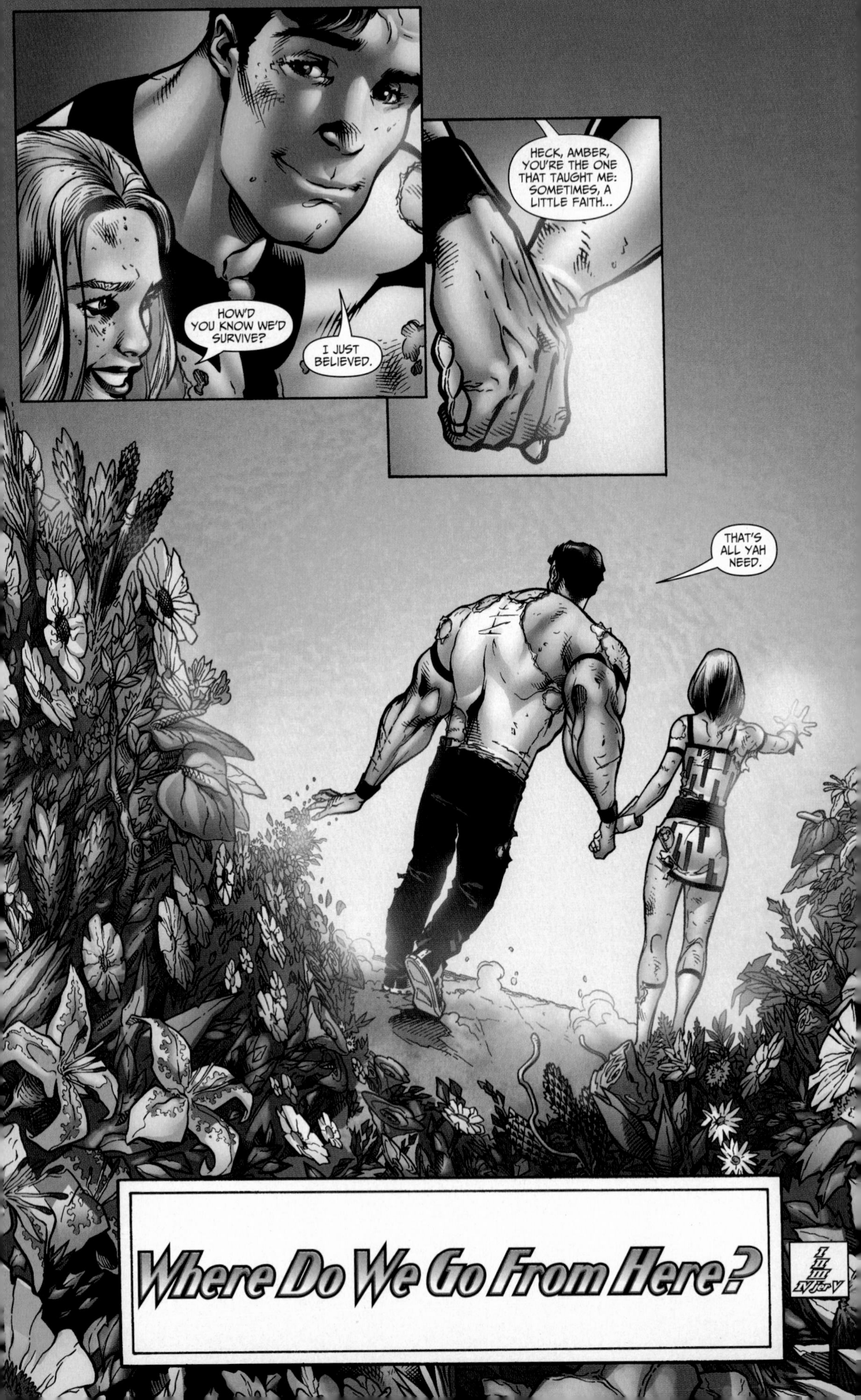
HOW'D YOU KNOW WE'D SURVIVE?
I JUST BELIEVED.
HECK, AMBER, YOU'RE THE ONE THAT TAUGHT ME: SOMETIMES, A LITTLE FAITH...
THAT'S ALL YAH NEED.
Where Do We Go From Here?

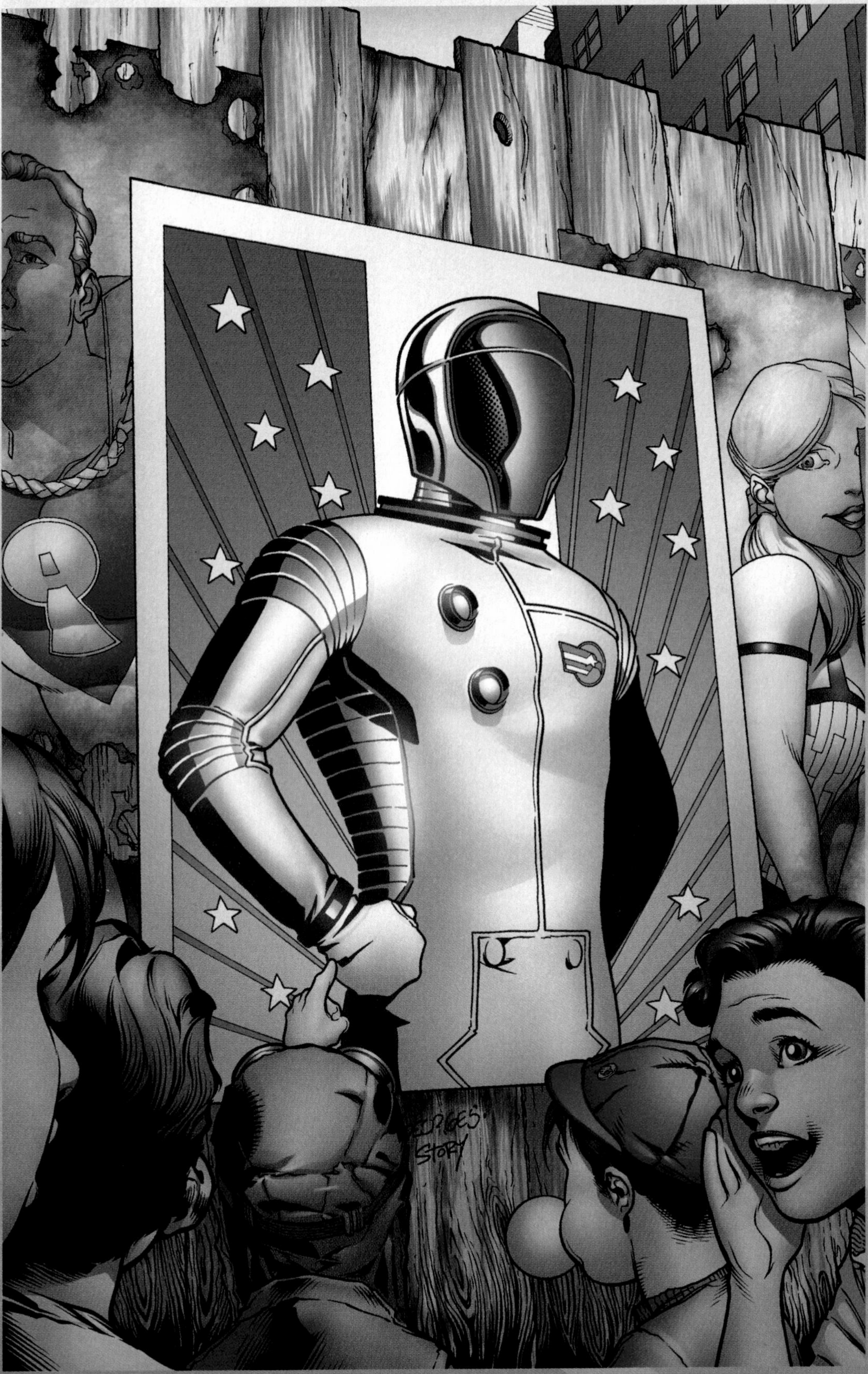

COVER #3

RIDLEY
NEW
WAR!
Abernathy Way.

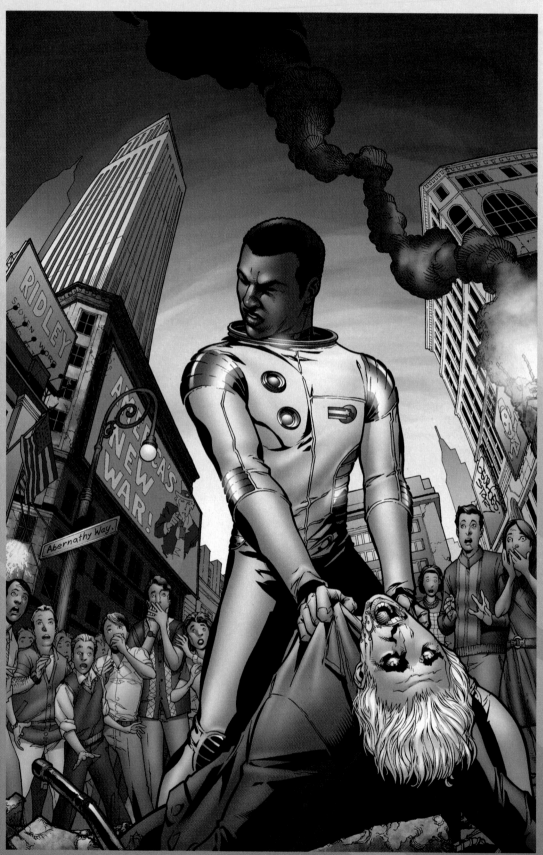

COVER #5

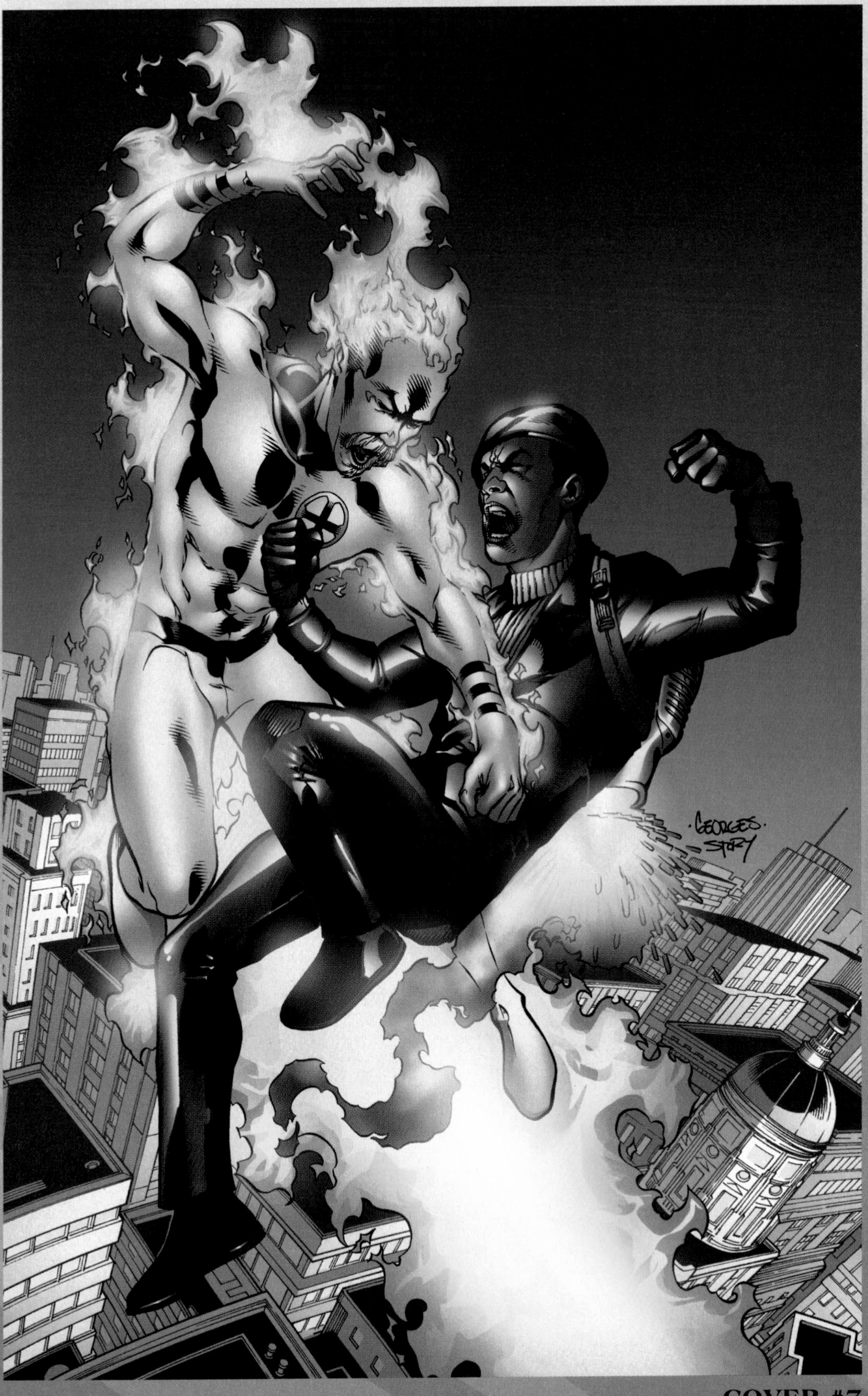
GEORGES STORY
COVER #7

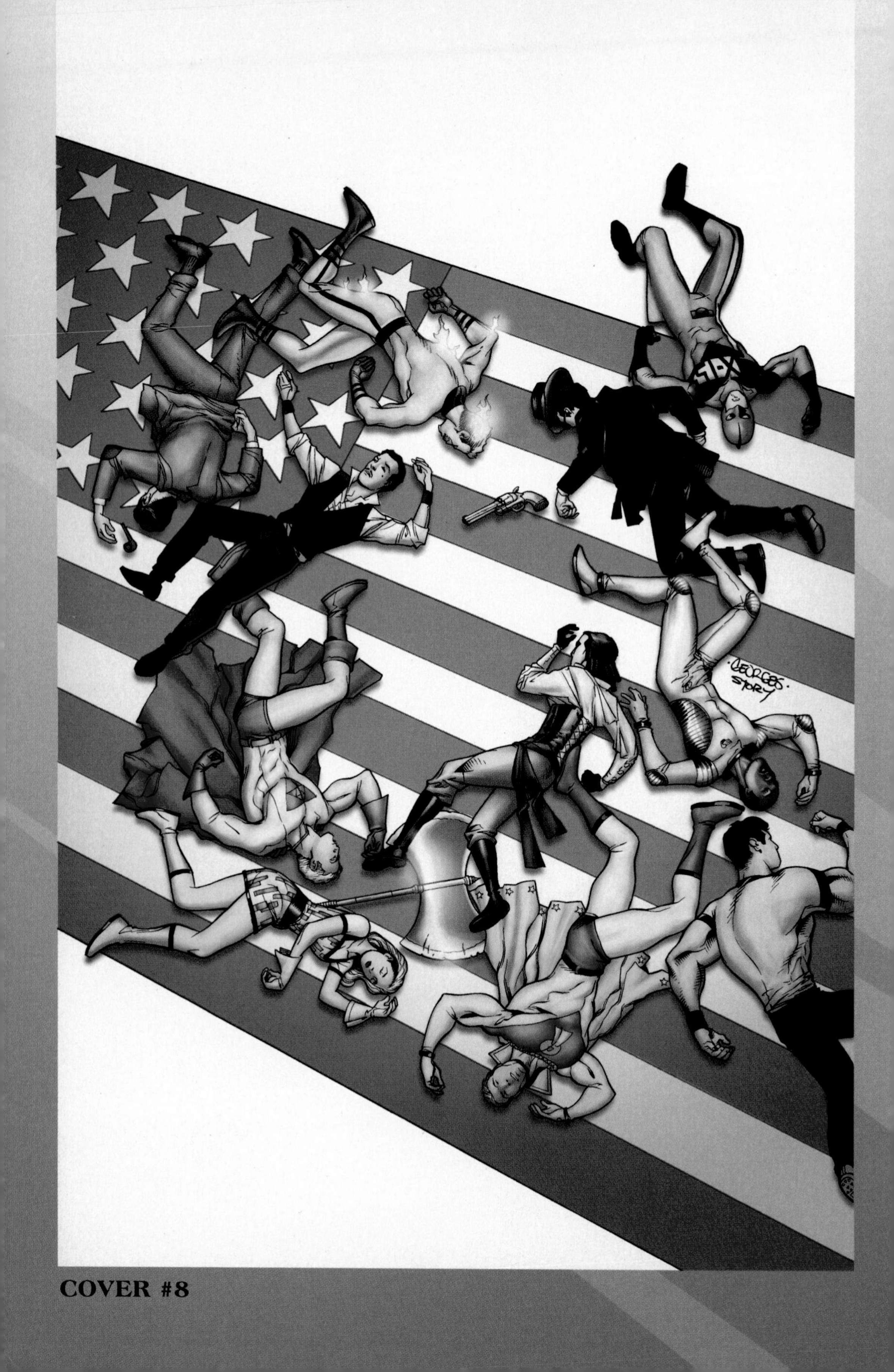
·GEORGES· STORY

COVER #8

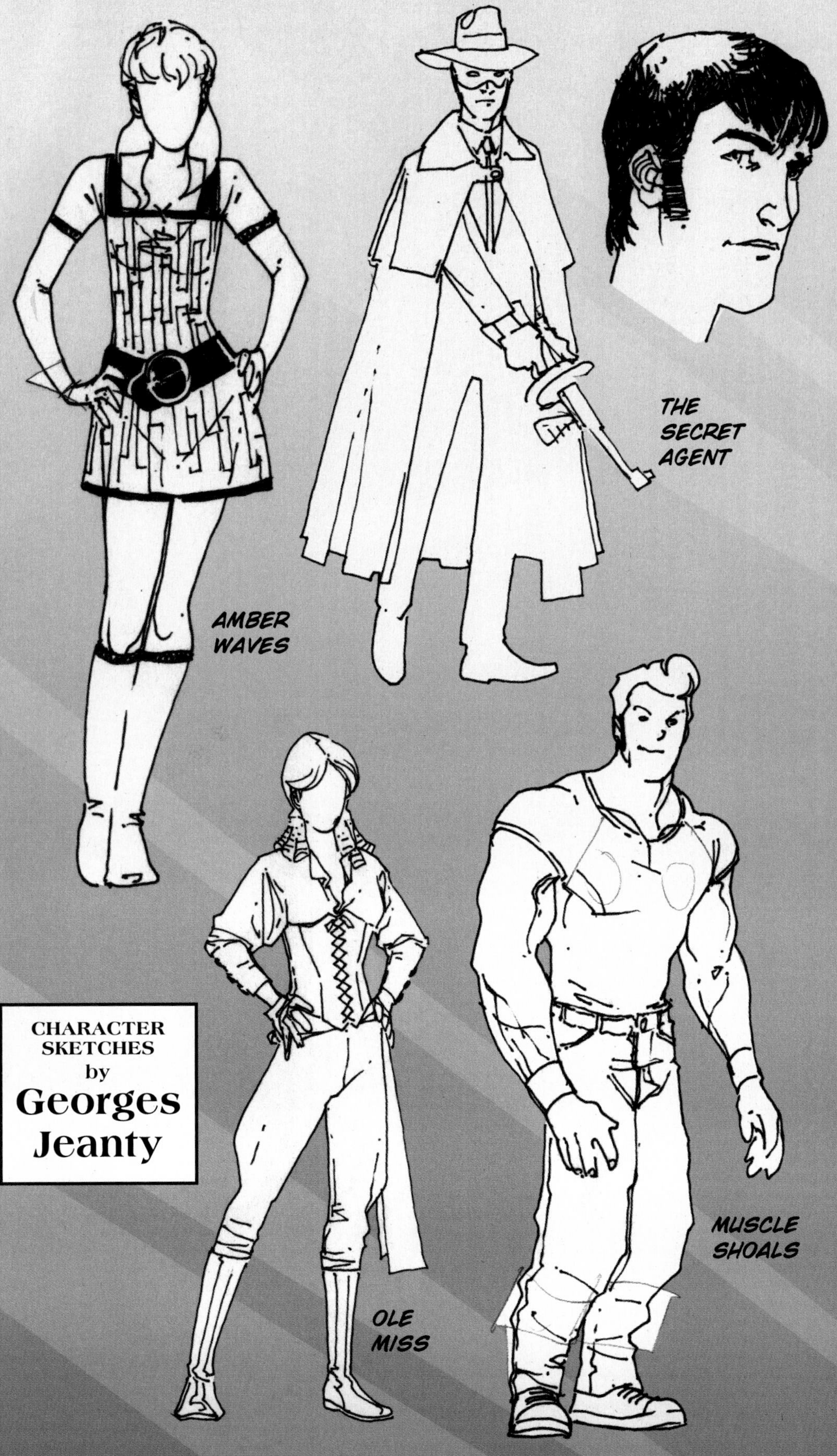
THE SECRET AGENT
AMBER WAVES
MUSCLE SHOALS
OLE MISS

CHARACTER SKETCHES by **Georges Jeanty**

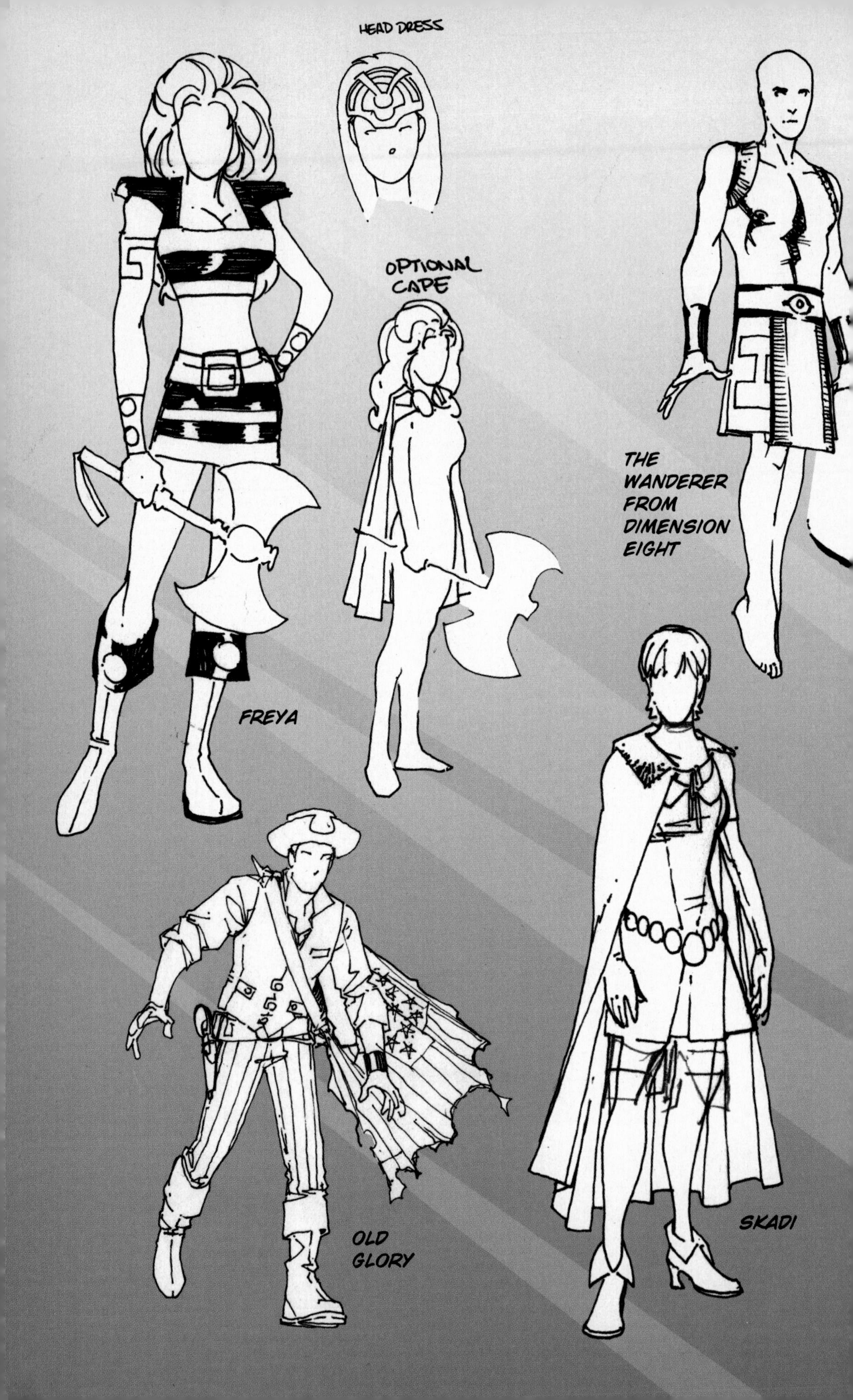
HEAD DRESS
OPTIONAL CAPE
THE WANDERER FROM DIMENSION EIGHT
FREYA
OLD GLORY
SKADI